2

POPULAR FRENCH ROMANTICISM

POPULAR FRENCH ROMANTICISM

Authors, Readers, and Books in the 19th Century

JAMES SMITH ALLEN

SYRACUSE UNIVERSITY PRESS
1981

Publication of this book was assisted by a grant
from the Publications Program of the National Endowment
for the Humanities, an independent federal agency.

Library of Congress Cataloging in Publication Data

Allen, James Smith.
Popular French romanticism.

Bibliography:　p.
Includes index.
1.　French literature—19th century—History and
criticism.　2.　Romanticism—France.　3.　Book
industries and trade—France—History—19th century.
4.　Books and reading—France—History—19th
century.　I.　Title.
PQ287.A4　　　840′.9′007　　　80-27129
ISBN 0-8156-2232-5

Manufactured in the United States of America

Pour ma famille partout

"Ce livre, je l'ai fait de moi-même,
de ma vie, . . . de mon coeur."
—*Jules Michelet*

James Smith Allen received the M.A. and Ph.D. in history from Tufts University and is Assistant Editor for the *Journal of Family History*.

CONTENTS

ILLUSTRATIONS

TABLES

FIGURES

PREFACE

"WHY ANOTHER BOOK ON ROMANTICISM?" an informed reader might well ask. After all, literally hundreds of books already exist on nearly every conceivable aspect of this literary, artistic, and intellectual phenomenon in Europe as well as France. It hardly seems necessary for another contribution: what more is there left to say about romanticism? Obviously, the present study needs some justification.

There are two primary reasons why I undertook this book. One of them is, simply put, the richness and variety of romanticism itself: the subject is its own justification. So long as readers and lovers of French literature remain, books and articles suggesting its significance will continue to be written. Although serious studies of romanticism often indulge in the celebration and elaboration of a literary tradition without much thought of the general reader, such work is still needed lest the literary texts themselves be forgotten. In returning to the original creations, for whatever reason, both the layman and the scholar become reacquainted with their common purpose—the appreciation and understanding of great literature that also underlie my consideration of French romanticism.

The second reason for the present volume, I think, lies in its approach that may shed some light on how and why we think as we do. In many ways we all owe much to the romantic movement. Indeed, our knowledge of complex human motives and consciousness derives, in part, from insights suggested by romantic writers in the eighteenth and nineteenth centuries. Thus romanticism, as one important source of the "modern ego," deserves the close study it has received. My investigation simply attempts to discuss this intellectual watershed from a historical perspective, one that aims to clarify what romanticism might have meant to the ordinary men and women of the past. By recognizing the way in which the movement participated in the lives of anonymous people in early nineteenth-century France, we may learn more about romantic ideas then and perhaps something about their part in our lives today.

In saying this I do not mean to claim too much for my work. An adequate elucidation of the many aspects of romanticism in Paris from 1820 to 1840, to mention nothing of its persistence in twentieth-century America, would require far more than a single monograph. The social, political, economic, and religious influences on the movement, and in turn the movement's impact on its immediate historical moment are incredibly difficult to sort out. No one can safely explain more than a few of the smaller problems posed by such study in the history of ideas. But by attempting to answer some basic questions—such as who wrote and read romantic works in early nineteenth-century Paris—this book suggests a useful way of conceiving the role that literature played at one point and place in French history. It is a beginning and perhaps justifies not only the book's publication, but also its perusal by a variety of people interested in both history and literature.

Consequently, this study is addressed to a rather diverse readership, social and literary historians, specialists and nonspecialists alike. I have deliberately chosen an interdisciplinary, some may say "structuralist," methodology that draws on the tools and sources of the social historian as well as the sensibilities and texts of the literary critic. Of course, nearly every specialist in his respective, well-defined field will find fault in this endeavor—the historian because of the limited role he ascribes to literature in "bread and butter" history, the critic because of the apparent "misplaced concreteness" he sees in the sociology of literature. But hopefully, they and the layman will still appreciate the merits of approaching romanticism in a more pragmatic fashion. Literature was a passionate subject in France, no less then than now: how and why this was so demand methods and sources unique to neither literature nor history. And its explanation should be intelligible to the reader with only a modest background in one discipline or the other. To this end a glossary is provided, lest the few technical terms in the text stand between the reader and the argument; for those interested in pursuing the issues further, ample footnotes and bibliography are also included.

I wish I could thank everyone who contributed to this project. Unfortunately, such acknowledgment would read like a New England family Bible—so many people helped whether or not they were asked. But I would be remiss in not expressing sincere thanks to Pierre-Henri Laurent, Howard Malchow, Howard Solomon, Frederic Shepler, Priscilla Clark, William Pencak, and a number of anonymous referees who read the entire manuscript at an early stage and provided shrewd, often very detailed critiques. Martin Green, Martine Loutfi, Pierre Orecchioni, Edgar Newman, Nathan Therien, Matthew Ramsey, Carol Fowler, Robert Davis, Jacqueline Wallace, Nancy Barker, Debra Perry,

Robert Darnton, and Robert Wheaton all read or listened patiently to parts of the book: their suggestions are appreciated as well.

None of the errors remaining in the text, or in the passages translated from the French, is any of these people's fault; I accept full responsibility for the mistakes, though not necessarily all the credit for the insights borrowed from so many sources. This volume has been improved immeasurably with their help.

I must also give special thanks to Tufts University for financial assistance and access to office space and equipment, during my graduate studies and after, without which this study would not have been undertaken; to Michael Richards at Sweet Briar College whose Symposium on Popular Culture in Nineteenth-Century Europe launched this book in March, 1978; to Peter Stearns, editor of the *Journal of Social History,* for his keen editorial eye and permission to publish portions of my article, "Toward a Social History of French Romanticism" (Winter 1979); and to the editors of the *Annales: E.S.C., Mouvement social,* Editions Pierre-Horay (Paris), Faber and Faber (London), University of California Press (Berkeley), and the Trustees of the Boston Public Library for allowing me to reproduce here original artwork or graphics in their possession. I thank as well all the many kind and helpful librarians at Wessell Library for their invaluable services.

Finally, I dedicate this book to my good family who endured and forgave my bookish indulgences. Their loving patience and sustenance made the present venture possible. This is their book as much as it is mine.

Somerville, Massachusetts   JSA
June 1980

POPULAR FRENCH ROMANTICISM

INTRODUCTION

$\mathcal{J}$N 1842 BENJAMIN ROUBAUD quite unintentionally portrayed a central issue in the social history of romanticism. His satirical vision, "Le grand chemin de la postérité," now in the Hugo Museum on the Place des Vosges in Paris, contrasts sharply with the views of romantic literature presented in many subsequent intellectual and literary accounts. No where in this flamboyant lithograph was depicted the *mal de siècle*, the *angst* of creative youth, the melancholy of lofty souls, the yearning to believe despite a faithless world, or the uncertainty in a changing society, all so evident in romantic literature. Nor was there included any apparent conflict between the rational and the irrational, between the universal and the particular, between the clarity and order of the classicists and the imagination and impulsiveness of the romantics. Little that has been emphasized in most writing about the climate of opinion in post–Napoleonic France appeared in Roubaud's strange vision.

Rather, the lithograph marches major and minor French authors alike in a gay procession behind the *enfant terrible* of the romantic movement in France: Victor Hugo, mounted on a dragon, carries a banner inscribed with the motto of the woolly-headed romantics, "le laid, c'est beau." After him in no particular order of distinction follow Théophile Gautier, Frances Wey, Paul Fouché, Eugène Sue, Alexandre Dumas, Frédéric Soulié, Léon Gozlan, Casimir Delavigne, Jules Méry, Alphonse Karr, Alfred de Vigny—an odd grouping of greater and lesser literary lights, some with no ostensible connection with romanticism except that they come in the wake of Hugo. The arch-melancholic Alphonse de Lamartine, holding a cross, is shown dreamily gazing off into the infinite near a bag bulging with 100,000 francs. In the second half of the lithograph, Roubaud portrayed another procession of authors even more curious than the first. Behind Eugène Scribe riding a steam locomotive, "fabricant dramatique de la vapeur: 30 pièces à l'heure," are the like-

1

1. "Grand Chemin de la Postérité" (ca. 1842). Lithograph by Benjamin Roubaud

nesses of Mélesvilles, Carmouche, Rochefort, Rosier, Masson, and other men of letters even less notable in literary history.

How is one to make sense of this assortment of apparently "romantic" authors? Few scholars read them, much less study all their work: how did so many of them lose their way on the road to posterity? The answer to these questions demands another approach to the history of nineteenth-century literature and ideas. More specifically, it lies in forgetting histories of French romanticism for the moment to view the movement through the peculiar lenses of contemporaries like Roubaud. Obviously their cynical perception of romanticism in the 1830s was not what scholars have characterized since then. By ignoring one side of the story, literary and intellectual historians have apparently perpetuated a

(1811–1847). *Courtesy of the Boston Public Library, Print Department.*

"culturomorphic distortion," one that involves the close study of works by the literary greats still deemed worthy of serious consideration, while neglecting the careful examination of titles by minor literati widely read in the early nineteenth century.[1] Romanticism was an enormously popu-

1. This is Robert Darnton's term for the study of ideas in a historical tradition of their own, a study often detached from a specific social and cultural context important to the shape and scope of the ideas themselves. The result of such an approach, a common one in the history of ideas since Arthur O. Lovejoy, may be a serious distortion of the intellectual life of a period. Many of the major French romantics, like Vigny and Musset, were published in minuscule editions generally neglected by readers in the early nineteenth century. Yet scholars mistake their importance to the history of French literature without also studying writers like Béranger and Ducray-Duminil who attracted much more popular attention

lar phenomenon in Paris from 1820 to 1840, especially among writers like J. A. de Norvins and Guilbert de Pixérécourt whose editions sometimes ran into the tens of thousands, even though they rarely rate more than a footnote today.[2] Yet intellectual and literary historians continue to define

and who consequently tell us more about the values and attitudes of the romantic reading public. For more on this problem in intellectual histories of the eighteenth century, see Darnton, "Reading, Writing, and Publishing in Eighteenth-Century France: A Case Study in the Sociology of Literature," *Historical Studies Today*, Felix Gilbert and Stephen Graubard, eds. (New York: Norton, 1972), pp. 238–80.

2. Production runs of nearly all Parisian authors published in the period may be found in Archives Nationales $F^{18}II*1$–35. "Déclarations des Imprimeurs. Paris. Années 1815–1845 [with lacunae]," crucial documents in the history of literary taste. Here it can be

the movement in terms of unread and unrepresentative authors in the early part of the century. Consequently, if French romanticism is to be understood, it must also be seen as Roubaud's contemporaries saw it—as part of popular culture in the patriotic songs, stormy melodramas, gothic

---

seen clearly how many copies of Lamartine, Hugo, and Lamennais were printed (frequently more than 1,500 per edition), but also how few copies of Gautier, Stendhal, and Musset (rarely more than 800). Meanwhile, according to these sources, the likes of Norvins, Ancelot, and Spazier all enjoyed multiple editions of 3,000 or better. To readers in the period, the latter authors merited a good deal more attention than many of the best-known romantics, yet they are largely passed over in silence in most histories of French romanticism.

Fortunately, recent scholarship has shown more interest in the historical and literary significance of popular writers in the past. For example, see, for France, Peter Brooks, *The*

romances, and national histories written, published, and read by men and women at the height of the movement.

To be sure, French romanticism in the low literature of the period was very different from that described in most histories. While Lamartine, Hugo, Vigny, and others of their stature explored new modes of feeling in response to personal and creative impulsions, their various imitators borrowed their modes of expression apparently with other things in mind. Upon close examination of popular titles in history and the *belles lettres*, the "new" literature revealed very little of the romantic sensibility, and much, much more of its formal innovation. In its immediate literary impact, romanticism was almost exclusively a matter of form. The vision of the *cénacles* existed only in their immediate productions, a very small portion of the literary marketplace despite some major successes. Meanwhile the emotional melodramas, gothic novels, and jolly *chansonniers* continued to express the entertaining concerns of ambition, love, and politics that only resembled the work of the romantic circles. Even though contemporary observers like Frances Trollope and Théophile Gautier described the poetic *Weltschmerz* of suicidal youth moved by the new literature, the literary market was actually flooded with lyrics, drama, and fiction which in their adoption of the new conventions were merely melancholic, or worse, bathetic.[3]

Only slightly less remarkable was the temporary nature of this vogue, for the more plebeian productions of the new literature appeared scarcely twenty years in the stalls of the *libraires* and *cabinets de lecture*. After 1840 the formulas soon changed emphasis: the new lyrics, *drames*, and historical settings no longer remained so important to adventure, mystery, sentimentality, and patriotism in the *belles lettres*. Eugène Sue, Paul de Kock, Jules Janin, and writers of serial novels, for example, concentrated much more or the popular effects of their work than on the

---

Melodramatic Imagination: Balzac, Henry James, Melodrama, and the Mode of Excess (New Haven: Yale University Press, 1976); for America, John Cawelti, *Adventure, Mystery, and Romance: Formula Stories as Art and Popular Culture* (Chicago: University of Chicago Press, 1976); and more generally, Northrop Frye, *The Secular Scripture: A Study of the Structure of Romance* (Cambridge, Mass.: Harvard University Press, 1976).

3. See what are now amusing accounts of romanticism's impact in Frances Trollope, *Paris and the Parisians in 1835* (New York: Harper and Brothers, 1836), pp. 31–32, 70–71; and Théophile Gautier, *Histoire du romantisme* (Paris: Charpentier, 1911), pp. 152–61, for example. It may be true that readers of romantic literature were indeed moved to the extent that these and other observers in the period claimed. But it is difficult to believe that such was the impact for all readers, especially in light of Alfred de Musset's equally amusing satire in "Lettres de Dupuis et Cotonet," *Œuvres complètes en prose*, Maurice Allem and Paul Courant, eds. (Paris: Gallimard, 1960), pp. 819–36, in which two provincial men of letters feel moved only to confusion and indignation by their reading of romantic works.

esthetic integrity that so worried the romantics still read today. Popular romanticism's decline followed rapidly upon its rise as the expanding book trade and growing readership demanded a purer emotional and dramatic interest than either authentic *romantiques* or their imitators were concerned with in their creations. Thus what was an influential movement in works by young, committed authors in search of a new mode of feeling and expression gave way to the productions of older authors in need of less innovative but more profitable forms. Ironically, the social and economic context that made for romanticism's success and influence on nonelite culture was the same milieu that a mere twenty years later made for its displacement, a context that favored popular sentimental songs, social melodramas, patriotic histories, and intriguing *romans-feuilletons* without the overlay of romantic conventions.

Such evidence provided by the study of popular titles certainly explains one aspect of the Roubaud lithograph, at least why all those long forgotten authors were portrayed on the road to posterity: many were literary hacks despite their apparent debt to the movement. Now, however, another problem remains. How is one to account for the large number of writers Roubaud included in this procession? Why was Lamartine so wealthy? And why was Scribe so productive? Evidently Roubaud depicted in this curious pictorial satire another neglected element in the study of French romanticism, namely, the commercialization of literature. The literary movement in post–Napoleonic France coincided with developments in publishing that handsomely rewarded many authors for their prodigious efforts. All the writers portrayed here were good bourgeois, despite Gautier's flowing locks of hair. They represented more than posterity to Roubaud and his contemporaries: they were on the road to prosperity as well.

Romanticism in the early nineteenth century must be viewed not only as people then saw it; it must also be considered in its extraliterary context of authors, publishers, and readers. More precise description and analysis of the production, distribution, and consumption of literature are needed to supplement the general accounts of elite romanticism everyone knows. On one level of analysis, climates of opinion, intellectual responses to changing social and political conditions, creative rebellions against the constraints of a sterile esthetic, and the like—the prevailing views of the romantic movement—are all adequate perhaps in explaining romanticism among elites. But they fail to explain its popular manifestations and their commercial success. Romanticism was good business, as Roubaud shows us: the question remains how and why this was so.[4]

4. Suggestions that romanticism was open to a brief, superficial, and commercial exploitation are found in the shrewd remarks of Victor Hugo, "Préface de *Cromwell*,"

This too is important in the social history of ideas. The commercial intrusion in literature made possible the extensive diffusion of romantic forms by authors no longer studied. Indeed, romanticism triumphed during a remarkable transformation in writing, publishing, and reading. With the rapid decline of patronage after the 1789 revolution, a new generation of authors born at the turn of the century learned to profit in the literary marketplace: their intellectual maturation and commercial apprenticeship in the period fostered the vogue of popular romanticism. Similarly, booksellers and publishers sought new modes of distribution just when the new writers came forward. Instead of producing expensive books for a known and limited audience, they promoted cheaper editions aimed at a larger, more diverse readership—a development that briefly profited the new literature. But also the increasing demand for books encouraged authors and publishers in their endeavors. Rising literacy and politicization among the Parisian populace nourished its intellectual curiosity, however ill informed and undiscriminating. Such a new audience probably read and may even have understood some of the more entertaining romantic innovations added to a more purely gothic, sentimental, and adventurous literature.

Perhaps because of these developments in the immediate social and economic context of books, the new literature effected a major cultural change in Paris during the middle years of the *monarchie censitaire*. Reaching a large, diverse audience romanticism not only exerted its intellectual and social influence on the cartesian rationality of the elites described in the literary accounts of the day. It also touched the popular culture of the lower orders evident in the plebeian titles they read. This movement in ideas and literature marked one of the first stages in the development of a "mass" culture in which the cultural cleavages between the bourgeoisie and the *menu peuple* began to disappear.[5] Despite the relatively broad appeal of earlier gothic and sentimental romances, often

---

Oeuvres complètes: théâtre (Paris: Imprimerie Nationale, 1904–52),1:49; C.-A. Sainte-Beuve, "Quelques vérités sur la situation en littérature," *Revue des deux mondes* 13(1843),4:5–20; and Saint-René Taillandier, "Simples essais d'histoire littéraire. La littérature et les écrivains en France depuis dix ans," *Revue des deux mondes* 18(1847),3:961–96. Such an approach as the present was never very far from the observations of the sharpest critics of the movement: romanticism *was* "low literature."

5. Of course, it is impossible to speak of *mass* culture in the romantic period; nearly all the elements necessary to the phenomenon, at least as sociologists define it, were lacking. Universal literacy, consumer-society leisure, postindustrial material standards of living, electronic media, etc.—none existed in Paris of the early nineteenth century. But evident then *was* an increasingly standardized literature making a socially heterogeneous appeal in less expensive books and newspapers. A new popular culture, resembling in certain crucial ways the mass culture of the twentieth century, had its origins in the romantic period. See Maurice Crubellier, *Histoire culturelle de la France, XIXe–XXe siècles* (Paris: Colin, 1974), pp. 9–23, for a fuller discussion of this problem in the French context.

criticized by propriety-minded *littérateurs,* elements of romanticism reached an even larger audience—from the Académie française to the street vendors on the quays. The new literature belonged to literary worlds both high and low and succeeded, however briefly, in appealing to a large group of authors and readers composing a diverse cross section of Paris. Thus romanticism's actual impact, both as a social and a literary phenomenon, was exerted not solely as a new sensibility among elites. Its emergence as a popular form also helped to blur the cultural distinctions among social classes in Paris of the early nineteenth century.

Romanticism also marked the crucial shift from traditional folklore to a more modern form of mass culture, a transition that appeared in the displacement of the *bibliothèque bleue, canards,* and oral literature of the eighteenth century by a standardized literature appealing to the largest possible audience in the nineteenth.[6] To be sure, political poetry, melodramas, *romans noirs,* and nationalistic histories had their origins in the eighteenth century. They were closely tied to the growth of a middle-class audience literate and wealthy enough in this early period to participate in the low life of literature. This literature appeared just as other elites were enjoying the *Encyclopédie,* and as peasants in and out of Paris were relishing the *bibliothèque bleue* before 1800. But with the rapid spread of literacy and the flow of cheaper books and newspapers in the nineteenth century, this urban middle-class literature began to command a disproportionate share of the book trade. It reached at last the hands of the *menu peuple*—greengrocers, artisans, even journeymen, and domestics—who had been the audience for the traditional almanacs, saints' lives, and broadsides. While the neo-classical canon of elite literature was giving way to romantic innovation, the titles in the *colporteur* baskets, in the countryside as well as in the city, increasingly included plebeian imitations of a new urban literature.

Romanticism participated in this transition from an essentially bifurcated culture of eighteenth-century elite and popular literatures (circulating in two generally separate social worlds and reflecting two very different mind frames), to a more homogeneous culture of nineteenth-century mass literature (reaching nearly every social level and heralding the demise of the traditional *mentalités*).[7] No doubt the movement first

6. This is a major historical problem that has received all too little attention. For initial discussions, see Robert Mandrou, *De la culture populaire aux 17ᵉ et 18ᵉ siècles* (Paris: Stock, 1975), pp. 183–95; Jean-Jacques Darmon, *Le colportage de librairie en France sous le second empire* (Paris: Plon, 1972), pp. 158–76; and Eugen Weber, *Peasants into Frenchmen: The Modernization of Rural France, 1870–1914* (Stanford: Stanford University Press, 1976), pp. 452–70.

7. Note contemporary observations of this cultural transition in Alexis de Tocqueville, *Democracy in America,* 2nd ed., Henry Reeve, trans., and Francis Bowen, ed. (Cambridge, Mass.: Sever and Francis, 1863 [1835–40]),2:56–74; and Jules Michelet, *Le peuple,*

shocked the elites by its deliberate iconoclasm, but it also appealed to the middle and lower classes in their thirst for distraction or political action. The romantics borrowed from all sources, high and low, to establish a new esthetic to rival the classicists; but the *chansonniers*, comedy-vaudevilles, romances, and popular histories borrowed even more from the romantics, the movement's conventions especially, in their expression of a whole other perception of concerns and the world, even though they were increasingly subject to commercial exploitation by the new entrepreneurs of literature for mass consumption.

In this, then, lies romanticism's revolution. The movement certainly effected a major change in intellectual paradigms among elites as historians have long characterized it: nearly all discourse, literary or otherwise, reflected a decisive deviation from the rational, universal, and secular world of the eighteenth-century *lumières*, in favor of the more emotional, particularistic, even mystical *Weltansicht* in the nineteenth century. This new sensibility, influencing subsequent generations of writers, has been well documented among serious authors and readers. But a parallel transition in the popular literature of the period also occurred and deserves more attention than it has received. Besides its influence on elites, romanticism affected ordinary men and women in the new kinds of literature they were now reading in common, for the first time, with their social betters. Such was a genuine cultural as well as social upheaval, a new notion of French literature, however unenduring, far more homogeneous than either the Enlightenment fifty years earlier or Naturalism fifty years later. Romanticism essentially was a privileged moment in the history of French literature *and* of urban popular mentalities. This cultural world crossed class lines well before the socially divisive political events of 1848, before industrialization in France created new and sharper class distinctions, before the French perceived their cultural differences in new social terms that are so evident today. It may well compare to a similar change in the French cultural climate during the German occupation of World War II when the poetry of the Resistance was read with the same fervor among all social classes, an equally brief interlude in the life of literature despite the variety of tastes evident in France since the last part of the nineteenth century.[8]

Robert Casanova, ed. (Paris: Julliard, 1965 [1846]), pp. 112–22. See also the reflections of one man only two generations removed from these developments in Edmond Goblot, *La barrière et le niveau: étude sociologique sur la bourgeoisie française moderne*, 2nd ed. (Paris: Presses Universitaires de France, 1968 [1925]), pp. 86–103.

8. The evolution of "taste cultures" often blurring class lines in periods of major transition is well characterized theoretically in Herbert J. Gans, *Popular Culture and High Culture: An Analysis and Evaluation of Taste* (New York: Basic Books, 1974), pp. 56–58;

Of course we know that by 1835 many contemporary observers were making similar claims, that the romantics were disrupting literary conventions on nearly every social level in Paris. The prim Frances Trollope actually likened the movement to an earthquake in the salons. One of Honoré de Balzac's shrewd *libraires* complained of the deluge of "incomprehensible verse, . . . of descriptive poems in which the new school believed itself innovative by imitating Delille."[9] After reading the baron de Barante's *Histoire des ducs de Bourgogne*, the school boys Maxime Du Camp and Louis Courier began writing their own history, replete with scenes of stabbings, rapes, burnings, and assorted tortures. "We were slaves, slaves to the romantic conventions," Du Camp noted later.[10] Shocked by the success of the new mode, guardians of the neo-classical virtues accused the romantics of deliberate vulgarity. Had he lived to 1835, one such critic, Louis-Simon Auger of the Académie, would not have been surprised to see popular lithographs of scenes from Alexandre Dumas and Victor Hugo sold in the streets of Paris.[11]

Moreover, literary evidence in the period also indicates the movement's impact on Parisian social life. Even before 1830 women's fashions adopted *manches à gigot* and *toques à créneaux* in imitation of dress during the Middle Ages. Similarly, the new expressive vocabulary of young writers crept into drawing room conversation. *Jeune-France, muguet, toupet, crocodile, rococo,* and *perruque*—slang from Théophile Gautier's *cénacle*—were used briefly during the July Monarchy to designate various age groups under forty-five.[12] Beyond such habits were new norms of bizarre behavior that many believed were encouraged by the new school of writers. Poses of languor and melancholy, heightened by draughts of vinegar to give a sickly pale to the poetic face, coincided with the vogue of

George H. Lewis, "The Sociology of Popular Culture," *Current Sociology* 26(1978),3:19; and more specifically in France of the romantic period, Maurice Agulhon, "Le problème de la culture populaire en France autour de 1848," *Romantisme* 13(1975),50–64; Adeline Daumard, "Le peuple dans la société française à l'époque romantique," *Romantisme* 13(1975),21–28; and Peter Burke, *Popular Culture in Early Modern Europe* (New York: Harper and Row, 1978), pp. 281–86.

9. Honoré de Balzac, *Illusions perdues* in *La comédie humaine*, Pierre-Georges Castex, ed. (Paris: Gallimard, 1977),5:368. See also Trollope, *Paris and the Parisians*, p. 71.

10. Maxime Du Camp, *Souvenirs littéraires* (Paris: Hachette, 1882),1:139–40.

11. Louis-Simon Auger, *Discours sur le romantisme*, prononcé dans la séance annuelle des quatre académies du 24 avril 1824 (Paris: Didot, 1824); Pierre-Louis Duchartre and René Saulnier, *L'imagerie parisienne* (l'imagerie de la rue Saint-Jacques) (Paris: Gründ, 1944), pp. 133–44.

12. Georges Matoré, *Le vocabulaire et la société sous Louis-Philippe...* (Genève: Droz, 1951), p. 76. See also Louis Maigron, *Le romantisme et la mode, d'après les documents inédits* (Paris: Champion, 1911), pp. 5–49.

femmes fatales and Byronic rakes. Etienne-Jean Delécluze claimed retrospectively that "the novels of Werther and of Herman and Dorothea by Goethe contributed in modifying the natural character of the French, giving them the trace of sadness that lingered for a long time in our literary productions."[13] Still others feared that the rash of recent suicides in the city were due to imaginations heated by romantic works.

Such remarkable accounts of the movement's effects indicate how pervasive were the new literary values after 1830. Besides its influence on literature, romanticism appears to have altered the outlook and conduct of its immediate Parisian audience, as well as the sensibilities of many subsequent generations of readers. Unfortunately, these anecdotes written by middle-class literati only suggest how far the phenomenon of romanticism reached among the general population of France. The romantic revolution affected many more people than the few depicted in formal texts, the traditional bases for most histories of the movement. But such literary accounts can be complemented by other sources and methods borrowed from social history to show more precisely what share the *menu peuple* also had in the new "world view." To discover just how lively the popular intellectual climate was in post–Napoleonic France involves a closer study of the diffusion and material circumstances of ideas among the common people and their particular culture. Once this central insight has been accepted, a new history of ideas and their social context becomes not only possible, with the wide range of evidence available, but necessary for a fuller understanding of the French romantic movement and the remarkable lithograph by Benjamin Roubaud.

In viewing romanticism in this way, this book argues a cultural upheaval whose nature has been debated, sometimes acrimoniously, by a long line of literary and intellectual historians. Since the movement's conscious inception in France, the romantics claimed to be creating an entirely new literature. Emile Deschamps declared in 1825 that "the truly talented men in every epoch are always gifted with an instinct that pushes them toward the new."[14] Yet the neo-classicists accused them not of originality but of bad taste during their emotional arguments with the leaders of the "new" literature. Long after its passing, the movement continued to divide opinion over its claim to revolution. During the Second Empire, Théophile Gautier appraised it nostalgically, C.-A.

---

13. Etienne-Jean Delécluze, *Souvenirs de soixante années* (Paris: Michel Lévy frères, 1862), pp. 36–37.

14. Emile Deschamps, *Un manifeste du romantisme* (Paris: Presses Françaises, 1923), p. 13.

Sainte-Beuve abrasively—just as they openly disagreed on the extent of the changes they witnessed as younger men.[15]

More recently scholars have responded with equal fervor to the same question. Irving Babbitt condemned romanticism as an old disease that Albert Béguin, to the contrary, thought new and pathetic. Even with a recent reassessment of the movement, intellectual historians still cannot agree. For instance, J. J. Saunders traced romanticism—"self-conscious, neurotic, and unbalanced"—back to the Middle Ages, but Jacques Barzun disagreed.[16] He believed the movement marked a true "biological revolution," that "by the end of the eighteenth century, new branches of knowledge—the science of man had come of age . . . offering new facts, new analogies, new modes of thought." For Barzun, then, romanticism was equivalent to neither "irrationalism, nor sentimentality, . . . indolence, nor feeblemindedness."[17] Thus with no apparent resolution in sight, the old problem of continuity and change in romantic ideas continues to be fiercely debated by twentieth-century intellectual historians.

The movement's definition has been no less an issue. This study is based, in part, on recent work in literary criticism that defines romanticism by its use of imagery. But this consensus has hardly gone unchallenged. Since the first self-conscious writers in the new vogue attempted and failed at their own definitions, it has been difficult if not impossible to find a common thread that tied them together. During the Restoration, the *Globe* ran a series of twelve articles, each proposing a different definition. And subsequent critics were quick to point out this diversity to the movement's disadvantage. Alfred de Musset claimed it was impossible to think of romanticism except as an "abuse of adjectives."[18] Such difficulty in precision, of course, was inherent in the nature of romanticism that valued the particular over the universal. As a result, Arthur O. Lovejoy demanded that the term be used in the plural, since he discerned not one but many romanticisms in France as well as Europe. Only very recently René Wellek, Morse Peckham, and others have seen this diversity as

15. Gautier, *Histoire du romantisme*, pp. 152–61; Sainte-Beuve, "Poésies complètes de Théodore de Banville," *Causeries du lundi*, 4th ed. (Paris: Garnier frères, [n.d.]),4:69–85. See also a witty critic of the movement in M. le baron d'Ordre, *Les classiques et les romantiques* (Paris: n.p., 1829).

16. Irving Babbitt, *Rousseau and Romanticism* (Boston: Houghton, Mifflin, 1919), pp. 306–52; Albert Béguin, *L'âme romantique et le rêve: essai sur le romantisme allemand et la poésie française*, 2nd ed. (Paris: Corti, 1960), pp. 47–86; J. J. Saunders, *The Age of Revolution* (New York: Hutchinson, 1949), p. 68; and Jacques Barzun, *Classic, Romantic and Modern* (Chicago: University of Chicago Press, 1975 [1943]), pp. 1–17.

17. Barzun, *Classic*, p. 54, 10.

18. Musset, "Lettres," p. 820. See also Pierre Trahard, ed. *Le romantisme défini par 'Le Globe'* (Paris: Presses Françaises, 1924).

purely relative. Nearly all romantic literature, for Wellek, had the "same conception of poetry and . . . [the] poetic imagination, the same conception of nature and its relation to man, and basically the same poetic style."[19] Still major exceptions to the rule complicate enormously this affirmation, and applying this precept in literary criticism remains a serious problem of study.

Perhaps wisely, social historians have attempted to rescue romanticism from the historical isolation of such arguments. Instead of evaluating or defining the movement, recent histories have tried to characterize its social context. Yet social historians have been no less immune to debate. As literary specialists with historical interests, Henri Peyre traced the origins of romanticism to the decline of the *ancien régime*, while Max Milner saw its roots in the Restoration and attempts to recreate the eighteenth century. Others like Pierre Barbéris described the movement less as a revolt against an anachronistic world, actual or reconstituted, than as an outgrowth of the bourgeois revolution whose contradictions pushed the movement from "a romanticism of the right to one of the left."[20] But J. L. Talmon argued that romanticism was a more ambivalent response to the idea of revolution: "[Romantic] man," he claimed, "was at once a *revolté* and a creature craving objective order; a being straining to express and assert itself and a social yearning for self surrender."[21]

The issue contested by these historical explanations, apparently, is not whether or not romanticism was revolutionary—that much they agreed upon—but *what* it revolted against. Did romanticism rebel against the rationality, the universality, or the cosmopolitanism of eighteenth-century elites? Or was it the vanity of the aristocracy, the pretensions of the middle classes, or the plight of the lower orders that provoked and sustained the movement in the nineteenth century? Which generation of

19. René Wellek, "The Concept of 'Romanticism' in Literary History," *Comparative Literature* 1(1949),2:147. See also Arthur O. Lovejoy, "On the Discrimination of Romanticisms," *PMLA* 39(1924),2:229–53; Wellek, "Romanticism Re-Examined," *Concepts of Criticism*, Stephen G. Nichols, Jr., ed. (New Haven: Yale University Press, 1963), pp. 199–221; Morse Peckham, "Toward a Theory of Romanticism," *PMLA* 61(1951),1:5–23; Henry H. H. Remak, "West European Romanticism: Definition and Scope," *Comparative Literature: Method and Perspective*, Newton P. Stallknecht and Horst Frenz, eds. (Carbondale: Southern Illinois University Press, 1961), pp. 223–59; and "Trends of Recent Research on West European Romanticism," *"Romantic" and its Cognates: The European History of a Word*, Hans Eichner, ed. (Toronto: University of Toronto Press, 1972), pp. 475–500.

20. Pierre Barbéris, "Le mal du siècle, ou d'un romantisme de droit à un romantisme de gauche," *Romantisme et politique, 1815–1851*. Colloque d'histoire littéraire. Ecole Normale Supérieure de Saint-Cloud, 1966 (Paris: Colin, 1969), pp. 164–87. See also Henri Peyre, *Qu'est-ce que le romantisme?* (Paris: Presses Universitaires de France, 1974), pp. 9–44; and Max Milner, *Le romantisme, I: 1820–1843* (Paris: Arthaud, 1973), pp. 27–30.

21. J. L. Talmon, *Romanticism and Revolt: Europe 1815–1848* (New York: Harcourt, Brace and World, 1967), p. 136.

romantic writers responded to the consequences of the 1789 revolution and which reacted to the failings of the constitutional monarchies? These questions have been answered various ways. The resulting confusion inherent in such analyses of historical climates has actually led to further conflict over the movement's social bases: was romanticism essentially bourgeois as Arnold Hauser implies, or antibourgeois as Paul Bénichou suggests?[22] And so the debate continues.

In 1955 Albert Joseph George took a less ambiguous approach to the social history of romanticism.[23] His analysis of the new literature's response to the industrial revolution had the merit of focusing attention on important economic relations overlooked in previous accounts of the movement. More specifically, George viewed romanticism as a literary response to industrialization and its social consequences. The industrial revolution in France not only provided romantics with a new social mythology, but it also promoted their publication and diffusion. Undoubtedly some aspects of French industrialization were painfully slow to develop in the nineteenth century; recent economic historians have even denied the existence of an industrial revolution in France.[24] Yet important changes in the social and economic context of writing and reading did occur in the period. George's most valuable contribution to romantic historiography was to show how material factors, on an appropriate level of analysis, influenced popular taste in the first half of the nineteenth century so given to new forms of prose fiction. As George noted, new patterns of production, distribution, and consumption of books; new relations between authors, publishers, and readers; new modes of writing, publishing, and reading all transformed the literate world of Paris just when romanticism was making its greatest impact. It was no mere coincidence, then, that in post–Napoleonic France, these two revolutions—the literary and the extraliterary—participated in new cultural developments: their connections deserve closer examination than George was able to offer in his study.

22. Arnold Hauser, *The Social History of Art*, Stanley Godman, trans. (New York: Vintage, [n.d.]),3:163–227; and Paul Bénichou, *Le sacre de l'écrivain, 1750–1830* (Paris: Corti, 1973), pp. 346–52.

23. Albert Joseph George, "The Romantic Revolution and the Industrial Revolution in France," *Symposium* (Winter 1952),281–89; and *The Development of French Romanticism: The Impact of the Industrial Revolution on Literature* (Syracuse: Syracuse University Press, 1955).

24. See Jean Marczewski, "Some Aspects of the Economic Growth of France, 1660–1958," *Economic Development and Cultural Change* 9(1961),369–86; Maurice Lévy-Leboyer, "Croissance économique en France au XIXe siècle," *Annales: E.S.C.* 23(1968), 788–807; and François Crouzet, "Essai de construction d'un indice annuel de la production industrielle française au XIXe siècle," *Annales: E.S.C.* 24(1970),56–99.

This problematic relationship between literature and its historical environment, though, has long interested literary critics more than social historians. The systematic analysis of the ties between literature and society may be said to begin in France with Germaine de Staël's *De la littérature considérée dans ses rapports avec les institutions sociales* (1800) which marked the origins of contemporary social-literary criticism. Since then, critics have come to recognize that a fruitful balance exists between study of the work and of its world, *pace* literary purists of the likes of Northrop Frye and Tzvetan Todorov. Some of the more useful explorations in literary sociology have examined literature as a commodity as well as a myth. While most students of the problem of literature and society have focused, quite naturally, on the issues raised in close consideration of the texts themselves, sociologists have also analyzed the extraliterary milieu of the text—its authors, publishers, and readers. Levin Schücking, Robert Escarpit, and Leo Lowenthal, among others, have studied the production, distribution, and consumption of literature and attempted to show that a work's immediate socioeconomic environment is an important influence on both its form and content.[25] Poetry, drama, and fiction are commodities, like shoes and soap, only in the shape of books. A study of *les faits littéraires* (Escarpit's term) not only clarifies external influences on literature, but also suggests a rich field of research on books as historical and cultural artifacts.

These insights have not been lost on recent social historians who have adapted some of these approaches of literary sociology, especially in their work on the French Enlightenment. *Annales* historians explored the intellectual climate of the *ancien régime* by looking not at the great works of the eighteenth-century *lumières*, read by only a small coterie of elites, but at the vast body of *colporteur* literature that was the reading matter of most French people until as late as the Second Empire. In this study they posed fundamentally new questions about the character of popular literary culture under the old regime: who produced books in the eighteenth century? what were they? and who read them? Consequently, their subjects were often the obscure grub-street authors of Paris, the provincial publishers of the *bibliothèque bleue*, the forgotten masses who read or listened to *colporteur* literature, as well as the popular titles and images peddled in the countryside. François Furet, Geneviève Bollème, Robert

---

25. L. L. Schücking, *The Sociology of Literary Taste*, Brian Battershaw, trans. (Chicago: University of Chicago Press, 1966); Robert Escarpit, *Sociologie de la littérature* (Paris: Presses Universitaires de France, 1958); Leo Lowenthal, *Literature, Popular Culture, and Society* (Englewood Cliffs: Prentice-Hall, 1961); and Hugh Dalziel Duncan, *Language and Literature in Society: A Sociological Essay on Theory and Method in the Interpretation of Linguistic Symbols* (Chicago: University of Chicago Press, 1953).

Mandrou, and others intended to locate the Enlightenment more precisely within the actualities of French society using methods and sources very different from those of older intellectual histories.[26] And the findings of this new line of historical investigation have largely revised many former notions of ideas and culture in early modern France.

These approaches to the history of ideas and literature are applied in the present study of French romanticism. Essentially, this examination of the sociocultural world of the early nineteenth century borrows from both literary sociologists and social historians. A wide range of questions is posed here that have already been asked, but only about other literary and intellectual movements, namely, what were French romanticism's popular manifestations? (Chapter 1); just how widespread were they? (Chapter 2); who wrote romantic works? (Chapter 3); who published them? (Chapter 4); what share of the book market did they have? (Chapter 5); who read them? (Chapter 6); what impact did revolution have on the new literature? (Chapter 7); and finally, what was the historical significance of popular French romanticism? (Chapter 8). In suggesting answers to these questions, like those already posed for the eighteenth century, an attempt is made to view romanticism as more a cultural than a literary phenomenon. Early nineteenth-century ideas are situated more in their social and economic context than in their intellectual tradition. Consequently, such an investigation depends upon methods and sources appropriate to social rather than intellectual history. The results, too, differ from those of older literary histories of romanticism. In contrast to the ambiguous study of written texts, not to mention the ambiguity of the texts themselves, the present study of their extraliterary milieu promises to show clearly the social character and cultural significance of the romantic revolution.

This approach also suggests clarification of the anomalous nature of formal French romanticism in the history of European literature. As opposed to the movement in Britain and Germany, in France it was relatively late and unenduring. German and English writers fashioned a literary response to neo-classical proprieties and celebrated the primacy of nature over art, for example, well before the nineteenth century. But elite French literati broke with their classical tradition much less perva-

---

26. Darnton, *The Business of Enlightenment: A Publishing History of the Encyclopédie, 1775–1800* (Cambridge, Mass.: Harvard University Press, 1979); Mandrou, *Introduction to Modern France, 1500–1640: An Essay in Historical Psychology*, R. E. Hallmark, trans. (New York: Harper and Row, 1975); Geneviève Bollème, *La bibliothèque bleue: littérature populaire en France du XVIIe au XIXe siècle* (Paris: Julliard, 1971); and François Furet et al. *Livre et société dans la France du XVIIIe siècle* (Paris: Mouton, 1965–70), 2 vols.

sively and only much later during the Restoration. Despite the brief
legacy of Rousseau—a truly exceptional figure—French romanticism
evinced a relative preference for order and clarity absent from the European movement generally. Even a leading romantic such as Chateaubri-
and argued the need for some esthetic principles, whatever the effusion of
feeling expressed in his own work.

A study of the movement among the *menu peuple*, on the other
hand, shows that popular French romanticism was much less at odds with
the European development of "mass" culture, if we can speak of it in this
early period. At least in the nineteenth century, romantic versions of
sentimental poetry, violent melodramas, gothic romances, and patriotic
histories existed in similar forms all over Europe. They were hardly
unique to France: witness the tremendous European vogue of works by
Schiller, Scott, and Manzoni in the 1820s. As a new mass culture began to
develop with widespread literacy, higher standards of living, and cheaper
newspapers and books—first in Britain, then on the continent—uniform
elements of romantic literature reached more ordinary people everywhere. Since it was far from specific to France, this problem deserves to
be seen in its Europe-wide milieu.

In focusing on Paris, however, the present study has singled out a
particularly clear example of these developments. Of course, this reflects
a definite bias. At the height of the new literature's success, Paris remained the center of important events on the continent, from insurrec-
tion to fashion. From here revolutions in many fields—political, social,
and cultural—spread to the rest of Europe that sometimes initiated less
than responded to matters of international importance. Moreover, Paris
attracted many of Europe's intellectual discontents, often in self-imposed
exile, from the nineteenth century onward. Since the romantic vogue was
no exception to this trend, the movement was likely to have a much more
evident impact in Paris of the *monarchie censitaire* than at any other place
or time. Nevertheless, it was only a few decades before similar developments began to occur elsewhere in France and Europe with similarly
dramatic consequences. Paris in the romantic epoch exemplifies the
historical pattern, a pattern that needs closer examination. The selective
focus, then, does not undermine its significance, while it greatly facili-
tates the necessary documentation. The bias of a study devoted solely to
Paris is instructive in an examination of cultural developments not only in
France, but also in Britain and Germany whose romanticisms still require
social histories.

But this leaves unanswered at least one very important question:
what did romanticism mean to the people who shared in this literary
phenomenon? We cannot actually trust accounts of major romantics and

their critics. Like Flaubert's satirical description of Emma Bovary's response to reading Walter Scott's novels, they exaggerated, either in horror or in defense of recent developments in the reading of the popular classes. And the largely mute lower orders leave the historian recourse to oblique approaches to the problem. Careful consideration of observers, diaries, and journals of working people, records extant of their reading activities, and the very works they well may have read (demanding a cautious exercise of the historical imagination) must serve as our only means to the life of plebeian minds in the past, otherwise inaccessible to the social historian.[27] We know that ideals and aspirations touched many people: the quest for "liberty" was strong among the men and women on the barricades during the 1830 revolution.[28] Only now we must determine what their more ordinary dreams were and what they meant during the romantic period. Undoubtedly this is a nearly impossible task, and the present volume will undertake only the immediately possible portion of it. Others will have to do more.

In the meantime, the conclusions that may be drawn from this analysis of romanticism demand a reassessment of the movement's debt to its historical context and its place in the history of French popular culture. While it remains difficult to prove the part played by the climate of opinion in post–Napoleonic France, it is easier to point out the elements of authorship, publishing, and readership that informed romanticism in a more immediately apparent way. Young writers in search of a viable career, sophisticated entrepreneurs in quest of marketable books, and larger numbers of naive readers in need of distraction contributed to the shape and scope of romanticism. Similarly, the evolution of production, distribution, and consumption of books in the period helped to foster a new literature for mass consumption, just as it promoted romanticism's influence, however brief, on Parisian literary taste. Moreover, the movement's participation in popular culture—the rise and fall of its vogue and the nature of its popular imitations—points up romanticism's role in mediating the transition from traditional to modern cultural patterns in Paris, perhaps in France and Europe as well, from 1820 to 1840.[29] In this

27. For example, Mandrou, *Introduction*, pp. 1–10; and Burke, *Popular Culture*, pp. 77–87.

28. See accounts of popular ideals in the 1830 revolution discussed in David Pinkney, *The French Revolution of 1830* (Princeton: Princeton University Press, 1972), pp. 252–73; and Edgar L. Newman, "What the Crowd Wanted in the French Revolution of 1830," in John M. Merriman, ed. *1830 in France* (New York: New Viewpoints, 1975), pp. 17–40.

29. Note that the term "culture" here denotes actually only one aspect, however important, of the larger conception studied by anthropologists. Literature and art share with

transition romanticism did not immediately change people's attitudes and behavior, as some commentators in the period would have us believe. What it did promote were developments in popular taste: romanticism shared in the way people wrote, published, and read in the early nineteenth century. The purpose of this book is to examine *how* it did so in more detail.

---

myth and ritual, gestures and conventions, "an historically transmitted pattern of meanings embodied in symbols, a system of inherited conceptions expressed in symbolic forms by means of which men communicate, perpetuate, and develop their knowledge about and attitudes towards life," according to Clifford Geertz. The present venture focuses on a very special system of signs, not on all of those that constitute such a culture. See Geertz, *The Interpretation of Cultures* (New York: Basic Books, 1973), pp. 3–30, 86–89, and 142–46.

FRENCH ROMANTICISM AND POPULAR LITERATURE

𝓛 ITERARY EVIDENCE AFTER 1820 suggests that romanticism owed its popular success less to its responsiveness to the prevailing intellectual climate than to its deliberate vulgarity. Many bitter critics, less committed observers as well, accused the movement of pandering to the lowest possible audience at the boulevard theaters where many of its plays were staged. "Write without rules and without art in the romantic fashion and you will create melodramas moving the multitude," claimed François Guizot in the preface to his translation of Shakespeare's works, ironically the very models claimed by the early French romantic dramatists.[1] When Alexandre Dumas wanted to stage *Antony* starring Marie Dorval at the Théâtre français in 1834, shocked neo-classicists demanded that the Interior Ministry ban the play, primarily because of this attempt "to foist the actors from the Porte Saint-Martin onto the Théâtre français and to naturalize absurd and filthy melodramas there."[2] These criticisms suggested by their very hysteria a secret envy of the romantics' success as well as a genuine outrage over their flouting of the neo-classical rules: critics seem to have recognized that the new theater succeeded largely because it ignored established literary conventions.

The romantics' conscious adoption of melodramatic effects, especially their emphasis on plots given to violence, intrigue, and chance, invited such a recognition, however damning its indictment of their esthetic. Many of the manifestoes and prefaces defending the movement from attack actually attempted to excuse such excesses. For some, these were the deliberate concessions they felt necessary for the establishment of a true literature of the present, as Stendhal argued in *Racine et*

1. François Guizot, ed., *Oeuvres complètes de Shakespeare* (Paris: Didier et cie., 1860), 1:126.

2. Quoted in Alexandre Dumas, *Mes mémoires*, Pierre Josserand, ed. (Paris: Gallimard, 1967), 4:317.

Shakespeare.[3] Even Alfred de Vigny the arch-elitist of the movement admitted as much in a preface: romantic history, he said, "is a novel authored by the people."[4] Consequently, in their creation of a new literary canon, romantics borrowed freely from popular literature to suit their needs: to this end George Sand, Gérard de Nerval, and Charles Nodier cultivated the study of provincial folklore.[5] In defense of the debt romanticism owed to the vulgar, Lady Sydney Morgan rationalized in 1830 that "the ambition to be useful to the many [had] superseded the desire of writing only for the refined and fastidious few."[6] In every genre the French romantics appeared to reflect an increasing attention to a larger, less lettered audience.

Such observations, however, are misleading. Because these criticisms were written mostly about elite romantic works and their apparent debt to literary low life, they overlooked the influence that romanticism itself exerted on truly popular literature. Many historians reading only the contemporary charges and countercharges by neo-classicists and the romantics have thus neglected the social and cultural role that the movement played in sentimental and jolly songs, melodramas and comedy-vaudevilles, gothic and adventure novels, and dramatic national histories. For a number of reasons, this world has simply not received the same careful attention critics have lavished on more "serious" works. While numerous histories and accounts of French romanticism detail the clear influence of popular literature on the romantics in the movement's quest to free elite literature of its sterile esthetic constraints, few if any study the favor romanticism enjoyed among works more generally available to a less sophisticated audience.[7]

The relationship between the romantic movement and popular literature was a rich one, and it requires an examination at least as extensive as that generally devoted to the debates between the romantics and the neo-classicists in most histories. Thus discussion here will focus not on the books aimed at the happy few, but on those obviously intended for the

3. Stendhal, *Racine et Shakespeare* (London: Oxford University Press, 1907), p. 21.

4. Alfred de Vigny, "Réflexions sur la vérité dans l'art," *Oeuvres complètes,* Ferdinand Baldensperger, ed. (Paris: Gallimard, 1950),2:22.

5. See George Sand, *Les légendes rustiques* (Paris: A. Morel, 1858); Charles Nodier, "Introduction," *Nouvelle bibliothèque bleue, ou légendes populaires en France,* A. J. V. Léroux de Lincy, ed. (Paris: Columb de Batine, 1842); and Gérard de Nerval, ed. *Chansons et ballades populaires du Valois* (Paris: Garnier frères, 1885).

6. Lady Sydney Morgan, *France in 1829–1830* (London: Saunders and Otley, 1830),1:270.

7. For surveys of French romanticism's debt to popular literature, see Hauser, *Social History*, 3:196–207; and George, *French Romanticism*, pp. 47–57.

anonymous many. After a brief definition of romanticism and survey of plebeian literature, this chapter takes a closer look at examples of popular titles in the genres most clearly influenced by the movement—poetry, drama, fiction, and history—to show how its ideas appeared to most readers in the period. In this way the place of elite ideas in popular culture, besides the debt romanticism owed to the low life of literature, may be assessed more accurately than what various contemporaries claimed so boldly.

ELITE ROMANTICISM AND THE NEW POPULAR LITERATURE

First, what do we mean here by *romanticism?* Even an examination of the social and cultural context of ideas must have some notion of its subject to avoid confusion, especially in an analysis of its influence and diffusion in plebeian literature. Unfortunately, the word has as many meanings as commentators, since the self-proclaimed romantics themselves were unsure what it signified even in the relatively narrow field of literature.[8] And the plethora of critical studies devoted to the problem since then offers equally little hope of a coherent definition: Ferdinand Baldensperger actually counted more than 600 different uses of the word, though his sources extended beyond the bounds of romantic France.[9] The term may be undefinable, short of what the movement was not. As Alexandre Dumas stated cleverly in his memoirs, "everyone agreed on one point, that if we did not know yet what it was we wanted, we knew at least what we did not want."[10] Such backhanded definitions, to be sure, will not suffice.

Nevertheless, Charles Baudelaire was probably right: "romanticism lies precisely in neither the choice of subject nor the depiction of truth, but in the manner of feeling," a manner of perceiving the world in terms very different from the objectivity, universality, and rationality cherished by the eighteenth-century *philosophes.*[11] Consequently, French romanti-

---

8. See Maurice Z. Shroder, "France: Roman-Romanesque-Romantique-Romantisme," in Eichner, ed. *"Romantic" and its Cognates*, pp. 263–92. Definitions of romanticism are as numerous as its histories. The debate between those who deny and those who attempt a definition is well represented by Lovejoy, "On the Discrimination of Romanticisms," and Wellek, "The Concept of Romanticism."

9. Ferdinand Baldensperger, *'Romantique': ses analogues et ses équivalents. Tableau synoptique de 1650 à 1840* (Cambridge, Mass.: Harvard University Press, 1937).

10. Quoted in C. H. Conrad Wright, *A History of French Literature* (New York: Oxford University Press, 1912), p. 652.

11. Charles Baudelaire, "Qu'est-ce que le romantisme?" *Œuvres complètes*, Y.-G. LeDantec and Claude Pichois, eds. (Paris: Gallimard, 1961), p. 879.

cism, the intellectual and literary movement, may be characterized by "the great endeavor to overcome the split between subject and object, the self and the world, the conscious and the unconscious."[12] Indeed when Lamartine wrote, "Et moi, je suis semblable à la feuille flétrie;/ Emportez-moi comme elle, orageux aquilons!" he captured this longing common among romantics to identify their emotions with natural imagery, real or poetic.[13] Also distinguishing this cultural vision from both the neo-classicism of the elites and the traditional *mentalités* of the peasantry, such a sentiment prescribed a reasonably narrow set of virtues: imaginativeness, individualism, originality, spontaneity, and to a more limited extent, religion, mysticism, *mal de siècle*, liberalism, and cosmopolitanism of time and place. Despite exceptions to the state of mind and its literary values—just how liberal *were* the early French romantics?—these elements are easily identified in the movement's major works from 1820 to 1840 that may well have been the source of the "modern ego" in the history of western ideas.[14]

Accompanying this distinctive sentiment was the new literature's frequent rejection of neo-classical forms.[15] The romantics often sought new modes of expression that were more appropriate to their view of the world than the formal literary constraints imposed in the seventeenth century. In time their bitter debates with the neo-classicists increasingly emphasized this poetic freedom, so by 1829 Hugo was declaring that "art has nothing to do with restrictions, gags, or manacles."[16] But the new

12. Wellek, "Romanticism Re-examined," p. 220. This assessment is largely corroborated for French romanticism by Albert Gérard, "On the Logic of Romanticism," *Essays in Criticism* 7(1957),262–73; and Georges Poulet, "Romanticism," *The Metamorphoses of the Circle*, Carley Dawson and Elliott Coleman, trans. (Baltimore: Johns Hopkins University Press, 1966), pp. 91–118. A useful survey of this recent consensus is Remak, "West European Romanticism."

13. Alphonse de Lamartine, "L'isolement," *Oeuvres poétiques complètes*, Marius-François Guyard, ed. (Paris: Gallimard, 1963), p. 4.

14. See Remak, "Trends." For discussion of romanticism as the origin of the modern psyche, see Barzun, *Classic*, pp. 115–31; Talmon, *Romanticism and Revolt*, pp. 135–65; and Peyre, *Qu'est-ce que le romantisme?*, pp. 221–88.

15. Most older literary historians of the romantic movement in France focus on this element of its development. See René Bray, *Chronologie du romantisme, 1804–1830* (Paris: Boivin, 1932); Pierre Moreau, *Le romantisme* (Paris: de Gigord, 1932); and N. H. Clement, *Romanticism in France* (New York: PMLA, 1939), for typical examples.

16. Hugo, "Préface," *Les orientales* in *Oeuvres complètes: poésie*, 1:615. For discussion of romantic stylistic changes, see, for poetry, G. Lotte, "Le vers romantique," *Revue des cours et conférences* 32(1930–31),1:44–58, 179–92, 214–26, 437–52, 538–51, 632–48, 689–704; for drama, W. D. Howarth, *Sublime and Grotesque: A Study of French Romantic Drama* (London: Harrap, 1975); for fiction, Maigron, *Le roman historique à l'époque romantique: essai sur l'influence de Walter Scott* (Paris: Hachette, 1898), pp. 235–432; and

literature did not consist entirely in this development of original forms and conventions. Lamartine and Vigny, for example, frequently expressed their visions within the traditional rules long after the movement was considered synonymous with literary license.[17] Yet contemporaries continued to identify these experiments in form, from *enjambement* in verse to medieval settings in fiction, with romanticism proper. Whether or not they developed a new poetic content, many popular writers seemed to represent the movement primarily because they used its conventions.

Consequently, complete strangers to the romantic sensibility earned reputations as "romantics," creating the *faux romantisme* that Hugo detected as early as 1827.[18] The blurring of the important distinction between *romanticism* the mood expressing a new world view and "romanticism" the mode employing only the new conventions underlies much of the difficulty in defining the new literature. Still, such distinctions suggest ways in which literary works influenced by the movement in ideas may be identified with a fair degree of accuracy. A definition sufficiently coherent to facilitate the study of romanticism's participation in popular literature may be attempted, whatever vagaries remain. Exceptions will always exist, of course, even for the most exacting of criteria, but a positive attempt must be made lest the whole notion of romanticism, as both mood and mode, be lost in sheer nominalism.[19] The critical literary game of finding inconsistencies in definitions of the movement must give way to more constructive approaches to the problem if romanticism is to have any meaning at all.

Thus the present study has adopted three criteria by which romanticism's influence on a broad range of popular works may be determined. They are admittedly selective and surely open to revision. But they do facilitate, in a heuristic way, a social history of French romanticism, one that requires an operational definition to characterize more precisely the movement's contribution to the lives and visions of ordinary people in the past.

---

for history, Emery Neff, *The Poetry of History: The Contribution of Literature and Literary Scholarship to the Writing of History Since Voltaire* (New York: Columbia University Press, 1947), pp. 116–49. Stylistic developments in each genre are well summarized in Paul van Tieghem, *Le romantisme dans la littérature européenne* (Paris: Albin Michel, 1969), pp. 347–457.

17. See, for example, Lamartine, *Méditations poétiques* in *Oeuvres poétiques complètes*, pp. 3–86; and Vigny, *Moïse* in *Oeuvres complètes*, 1:59–62.

18. Hugo, "Préface de *Cromwell*," *Oeuvres complètes: théâtre*, 1:49.

19. E.g., Joseph Aynard, "Comment définir le romantisme?" *Revue de littérature comparée* 5(1925),641–58; and Jean-Bertrand Barrère, "Sur quelques définitions du romantisme," *Revue des sciences humaines*, Fsc. 62–63(1951),98–110.

1. Declaration. Because of the very strong classical tradition dating from the seventeenth century, and because of the pervasiveness of the Enlightenment among elites, the lines between the neo-classicists and the romantics were sharply and self-consciously drawn in their acrimonious debates during the Restoration. For nearly every manifesto, preface, introduction, or work by an ardent adherent of the new literature, there appeared a stinging rebuke by a defender of neo-classical esthetic principles. As the *romantiques* grew more numerous and assertive, new journals like *La muse française* and *Le conservateur littéraire* adopted their cause largely in response to the resistance of more established periodicals that refused to provide them a forum. Members of the Académie française in turn attacked the productions of the *cénacles* maintained by Charles Nodier at the Arsenal or Victor Hugo on the rue Notre Dame des Champs. At stake in all this, however far astray the intense exchanges went, were the enduring beliefs in order and balance in literature, the hallmarks of French poetry and drama from the age of Louis XIV, in marked contrast to the spontaneity and imagination of the nineteenth century advocated by the men and women of the new literature.

It is evident, then, that authors engaging in the debate between romantics and classicists knew at least of the new mode, and perhaps even the sensibility of romanticism. Thus those popular works declaring an allegiance to the movement at some point in the text, comparing their accomplishment to known romantic works or contrasting it to known neo-classical pieces, may be considered "romantic" whether or not they actually used the appropriate conventions or expressed a corresponding mood of melancholy, memory, or enthusiasm. Participation on one side of the argument appears to be explicit documentation of the movement's influence. Certainly without such literary rebels like Emile Deschamps and Louis Vitet expressing their opposition to an earlier tradition defended by established men like Louis-Simon Auger and the baron d'Ordre, the notion of a change in ideas would not have had the impact it did in France—rather a special case in the panoply of European romanticisms thanks to these combative *littérateurs*.

2. Mood. Even more important to the identification of titles influenced by the movement was the romantic sensibility. Since its inception, critics have characterized romanticism's impact on attitudes and values.[20] The yearning to believe despite a faithless society, the despair of living in a rapidly changing and uncertain world, the recognition of time

---

20. E.g., H. G. Schenk, *The Mind of the European Romantics: An Essay in Cultural History* (Garden City: Anchor Books, 1969), pp. 49–77; Hermine Riffaterre, *L'orphisme dans la poésie romantique: thèmes et style surnaturalistes* (Paris: Nizet, 1970), pp. 39–82; and Poulet, "Timelessness and Romanticism," *Journal of the History of Ideas* 15(1954),3–22.

and history through personal memory, the enthusiasm and energy admired in dynamic historical figures, the primacy of the artist's imagination over the canon of esthetic rules and constraints, and a host of other notions expressed in literary works bear witness to the pervasive impact of the romantic movement even in the late eighteenth century. Such undoubtedly marked a major shift in intellectual paradigms that romanticism represented in Europe as well as France. Unfortunately, historians of ideas have cited a wide range of such perspectives, too numerous to use effectively in the present study. The contradictions among them, as Arthur O. Lovejoy noted, only complicate the problem.

But the recent consensus documented in the work of René Wellek, Morse Peckham, and Henry Remak has posited a more convenient definition: the attempt to identify a personal state of mind with natural imagery.[21] Again and again among recognized romantics, this singular longing to overcome the split between subject and object, between the self and the world, between conscious and unconscious appeared in the relationship, for example, between the mood of the narrative voice and its descriptions of a particular setting. In Musset's *La confession d'un enfant du siècle* Octave and Brigitte found the sadness of their impossible love reflected in the somber forest scene of their attempted reconciliation. "While by a strong moonlight we traversed the woods slowly, we both felt ourselves captured by a profound melancholy."[22] Octave remarks here, as he does numerous times, the power of the nocturnal forest to represent his most intimate thoughts about himself and his perversely contradictory feelings for Brigitte. At times this connection between mind and matter was reversed to give inanimate objects their own humanlike emotions: Octave evoked the emotive power of the moon often enough to suggest its participation in his ambivalent love. In fact, such an indulgence in the pathetic fallacy was just another manifestation of the larger attempt to establish a new sensibility in the development of new patterns of images and symbols in romantic literature.

Consequently, the present study sought the essence of the romantic revolution in this relationship between a state of mind and specified literary images. Of course, the contradictions in the sensibility, as well as its definitions, posed serious problems. But the consistency in the use of particular images—the twilight, the mountain, the moon, the sea, and the color blue, for example—permitted a more precise identification of the romantic mood captured by them. This mentality defined in the treat-

21. See Remak, "Trends"; Wellek, "The Concept of Romanticism," and "Romanticism Re-Examined"; and Peckham, "Toward a Theory of Romanticism," and "Toward a Theory of Romanticism, II: Reconsiderations," *Studies in Romanticism* 19(1961),1:1–8.

22. Musset, *Oeuvres complètes en prose*, p. 208.

ment of imagery made the movement's diffusion in the popular literature in the period much more tangible. The explicit manifestations of romanticism's profound presence in the public mind could then be discovered, and the expression of its most poignant attitudes—those of personal introspection, anguished melancholy, and extraordinary enthusiasm—assessed. Such an outlook embodied in a distinctly symbolic pattern was largely unique to romantic poetry, drama, fiction, and history; and it clearly distinguished much of the literary upheaval that has deserved and continues to deserve close critical attention.[23]

3. Mode. Finally, the movement was sought in the forms most appropriate to its sensibility. Constrained by a well-established neoclassical esthetic, romantics often created new literary conventions to facilitate their expression of a new view of man and his world. Some like Hugo considered another mode fundamental to their new perceptions, while others like Pétrus Borel developed a deliberate iconoclasm more for its own sake. Whatever the reasons, the movement meant a certain experimentation in form as well as feeling. Although the experiments specific to romanticism have been the source of much literary historical contention, a few conventions in each genre still stand out, and they may be considered more or less representative of the movement. Surely the renewal of literary forms in France remains one of romanticism's major contributions to the history of literature.

In poetry, freer versification—*enjambement*, approximate rhymes, displacement of the caesura in the alexandrine, conscious prosodic experimentation in less defined poetic forms, and wider vocabulary—were hallmarks associated with the French romantics. In verse drama the flouting of the three classical unities of time, place, and action, and in prose drama, the melange of the comic and the tragic served as useful guides to romantic theatrical forms in which no subject matter was eschewed because of its inappropriateness to classical virtues or values. In fiction the historical novel *à la* Walter Scott was the model for works often set before the classical age of the seventeenth century. Such "medievalism" was very loosely conceived among romantic writers and also appeared in their colorful, dramatic stories set in well-defined, frequently exotic locations.

23. See studies of romantic imagery in Marion Elizabeth Carter, *The Role of Symbolism in French Romantic Poetry* (Washington, D.C.: Catholic University Press, 1946); James Doolittle, "Four Elements in Romantic Writing: Mountain, Blue, Twilight, I," *Symposium* (Winter 1969),216–24; Paul de Man, "Structure intentionnelle de l'image romantique," *Revue internationale de philosophie* 14(1960),60–84; and Victor Brombert, "The Happy Prison: A Recurring Romantic Metaphor," in David Thorburn and Geoffrey Hartman, eds. *Romanticism: Vistas, Instances, Continuities* (Ithaca: Cornell University Press, 1973), pp. 62–82.

In history the adoption of the Middle Ages, its strong figures, dramatic conflicts, and stage paraphernalia were the focus of interest in many romantic studies resuscitating pre–Bourbon France as a subject worthy of serious consideration. And, of course, Napoleon also became an object of romantic admiration after 1820. All works deliberately using these and other iconoclastic conventions too numerous to list here, but discussed in detail elsewhere, were chosen to represent the movement's influence on the popular literature in the period.[24]

It must not be assumed that these elements of French romanticism appeared without a development important to the history of literature in the nineteenth century. Throughout the previous century strands of the movement grew increasingly apparent to an elite audience.[25] One can mention a host of these romantic precursors, viz., the sentimentality of Richardson and Gessner, the meditations on solemn and melancholy subjects in Gray and Young, the appeal of nature's wilder majesty in the pseudo-epics of Ossian—all translated into French. Moreover, there were the transfer of the author's focus from the universal to the particular (often himself) in Rousseau, the growth of elegaic tones in the lyricism of Parny and Millevoye, the exploration of new and exotic landscapes (both real and emotional) in Saint-Pierre and Chateaubriand, and the celebration of chivalry and troubadours in Madame de Staël who helped introduce Schiller and the Schlegel brothers into France, just as many other émigrés during the revolution and empire brought back with them at the Restoration their enthusiasm for Shakespeare, Byron, and the Lake Poets. By the time André Chenier's poetry was published posthumously in 1819 and Lamartine's *Méditations poétiques* appeared in 1820, authors and readers of literature among the social elites of Paris were prepared for the romantic revolution that was to characterize much of the nineteenth century.

Coinciding and even paralleling this evolution in the literary realm of the middle classes and their esthetic betters, however, was another development, one much less studied and still little understood. At roughly the same time romanticism appeared in the works for serious-minded readers, new poetry, drama, fiction, and history were being writ-

24. For titles discussing romantic stylistic changes, see note 16. The method of using these conventions and images, expressive of romanticism in France, is adopted from similar approaches to the problem of documenting literary and artistic trends. See Cawelti, *Adventure*, pp. 5–36; Erwin Panofsky, *Studies in Iconology: Humanistic Themes in the Art of the Renaissance* (New York: Oxford University Press, 1939), pp. 3–31; and John Porter Houston, "Toward a Romantic Iconology," *The Demonic Imagination: Style and Theme in French Romantic Poetry* (Baton Rouge: Louisiana State University Press, 1969), pp. 43–69.

25. Studies and histories of French pre-romanticism and romanticism are numerous. A basic topical bibliography is available in Milner, *Le romantisme*, pp. 363–81.

ten for many in the lower orders. Even before the revolution of 1789, such a plebeian literature had, in fact, been evolving into a literary tradition of its own, almost independent of the monuments still studied by intellectual historians. The turn of the eighteenth century actually marked the decisive transition from a much older popular culture that would have been incapable of participation in an elite intellectual development such as romanticism.

Earlier during the eighteenth century what had circulated among the common people in and out of the cities—broadsides, calendars, saints' lives, fairy tales, and images—expressed a distinct folk culture largely untouched by elite values, as it had since time out of mind.[26] The literature peddled by *colporteurs,* hawked from the baskets hanging from the necks of itinerant agents of booksellers in Epinal, Troyes, and Paris, followed in a peasantlike oral tradition whose vintage still remains a subject of historical debate. But clearly the *canards,* garnished with crude woodcuts and composed in the easy verse of *complaintes,* continued a standard form of urban street literature relatively unchanged from the sixteenth century onward.[27] And the fact that they were often sung by the hawker to attract the single sou paid for broadsides tied them closely to an even older oral literature using many of the same formulas, if not the same details, as the *canards.* The same may perhaps be ventured about other items in the famous blue-covered *bibliothèque bleue:* the simple calendars relied on well-known folk symbols and the brief accounts of the four sons of Aymon and the good king Louis IX, for instance, perpetuated many time-honored subliterary forms.

In the place of this long-standing tradition appeared increasingly a new popular literature far more responsive to elite intellectual influence, a literature that would displace the much older folk literature, oral and written, almost entirely by the Third Republic.[28] For example, where mimes accompanied by music had been common in the streets of Paris during the *ancien régime* (primarily because of the stranglehold maintained by the Théâtre français' monopoly over all theatrical productions),

26. See studies of premodern French popular literature by Mandrou, *De la culture populaire;* Bollème, *Les almanachs populaires aux XVIIe et XVIIIe siècles* (Paris: Mouton, 1969); Pierre Brochon, *Le livre de colportage en France depuis le XVIe siècle* (Paris: Julliard, 1954); and the classic account, Charles Nisard, *Histoire des livres populaires, ou la littérature de colportage depuis l'origine de l'imprimerie* (Paris: Amyot, 1854), 2 vols.

27. See Jean-Pierre Seguin, *Canards du siècle passé* (Paris: Horay, 1969); and *Nouvelles à sensation: canards du XIXe siècle* (Paris: Colin, 1959).

28. See Michel Ragon, *Histoire de la littérature prolétarienne en France* (Paris: Albin Michel, 1974), pp. 73–128; Darmon, *Le colportage de librairie en France,* pp. 159–62; and Weber, *Peasants,* esp. pp. 452–70.

more elaborate musical vaudevilles and comedies were played instead in theaters to a much broader audience in the nineteenth century.[29] The melodrama also originated in the years following the 1789 revolution that had altered radically the political and social foundations of the theater and made possible the staging of such new dramatic forms. With the rapid growth of Parisian playhouses from only twenty-three on the eve of the revolution to forty-four at the end of the Restoration—a growth briefly interrupted by Napoleon's restrictions and neo-classical taste—accommodation was made for sophisticated versions of dramas, topical vaudevilles, fantasies, and pantomimes alike in the romantic period. The establishment of the melodrama with the commercial success of such dramatists as Guilbert de Pixérécourt, "the Corneille of the Boulevards," gave legitimacy to the new popular theater in general with a tradition of its own distinct from both that of the street mime and the neo-classical drama, even though their audiences frequently overlapped during the constitutional monarchies.

Similarly, the novel was evolving into a more plebeian genre after 1800.[30] Simple folk tales, like those collected by Charles Perrault in the seventeenth century, soon gave way to the gothic and adventure novel, both longer and more entertaining to its more literate audience in the cities. A nineteenth-century catalog of such books detailed their various attractions: "passions of the black cloak, . . . loves and elopements, young persecuted heiresses who faint in ballrooms, . . . somber forests, diabolical medallions, secret oaths, tears and kisses, gondollas, young fiancés more courageous than lions [yet] gentle as lambs, suicides out of delicacy, [and] self-sacrifices of all sorts."[31] The development of prose romances as the staple literature of Parisian women, the primary clientele of the lending libraries, began with the *romans noirs et terrifiants* in the first years of the nineteenth century, and joined the more sentimental productions of domestic bliss that had appeared late in the eighteenth century. Despite the often explicitly didactic tones their authors employed frequently to emphasize the "moral qualities" of their novels, they

29. On developments in the drama for this period, see Maurice Albert, *Les théâtres des boulevards, 1789–1848* (Paris: Société française d'imprimerie et de librairie, 1902); E. C. van Bellen, *Les origines du mélodrame* (Utrecht: Kimink and Zoon, 1927); and David Owen Evans, *Le drame moderne à l'époque romantique, 1827–1850* (Paris: Vie Universitaire, 1923).

30. On developments in the novel for this period, see Alice Killen, *Le roman terrifiant, ou roman noir de Walpole à Ann Radcliffe et son influence sur la littérature française jusqu'en 1840* (Paris: Champion, 1923); André LeBreton, *Le roman français au XIXe siècle, avant Balzac* (Paris: Boivin, 192?); and John S. Wood, *Sondages, 1830–1848: romanciers français secondaires* (Toronto: University of Toronto Press, 1965).

31. Cited in Mandrou, *De la culture populaire*, p. 185.

continued to appeal to coarser sensibilities anxious more for distraction than for instruction. Works, for instance, by Madame Cottin, Madame de Genlis, Pigault-Lebrun, Ducange, and Ducray-Duminil, and translations from the English of Samuel Richardson, Horace Walpole, Monk Lewis, and Maria Porter during the Restoration composed a large portion of the "new" fiction soon replacing the *bibliothèque bleue* in nineteenth-century Paris.

An equally remarkable transformation was accomplished, though mainly after the First Empire, in popular histories. Just when the romantics were discovering the Middle Ages, accounts of Charlemagne and the good kings of medieval France ceased to be the sole plebeian histories: Saint Louis dispensing justice beneath his oak tree, the Templars burning at the stake, and the like—long the basis for much *colporteur* literature in the eighteenth century—shared room increasingly with tales of the heroic exploits of Napoleon Bonaparte: his victorious battles, his touches of human kindness, his grand march across the map of Europe, even his less glorious moments such as the retreat from Russia and the exile to Saint Helena.[32] Undoubtedly these versions of recent French history coincided with the accounts that veterans told of their experiences in the *Grande Armée*. Although this new subject matter apparently conflicted with the former glories of France during the Middle Ages, it actually complemented their focus on the ruler, be he king or emperor, that was treated more dramatically and more fully in narratives devoted to his fortunes. Tales of both Napoleon and medieval figures participated in this new emphasis on a single individual attempting to turn the course of history after his own fashion, a new attitude also reflected in the political pamphlets disguised as "histories" or "biographies" that circulated despite police surveillance of the book trade before the Third Republic.

Poetry, too, shared in this development of a new popular literary culture.[33] In lieu of the favorite ballads and ditties sung at rural *veillées* in the eighteenth century, another form of popular poetry, the *chansonnier*, attracted the attention of people in many Parisian homes. Edmond Goblot in his study of the French bourgeoisie recalled his grandparents and their dinner guests during the *monarchie censitaire* singing not only

32. On the Napoleonic myth, see Albert L. Guerard, *Reflections on the Napoleonic Legend* (London: Unwin, 1924); Jean Lucas-Dubreton, *Le culte de Napoléon, 1815–1848* (Paris: Albin Michel, 1959); and Barbéris, "Napoléon: structure et signification d'un mythe littéraire," *Revue d'histoire littéraire de la France* 70(1970),5–6:1031–58.

33. On developments in poetry for this period, see Henri Avenel, *Chansons et chansonniers* (Paris: Marpon et Flammarion, [1889]); Georges Mazinghien, *Les ouvriers poètes* (Versailles: Impr. Vve. E. Aubert, 1893); and Edgar L. Newman, "L'Arme du Siècle, C'est la Plume: The French Worker Poets of the July Monarchy and the Spirit of Revolution and Reform," *Journal of Modern History* 51(1979),4: offprint.

the socially acceptable songs of love and family life, but also the politically "dangerous" ones written by Béranger and other Bonapartists.[34] Sentimental, jolly, and political songs soon became a common sound among the *menu peuple* in the first half of the nineteenth century. To be sure, such chansons were not so far removed from an earlier oral folk tradition—the illiterate could participate equally well in the old and new poetry—but they clearly differed from the songs of times past in both subject and form fixed now by a printed text. In time the song books helped support *goguettes* in the cafés, and later *orphéons,* the quasi-professional singing societies during the Second Empire and Third Republic. By then song had moved more firmly into the realm of business to become something more for common people in the city to hear than to sing.

Taken as ideal types, the poetry, drama, fiction, and history in the nineteenth century reflected the shift from a traditional folk to a more modern popular culture.[35] Where earlier works had been simple in form, anonymous in origin, and freely available in the public domain, literary titles became moderately more complex productions by known authors and available only at cost. This marked a decided commercialization in popular literature. The production and distribution of such work were no longer in the hands of amateur producers little different from their audience, but in those of professional writers and mediators clearly distinguished from the consumers of their wares. Of course, the *bibliothèque bleue* did not truly represent a genuine folk culture: in printed form and sold at a modest price, it was much closer to the literate world of later centuries. But its values were closely tied to a much older social and cultural milieu, values not expressed in the new literature that appeared in its place in the course of the nineteenth century.

The remarkable changes apparent in the literature of the common people from the eighteenth to the nineteenth century coincided with a change in literary vision: from literature expressive of the mythical structures adapted by a specific group in a relatively closed peasant community, the new popular titles developed another set of esthetic formulas appropriate to a more heterogeneous, urban, atomized society. Although this transition from the folk to the popular, like the development of romanticism among elites, was far from sudden and uniform, it did become increasingly apparent to observers in the early nineteenth century, to the alarm of many conservatives such as the neo-classicists and to the

34. Goblot, *La barrière,* p. 133.

35. Theoretical considerations of this problem appear in Gans, *Popular Culture and High Culture,* pp. 52–55; Lewis, "The Sociology of Popular Culture," 3:19; and Crubellier, *Histoire culturelle,* pp. 52–308.

delight of many others willing to enjoy the new literary world offered to them. In time, neither the *colporteur* literature nor the elite titles, both neo-classical and romantic, appealed as well to the Parisian audience as *chansonniers*, melodramas, romances, and dramatic histories.

INSTANCES OF POPULAR ROMANTICISM

It was on precisely this literature that romanticism had its greatest impact in the middle years of the constitutional monarchies. Despite the growth of popular titles independent of immediate elite influence, there appeared a brief romantic fashion on a much lower level of literary achievement than that contemporaries often praised or damned. The popular manifestations of romanticism were even confused with the works by more sophisticated authors; such distinctions among their titles were increasingly difficult to make as the literary marketplace grew and commanded the attention of more and more writers anxious to see their work in print. Nonetheless, a close look at titles destined for a distinctly plebeian audience reveals a clear romantic character, one deserving careful attention not just because it has been ignored, but because it was the primary form of romanticism that ordinary French men and women were most likely to have known in the period. To read these popular *romantiques* is to see aspects of the movement most appreciated by their widespread readership.

In one popular song book, 2,500 copies of which were published in 1820, for example, may be found a remarkable piece entitled "La mélancolie" by Pauline de Brady (see Illustration 2).[36] Although it appeared very early in the romantic period, it expressed a sentiment evidently drawn from sources of feeling and expression shared by major figures in the movement still studied today. The ostensible cause of this poem's sadness and longing was a love, perhaps frustrated by death, which the poet used to create a mood like that of Lamartine's "Le lac" also published in 1820. Moreover, Madame de Brady chose to capture this intense sentiment aptly in a setting conducive to melancholy: not only did she express an extraordinary frame of mind, but she also developed it in a curiously sophisticated pattern of imagery often found in elite literature after 1820.

---

36. Pauline de Brady, "La mélancolie," in *Le rendez-vous, ou le moment d'amour. Chansonnier pour tous les âges* (Paris: Tiger, 1820), p. 4. See A.N.F¹⁸II*7 "Déclarations des Imprimeurs" (1820), for the number of copies printed of this particular song book.

2. "Comtesse de Brady" (ca. 1820). Lithograph by Charles-Edouard Crespy le Prince (1784–1841). *Courtesy of the Boston Public Library, Print Department.*

In short, her poem seems to have participated in the romantic movement, in both form and content, even though it was published in a collection of popular poetry for rather modest readers who would not ordinarily have read either the romantics or the neo-classicists. The poem itself deserves closer examination.

> Vague mélancolie, es-tu peine ou plaisir?
> En me livrant à toi je sens couler mes larmes;
> Mais cette douleur a des charmes:
> Pleurer n'est pas toujours souffrir.
>
> D'une sombre forêt je cherche le silence;
> Au pied d'un froid tombeau j'aime à me recueillir:
> Là, je vois qu'il faudra vieillir;
> Là, je vois la mort qui s'avance.
>
> Lorsque l'oiseau nocturne a quitté le beffroi,
> Qu'à l'airain gémissant il joint sa voix plaintive,
> Je viens méditer sur la rive,
> Et je l'écoute sans effroi.
>
> L'air est calme et serein, la rive est solitaire;
> Seule, assise à l'écart, il m'échappe un soupir . . .
> Hélas! quel triste souvenir! . . .
> A de plus doux je le préfère.
>
> Je cacherai toujours mes plaisirs, ma douleur;
> Ah! qui partagerait la crainte, l'espérance,
> Et le bonheur et la souffrance,
> Qui viennent agiter mon coeur.
>
> Je ne confirai pas, douce mélancolie,
> Tes aimables secrets; on ne m'entendrait pas;
> Seule, je chanterai tout bas
> Les charmes de la rêverie.
>
> Brillant astre des nuits, affaiblis ta clarté,
> Tu troubles les plaisirs dont mon âme est éprise;
> Je n'ai point changé de dévise:
> Le silence et l'obscurité.

After the brief apostrophe to melancholy, the poet claims here to find solace in sadness and longing which invite explicit indulgence in feeling for its own sake. To underscore this emotional ambivalence between pain and pleasure, life and death, past and present, she emphasizes the imagery necessary to convey it in the following stanzas: the somber forest, the cold tomb, the nocturnal bird, the moaning bell, and the solitary shore. These important images express a decidedly romantic state of mind given to the recognition of time through personal revery. In the fourth stanza the poet restates the reflective mood she takes so much pleasure in experiencing and expressing, the bitter sweet memory that has apparently provoked this poetic outpouring. The private world of her enjoyments, doldrums, fears, hopes, happinesses, and sufferings is centered in the agitation of her heart before the poet addresses the charming melancholic muse once more in the sixth stanza. Finally, she admonishes the brilliant star of the night for disturbing her favored condition, in silence and obscurity, that ends the poem on an even more somber note.

Throughout the piece, however, the poet evidently attempted, with her use of striking romantic images, to capture the essence of her emotional state that resembled closely, in intention if not achievement, the intense moments expressed by more accomplished romantic poets in the same period.[37] This pose, of course, owed much to a tradition of pastoral and melancholic poetry evident since the end of the eighteenth century among the likes of Delille and Millevoye, as well as among the later romantics Lamartine and Hugo. But it was presented here clearly for one of the first times in the verse of poetry intended for a much larger and less erudite readership, an audience likely to have encountered little difficulty with either the vocabulary of such poems or the price of the books in which they appeared. Madame de Brady's romantic achievement marked an important development in French popular culture.

Romanticism's influence on more plebeian literature appeared no less remarkably in the drama written for the boulevard theaters in Paris. Played for the first time at the Théâtre de Madame in July 1827, for example, a hybrid comedy-vaudeville-drame (Le paysan perverti, ou quinze ans de Paris) deliberately adopted romantic conventions despite their apparent inappropriateness to the dramatic genres in which the playwright normally wrote.[38] Author of more than fifteen other comedies and melodramas, Léon Théaulon stated explicitly in the preface to his new work that he was the first to introduce the movement into the French popular theater.[39] Moreover, in the epilog he discussed at greater length

37. See Lamartine, *Méditations poétiques* in *Oeuvres poétiques complètes,* pp. 1–4.

38. M. E. G. M. Théaulon de Lambert, *Le paysan perverti, ou quinze ans de Paris,* drame en trois journées (Paris: Barba, 1827).

39. See the entries under Théaulon de Lambert in the Paris, Bibliothèque Nationale, *Catalogue général des livres imprimés* (Paris: Imprimerie Nationale, 1949), 185:266–303.

the importance of the quintessentially romantic *drame* to the development of the comedy, the vaudeville, and the melodrama. "As society in our day has been the subject less to travail and ridicule than to vices and hatreds, the *drame* has become our truest comedy," Théaulon concluded after he had distinguished the various elements of popular drama, apportioned their share in the new literature, and linked them to contemporary social and political events.[40] Thus this dramatist of the boulevards conceived *Le paysan perverti*, however hackneyed its theme borrowed from the eighteenth century, as part of the romantic movement; and he claimed to present a genuine example of it to an audience otherwise unaware of the neo-classical esthetic or its conflict with the new literature in France.

The action of the play points up both the popular and the romantic aspects of Théaulon's work. In the first *journée*, as the playwright called his acts, the sole heir to 500,000 francs, Gervais arrives in Paris to buy a farm and to marry his village sweetheart, now a domestic in the city. But before he can entrust his money to Germont the *notaire*, he meets Robert from the same village who convinces Gervais to spend his money on the pleasures of the city instead. The second *journée*, set seven years later, shows the chevalier de Saint-Gervais (the hero socially transformed) living the gay life, betrothed to a comtesse, and dependent upon Roberville, his village friend who has also assumed a more socially acceptable name (whatever its popular association with Pigault-Lebrun's salacious novel).[41] But Roberville has lost all Gervais' money in risky speculation, and he escapes just as Gervais is arrested for his debts. Meanwhile, Gervais' sweetheart Justine has married the aging Germont despite her enduring love for her former fiancé. By the last *journée* eight years later, all is set to right in a dramatic climax in which chance brings the penniless Gervais into the baronne d'Oberval's hôtel where he is recognized by the baronne, i.e. Justine. The large inheritance Gervais had lost to the unscrupulous Robert is finally returned to him by his marriage to Justine, the widow of the enormously wealthy *notaire* who had fleeced Robert. And so the play ends just as it was to have begun.

In this stock social comedy Théaulon aimed to achieve his ambitious program: he clearly attempted to violate the integrity, not of the classical distinctions between comedy and tragedy, but of the popular distinctions between melodrama, comedy, and vaudeville. Characteristics properly

40. Théaulon, *Le paysan perverti*, p. 87.

41. Pigault-Lebrun's notorious novel, *Monsieur Roberville* (Paris: Barba, 1824 [1809]), was placed on the Interior Ministry's list of obscene books in 1825. See E. H. Whitmore, "The Cabinets de Lecture in France, 1800–1850." Unpublished Ph.D. dissertation, University of Wisconsin-Madison, 1975, p. 102.

belonging to each of these latter dramatic forms were incorporated into the piece in order to create an entirely new genre of popular theater. Unfortunately, the playwright did not actually accomplish what he claimed: instead of integrating the various elements throughout, he separated them into three acts, each of which remained in effect a separate dramatic form. Nevertheless, the "play in three days" also marked a conscious attempt to imitate the romantic flouting of the neo-classical unities of time, place, and action: all three acts were set in different times (1812, 1819, and 1827) and in different places in Paris (an isolated square, a richly decorated salon, and a quay near the Pont des Arts). None of the action or characters would have been acceptable in a neo-classical play, to be sure, though there was nothing unusual about his work in boulevard theater except its conscious imitation of elite developments in literature. Although the play was essentially structured as a melodrama—with its sharply drawn characters identified with good and evil, its depiction of fair virtue's persecution by villainous machination, and its resolution in the marriage of the hero and the heroine after evil and misunderstanding had been vanquished—Théaulon's creation adopted romanticism's conventions and made clear to his audience how appropriate he thought they were to the popular theater.[42]

Another variation of the movement's influence appeared in the fiction that filled the shelves of the *cabinets de lecture* in the romantic period. In 1834 Maurice de Viarz wrote his *Neuf jours d'hymen, ou la cour en seize cent dix*, published in a special multivolumed edition intended for the city's lending libraries.[43] The author of two other novels, similarly aimed at a relatively large audience, prefaced his historical novel in a clearly romanticlike justification of his attention to a period still considered medieval: France before the reign of Louis XIV. "The sixteenth century," he wrote, "appears to us wild and austere, chivalrous and fanatic; generous and cruel; superstitious and bold. . . . Even the most unhappy periods possessed something good: I envy the sixteenth century its great genius, its moral energy, its heroic vigor which would have been directed more easily today toward virtue."[44] His colorful and

42. See Brooks's study of melodrama in this period, *The Melodramatic Imagination,* esp. Ch. 2.

43. A. E. R. de Serviez wrote under the pseudonym of Maurice de Viarz. His *Neuf jours d'hymen, ou la cour en seize cent dix* (Paris: Lachapelle, 1834), was published in two volumes, an edition of 500 copies each, whose blanched pages and duodecimo format indicated that the publisher intended the title primarily for the city's lending libraries. Since the lending libraries rented by the volume, their proprietors prefered such multi-volumed novels to increase rental revenues. See A.N.F[18]II*24 "Déclarations des Imprimeurs" (1834), for the press run of this title.

44. Viarz, *Neuf jours d'hymen,* 1:2–3.

dramatic account of important historical figures was expressed with a genuine sympathy for the period and with an eye to defending it as a subject worthy of the reader's serious consideration. The novel's subject, he stated, was not a barren era in French history as the neo-classicists would have believed, but one rich and instructive to the present, an argument often made by many romantic creators of historical novels in the early nineteenth century.[45]

The story of Henri IV's last days certainly captures this romantic spirit, one generous to events and figures from France's "medieval" past within an otherwise gothic novel of intrigue. The wise and heroic character of the king is quickly established in the opening chapters devoted to his provisions for the less fortunate members of his court, as well as to his even-handed policy that resisted the fanaticism of Austria in its attempt to destroy the Protestant states in Germany. Henri IV is contrasted sharply with the selfish and conniving Marie de Medicis, surrounded by the most brilliant members of the court (all introduced, described, and amply footnoted for authenticity by the author). An important subplot is given over to Léonora de Sommereuil whose devotion to her murdered husband stands out against Léonora Galigai's flirtatious affairs among the gentlemen of the court: when Léonora Galigai bemoans her lover lost to a rival, Léonora de Sommereuil, dagger in hand at the dead of night, seeks to revenge her dead husband by attempting to kill Elzéar de Verrières, his murderer. Meanwhile, the fanatic Catholic Leaguers plot the assassination of Henri to protect France's religious purity and obedience to the pope. Ravaillac's dramatic knifing of Henri on the way to see the ailing Sully is described as the close of an era of wise, effective rule and the beginning of a new period of open political intrigue. Marie de Medicis and her sycophant Richelieu seize power, but they reluctantly recognize the necessity of an alliance with the still powerful Sully to guard France against complete chaos.

Strains of both the romantic and the gothic are apparent in this extended historical and suspenseful narrative. Besides the author's open sympathy for the reign of Henri IV, a common one among elites during the Restoration, there is his clever use of events, real and fictive, to strike terror in the hearts of his readers, an equally common device among popular novelists. Interspersed among his ample descriptions of the court, the author passes judgment to distinguish good from evil, characterizing Henri as "the protective guardian of humanity's universal repose"[46] and Marie de Medicis as "the totally Italian princess who passed

---

45. *Ibid.* Compare this statement with Vigny's "Réflexions," *Oeuvres complètes,* 2:19–25.

46. *Ibid.*, 1:116.

half her life at the foot of altars."[47] The heroes and villains, as in most popular fiction, are clearly identified from the start, despite their far more ambiguous place in French history. The novel builds suspense with all the implied terrors of the midnight hour, curiously touched occasionally by more complex, almost romantic moods. For instance, Ravaillac's nocturnal musings as he prepares to assassinate the good king are reflected in Viarz's gloomy imagery:

> The moon resembled a great open eye in the midst of heaven; its rays brightened the triangular roofs of the city as well as all the innumerable prisons and dungeons that dominated Paris; the trembling light of the mysterious star, spreading over the straight lines of sharp-pointed paving stones which trace the middle of deserted streets, struck the dazzled eye as a broad expanse of snow . . .

a description appropriate, of course, to Ravaillac's state of mind on his way to kill the king, at once dramatic and romantic in its effect.[48]

A similar incorporation of the elite and the popular, albeit with a decidedly different emphasis, informed much of the historical writing in the romantic period. This same fascination in things both medieval and ghoulish may be found in many popularized histories clearly affected by romantic values. For example, an explicit imitation of Augustin Thierry's *Histoire de la conquête de l'Angleterre* (1825), Louis Edouard Gauttier du Lys d'Arc's *Histoire des conquêtes des Normands, en Italie, en Sicilie, et en Grèce* (1830) made effective use of the dramatic quality of the Middle Ages.[49] Just as the historical was introduced into the gothic romance, the gothic was brought into history, especially one anxious to reach a broad readership. Gauttier d'Arc claimed for his work "the colors of fable" that made it entertaining as well as informative. Though the actual press run of the book is not known, it was clearly in the current of popular historical writings deliberately adopting romantic elements, and it closely resembled the mixture of the elite and the popular in poetry, drama, and fiction published between 1820 and 1840.[50] Beyond sympathetic consideration of medieval subjects, such histories cultivated strong nationalistic feeling, use of local color, dramatic treatment of events, and imaginative

47. *Ibid.*, 1:218.

48. *Ibid.*, 2:119–20. See discussion of such imagery in Doolittle, "Four Elements of Romantic Writing."

49. Edouard Gauttier d'Arc, *Histoire des conquêtes des Normands, en Italie, en Sicilie, et en Grèce* (Paris: L. de Bure, 1830). The size of the title's edition is not listed in the Interior Ministry archival records.

50. *Ibid.*, p. viii.

reconstruction where primary documentation failed to provide the information necessary for vivid storylike accounts of the past.[51]

Perhaps the best introduction to this kind of historical writing lies in a brief passage from Gauttier d'Arc's work in which the mood of the tenth century is discussed as a prelude to the crusades and the Normand conquests that followed.

> Sinister forebodings [it notes] had promoted dread in the breasts of Christians in the last years of the tenth century. It was said—and this disturbance propagated by a less than disinterested zeal was quickly entertained by a superstitious ignorance—that a thousand years had passed, the time was ripe, and the universe approached its destruction. Several frightening phenomena had given more than credence to these woeful predictions. Long and repeated earth tremors had shaken the land to its very foundations; the sky was seen traced by long furrows of flame that, borrowing the forms of the Evil Genius, had struck the sun with a noise like that of thunder; finally a brilliant comet excited among the common people that instinctive fear which, judged today by a sane philosophy, can still find some rationale in our eyes.[52]

Here the historian displays an engaging style combining a clear detachment from events, permitted by the passage of several centuries, with a sympathetic understanding of the period, encouraged by developments in nineteenth-century historiography. Moreover, he does not disdain the medieval world, no more so than he eschews the details of men's imaginative susceptibilities, past and present, for dramatic and rhetorical effect. In this brief passage the historian has played on the reader's own fears of supernatural occurrences, still alive in the nineteenth century, at the same time he has attempted to protect his account from immediate condemnation by the more enlightened members of his audience: Gauttier d'Arc's appeal to his readers lies as much in his novelistic story about the Middle Ages as in his scholarly observations about them.

The author was more explicit in the preface to his work: "the exploits of the Norman explorers surpassed the burgeoning imagination, pushed to its extremities. . . . Never has a novelist dared to invent anything more astonishing than what they did. The only account of so many feats of arms, as they have been reported to us . . . seems to belong more to fiction than to history. Heroes gifted with a superhuman force surprise the spirit by such unbelievable yet true adventures."[53]

51. See Neff, *The Poetry of History*, pp. 116–49.

52. Gauttier d'Arc, *Histoire des conquêtes*, pp. 15–17.

53. *Ibid.*, p. vii.

Undercurrents of national feeling, local color, as well as elements of imaginative and dramatic action clearly appeared in Gauttier d'Arc's history, in essence a genuinely romantic work despite its direct appeal to an audience less sophisticated than that sought by better known historians published in the period. The almost bifurcated achievement of *Les conquêtes des Normands* was perfectly obvious to the author: "one notices even here two particular characteristics that I have strived to retain in my account: the first consists in the faithful and frequently minute description of the places which engage the writer; the other [lies] in a particular coloring from which their style and their works are borrowed."[54] It is this scrupulous yet decorative intention in a popular work obviously affected by the new literature that was achieved in Gauttier d'Arc's historical creation and in that of many equally engaging historical writers in early nineteenth-century Paris.

What we see in these four titles is the profound impact romanticism had on selected examples of a more plebeian literature. Although the actual romantic revolt was aimed at the neo-classical canon, an elite literature by self-definition, and although the movement wished to create a more eclectic esthetic appealing to a variety of tastes, romanticism reached an ironically more catholic audience than perhaps its advocates realized or even wanted. Popular literary titles incorporated and adapted to their own esthetic—one very different from that of elite literature—the values and conventions, the deeply personal mood, and the deliberately iconoclastic forms increasingly common among leading romantic writers in France after 1820.

In nearly all cases this wholesale adoption of romanticism by plebeian-minded authors was hardly identical with the movement, as is apparent in the works examined here briefly: their authors borrowed freely the elements that would not change the essential structure and content of the popular genres in which they worked. Madame de Brady kept her very simple verse stanzas, despite the prosodic pyrotechnics of the later romantics; Théaulon retained his violent melodramatic prose, even though romantics also explored the richer possibilities of poetic language on the stage; Viarz still enjoyed chilling his readership with medieval gothic horrors, while more talented novelists were turning to the contemporary novel of manners and mores; and Gauttier d'Arc played on the susceptibilities of his audience, whatever the more sophisticated histories written by romantic historians.[55] Popular authors simply singled out the elements

54. *Ibid.*, p. xxv–vi.

55. See for comparison, the poetry of Hugo in *Les orientales* (1829); the drama of Louis Vitet, *Les États de Blois* (1827); the fiction of Balzac, *Eugénie Grandet* (1835); and the history of Augustin Thierry, *Dix ans d'études historiques* (1834).

of the romantic movement most compatible to their own established genres.

This much was certainly true in much French popular literature published between 1820 and 1840, at the height of the first phase of romanticism in France. Even though any definition of such an important, though amorphous phenomenon in literature and ideas must be based almost exclusively on the productions intended for an elite audience, at least in the early nineteenth century, it is apparent that the movement actually reached a much larger readership; many of its elements pervaded the songs, melodramas, romances, and histories consumed by a much less sophisticated audience, belying the numerous critics in the period who believed that romanticism was pandering to vulgar tastes. In a way, of course, they were right: the movement was far more popular than either they or their romantic opponents realized. But the extent to which this influence penetrated the titles in a new popular culture eluded them and the historians of French literature since then.

Still, a more accurate assessment of romanticism's diffusion is needed, one using sources and methods more appropriate to the problem than a brief examination of a few titles aimed at a plebeian audience. No doubt such instances reflected the movement's pervasive impact in the literary culture of a very heterogeneous readership in Paris from 1820 to 1840. But no one knows yet just how broad romanticism's impact was, nor has anyone studied its precise nature outside elite literary circles. These issues must be addressed and consequently are the subject of the next chapter devoted to a more extensive consideration of romantic values in the new popular literature.

ঙ 2 ও

THE DIFFUSION OF ROMANTICISM

THROUGHOUT THE PERIOD commentators often confused romantic ideas with the movement's more popular devices. In 1829 Lady Sydney Morgan reported the opinion of one melancholy writer mistaking widespread changes in the theater for expression of new verities. "Our great historic dramas," he said, "[are] written not in pompous Alexandrines, but in prose, the style of truth, the language of life and nature."[1] Yet such a vocabulary, apparently necessary to new ideas, appeared in ordinary social conversation as well. In 1830 Balzac characterized this fashion in words obviously taken from romantic usages. " 'Now that's a *drame!'* With this phrase you can strangle without mercy every literary dispute. With that you throw a whole century and its thought at your listeners."[2] This confusion of form with content was natural, of course, given the emphasis many leaders placed on their deliberate iconoclasm intended to bait their neo-classical critics. But the mistake certainly made the distinction between a profoundly new literature and an ephemeral literary fad enormously difficult to make.

Some literary reputations were actually made by such nonconformity. Victor d'Arlincourt, the author of mostly gothic novels, represented to many "the Prince of the Romantics," a kind of popular Chateaubriand. The two authors even looked alike, to the further embarrassment of Chateaubriand who wanted nothing to do with the movement despite the romantic vision of his work.[3] Still others believed the romantic mode was literally synonymous with poses of melancholy fashionable among the young, in contrast to the more heroic postures adopted by the old, as

1. Morgan, *France in 1829–1830,* 1:171–72.

2. Balzac, *Oeuvres diverses,* Marcel Bouteron and Henri Longnon, eds. (Paris: Conrad, 1935–40),2:36.

3. Note Frances Trollope's confusion of the two before a portrait of Victor d'Arlincourt in *Paris and the Parisians,* pp. 249–50.

Maxime Du Camp noted in his memoirs. "My heart is worn like a whore's staircase" became a stock phrase, however shocking to bourgeois sensibilities, that was as much a convention as the romantic literary forms.[4] Evidently, contemporaries identified the movement's message with its more striking medium.[5]

These commentaries on the movement's frequent and intentional confusion of its form and content suggest the nature of romanticism's immediate diffusion: the new literature appears to owe its success to entirely new conventions.[6] The romantics developed iconoclastic forms, as much to spite the rules as to create a new esthetic, to imply the revolutionary temper noted by observers. To many, sometimes even the movement's leaders, formal experiments represented romanticism's new view of the world whether or not they actually expressed it. Similarly, these literary conventions were derived from more than the romantics' revolt against older literary conventions; they also owed to the romantics' initial need for acceptance by a large and appreciative audience. The borrowing of popular devices, from the melodrama and the gothic novel, for example, was in some cases a deliberate attempt to encourage more spectators and readers unaccustomed to the classics.[7] The movement triumphed, esthetically and commercially, on the basis of its new forms more suited to a general public than those of the neo-classicists. Thus romantic works stand between the exclusiveness of the neo-classical on the one hand, and the broad appeal of the popular on the other. As opposed to formal neo-classical poetics, the new literature adopted the language and style of the prosaic, which for contemporaries was both the symbol of a new content and the debt to a lower literature.

To test this idea—that romanticism as a mode of expression, rather than an intellectual sensibility, was popularly diffused—a systematic examination of a wide range of titles in literature and history is needed. Was there actually an emphasis on form instead of content in most works affected by romanticism? Was it as widespread as observers in the period claimed? Such an examination should provide a picture, perhaps clearer than that offered by the literary evidence, of the nature of the movement and what it meant in actual practice to authors in the period. Although the

4. Du Camp, *Souvenirs*, 1:162.

5. This has been remarked by other scholars as well. See Guillaume de Bertier de Sauvigny, *The Bourbon Restoration*, Lynn M. Case, trans. (Philadelphia: University of Pennsylvania Press, 1966), p. 353.

6. This common observation about the romantics is well summarized in Theodore Zeldin, *France, 1848–1945* (New York: Oxford University Press, 1977),2:793–809.

7. See Hauser, *Social History*, 3:196–207; and George, *French Romanticism*, pp. 47–57, on the debt of the romantics to popular literature.

notion of romanticism as a widespread and popular literature is hardly new—it was assumed by the romantics and their critics from the start— the precise role played by the movement in plebeian literature remains for serious study.

Immediately, however, the problem of selection arises. *Which books should be examined?* Surely writers belonging to the relatively exclusive *cénacles* were not the only producers of romantic works. A fair study of the question requires literary and historical titles more representative of the market than those generally discussed in literary histories. If romanticism did indeed become a popular movement, it must have appeared in the writings aimed at audiences both high and low—a diverse audience the known romantics did not always enjoy despite their intentions. Unfortunately, this issue involves a methodological procedure that must be discussed, at least briefly, so that later generalizations will be reasonably founded on a well-defined approach.

A solution to the problem of representativeness was found by taking random samples from the *Bibliographie de la France,* the national trade catalog for new titles, published since 1811.[8] Edited by A. J. Q. Beuchet from 1811 to 1847, the *Bibliographie* constitutes the most complete list of titles published in Paris, where enforcement of the 14 October 1811

8. For discussion of the value of this source, see Philarète Chasles, "Statistique littéraire et intellectuelle de la France pendant l'année 1828," *Revue de Paris* 7(1829),195– 96; Victor Zoltowski, "Les cycles de la création intellectuelle et artistique," *L'année sociologique* 3(1952),178–82; and D. Bellos, "The *Bibliographie de la France* and its Sources," *The Library: Transactions of the Bibliographical Society* 28(1973),1:64–67.

Unfortunately, this source did not include pirated, contraband, or smuggled titles, a growing proportion of the book trade. But evidence from a study on the Belgian *contrefaçon* indicates that most such titles were copies of successful works already published in France. See Herman Dopp, *La contrefaçon des livres français en Belgique, 1812–1852* (Louvain: Librairie Universitaire, 1932), pp. 106–14. Moreover, the manual frequently repeats titles and announces bogus re-editions as advertising ploys on the part of booksellers anxious to push a slow moving work. Nevertheless, this source is indexed by author, genre, and title so that these errors could easily be identified in the sampling process. Gratuitous additions of previously published titles were thus eliminated.

One further complication with this source concerns titles omitted as a consequence of the Interior Ministry's administrative lapses. Publications under twenty pages (the legal definition of a book in the period) and illicit works obviously were not included and surely made the *Bibliographie's* listings far from exhaustive, especially in the provinces during years of political turmoil. But this major defect in the source's completeness—and the representativeness of the present study's samples—was minimized by the relatively apolitical nature of the literary genres considered (poetry, drama, fiction, history), by the comparatively quiescent years for which the titles were sampled (1820, 1827, 1834, 1841), and by the closer political surveillance of the book trade within the geographical limits of the study, i.e., in Paris. See Bellos, "Le marché du livre à l'époque romantique: recherches et problèmes," *Revue française d'histoire du livre* 47(1978),648–51, for a scrupulous discussion of the *Bibliographie's* limitations.

decree was the strictest. By this directive, largely maintained until the Third Republic, all publications were to be placed on deposit with the Interior Ministry for censorship purposes. It was on this collection that Beuchet largely based his monthly notices of new books, compiled and indexed annually. Besides the legal force behind the *Bibliographie*, however, the advantage of advertising naturally encouraged publishers to place their titles in the city's most important catalog of new works for sale. Better forms of marketing books were unavailable in the trade until late in the period, as will be discussed in Chapter 4. This source thus served the commercial needs of the booksellers, as well as the political interests of the regimes from Napoleon onward, to ensure the completeness of its listings from year to year.

But between 1820 and 1840 more than 100,000 new titles appeared, far too many for any one scholar to examine alone: sampling was imperative. So a random numbers table provided the order for the selection of 120 titles in indexes at the back of four annual volumes of the *Bibliographie*—1820, 1827, 1834, and 1841—equidistant years spanning the height of romanticism's first phase in France. The thirty titles per year in each of the genres most appropriate to the movement (poetry, drama, fiction, and history) constituted a statistically significant sample of approximately 10 percent of all works published in the *belles lettres* and history. Only those titles not published in Paris or not available for examination in the Bibliothèque Nationale were eliminated from the samples. (Additional titles were sampled as necessary to complete the sample sets.) Because the Bibliothèque contains nearly all those titles consigned by law to the Interior Ministry during the constitutional monarchies,[9] the titles examined probably represented a fair cross section of the city's total production of works in literature and history in the romantic period, or at least in each of the sample years.

Of course, leafing through the *Bibliographie* and reading the titles sampled in a systematic fashion were only the most mechanical parts of this assessment of romanticism's influence. A much more difficult task was deciding which of the works reflected a discernible debt to the movement. Even with the reasonably precise criteria defining romanticism in

9. The first law requiring that two copies of all new publications printed in France be deposited with the Interior Ministry was passed by the Conventional Assembly in 1793. Modifications to this law issued by the Napoleonic decree of 5 February 1810 and the royal ordinance of 21 October 1814 raised the number of copies to five, only to be lowered again to two by the royal ordinance of 9 January 1828. The July Monarchy continued this Restoration policy of demanding one copy for the Bibliothèque Royale and another for the Interior Ministry, ostensibly for censorship purposes. See discussion of this legal requirement in Jean-Alexis Neret, *Histoire illustrée de la librairie et du livre français* (Paris: Lamarre, 1953), pp. 117–18.

France outlined in Chapter 1, their application can never be quite so straightforward. For example, how "romantic" was a collection of 200 songs only 5 of which borrowed subjects or verse from recognized romantics? What made fiction and history clearly part of the movement which focused so much of its attention on poetry and drama? There is no way of avoiding the selection of titles on the basis of the authors' apparent emphases, some only slightly more expressive of the movement's influence than others. Obviously such a procedure does not make these works part of the literary movement per se. Rather, it places them in a category that is romantic by definition, one intended to approximate as best as possible the meaning the movement had to contemporaries. Throughout the research for this chapter, therefore, the danger of "misplaced concreteness" arose repeatedly, even though the procedure, however flawed, promised clarification of an important issue in the social history of ideas.

Not every book examined here satisfied the three romantic criteria as well as the major figures on whose work the operative definition was based. Most samples simply failed to express an identifiably romantic mood, even though they may have used many of the same images. Even fewer joined the debate between romantics and classicists in their prefaces. Accordingly, most titles here were chosen for consideration because they satisfied one important criterion, that of an innovation in form. But what constituted a "deliberate" use of the new fashion lay in the admittedly fine, perhaps even subjective distinction between the model romantics and the works simply borrowing their literary devices. In fact, a careful reading of each work was necessary to distinguish these particular titles from the rest that had still less to do with romanticism. For these reasons, an analysis of such history and literature may appear rather far removed from other critical examinations of important and well-known romantic works, even while it comes much closer to romanticism's actual state among popular titles. Though their selection was certainly not arbitrary, this approach to plebeian versions of the movement can only suggest, not decide, an answer to the nature of its diffusion in a wide variety of titles representative of French literature in the period.

This said, the random samples from the *Bibliographie de la France* present a very different impression of romantic influence than expected from both the creative masterworks and the literary evidence (see Appendix A for a list of samples classified by romantic influence). In contrast to the productions of the *cénacles* and various commentaries whose expressions form the basis of the romantic revolution, the evidence of 480 titles in the *belles lettres* and history reveals the existence of something else, of a "popular romanticism" that was clearly more a matter of form than feeling among the works obviously intended for a plebeian audience.

THE NEW LITERATURE'S INNOVATION AND BREVITY

The adoption of romantic conventions—especially freer versification in poetry, violation of the three unities in drama, medieval settings in fiction, and local color in history—was indeed widespread. More than 30 percent of the titles evinced at least some sign of this romantic influence. But curiously enough, these forms were largely incorporated into a new popular literary tradition in the process of becoming established in its own right, on a level quite independent of elite literature. The innovations simply overlay a culture whose entertaining vision of love and social conflict communicated little of the romantic sensibility. The revolt was reduced to a literary code, a "romanticism" in name only largely emptied of its original significance among leaders of the more exclusive *cénacles*. This extensive bastardization of romantic influence, however different from that detailed in literary accounts, indicates how romantic conventions literally became the fashion from 1820 to 1840.

In poetry the samples show clearly this widespread adaptation of romantic forms to popular content. Most works in verse, of course, continued a tradition irrelevant to the new movement. Political poetry in imitation of Béranger, *chansonniers* both amorous and patriotic, elegies and odes in more or less proper neo-classical style, as well as dabblings by eccentric poetasters dominated production in the period (80 percent). But romantic elements did appear, though modified to suit purposes different from what the romantics intended. Thus in one *chansonnier* published in 1827, poetic romances developed historical themes often associated with the new literature.[10] Amable Tastu's "Marie Stuart," Benjamin Antier's "Clement Marot et Marguerite de Valois," and Eugène Scribe's "Ballade de la Dame Blanche" used medieval settings and characters in celebrating the ordinary frustrations of love, far removed from the soul searching historical and mythical memories elaborated in Hugo's and Vigny's work.[11] After 1830 numerous poems on Napoleon evoked a romantic flavor in their parallels with social romantic poems. An anonymous "Napoléon sur la colonne" was obviously an imitation of Hugo's famous "Ode à la colonne" on the same theme.[12] Consequently, by 1841 popular verse had incorporated romantic license sufficiently to establish an informal, almost chatty style. As a word, "romantic" no longer meant the

10. Charles Malo, ed. *Chansonnier des dames* (Paris: Janet, 1827).

11. E.g., see Hugo, *Odes et ballades* in *Oeuvres complètes: poésie*, 1:37–92; and Vigny, *Le cor* in *Oeuvres complètes*, 1:137–40.

12. Hugo, *Les chants du crépuscule* in *Oeuvres complètes: poésie*, 2:194–202.

movement—it became for one self-styled *vieux romantique* what it means today: vague and amorous.[13]

Similarly, many samples in drama borrowed freely from the romantic theater. Even though nearly a third of the plays were comedy-vaudevilles—a popular dramatic form in a tradition all its own—the influence of the new literature was clearly evident in the common use of the term "drame" in lieu of "mélodrame" by 1841.[14] This did not actually mean a change in the melodramatic convention, no more than it meant a genuine respect for the romantics who were often the object of amusing satires on the popular stage. *Les folies du jour* (1820), for example, stars Mademoiselle Romantique, "that amiable fool . . . recently arrived from England and Germany" given to uncontrollable raptures in gloomy forest scenes.[15] But the new mode did creep into the habits of more respectable characters. The baronne d'Orvant in Merville's *L'homme poli* (1820) wrote "how the poetry of my romantic prose suggests the charming eclat of verse . . . without rhyme and feet."[16] Romantic drama seems to have suggested to the boulevard theaters the use of historical settings as well. Louis Vitet's *Les Etats de Blois* (1827) and Julien de Mallian's *Les dernières scènes de la fronde* (1834) represented this widespread interest in "scènes historiques" that often violated the three unities. In his preface to Schiller's *Marie Stuart* (1820), Henri Latouche wrote of the German playwright in terms equally applicable to his popular French imitators: "Like Shakespeare he does not disdain to employ the ways of nature, and he rarely affects to reveal with more delicacy than truth."[17] From 1820 to 1840 this was more or less the vogue in French drama.

Romantic influence in fiction appeared most explicitly in the numerous imitations of Walter Scott. Here historical novels made up nearly a third of all the samples, most of which blended the historical in equal doses with the sentimental and the gothic. Joseph Quantin's *Le pâtre tirolien* (1820), for instance, developed the story of a virtuous love between a humble shepherd for the manor lord's daughter, a plot little different from those of popular novels since the eighteenth century; the emphasis

13. L. Achem (Un vieux romantique) *Théorie-poème en huit leçons: la boussole du mariage, ou l'art poétique de Boileau revu et détérioré* (Paris: Charpentier, 1841).

14. See, for example, *Lucie de Lammermoor*, drame tragique (Paris: Lange-Lévy, 1841); Michel Masson et Valory, *Deux soeurs, ou une nuit de mi-carême*, drame-vaudeville (Paris: Tresse, 1841); and Joseph Bernard Rosier, *Zacherie*, drame (Paris: Marchant, 1841).

15. Léon Théaulon, Menissier, et Martin, *Les folies du jour*, extravagance (Paris: Barba, 1820), p. 16.

16. Merville (Pierre-François Camus), *L'homme poli, ou la fausse bienveillance*, comédie (Paris: Barba, 1820), p. 18.

17. Henri Latouche, "Préface," in Frédéric Schiller, *Marie Stuart*, tragédie. Henri Latouche, trans. (Paris: Barba, 1820), p. xvi.

GARDE À VOUS.

3. *Le Chansonnier des Grâces, Pour 1822.* Frontispiece and title page.

LE
CHANSONNIER
DES
GRACES,
Pour 1822.

Avec les Airs nouveaux gravés.

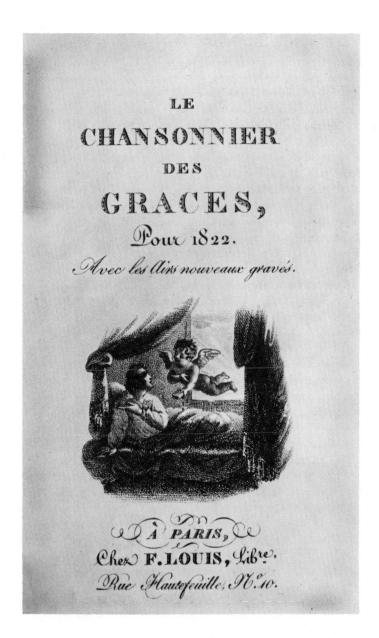

À PARIS,

Chez **F. LOUIS,** *Libre.*

Rue Hautefeuille, No. 10.

of the novel on the local color of medieval Lombardy made it the "romantic" variation of an otherwise sentimental tale. The pretense to historical authenticity, often in the form of "discovered" documents and occasional footnotes, was also used in these popular novels, as much to anticipate the reader's disapprobation as to mimic the romantics' search for a poetry of history.[18] "I have attempted to approach the historical truth as much as possible in my work where imagination supplies [only] that which the past omits," wrote Anna Maria Porter in her preface to *Don Sébastien, Roi de Portugal* (1820), a gothic novel set in the eighteenth century. Such a perspective was repeated seven years later in Vigny's preface on the historical imagination in *Cinq-Mars*.[19] Moreover, the romantic preference for epigrams at the head of every chapter recurred in novels with only the remotest resemblance to works at the heart of the movement. Accordingly, Carl Spindler's *Soirées de Dresde* (1834), a series of anecdotes in the fashion of Nodier's early work, lavishly sported quotations from Byron, Coleridge, and Shakespeare.[20] Thus romantic literary innovations were easily adopted by didactic, sentimental, gothic, and picaresque stories that dominated the fiction published in Paris from 1820 to 1840.

Fascination with the historical novel set in the Middle Ages also found a comparable development in history. A large number of titles devoted to accounts of events prior to the seventeenth century appeared in the sample; M. G***'s *Beautés de l'histoire des croisades* (1820), Adhelm Bernier's *Monumens* [sic] *inédits de l'histoire de France, 1400–1600* (1834), and Mademoiselle Vauvilliers' *Histoire de Blanche de Castille* (1841) represented this remarkable interest in things medieval. But the past shared a similar emphasis on the national that hinted equally at romantic concerns in history. "The glory of the golden ages of Pericles and Augustus is entirely alien to us," wrote E.-Hyacinthe Langlois in his description of an eleventh-century abbey. "They hardly reflect the eclat of our political existence; to the contrary, we reclaim our national patrimony by reminding ourselves that Charlemagne and Saint Louis were French like us."[21] Similarly, histories featuring Napoleon, the modern French prometheus, shared a large portion of the sampled titles, especially

18. One sampled novel reportedly based on "discovered" documents is Georges Touchard-Lafosse, *Hélène de Poitiers*, roman historique (XIVe siècle) (Paris: Sandré et cie., 1841), p. x; and for a novel using extensive footnotes, see Viarz, *Neuf jours d'hymen.*

19. Anna Maria Porter, *Don Sébastien, Roi de Portugal*, roman historique (Paris: F. Louis, 1820). See also Vigny, "Réflexions."

20. Karl Spindler, *Soirées de Dresde*, Paquis, trans. (Paris: Dumont, 1834).

21. E.-H. Langlois, *Essai historique et descriptif sur l'Abbaye de Fontenelle* (Paris: Dupont, 1834), p. xix.

after the return of the emperor's ashes in 1840. Such histories of Napoleon's essentially romantic nature and fate were published throughout the period. In 1827 J. A. de Norvins wrote, "The study of Napoleon's life . . . is dominated by three great characteristics: the excess of genius, the excess of fortune, and the excess of misery . . . . The writer, as he must, trembles before dimensions so colossal."[22] Still, these concerns with the Middle Ages and the more recent genius of French history coincided with more immediate concerns. The assassination of the duc de Berri, the Greek war of independence, the revolution of 1830, and the possible conflict with Britain over Egypt earned less romantic treatment in a genre otherwise given as much to political as literary controversy.

In the samples, then, this selective adoption and adaptation of romantic forms to the popular tradition reveals the pervasive influence of the new literature. Contrary to the literary evidence, however, the impact of romanticism was more a fashion than a true intellectual movement. The ideas behind the use of romantic innovations reflected the mentality of popular culture—its entertaining vision of social ambition, all-conquering love, and political polemic far removed from intellectual developments among elites. While romantic content did not become as widespread as its conventions, the pervasiveness of the movement's influence still indicates the extent to which elites provided models for others to follow. Indeed, the samples show clearly the flow of influence from higher to lower literature, a direction contrary to that frequently noted in contemporary accounts.[23] Romanticism proper clearly differed from the *chansonniers*, melodramas, gothic novels, and local histories; the actual movement was much less vulgar than its imitators. Its compelling view of the world was neither borrowed nor lent, but its original experiments in form were widely imitated from 1820 to 1840 by a broad range of works intended for popular consumption.

On the surface a parallel development appears to have occurred; both high and low brow literature seemed to have evolved. Just as elite romantics were changing the form and content of works read by the well-educated, popular writers were borrowing from them to effect no less remarkable changes in pieces consumed by a less lettered audience. New themes, characters, and settings in all genres were developed on all levels of literary achievement. Yet the patterns of apparent romantic influence hid the actual nature of cultural continuity and change in early

22. J. A. de Norvins, *Histoire de Napoléon* (Paris: Dupont, 1827), 1:i–ii.
23. See Brooks, *The Melodramatic Imagination,* pp. 81–109, on the popular elements used in the romantic *drame*, reflecting the usual scholarly interest in the flow of influence from the bottom up.

Bailli, proclamez au village

Que demain j'épouse mon page

4. *Le Chansonnier des Grâces, Pour 1830.* Frontispiece and title page.

LE
CHANSONNIER
DES
GRACES,
Pour 1830.

Avec les airs nouveaux gravés.

A PARIS,

Chez F. LOUIS, Libraire-Éditeur,

Rue du Paon, N.º 2.

nineteenth-century France. The most significant transformations actually occurred in the exclusive realm of elite literature. The production of works expressing the romantic sensibility, whether or not they used the new forms, marked the evolution of ideas in western history—this much intellectual historians have well recognized. At the same time popular literature hardly evolved at all despite its adoption of certain romantic innovations. Beneath the façade of experiments in versification, historical dramas and novels, and colorful histories, the vast production of literature remained largely what it had been since the turn of the century: merry songs, stormy melodramas, sentimental tales, and political polemic.[24] Evident in the samples was the important distinction between the *romantic* mood, an exclusive phenomenon, and the "romantic" mode, a widespread adoption of form—a distinction that points up the evolution of elite and the persistence of popular culture in the period.

This point is even more apparent in the development of book illustration. It is well known that the book trade created a romantic format in binding, illustration, and design to promote the sale of expensive books.[25] Many of the original editions of the great romantic authors sported gothic cathedrals on the cover and elaborate vignettes on the title page. But in the samples, new designs and lithographs also appeared in titles intended for popular consumption, just as they adopted changes in literary style. For example, from 1820 to 1830 the frontispieces to song collections moved from neo-classical to romantic motifs (see Illustrations 3 and 4). The traditional classic symbol of love, the cupid, common in 1822 was replaced by the dark perspective on a medieval castle and ladies in waiting current in 1830. Of course, sentimental love remains of primary interest, but the front illustrations indicate a fashionable "romanticism" in book design much like that of literary forms in popular literature. In fact, by 1830 most popular titles appeared with similar stylized letters and exotic vignettes appropriate to the new literary conventions. Evidently, the movement developed a widespread interest in innovation, captured in book design as well as literary forms, even if the contents of popular literature remained what it had been since the revolution. The romantic fashion produced a new façade, both literary and artistic.

24. The continuity of popular culture in the period is also argued in the works synthesized by Crubellier, *Histoire culturelle*, pp. 125–41.

25. See Henri Girard, "Le livre, l'illustration, et la reliure à l'époque romantique," in Louis Hautecoeur et al., *Le romantisme et l'art* (Paris: Laurens, 1928), pp. 288–317; Léopold Carteret, *Le trésor du bibliophile romantique et moderne, 1801–1875* (Paris: Carteret, 1924–28), 4 vols.; Léopold Dérôme, *Causeries d'un ami des livres, les éditions originales des romantiques* (Paris: Rouveyre, 1886–87), 2 vols.; and Jules Fleury, *Les vignettes romantiques: histoire de la littérature et de l'art, 1825–1840* (Paris: Dentu, 1883).

Further study of the samples suggests another important aspect about the new literary vogue: not only was it a matter of form, in literature and book design; it was also very brief. The romantic fashion lasted scarcely more than twenty years among the titles taken from the *Bibliographie de la France*. Whatever its initial appeal, popular authors apparently did not continue to use the movement's more striking literary conventions after 1840. This temporary feature of popular "romanticism" even appeared in the frontispieces where the letters, vignettes, and illustrations characteristic of the new literature gave way to another set of pictorial conventions. For example, a *chansonnier* in 1838 retained the amorous suggestions, to be sure, but none of the motifs peculiar to the movement: the frontispiece here no longer stressed even the superficial influence of romanticism (see Illustration 5). In this book and most others the movement had passed, a fall from popular favor even more clearly evident in a survey of the samples from 1820 to 1840.

Early in the period, few samples evinced any signs of the new literature. Nearly all the poems in 1820 obeyed the neo-classical rules—every one of the seventeen elegies on the assassination of the duc de Berri was composed in alexandrine verse. Popular songs had not yet adopted romantic subjects, and their treatment of potentially romantic themes failed to evoke an appropriate mood. As seen in Chapter 1, Madame de Brady's melancholy, for example, was not exactly a mood of personal introspection but a lament for her lost love: "Mais cette douleur a des charmes;/Pleurer n'est pas toujours souffrir."[26] In the theater only Schiller's *Marie Stuart* appeared, largely purged of its romantic improprieties by Lebrun's translation. Most plays were classical or neo-classical tragedies and comedies such as Sophocles' *Electra* and Arnault's *Germanicus*, although fully one-third of the drama titles were also popular comedy-vaudevilles unaffected by either romanticism or neo-classicism. The seventeenth century remained the model for dramatic achievement, as Népomucène Lemercier noted in the preface to his *Clovis*: "Of all dramatic works, the most perfect is uncontestably Molière's *Tartuffe*."[27]

Similarly, very few of the sampled novels in 1820 reflected the impact of romanticism—only a translation of Scott's *Ivanhoe*, a gothic tale by Charles Nodier, *Paul et Virginie* by Bernardin de Saint-Pierre, and three sentimental novels set before the seventeenth century. Obviously the vogue of the historical novel had not yet begun in 1820. Rather, most were didactic tales whose tenuous reputation forced novelists to draw an explicit moral lesson from their stories; however threatened, virtue al-

26. Brady, "La mélancolie," p. 4.

27. L. J. Népomucène Lemercier, "Préface," *Clovis*, tragédie (Paris: Baudouin frères, 1820), p. xiii.

Sire,

pardonnez à mon père!

5. *Le Chansonnier des Grâces, Pour 1838.* Frontispiece and title page.

LE
CHANSONNIER
DES
GRACES,
Pour 1838.

Avec les Airs Nouveaux gravés

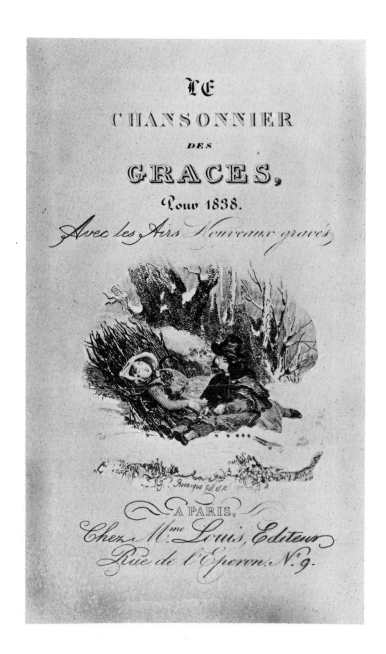

Bouaique *del. et sc.*

À PARIS,

Chez Mme Louis, Éditeur

Rue de l'Éperon, N.º 9.

ways triumphed over vice.[28] Among all the histories given to detailed accounts of the duc de Berri's assassination, there was only one colorful history of the crusades: "Peter the Hermit travelled throughout Europe," stated the anonymous work, "seated on a mule, crucifix in hand, feet bare, head uncovered, his body encompassed by a large rope and dressed in a long monk's robe of the coarsest material. The singularity of his clothes was a spectacle for the people," as was this predecessor of romantic history.[29]

Among the samples in 1827, the year of Hugo's famous preface to *Cromwell*, there was a decided rise in romantic influence. Most poetry collections continued to follow the neo-classical models established by Boileau's *Art poétique; épîtres, poèmes héroiques*, elegies and pieces in alexandrine couplets, both in Latin and French, accounted for nearly half of the poetry titles. But Lamartine, Desbordes-Valmore, and Ulric Guttinguer were anthologized in the *chansonniers;* and a few other poets, like Augustin André in *Les étrennes du troubadour*, actually tried to express the anguish of the new century.[30] Drama also included some examples of recent changes in form and sentiment. One play explicitly claimed to be "the fruit of this foreign import, termed the romantic genre, that we seek to adapt to our own soil."[31] This work coincided with an edition of Shakespeare's *Othello,* then being staged in Paris by a renowned English troupe, for the attention of those who ordinarily might have attended performances of popular comedy-vaudevilles less influenced by the romantic fashion.

In the prose fiction of 1827 the vogue of "medieval" history was more advanced than it was in poetry or drama, with numerous translations and imitations of Walter Scott. The baronne d'Ordre's *Les suisses sous Rodolphe de Habsbourg*, Kératry's *Frédéric Styndall,* and van der Velde's *Christine et sa cour* were among the more French representatives of this important new form in the sample. The historical novel now shared in the mainstream of sentimental and gothic tales. Despite Achille

---

28. E.g., Madame la comtesse du Nardouet (Ruault de la Haye) *Vice et vertu, ou l'heureuse séduction* (Paris: Brianchon, 1820), 3 vols.

29. M. G***, *Beautés de l'histoire des croisades*, 2nd. ed. (Paris: Eymery, 1820), p. 10.

30. E.g., in one of Augustin André's poems found in his *Les étrennes du troubadour* (Paris: Rusand, 1827), p. 4:

> Le buffle qui mugit immobile d'horreur...
> Les arbres élevés que l'ouragan déchire...
> L'insensible rocher qui s'anime et soupire...
> Le trouble universel ne peut rien sur mon coeur!

31. Théaulon, "Prologue," *Le paysan perverti*, p. i.

Roche's response to romantic excess, warning fellow authors to "submit to the approval of reason the fantasies that a nebulous imagination leads you," the persistent current of such fiction continued, whatever its historical overtones.[32] Similarly, a half dozen colorful histories with appropriate lithographs appeared among the thirty sampled, indicative of the movement's impact on a genre given over to political commentary whether or not it considered medieval subjects.

In 1834 when Lamennais published his enormously successful *Paroles d'un croyant,* the influence of romanticism was most clearly apparent. The neo-classical models in poetry no longer had the hold they did in the 1820s: here only four of thirty samples in poetry obeyed the classical rules. Although the rise in popular poetry was much greater, pieces experimenting in form and feeling were much more prominent than they had been only seven years earlier. In *Le nouveau chansonnier des grâces* was actually found an explicit imitation of Lamartine's "Le lac": "J'aime à rêver sur le bord du rivage."[33] Even the political poetry utilized the new poetic freedom permitted budding poetasters. A sampled play by Casimir Delavigne, member of the Académie française since 1825, was also influenced by recent developments: his *Louis XI* violated the three unities even though it scrupulously observed neo-classical language and meter. Furthermore, the popular theater showed signs of adapting new subjects and conventions to its purposes: Léon Théaulon's *Les quatre âges du Palais-Royal* and Jacques Arago's *Un noviciat diplomatique* employed historical settings that had nearly become stock to the genre.

Seven historical novels, also set in the Middle Ages, appeared among the thirty sampled in 1834, while Auguste Rogeau joined the ranks of the young prosateurs in his own bizarre way: "There is absolutely no order in my work. All that is certain is that the final sentence that ends the piece will be complete."[34] Histories employing local color became more evident as well, like Augustin Thierry's *Dix ans d'études historiques* and R. O. Spazier's *Histoire politique et militaire de la révolution polonaise.*

32. Achille Roche, *Le fanatisme,* extrait des mémoires d'un ligueur (Paris: Chaigneau, 1827), 1:xxx.

33. "J'aime à rêver sur le bord du rivage," *Le nouveau chansonnier des grâces* (Paris: Denn, 1834),2:28. Compare this line with Lamartine's "Le lac," *Oeuvres poétiques complètes,* p. 14:

> Ainsi, toujours poussés vers de nouveaux rivages,
> Dans la nuit éternelle emportés sans retour,
> Ne pourrons-nous jamais sur l'océan des âges
> Jeter l'ancre un seul jour?

34. Auguste Rogeau, *Sardanapale,* essais rétrogrades (Paris: Imp. Delacombe, 1834), p. 13.

Such accounts of peoples united in dramatic historical events were certainly new in both subject and tone. In this way 1834 marked the high point of the movement.

But by 1841, the year before Balzac's "Avant-Propos" to *La comédie humaine,* the published manifestations of romanticism were in eclipse. In their place were popular productions pretending to no imitation of either classical or romantic form or feeling. Easy verse relating an amusing anecdote appeared in increasing numbers in poetry; titles evincing clear signs of romantic influence declined to only four of the thirty sampled. The passing of the *drame* was especially marked two full years before the failure of Hugo's *Burgraves;* two of the thirty plays taken randomly from the 1841 *Bibliographie de la France* evinced positive evidence of the movement—both, ironically, by Hugo himself. Moreover, more than 53 percent of the drama titles were comedy-vaudevilles, none of which acknowledged the movement's conventions.

The slide in the new literature's impact was only slightly less marked in fiction where the historical novels in the vein of Walter Scott gave way to novels of manners and mores in the Parisian literary market. Pieces like Frédéric Soulié's *Le conseiller d'état* and *Si jeunesse savait!* and Auguste Ricard's *Le viveur* and *J'ai du bon tabac dans ma tabatière,* besides the still engaging sentimentality of Madames Cottin and de Genlis, accounted for more than half of the novels published. It was in history, however, that romanticism seems to have retained its greatest appeal. Dramatic versions of the Middle Ages and the exploits of Napoleon numbered fourteen of thirty titles sampled, though of course, the return of the emperor's ashes in 1840 explains much of the interest in this easily idealized historical figure.

In sum, evidence of a shift away from earlier innovations in popular literature indicates that by the early 1840s, romanticism no longer remained the model for authors it had been less than ten years before (see Table 2.1). Moreover, the impact of these samples includes more than a reasonably precise accounting of romantic influence and its duration. It is equally evident in the almost exclusive adoption and adaptation of its styles and conventions: freer verse, historical *drames,* medieval settings, and local color. To be precise, most titles imitative of new images and forms here did *not* express the manner of feeling that Baudelaire spoke of, presumably the heart of the romantic revolution. Rather, they appeared to develop a kind of fashion largely irrelevant to recent changes in literary vision among a select group of authors. It was the movement's more common stylistic and generic experiments, not its sensibility and imagination, that attracted the greatest imitation at the height of the romantic period.

TABLE 2.1
Percentages of Sampled Titles Reflecting
Romantic Influence, by Genre, 1820–1841

	Poetry	Drama	Fiction	History	Total
1820	—	3.3%	20.0%	3.3%	6.7%
1827	10.0%	13.3	26.7	16.7	16.7
1834	33.3	40.0	46.7	26.7	36.7
1841	13.3	6.7	23.3	36.7	20.0

Source: See discussion, pp. 47–49, 59–64.

A SYSTEM OF ROMANTIC SIGNS

Marking only an apparent change in intellectual paradigms, popular romanticism was mostly a conscious rejection of neo-classical forms and conventions, while romanticism proper eschewed the classical values established in the seventeenth century almost incidentally in its new vision of the self and the world. What evidence there is of the movement's impact appears to be not romantic as literary historians know the term, but centered on its most popular devices—all that was readily adopted without expressing the movement's distinctive sentiment. In its prime, romanticism, as most contemporaries must have known it, was in effect a superimposition upon the new popular literature developing since the revolution.[35]

Thus the importance of this influence, however brief, lies not in the vision of the world developed by elite romantics. Rather, it exists in the remarkable extent to which their conventions were used in popular works. However banal and short-lived its imitations, the movement affected public literary taste on a scale unknown to any previous trend in ideas, far beyond even the impact of the eighteenth-century Enlightenment.[36] With romanticism intellectual values of elites filtered downward

35. For discussion of the new urban popular culture since the 1789 revolution, see Crubellier, *Histoire culturelle*, p. 125–41.

36. See Daniel Mornet, "Les enseignements des bibliothèques privées (1750–1780)," *Revue d'histoire littéraire de la France* 17(1910),449–92, in which doubt is cast on the actual influence of the Enlightenment. Very few of the *lumières* seem to have reached the hands of even the elite, much less the illiterate lower orders. Recent work by François Furet and Robert Mandrou has shown that popular literature was nearly untouched by the Enlightenment during the eighteenth century. See Furet et al., *Livre et société*. But see also the relatively wide diffusion of the *philosophes* argued in Darnton, "Le livre français à la fin de l'ancien régime," *Annales: E.S.C.* 28(1973),3:735–44.

to a much larger portion of the literature aimed at a plebeian audience, influencing the usages if not the sensibilities of its authors with remarkable intensity for nearly twenty years. Given the nature of both the movement and the popular literature it affected, romanticism took on all the appearances of a brief, commercial fad.

Surely with its interest in distinguishing itself from neo-classicism, elite romanticism itself was not untouched by popular influence: witness Hugo and Dumas's dramatic success at the boulevard theaters.[37] But the pervasiveness of high romantic influence on the vast production of poetry, drama, fiction, and history for nonelites, on the other hand, was much more significant, for it breeched decisively the former cultural distinctions between the "great tradition" of the middle classes and the "little tradition" of the *menu peuple* that had existed almost since the origins of printed literature.[38] So widespread was this development that even the romantics, long anxious for the largest possible audience, became alarmed at the dilution of their original intentions. In 1843, the movement nearly passed, Sainte-Beuve spoke in strident terms about the victimization of the new literature by its imitators. Moved apparently more by commercial than esthetic considerations, these literary "parasites" re-

37. As much as 15,000 francs per play, according to Milner, *Le romantisme*, p. 35.

38. On the eighteenth-century cultural cleavage between social orders, see Burke, *Popular Culture*, pp. 270–81; and Philippe Ariès, *Centuries of Childhood: A Social History of Family Life*, Robert Baldick, trans. (New York: Vintage, 1962), pp. 62–99.

The bifurcation of French society and culture from the seventeenth to the nineteenth centuries, of course, was not absolute. Throughout this period, elites frequently indulged in popular cultural activities, from country fairs to street dramas. Only the lower orders of society were unable to reciprocate in any genuine way; they could not participate in salon life, the theater, and printed literature especially, largely as a consequence of poverty and illiteracy, as well as major differences in taste and perception. It was not until politicization and literacy in the nineteenth century that a mass culture was capable of bridging this one-sided cultural participation, one that was indeed a gulf for nearly all but a very special few in France during the *ancien régime*. By the romantic period, however, distinctions between high and low culture were rapidly changing, as shown by the evidence in the samples.

A similar qualification in the dichotomy between rural and urban popular cultures must also be made. Undoubtedly, many workers in Paris perpetuated "premodern" modes of thought well into the nineteenth century, just as many seasonal migrants carried back to their home villages the new ways they had learned in the city. But there were in the nineteenth century, and there continue today, important cultural, political, and social differences between Paris ("l'autre pays") and the provinces still cherishing rapidly vanishing local heritages. This conflict between the capital and the country surely owes to developments in Paris, as well as those in the hinterlands, and bears serious consideration. For fuller discussion of this problem, see Zeldin, *France, 1848–1945*, 1:365–92.

placed romanticism with the products of "fatuity combined with cupidity" that it ironically helped to foster.[39]

Much of Sainte-Beuve's alarm owed to the development of a new popular culture. Besides marking the rise and fall of romantic influence on nearly every social level, the sampling evinced the consistent growth of a literature intended for a plebeian audience. The literate world no longer remained the exclusive realm of the classically educated; it now shared an increasing portion of its limited literary production with works by authors unconcerned with either romantic or neo-classical proprieties. From 1820 to 1840 an entirely new literary etiquette was being established, as noted in Chapter 1. The easy verse of songs and patriotic poetry, the melodramas and comedy-vaudevilles, the adventure stories and gothic novels grew from less than a quarter of the samples to nearly half of the market in *belles lettres*. Literature for elites was giving way to one for the greatest possible readership (see Table 2.2).

Moreover, the older tradition of the *bibliothèque bleue* and the *canards* shared a similar fate before this new urban literature.[40] Already *colporteur* literature was being banned to the provinces where it was increasingly produced and consumed in a literary domain unto itself. Similarly, the sensational events celebrated in the broadsheets sold in the streets appeared as well in the theater and fiction that now became new sources of rivalry to the *canards*.[41] Although these early developments in mass culture did not originate in the period, they *did* grow remarkably, amusing the peasantry come to the city and alarming the lettered pretensions of middle-class critics like Sainte-Beuve. It is in this trend toward a more modern popular literature that romanticism as fashion enjoyed its early success and saw its later decline.

This much the samples show clearly. Popular romanticism appeared to benefit briefly from the growth of a new mass culture. Romantic and popular literary conventions certainly overlapped and the extent of the movement's diffusion among the titles can even be measured. But a much more difficult task is to assess the significance these conventions had for their authors. Did they perceive the forms they used only as popular devices to insure the success of their work? Or did these authors share

39. Sainte-Beuve, "Quelques vérités," p. 13. Note the traditional discussion of the movement's rise and fall, independent of its sociocultural context, in Milner, *Le romantisme*, pp. 49–70, among others.

40. See Crubellier, *Histoire culturelle*, pp. 81–102.

41. See Seguin, *Nouvelles à sensation*, which argues the demise of the French broadside for many of the same reasons.

TABLE 2.2
Classification of Sampled Titles by Genre, 1820–1841

	1820	1827	1834	1841	Total
Poetry					
Greek and Latin Titles	2	3	2	6	13
Collected Works	1	3	1	2	7
Elegies, Odes, Chants	15	11	6	3	35
Epistles, Essays in Verse	4	5	6	5	20
Songs and Stories in Verse	7	5	11	10	33
Miscellaneous	1	3	4	4	12
Total	30	30	30	30	120
Drama					
Greek and Latin Titles	2	1	1	2	6
Collected Works	3	4	3	2	12
Tragedies and Comedies	14	4	4	4	26
Melodramas and *Drames*	2	2	9	4	17
Comedy-vaudevilles	6	10	7	13	36
Miscellaneous	3	9	6	5	23
Total	30	30	30	30	120
Fiction					
Greek and Latin Titles	0	3	0	2	5
Picaresque Tales	4	3	3	2	12
Memoirs	5	1	1	0	7
Historical Novels	3	4	8	6	21
Other Novels	14	10	11	15	50
Stories and Scenes	4	9	7	5	25
Total	30	30	30	30	120
History					
Historical Works	5	7	9	12	33
Textbooks/Chronologies	2	2	4	3	11
Contemporary Events	15	5	10	7	37
Memoirs and Petitions	4	7	2	3	16
Atlases and Almanacs	4	6	4	4	18
Miscellaneous	0	3	1	1	5
Total	30	30	30	30	120
Total Titles	120	120	120	120	480

Source: Random samples from the genre indexes in *Bibliographie de la France*, 1820–1841.

with observers and critics the feeling that they were actually participating in a larger intellectual movement? There is perhaps no way of knowing short of studying the biography of every borrower of romantic innovations.

But literary evidence, with a few exceptions, still suggests their sincerity, despite the imitators' apparent cynicism as a group in the samples. Although their presence was rare, plebeian imitators of romantic sensibility did exist, such as the worker poets in Olinde Rodrigues' collection sampled in the 1841 *Bibliographie*.[42] Nearly all of their poems expressed a deeply felt emotion akin to that of the social romantics after 1830, perhaps because their authors had personally experienced the injustices they poeticized. Surely the four examples of popular romanticism examined in Chapter 1 expressed an apparently genuine romantic tendency; Pauline de Brady, Léon Théaulon, Maurice de Viarz, and Edouard Gauttier d'Arc at least shared in the movement as many literary historians have characterized it. Nevertheless, such sincerity is nearly impossible to establish among all the titles, even in strictly literary terms; the actual impact of ideas must remain elusive, however clear the trends in the available texts.[43]

The samples also fail to show the movement's influence in other creative endeavors, both intellectual and artistic.[44] Although romanticism appeared in France most explicitly in the *belles lettres* and history, it also affected the style and vision of works in science and theology, only in a much different manner difficult to document. Intellectual historians are far from a coherent definition of romantic values in either field.[45] Without such a notion, sampling alone is unlikely to assess the movement's influence on phrenology or Protestantism, for example, in the early nineteenth century. Similarly, study of the diffusion of the new sensibility in memoirs requires an equal effort in imagination: how common was Agricol Perdiguier's account of his rapture by the sea in Marseille? "The wind blew with extreme violence, the waves crashed against the shore. I was alone. I had before me only the rocks, the sea, the sky."[46] Similar effusions are easily identified in the journals of major romantic authors, but are rare among the few published diaries of more ordinary people.

Perhaps more difficult to assess is the diffusion of romantic feeling among dancers, musicians, and actors. Obviously these people were

42. Olinde Rodrigues, ed., *Poésies sociales des ouvriers* (Paris: Paulin, 1841).

43. The problem of sincerity in European literature, generally, is discussed more fully by Lionel Trilling, *Sincerity and Authority* (Cambridge: Harvard University Press, 1972).

44. On the larger question of the diffusion of romanticism among other creative endeavors, see Malcolm Easton, *Artists and Writers in Paris: The Bohemian Idea, 1803–1867* (New York: St. Martin's, 1965); Pierre Moreau, "Le romantisme et la 'fraternité' des arts," *Symposium* (Winter 1969), 319–24; and Hautecoeur et al., *Le romantisme et l'art.*

45. E.g., see the discussion of early nineteenth-century science as seen by poets in Alfred North Whitehead, "The Romantic Reaction," *Science and the Modern World* (New York: The Free Press, 1953), pp. 75–94.

46. Agricol Perdiguier, *Mémoires d'un compagnon* (Paris: Librairie de Compagnonnage, 1964), p. 83.

touched by the movement: witness the great actor Talma for whom Hugo wrote *Cromwell*. Except for their and others' accounts of their performances, however, such responses to romanticism have gone largely unrecorded. The new literature's sentiments and conventions must surely have affected a wide range of creative activity. More than a literary phenomenon, romanticism high and low pervaded the practice of all the arts, a practice that cannot be known more precisely without another approach to the problem in early nineteenth-century France.

Nevertheless, what evidence there is indicates that the romantic movement did reach a large number of authors. Their production of poetry, drama, fiction, and history was apparently influenced by the values of a relatively select group of writers who championed the new literature among elites. Romanticism was indeed widely diffused, in both senses of the word: widespread and diluted. Authors of popular titles adopted and adapted the romantic conventions most appropriate to their genres, omitting or even changing the movement's devices to suit their needs. But this brief and relatively superficial romantic patina in many popular works in the period had a far deeper meaning than appears at first glance. The romantic movement's historical significance is generally believed to lie in its new vision of man and his relationship to himself and the world around him. Instead of conceiving in the mechanistic analogies adored by the eighteenth-century *lumières*, for example, the nineteenth-century *romantiques* thought more in organic metaphors that marked one element of this watershed in the history of ideas. Despite this, the movement's immediate impact, beyond the small circle of elites participating in this new intellectual paradigm, was not its world view but its iconoclastic forms whose meaning lay elsewhere, "encoded" in à system of signs perhaps, not readily apparent to everyone on a clearly articulated level.

What was this romantic literary code and what did it express implicitly?[47] Since the more profound mood of the known romantics was

47. This analysis of the meaning of the popular romantic "code" owes much to the structuralist methodologies developed by Claude Lévi-Strauss, Michel Foucault, and Roland Barthes. See useful discussions of their work and its applicability to the study of popular culture in Hayden White, "Structuralism and Popular Culture," *Journal of Popular Culture* 7(1973),759–75; and G. R. Kress, "Structuralism and Popular Culture," in C. W. E. Bigsby, ed., *Approaches to Popular Culture* (Bowling Green: Popular Press, 1977), pp. 85–105.

Such an approach also finds theoretical support from the semiotic interpretation of culture, in its larger anthropological sense, characterized in Geertz, *The Interpretation of Cultures*, pp. 3–30, 412–53. Although Geertz examines aspects of primitive cultures more crucial to their functioning, his work does suggest the interpretative possibilities of the romantic conventions explored here.

largely absent from popular works affected by the movement, the romantic mode must have embodied a significance that may well have eluded contemporaries who only remarked the bastardization of the movement, not what it could have represented to those who experienced it. If this widespread adoption of elite literary conventions, from the romantics' freer versification in poetry to their use of local color in medieval history, meant anything, it must have underscored a remarkable cultural ambivalence on all social levels in Paris during the middle years of the *monarchie censitaire*. The selective use of romantic innovations in literature could have reflected a comparable acceptance and rejection of social and political changes occurring in France since the eighteenth century. Indeed, the preference writers and readers evidently had for the movement and its celebration of both a medieval world and a renovated literary practice seems to parallel their feelings about the constitutional monarchies and the Revolution that these regimes hoped to modify or accommodate to a more stable social and political structure.

This historical ambivalence is clearly apparent in the conventions that the popular romantics used. The façade of the movement's formal devices in jolly and sentimental songs, melodramas and comedy-vaudevilles, gothic and adventure stories, and dramatic national histories actually intensified the nostalgic longing for the apparent social, political, even moral stability of the *ancien régime*. At least as many people then conceived it, such as Balzac in the occasionally intrusive voice of *La comédie humaine*, there had been a more orderly world before the Revolution, before the Bourbons, in fact, who had only made matters worse both in the eighteenth and nineteenth centuries. The need for some secure moment in history where people presumably knew their place in the hierarchy of deference, power, and faith occurred to many readers as well as writers in the aftermath of twenty-five years of revolutionary and imperial adventures. And this widespread desire for stability and order, even an archaic one, appeared in the medievalism and melancholy captured in popular titles imitating the romantics' more profound historical and personal vision. Although the ostensible source of such a pose in poetry, for example, was almost always far more trivial, the popular romantic conventions did approximate a larger historical conscience in the nostalgia and sentimentality invested in a better world, one long ago and far away, like that sought by Lamartine, Vigny, and Hugo in their more remarkable achievements.

The other side of this ambivalence, however, lay in the optimism and innovation also evident in the popular imitators of romanticism. While many of them focused their regrets on the passing of a better age, others wholeheartedly embraced the new world of revolution and empire. This certainly appears among elite romantics who at first expressed an ardent royalism that in time waned and disappeared altogether by the end of the Restoration. Then they turned increasingly to a variety of political attitudes heralding a new, or at least a reformed, order. The popular romantics seemed to have expressed this aspect of the movement as well: the striking new devices in the different genres—the experimentation in poetry, the new forms of drama, the realistic touches in gothic romances, and the novelistic features in history—all seemed to express the exciting possibilities, historical as well as literary, inherent in the vast changes shaking the country. The very enthusiasm with which so many new conventions were used in popular literature, at least temporarily, coincided with the energies of men and women anxious to establish liberty in France during the 1830 revolution. It is certainly no accident that rapid changes in literature, however superficial and brief, shared in rapid changes in politics, society, and values during the romantic period.

Thus a deep-seated ambivalence in attitudes towards change, both literary and historical, occurred in what must have been something of a brief *prise de conscience* on the part of popular writers and perhaps even their readers. Quite obviously this larger awareness of change, greeted at once by fear and by joy, marked all romantic literature, only in rather different ways. While the romantics still known and studied today expressed dread and enthusiasm in the mood captured in the imagery of their work, giving it its distinctive revolutionary quality, the popular romantics unremembered and unstudied only implied this Janus-like attitude toward historical change suggested in their adoption and adaptation of romantic conventions. Much of the fascination of romanticism for many writers and readers in the nineteenth century must have derived from their complex feelings about the breakup of long established political, social, and spiritual hierarchies in France. In place of the traditional centers of authority in the monarchy, the guilds, and the Church, the ethos of individualism, the ideal of the Christian family circle, and scientific rationalism were on the way to becoming dominant centers of value and feeling. Of course, all this grossly exaggerates the meanings implicit in the popular imitations of romanticism, and oversimplifies the historical developments taking place in Europe as well as France in the period. But it does suggest the historical place the movement had, even on the relatively superficial level of forms and conventions found in popular literature for a very short time. Certainly this ambivalence, if it was actually felt in the plebeian world, was of short duration. Why this was so remains for further study.

This remarkable spread of romantic conventions, though not their more exclusive sensibility, owed to factors not immediately apparent in the samples or their historical context. How did this profusion of romantic forms come about? Who were their authors? Who published them? Who read them? What role did the extraliterary milieu of authors, publishers, and readers play in this development? Admittedly the climate of opinion, the conflict of social class values, and the continuation of political revolution contributed, but in a manner impossible to assess with precision. Whatever their merits, traditional accounts of French romanticism's success simply fail to explain how its books were produced, distributed, and consumed in the early nineteenth century. Before the movement can be understood, it must first be placed in its more immediate social context. Romantic ideas did not exist in a vacuum without men and women to write, publish, and read them. Although such elements did not determine diffusion, they did make it possible—a sufficient reason for their closer study in the following chapters on authors, publishers, and readers.

❧3❧

ROMANTIC AUTHORSHIP

$\mathcal{S}$INCE THE ROMANTIC PERIOD the author and the artist have often been portrayed as lonely youths in conflict with society, promethean visionaries martyred to an unappreciative public.[1] For many romantics, and others since, the mythical figure of Icarus embodied the ambivalent state of the creative man in the modern world—the daring apprentice in quest of the impossible, foiled in flight by the ecstasy that took him too close to the sun, and ignored by all once he had fallen in the sea.[2] In the nineteenth century, however, "the fate of Icarus frightened no one. Wings! Wings! Wings! they cried from all sides, even if we should fall," Théophile Gautier wrote, less of aspiring authors in general than of the romantics in particular.[3] The romantic man of letters had incurred the sacred duty to create, despite the risks, despite the obstacles placed in his way by a materialistic world skeptical of his self-assumed priestly functions.[4]

For those unequal to the task, there was but one other course permitted this divinely inspired aristocracy: esoteric retreat. So wrote Gérard de Nerval: "Our period was a mixture of activity, hesitation, and idleness; of brilliant utopias, philosophic, or religious aspirations, vague enthusiasms, . . . boredom, discord, and uncertain hopes. Ambition

1. For discussion of modern literary images of artists and authors in the romantic period, see Easton, *Artists and Writers in Paris*; Geraldine Pelles, *Art, Artists, and Society: Origins of a Modern Dilemma. Painting in England and France, 1750–1850* (Englewood Cliffs: Prentice-Hall, 1963); and Maurice Beebe, *Ivory Towers and Sacred Founts: The Artist as Hero in Fiction from Goethe to Joyce* (New York: New York University Press, 1964), pp. 3–171.

2. See Shroder, *Icarus: The Image of the Artist in French Romanticism* (Cambridge: Harvard University Press, 1961), pp. 1–59.

3. Gautier, *Histoire du romantisme*, p. 153.

4. For a fuller discussion of the author's self-assumed priestly role in the early nineteenth century, see Bénichou, *Le sacre de l'écrivain*, pp. 275–352, 419–62.

was not of our age. . . . There remained to us only the poet's ivory tower."[5] This pose naturally went hand in hand with the development of an exclusive art, as much for the sake of the disaffected artist as for art itself. Nevertheless, the two romantic artistic ideals of the ivory tower and purity of art on the one hand, of the sacred fount and orphic mission on the other, implied the deep-seated ambivalence between inspired creation and social alienation inherent in the image of modern creative genius.

Yet this popular view of romantic artists and authors against themselves and the world contrasts sharply with another image current in the period: the worldly man of letters. The empty pretensions of the penniless poet, especially, was often the object of bitter satires.[6] "Vanity! the favorite sin of the poet! As soon as the school boy scribbles his first quatrain celebrating his teacher, he believes his pen the source of glory and fortune," wrote Emile de la Bédolierre in an article on the French versifier, a type he believed most given to the foibles of pride and ambition.[7] A few years later Saint-René Taillandier mocked the same figure: "Priest, legislator, man of state, the poet claims for himself all spiritual powers, he is first and final cause, the supreme hierophant."[8] In these scathing commentaries creative heroism suffers for all its foolish egotism.

Perhaps the self-elected deities did not deserve this harsh criticism. But in the case of the vaunting man of letters, there was little room for pity. This is certainly true for the successful author portrayed in Benjamin Roubaud's lithograph, "Le grand chemin de la postérité," where a dreamy Lamartine leans on a bag of 100,000 francs—or more tellingly in Roubaud's "Panthéon charivarique" where he satirizes a host of successful authors.[9] In 1841 Elias Regnault could only lament, "Certain men in this century [who] accumulate the glories of Parnassus as well as the material profits of their work . . . [only] give the muses their hours of leisure."[10] In such almost envious accounts of the philistine poet, the nineteenth-century idealist, at least as he would like to have been seen, is no where to be found.

5. Gérard de Nerval, "Sylvie," *Oeuvres*, Albert Béguin and Jean Richer, eds. (Paris: Gallimard, 1960), 1:242.

6. See the amusing satirical articles on "L'homme de lettres," "Le poëte," "Le débutant littéraire," "Le journaliste," and "L'auteur dramatique" in Léon Curmer, ed. *Les Français peints par eux-mêmes* (Paris: Curmer, 1841), 4 vols.; and Louis Reybaud, *Jérôme Paturot à la recherche d'une position sociale* (Paris: Michel Lévy frères, 1876), first published 1842.

7. Emile de la Bédolierre, "Le poëte," in Curmer, ed. *Les Français*, 2:82.

8. Taillandier, "Simples essais d'histoire littéraire," p. 976.

9. See Illustrations 1 and 5.

10. Elias Regnault, "L'homme de lettres," in Curmer, ed. *Les Français*, 3:226.

Despite this competing image, the youthful Icarus remains the primary representative of the romantic man of letters. His deep personal anguish is remembered by literary historians more than his greedy ambitions, perhaps because the new literature itself emphasized the poet's martyrdom instead of his bills of credit. Alfred de Musset's *mal de siècle* was enshrined in his *Confession* still read today, while A.-H. de Kératry's literary chicanery disappeared with his largely forgotten novels. Yet this portrait of the overweening poet in open quest of fame and fortune appeared concurrently with the more romantic image of the visionary artist, one starving in his garret rather than compromising to a vulgar public. Obviously, such a clash of conceptions, the creative man as youthful dreamer and as cynical rake, obscures the actual nature of authorship in the period. Indeed, which of these portraits is the most appropriate to the romantic writer? What was more typical, the wounded anger of Alfred de Vigny's *Journal* or the self-satisfaction of Victor Hugo's correspondence?

Such ambiguity clouds the romantic author's contribution to the new popular literature. It may well be that these two responses to the new literary marketplace coincided with the distinctions between romanticisms high and low. The rather superficial patina of romantic conventions adapted in the more popular titles suggests a freer acceptance of the commercial side of literature, something that the intense sensibility of less popular works does not. The authors in the romantic mode seem far more cynical or less principled than those in the corresponding mood. Only a close study of authors in the period promises clarification of this ambiguous image and some understanding of the brief but significant appearance of popular romanticism.

THE "GENERATION" OF 1830

One approach to this problem lies in an examination of the demographic context of authorship, especially of the phenomenon of historical and literary generations.[11] Writers' differing attitudes toward their work and audience may have derived from a significant age factor; the older author remembered and probably preferred the patronage of the eighteenth

---

11. For discussion of this problem, see Peyre, *Les générations littéraires* (Paris: Boivin, 1948), pp. 7–44; and Albert Thibaudet, *Histoire de la littérature française de la révolution à nos jours* (Paris: Stock, 1936), pp. 105–22. See for a more general historical treatment, Alan Spitzer, "The Historical Problem of Generations," *American Historical Review* 78(1973),5:1353–85; and John R. Gillis, *Youth and History: Tradition and Change in European Age Relations, 1770–Present* (New York: Academic Press, 1974), pp. 37–93.

century, while the younger writer did not and looked forward to a more commercially acceptable esthetic in the nineteenth. Such a generational conflict between the old and the young certainly appears behind some of the literary differences between the neo-classicists and the romantics in general, a problem frequently addressed in literary histories of the movement. But it could also be a factor in the ambivalent images of romantic writers. The idealism of a youthful romantic sensibility, despite commercial reality, could well have given way in time to the cynicism of a more mature romantic convention, one more pleasing to a paying audience. The aging of the romantic generation, as well as its conflict with the older generation of neo-classicists, explains in part the movement's more popular though temporary manifestations. Any study of authorship in the romantic period must, in any case, address this important demographic phenomenon.

But first, what *is* a generation? Like romanticism, "generation" demands definition. Fortunately, more consensus exists here than on French literature in 1830.[12] To explain historical periods of continuity or change, theorists have often cited the importance of the biological life cycle. Clearly the aging of elites not only modifies their individual desire for change but also affects their collective relationship to the rest of society. In their maturation from youth (birth–age 15), initiation (ages 15–30), maturity (30–45), dominance (45–60), to old age (60–death), influential figures advocate change appropriate to their age-specific interests until they have taken "possession" of society, politics, business, and the arts. Having achieved such dominance they are much more likely to consolidate and conserve the institutions and ideas they have established, especially in the face of changes demanded by younger elites. But in time members of the conservative, older generation retire and die, giving way to those of the innovative, younger cohort anxious to take their place. Consequently, according to this theory, historical continuity is maintained by the succession of very similar elite age groups, while change must occur in the transition between groups widely different from each other.

A generation is thus defined by the maturation of contemporaneous and coetaneous cohorts, by those of the same age and those of different ages living at the same time, with visions of the world largely unique to each age group. Such a common trait among people born within a fifteen-year period is delimited by what Ortega y Gasset has called *vigencia,* the

12. See Vilfredo Pareto, *The Rise and Fall of the Elites: An Application of Theoretical Sociology* (Totowa: Bedminister Press, 1968), pp. 25–101; S. N. Eisenstadt, *From Generation to Generation: Age Groups and Social Structure,* rev. ed. (New York: The Free Press, 1971), pp. vi–xlix; and for an excellent survey, Julián Marías, *Generations: A Historical Method,* Harold C. Riley, trans. (University: University of Alabama Press, 1970).

prevailing social customs at the formative age before maturity that often mold an age group's outlook for the rest of its life cycle.[13] Because of this, each cohort has a distinctive character, however much its interests resemble or differ from those of others at the time. But this recognition of generational solidarity derives from more than a crucial social or psychological influence early in life; it is also an enduring awareness, shared by both contemporaneous and coetaneous groups, that such generational boundaries exist, that any one individual belongs to a specific and commonly recognized generation with a special historical role to play. This consciousness is as essential as biological fact to the theory.

The application of this view of continuity and change has obvious uses in explaining literary developments. As Levin Schücking observed in 1923, a new literary mode is not so much a change in taste as the consequence of "other persons [who] become the advocates of a new taste. . . . The completely new trend in art [demands] new men and women, the most confirmed supporters of the new trend being found entirely outside the supporters of the old."[14] What this means to the study of French romanticism is that the age group of literary elites embracing the new literature was born around 1800, experienced the disillusionment of the Restoration in 1815, challenged neo-classicism and its politics during the 1830 revolution, and dominated art, society, and politics by 1845 until old age permitted another generation to succeed it during the Second Empire. Such were the advocates of romanticism during the constitutional monarchies.

These "biological data constitute the basic stratum of factors determining generational phenomena," stated Karl Mannheim, "but . . . we cannot observe the effect of biological factors directly; we must, instead, see how they are reflected through the medium of social and cultural forces."[15] This, too, is evident in the rise and fall of French romanticism. The romantic vision conceived by this demographic cohort first received widespread attention with Lamartine's *Méditations poétiques* in 1820, triumphed with Hugo's dramatic victory at the Théâtre français in 1830, and was itself attacked in 1843 by a new literary generation. Thus the traditional dates of French romanticism's first phase (1820–1830–1843) roughly coincide with the crucial transitions in the life cycle of the cohort born in 1800 (1815–1830–1845). Despite slight variations, literary and demographic developments parallel and lend credence to the idea of a French romantic generation of 1830.

13. See José Ortega y Gasset, *Man and Crisis*, Mildred Adams, trans. (New York: Norton, 1958), pp. 30–84.

14. Schücking, *The Sociology of Literary Taste*, p. 82.

15. Karl Mannheim, "The Problem of Generations," *Essays on the Sociology of Knowledge*, Paul Kecskemeti, ed. (Oxford: Oxford University Press, 1952), p. 311.

But such an examination of authorship needs elaboration: for one, it obviously fails to account for the larger consciousness of age groups in the period.[16] Many observers during the Restoration worried about a political leadership, personified by the ailing Louis XVIII, too old to lead a France rejuvenated by revolutionary upheaval and Napoleonic conquest. James Fazy, among others, characterized the regime as a gerontocracy reduced to "seven or eight thousand asthmatic, gouty, paralytic eligible candidates with enfeebled faculties."[17] Similarly, concerned amateur statisticians found in their study of demography convincing evidence of an aging population: Charles Dupin, the Saint-Simonian baron, calculated that in 1827 more than one-ninth of France was over fifty-seven years old, but because of the electoral laws, they constituted more than one-half of the French polity.[18] This situation meant to many like Balzac a growing social division between young and old. For him Paris had "only two ages, youth and senility, a wan and colorless youth, a senility bedizened in an attempt to look young," locked in struggle for political as well as social prominence.[19]

In the romantic period such open conflict clearly reflected a sensitivity to the aspirations of the young frustrated by older men in established positions, a conflict between age groups that others besides Balzac recognized. Delacroix's painting of "Liberty Leading the People," for example, portrayed a pistol-waving adolescent and a student from the Ecole Polytechnique, the very youths Caleb Cushing claimed led the fight on the barricades during the July revolution.[20] Although this was not an accurate rendering of the participants—one recent historian found their ages actually ranged between twenty and thirty-five—the tableau still depicted a common belief among the painter's contemporaries about the rebelliousness of youth.[21] The idea of this conflict between generations lingered well into the July Monarchy. After an abortive uprising in Paris, one youthful republican on trial before the much older Chamber of Peers in 1834 stated, "We do not feel the same, we do not speak the same

16. See Bertier de Sauvigny, *The Bourbon Restoration*, pp. 328–62; Anthony Esler, "Youth in Revolt: The French Generation of 1830," *Modern European Social History*, Robert J. Bezucha, ed. (Lexington: D. C. Heath, 1972), pp. 301–34; and Louis Mazoyer, "Catégories d'âge et groupes sociaux: les jeunes générations françaises de 1830," *Annales d'histoire économique et sociale* 10(1938),385–423.

17. Jean-Jacob Fazy, *De la gérontocratie, ou abus de la sagesse des vieillards dans le gouvernement de la France* (Paris: Delaforest, 1828), p. 5.

18. Charles Dupin, *Forces productives et commerciales* (Paris: Bachelier, 1827), pp. 111 ff.

19. Balzac, "La fille aux yeux d'or," *La comédie humaine*, 5:1039.

20. Caleb Cushing, *Review, Historical and Political, of the Late Revolution in France* (Boston: Carter, Hendee, 1833), 1:159–60.

21. Pinkney, *The French Revolution of 1830*, p. 257.

language. . . . None of those things that constitute a society, not even the heavens and the earth look the same to us." The difference between the defendants and their judges was obviously more than ideological; it was one of another social perspective largely conditioned by the significant difference in their ages.[22]

Naturally, commentators in the period characterized the conflict between the old and new literatures in similar terms. The romantics were identified with the idealism of *les jeunes gens*, the classicists with the cynicism of *les perruques*. According to Théophile Gautier, after age forty one became "the ultimate in decrepitude: an academician and member of the Institut." But even Gautier in his more serious moments believed that the new literature could only be created by younger men and women.[23] Stendhal, of course, had claimed as much fifteen years earlier: romanticism appealed to the present generation just as neo-classicism did to its grandparents.[24] The movement's leaders were very conscious that most of them were born during the Empire, "conceived between battles, taught in schools to the rolling of drums." According to Musset such a crucial period in European history shaped these writers together at an impressionable age.[25] To Hyacinthe Azaïs, a more detached observer, romanticism was indeed the response of "a large number of men constrained by too narrow a sphere for their aspirations" that had been aroused in the bloom of youth during the Napoleonic Wars.[26] Thus the literary conflicts of the period, like those between political ideologies and social classes, were partly extensions of the larger clash of old and young in France of the *monarchie censitaire*.[27]

More statistically minded contemporaries, looking at birth dates, attempted to define the romantic generation more precisely.[28] They were not surprised to discover that most of the new literature's creators were born between 1795 and 1805—Mignet first saw light in 1796; Vigny, 1797; Michelet, 1798; Balzac, 1799; Hugo, Dumas, and Lacordaire, 1802;

22. Quoted in Sébastien Charléty, *La monarchie de juillet (1830–1848)* in *Histoire de France contemporaine depuis la révolution jusqu'à la paix de 1919*, Ernest Lavisse, ed. (Paris: Hachette, 1922),5:118–19.

23. Gautier, *Les Jeunes-France,romans goguenards* (Paris: Champion, 1875), p. 87.

24. Stendhal, *Racine et Shakespeare*, p. 21.

25. Musset, *La confession d'un enfant du siècle*, in *Oeuvres complètes en prose*, p. 81.

26. Hyacinthe Azaïs, *Comment cela finira-t-il?* (Paris: Vve. Cellis, 1819), p. 7.

27. See discussion of this mood in the romantic period in Barbéris, *Balzac et le mal du siècle, contribution à une physiologie du monde moderne* (Paris: Gallimard, 1970), 1:31–139.

28. Dupin, *Forces productives*, p. xxxi.

Mérimée and Quinet, 1803; and George Sand in 1804, to name the more prominent writers. On the other hand, not a single member of the Académie française in 1824 had been born after 1790. The best known authors of the "movement" were noticeably younger than the classicists, and the literary and social consequences seemed obvious. "The new world, regenerated by the baptism of blood [during the Empire] is now still in its youth," commented Alexandre Guiraud in 1824. "We no longer doubt that our literature feels itself as well the poetic expression of the new life that animates our society."[29] In ironic comment on his image as champion of the new generation, Stendhal the middle-aged diplomat felt compelled to lie about his age before publication of *Racine et Shakespeare* in 1823.[30] Perhaps then Sainte-Beuve's disaffected snipes at Hugo's *cénacle* implied more than a sacrilegious comment on the literary group; they probably referred as well to the youth of the fawning disciples to the French Childe Harold of romanticism in Paris.

Thus literature, like politics and society, was often seen in terms of conflicting generations. There need not have been a major revolution in literary taste comparable to 1789 or even 1830; older generations would pass. It was only a matter of time before the values, perhaps too the visions of *les perruques* would give way to those of *les jeunes gens*. So predicted Théodore Jouffroy in 1825: "The generation of those who have lived the old faith must pass. Its task was to destroy, it will never be given to reëstablish its faith. . . . [But] a new generation arises" that will fashion a new way of writing.[31] Romantics and their literature would surely triumph when the neo-classicists died and took their books with them to the grave. This confidence in eventual victory, however, was undermined by the intense climate of opinion during the constitutional monarchies. It is certainly no accident that classicists and royalists alike resisted romantics and revolutionaries in 1830. The impatience of young authors to publish their books, to stage their plays, and to receive the honors and recognition they felt was their due shared in the sharp social and political conflicts of the period. The romantics lived in a contentiously age-conscious world.

At this unique historical moment given to a widespread awareness of age groups, did such a new literary generation exist in biological fact?

---

29. Alexandre Guiraud, "Nos doctrines," *La muse française, 1823–1824*, Jules Marsan, ed. (Paris: Cornély, 1909),2:20–21.

30. "On rappelle que je n'avais que vingt ans en 1821." Actually he was 37. Stendhal, *Souvenirs d'égotisme* in *Oeuvres intimes*, Henri Martineau, ed. (Paris: Gallimard, 1955), p. 1453.

31. Théodore Jouffroy, "Comment les dogmes finissent," *Le cahier vert*, Pierre Poux, ed. (Paris: Presses Françaises, [n.d.]), pp. 72–73.

Perhaps so, for demographic evidence *does* point to a generationlike phenomenon. Random samples of authors publishing history and the *belles lettres* listed in the *Bibliographie de la France*, the national trade catalog, provide data to support the general age patterns that contemporaries often noted (see Table 3.1).[32] Authors in the romantic period were

TABLE 3.1
French Authors by Age-Group Percentage, 1820–1841

Age	1820	1824	1827	1830	1834	1838	1841
20–29	19.1%	16.7%	14.5%	16.3%	12.3%	10.0%	9.1%
30–39	13.9	16.7	21.8	37.5	40.3	38.3	27.3
40–49	20.3	21.7	20.1	18.7	15.8	26.6	27.3
50–59	29.1	26.6	23.6	15.0	15.8	8.4	20.8
60–69	11.4	13.3	16.3	10.0	7.0	10.0	9.0
70+	6.2	5.0	3.7	2.5	8.8	6.7	6.5
Mean	47.5	47.6	46.6	41.3	43.6	44.3	46.6
Median	48	48	47	36	39	41	43

Source: See fn. 32, p. 82.

indeed younger: the mean ages of writers published during the Restoration dropped from a high of 47.5 in 1820, to a low of 41.3 in 1830. Apparently larger numbers of younger men and women joined the ranks of fewer older writers just when the movement came into its own. But during the July Monarchy, the trend reversed itself: the mean ages rose again from 43.6 in 1834, back to 46.6 in 1841. It seems that fewer young authors were enlisted after 1830 and the cohort of recently established writers simply grew older. Authors were generally older before and after romanticism triumphed in 1830.

In 1897 Alfred Odin, a nineteenth-century social critic using other sources, plotted this demographic peculiarity on a graph that shows a

32. Random samples of authors were taken from the genre index in the back of the *Bibliographie de la France*, the most complete trade manual in France. Twenty living authors in each of the major genres most likely to be influenced by romanticism (poetry, drama, prose fiction, French history) were drawn using a random numbers table from volumes for 1820, 1824, 1827, 1830, 1834, 1838, and 1841, for a total of 560 authors. Ages were located in appropriate biographical dictionaries: Joseph-Marie Quérard et al., *La France littéraire, ou dictionnaire bibliographique des savants, historiens et gens de lettres de la France* (Paris: Didot frères, 1827–39), 10 vols.; *La littérature française contemporaine, 1827–1849* (Paris: Daguin and Delaroque, 1840–57), 6 vols.; *Les supercheries littéraires dévoilées* (Paris: Editeur, 1845–53), 5 vols.; and Pierre Larousse et al., *Grand dictionnaire universel du XIXe siècle* (Paris: Larousse, 1865–88), 22 vols. In each mean calculated here, the standard deviation was between fourteen and fifteen; median ages showed the same patterns as the means.

large swell in the number of authors born slightly later between 1795 and 1810.[33] This fifteen-year period, according to Odin, produced nearly one-sixth of all authors born in France from the fourteenth to the nineteenth centuries (see Figure 3.1). Although this evidence by itself still does not define a generation, it does indicate a suggestive temporary shift to younger writers at the height of the movement. There is even some

FIGURE 3.1

The Numbers of French Authors Born in Five-Year Intervals, 1775–1830

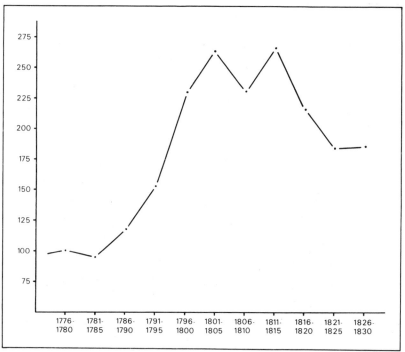

Source: See fn. 33, p. 83.

evidence that authors publishing romantic works were younger than the norm. The mean ages of sampled authors using the new conventions ranged between 37.5 in 1830 and 51.5 in 1841, from two to eight years below that of all authors published in the same years (except 1841 when the sampled romantics seemed to have aged considerably). They also appear to follow the same pattern, the youngest romantics generally publishing in the 1830s (see Appendix B).

33. Alfred Odin, *Genèse des grands hommes: gens de lettres français modernes* (Lausanne: Mignot, 1895),2:Tableau 2, Planche 1.

The significance of these data appears more clearly in a comparison of age structures (see Figure 3.2). Percentages of the total population 20 years or older, broken into ten-year intervals, were compared with percentages of published authors, sampled randomly from the *Bibliographie de la France* history and *belles lettres* indexes, in the same age intervals. (Deceased authors accounting for less than 15 percent of the samples were excluded.) For 1820 the graph indicates a disproportionately large number of living authors age 40 and older; nearly 30 percent were in their 50s alone. Just ten years later in 1830, however, the graph shows a

FIGURE 3.2

Comparative Age Structures, Authors and General Population, for France in 1820, 1830, and 1841

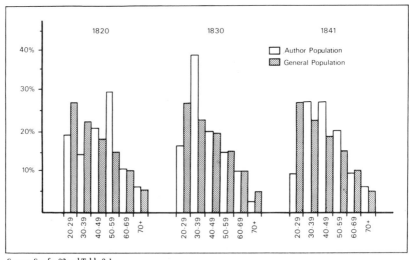

Source: See fn. 32 and Table 3.1.

remarkably high percentage of younger writers. Nearly 40 percent of the sampled authors were only in their 30s when romantic works were flourishing. By 1841 some of this cohort finally passed into the next age interval, raising the relative numbers of older writers; again over 20 percent were in their 50s. Thus there does seem to have been a brief wave of authors born at the turn of the century, between 1790 and 1805, who joined the published world of history and literature in 1830 and grew older in the next ten years. Although the percentage of writers in the youngest age interval decreased throughout the period—from 19 to 9 percent—young men and women at the height of the romantic movement were published in numbers entirely disproportionate to their presence in the rest of the population: more than 52 percent of the sampled authors in 1830 were under age 40 as opposed to only 36 percent in 1820 and 1841.

If the age data on the samples from the *Bibliographie de la France* can be believed, literary interest among more youthful authors rose significantly at the end of the Restoration and in the early years of the July Monarchy. Of course, in 1830 much of the participation of younger authors may also owe to the revolutionary climate of the "three glorious days," but such an impact would have only come very close to the revolutionary events. Old and young alike were surely attracted to the polemical swirl during the most intense moments of the conflict in July and August. Actually the trend is evident both much earlier and later in the period. These changes in the author's age structure from 1820 to 1841 suggest rather a brief rejuvenation of authorship more appropriate to romanticism than to revolution.

Initially younger writers appeared in increasing numbers, as authors did generally in the nineteenth century with the rapidly expanding literary marketplace in France.[34] Their relatively immature works presumably reflected romanticism's formative influence. As they grew older and were joined by more mature authors, their writings indulged less in the youthful excesses and dogmatism associated with the movement's early taste, a suggestion Sainte-Beuve made in 1843.[35] Indeed, the rise and fall of young writers seem to follow that of romanticism in most early histories. As observers correctly remarked, a large number of authors at their most creative age coincided with the vogue of the new literature in the early nineteenth century.[36]

More general demographic data in the period also support this brief trend towards a younger population.[37] Even Restoration demographers noted a shift in the age structure after 1827 when the percentage of the

34. Compare Quérard's six volumes covering only twenty-two years of French publishing (1827–49) to his ten volumes covering 250 years (16th century–1826) for a sense of the expansion of the book trade in the period.

35. Sainte-Beuve, "Quelques vérités," p. 5. This was noted by others in the period. See Taillandier, "Simples essais d'histoire littéraire," p. 975.

36. In 1936 Harvey C. Lehman averaged the ages of four hundred men and women prominent in various intellectual fields to determine their most creative years. He found that poets, literati, and playwrights achieved eminence by age forty-five after a decade of endeavor. This period of intellectual activity seems to correspond to the data here on the sampled authors who, though not yet (if ever) prominent, were struggling to make their names in literature during the romantic period. See Lehman, "The Creative Years in Science and Literature," *Scientific Monthly* 43(1936),151–62. See also Escarpit, *Sociologie de la littérature*, pp. 35–36.

37. Wesley D. Camp, *Marriage and the Family in France Since the Revolution* (New York: Bookman Associates, 1961), pp. 23, 101, 148–50; Charles Pouthas, *La population française pendant la première moitié du XIX*ᵉ *siècle* (Paris: Presses Universitaires de France,

French population over age 40 began to decrease noticeably.[38] Despite more recent evidence of declines in fertility and mortality that began to age the population as early as the end of the eighteenth century, net reproduction rates climbed from 1785 to 1800 and then declined steadily until the Second Empire. This fact in addition to the long trough in the net birth rate from 1804 to 1813—due to the loss of marriageable men during the Napoleonic wars—did produce a slight bulge in the age structure with the cohort born between 1795 and 1805 (see Table 3.2). A slight rippling effect is evident throughout the period as the 1801 cohort aged: within every ten-year age group it was always the largest, a fact noted in italics by the table.

TABLE 3.2
French Population by Age-Group Percentage, 1801–1851

Age	1801	1811	1821	1831	1841	1851
0–9	23.37%	22.37%	22.46%	21.72%	21.17%	20.54%
10–19	18.57	19.32	18.47	18.31	18.18	17.97
20–29	15.36	15.52	16.19	16.09	16.14	15.96
30–39	13.68	13.23	13.19	13.98	13.83	13.82
40–49	11.84	11.34	11.08	11.07	11.87	11.82
50–59	8.46	9.25	8.83	8.84	8.90	9.65
60–69	5.63	5.69	6.30	6.16	6.15	6.30
70+	3.09	3.28	3.38	3.83	3.76	3.84

Source: J. Bourgeois-Pichat, "The General Development of the Population of France Since the Eighteenth Century," Population in History, D. V. Glass and D. E. C. Eversley, eds. (London: Arnold, 1965), p. 498.

Moreover, the anomalous demographic characteristics of Paris, the heart of French literature and publishing, contributed to this effect. Between 1817 and 1836 there was a 41 percent increase in the number of men and women aged 30 to 39, while from 1836 to 1851 this same age group dropped 8 percent.[39] Apparently a rejuvenation, fostered by rural-to-urban migration, occurred among the Parisian population simultane-

---

1956), pp. 22–23; and J. Bourgeois-Pichat, "The General Development of the Population of France Since the Eighteenth Century," Population in History, D. V. Glass and D. E. C. Eversley, eds. (London: Arnold, 1965), pp. 474–506.

38. Dupin, Forces productives et commerciales, pp. 111 ff.

39. Louis Chevalier, Dangerous Classes and Laboring Classes in Paris during the First Half of the Nineteenth Century, Frank Jellinek, trans. (New York: Fertig, 1973), pp. 234–35. See also his La formation de la population parisienne au XIX ͤ siècle (Paris: Presses Universitaires de France, 1950), pp. 58–59.

ously with the wave of younger authors and others in the national population. It is also known that alongside this largely working-class migration to the city, there was another brief immigration of middle-class occupational groups, authors included, whose mean ages were in the 30s during the constitutional monarchies.[40] Thus both the French and the Parisian populations in the romantic period experienced a temporary infusion of youth parallel to that among published authors: in effect, age data on the samples from the *Bibliographie de la France* reflected a larger demographic trend.

A French romantic generation of 1830 apparently did exist. Unfortunately, this timely rejuvenation cannot be defined more precisely, because not all the data on authors fit perfectly the strict theoretical patterns defined by most students of historical generations. Among romantics recognized by literary historians, there are a number of demographic anomalies that fall outside the 1795–1805 cohort: Guttinguer, Desbordes-Valmore, and Lamartine were alive before 1791, while O'Neddy, Houssaye, and Musset were born after 1809. And the notion of some historians that there were two romantic generations suffers from the same kind of exceptions (though this demographic phenomenon has no basis in fact among either authors or the general population). Anyway, to divide the movement into two groups, born 15 years before and after 1800, includes Béranger, Nisard, and Ponsard—adamant antiromantics, while it excludes Delécluze, Lamennais, and Nodier—close to the heart of the movement's sensibility. Contrary to the theorists, it would be impossible to contain all of romanticism within such arbitrary dates. What are we to do with Rousseau and the later Hugo? Still it is true that the evidence points to an undeniable demographic trend which may well have contributed to the shape of literature in France during the *monarchie censitaire*.

A similar difficulty in the definition of one or more romantic generations arises with the different ages at which authors published and with the unequal duration of their influence on other writers. For example, Chateaubriand (1768–1848) continued a powerful presence in French literature long after his *Atala* and *René* were published during the First Empire. Madame de Staël (1766–1817), on the other hand, ceased to be a major influence long before the movement triumphed in 1830, even though she had published many of her important works at the same time as Chateaubriand. Besides these exceptions to the generational cohort and its influence on writers, there is the problematic timing of the new literature: its vogue was apparently too brief to support the progression of

40. Daumard, *Les bourgeois de Paris au XIX*e *siècle* (Paris: Flammarion, 1970), pp. 111–14.

generational change. Why did romanticism in France fade just when its authors were coming into their own in 1845? In theory they should have maintained the dominant literary mode until 1860.

Thus a theoretical romantic generation does not fit what we know about the literature and its authors. But if the preconceived idea of generational movement in history is cast aside and the pattern of evidence examined, a self-conscious rejuvenation *does* appear in 1830—and its significance to the development of popular romanticism is apparent: just as a younger generation of authors challenged the esthetic of one older and better established in the battle between the early romantics and the last neo-classicists, the younger romantics indulging in a commercially disastrous elite sensibility also grew older, and perhaps wiser, to produce a more lucrative romantic convention in their adoption of more popular literary expression. Too, they may have cast all romantic pretense aside when readership interest in things romantic faded after 1840. Such speculation on the role of age in literary creation remains intriguing, to say the least.

AUTHORS IN THE LITERARY MARKETPLACE

Given the difficulties in definition with the available data it may be more fruitful to examine other factors affecting these younger authors. It is evident that this so-called generation was influenced less by biological facts, interesting as they are, than by their social context. The maturation of a demographic cohort constituted only one element, however basic, in the rise and fall of the popular romantic movement. Younger authors worked under new commercial circumstances that also effected changes in literary taste and need closer examination for a clarification of the actual state of romantic authorship and its contribution to popular literature. Clearly the ambivalent images of the French man of letters, as aspiring apprentice and as cynical versifier, were derived not solely from contemporary perceptions of a new generation of foolhardy authors in conflict with one older and more vain. They also came from the social and economic world in which these writers functioned from 1820 to 1840. An examination of this context may help explain their preference for form over feeling that characterized the brief, popular romantic movement.

Almost until the 1789 revolution most authors did not actually live on a direct return from their writings; production costs were too high and the number of readers too small. Only a select few managed an income, meagre at best, from the sale of their books aimed at the largest possible market. These grub-street authors resorted to radical politics and more or less explicit pornography, the most reliable genres beside fiction for profit in this largely illicit trade. Most other writers, on the other hand, profited from the indirect benefits of their work: gifts, pensions, benefices, and sinecures from appreciative patrons. To earn a livelihood, the *lumières*, for example, did not have to sell so much as be admired by the right people, or failing that, attend another occupation insuring the income that writing alone normally could not provide. Even Voltaire did not live by his pen; he earned most of his money from properties, banking transactions, commodity speculations, as well as a royal pension as gentleman of the bedchamber to Louis XV.[41] Despite the rapid growth of the book trade, it was not enough to support more than a relatively small covey of vulgar *littérateurs*.

Commented Balzac, a man of affairs as well as of literature, "before the Revolution seven out of twelve writers received considerable pensions paid by foreign sovereigns, by the court, or by the regime."[42] But unlike the *philosophes*, the writer in post–Napoleonic France had few choices other than to accept the sale of his work as a commodity. He was caught in the shift from the former system of royal and aristocratic patronage to the literary marketplace. Dependent upon a largely middle-class audience, the early nineteenth-century author increasingly needed to please a new, often fickle public in order to survive. Romantic idealists were certainly no less immune to this imperative, one that Vigny characterized in his poem of advice to a young poet: the author now must cast his work before a vast, anonymous audience, like a shipwrecked sailor who throws his bottled message into the sea, with only the hope of material survival.[43]

Nevertheless, in the nineteenth century new commercial and political conditions permitted larger numbers of writers to live without the patronage that had largely disappeared with the *ancien régime*. More numerous readers, cheaper books, and less repressive censorship enabled literary professionalism to appear in its stead, even though not all nineteenth-century authors did well by the sale of their writings. The post–Napoleonic period did see a remarkable expansion of the literary mar-

41. Georges d'Avenel, *Les revenus d'un intellectuel de 1200 à 1913: les riches depuis sept cent ans* (Paris: Flammarion, 1922), pp. 301–302.

42. Balzac, *Oeuvres diverses*, 3:236.

43. Vigny, "La bouteille à la mer (conseil à un jeune homme inconnu)," *Oeuvres complètes*, 1:213–15. For detailed discussion of this transition from patronage to market in the nineteenth century, see John Lough, *Writer and Public in France from the Middle Ages to the Present Day* (London: Clarendon Press, 1978), pp. 164–274.

ketplace, warmly welcomed by many in the younger generation. "Thank heavens we no longer live in those times when talent produced only for some rich patron," a writer rejoices in Eugène Scribe's *Mariage d'argent* (1827). "Artists today in quest of fame and fortune have no need to resort to such means; true artists . . . remain true to themselves and work, while the public judges and rewards them."[44]

Many other writers were hardly as enthusiastic or as successful as Scribe, and for good reasons. The literary market could still be a source of income neither reliable nor honorable to the early nineteenth-century man of letters who continued to seek viable alternatives even though circumventions were largely unavailing.[45] Very few writers enjoyed private resources from inherited family properties or shrewd marriages. With mixed motives, Lamartine and Vigny both took rich English wives when few others were willing to make such a compromise. Similarly, the attraction of royal patronage waned, as did its generosity, during the constitutional monarchies. After publication of his flattering *Odes et poésies diverses* in 1822, Hugo was fortunate to receive a royal pension of 2,000 francs from the Interior Ministry and an additional 1,200 francs a year from the King's privy purse.[46] Such handsome treatment for sycophants provided an irregular income, subject to shifting political winds, for only a small number.

Frequently, authors found government positions or chose the liberal professions that permitted them time to write: Nodier was a librarian, Stendhal a diplomat, and Mérimée an inspector of historical monuments. Such occupations were common among authors before 1850.[47] Still, administrative sinecures were difficult to secure and paid poorly in the period. Michelet remarked that a middling bureaucratic functionary earned less than a journeyman baker.[48] Another possible retreat, the Académie française, assumed that its lifetime members were already wealthy, offering only 1,500 francs annually to each of the "immortal" forty. Before 1835 literary prizes were few and small, except for the Montyon Prize endowed for 10,000 francs in 1820 and awarded annually

44. Eugène Scribe, *Le mariage d'argent*, comédie (Paris: Bezou, 1828), Act I, Scene iv, p. 21.

45. For discussion of authors' various attempts at circumvention of the literary market during the nineteenth century, see Priscilla P. Clark, "Stratégies d'auteur au 19ᵉ siècle," *Romantisme* 18(1977),92–102.

46. André Maurois, *Olympio: The Life of Victor Hugo*, Gerard Hopkins, trans. (New York: Harper and Brothers, 1956), pp. 74, 81. See also Patrice Boussel and Madeleine Dubois, *De quoi vivait Victor Hugo?* (Paris: Deux Rives, 1952).

47. Clark, "Stratégies," pp. 94–95.

48. Michelet, *The People*, John P. McKay, trans. (Urbana: University of Illinois Press, 1973), p. 77.

by the conservative Académie. But individual awards were diminished often by the number of winners each year who divided the prize money into small, mostly symbolic sums.[49] All other avenues exhausted, authors like Balzac's Lucien Chardon turned to the shifting fashions of publishing and journalism, perhaps even to romanticism to live by their literary work.

The ambivalent attitude among romantic authors towards the literary market may well have been based on bitter experience. Conditions of the early literary market, even for successful writers, were indeed hazardous. Rapid fluctuations in demand sometimes made an author's career a matter of chance, as Stendhal noted ruefully: "I have always regarded my works as lottery tickets."[50] Moreover, the Paris book trade remained a largely anachronistic world of small family enterprises, cautious publishers, and artisanal printing practices that limited the marketability of literary works too expensive for a large audience.[51] Choice of genre sometimes helped. As a general rule, most money was made in drama, as much as 15,000 francs for a long running play. The best selling novel rarely netted 5,000 francs, the best selling history 1,000, and the best selling poetry only 500.[52] But even these figures varied greatly. In 1830 Gautier published his *Poésies* at his own expense, the same year Lamartine sold his *Harmonies poétiques* for 27,000 francs.[53] Obviously, the name made a big difference in sales and profit, as Balzac's *libraire* Dauriat remarked.[54]

The size of their editions varied accordingly, from 2,500 to 300 copies or less, very low in comparison to present-day paperback editions in the tens of thousands. Re-editions of successful works were decisive. Successive editions of Lamennais' *Paroles d'un croyant* in 1834, for example, easily boosted its production past 35,000 within a year, though this was exceptional.[55] Most titles saw only one edition of 1,000 copies or

49. A. C. F. de Franqueville, *Le premier siècle de l'Institut de France* (Paris: Rothschild, 1896),2:381–82.

50. Stendhal, *Souvenirs*, p. 1456.

51. For discussion of the premodern literary market, see David Pottinger, *The French Book Trade in the Ancien Regime, 1500–1791* (Cambridge: Harvard University Press, 1958); Darnton, "Le livre français," and *The Business of Enlightenment*, esp. pp. 1–37.

52. Avenel, *Les revenus*, p. 285. Avenel calculates in 1913 francs; the figures in the text have been converted into 1830 francs.

53. Arsène Houssaye, *Les confessions, souvenirs d'un demi-siècle, 1830–1880* (Paris: Dentu, 1885),1:306; and Francis Dumont and Jean Gitan, *De quoi vivait Lamartine?* (Paris: Deux Rives, 1952), pp. 20–21.

54. "Je ne suis pas ici pour être le marchepied pour les gloires à venir, mais pour gagner de l'argent et pour en donner aux hommes célèbres." In Balzac, *La comédie humaine*, 5:367.

55. Neret, *Histoire illustrée*, p. 151.

less. Publishing contracts were written for one edition at a time, rarely stipulating more than 500 copies, in which the author either leased or sold his rights to the work.[56] Until a writer established a popular reputation, he remained largely at the mercy of the publisher and the terms he set for each manuscript. Under such circumstances, the life of the author in the period was at best difficult and explains much of his ambivalence towards a career in literature.

These risks aside many young men felt they had little choice but to write for profit, given a society whose values encouraged overcrowding in a few socially acceptable careers.[57] Positions as lawyers, doctors, and government officials were at a premium in post–Napoleonic France, a fact Stendhal's Julien Sorel learned to his dismay. The educational system, emphasizing the Greek and Latin classics, ill prepared its students for the business world, even if they chose such a base course in life. Squeezed by incredible competition for limited opportunities in the liberal professions and educated for little else, young men saw in journalism, literature, and the arts acceptable careers *relatively* open to the socially aspiring. Under the circumstances, "there [were] only three possible avenues in a civilization as advanced as ours," remarked Gautier half seriously, "thief, informer, writer."[58] The expanding literary market did afford a haven for a select few from the brutal competition for honorable positions. Some, like Maxime Du Camp's school teacher, were drawn away from their poorly paying and lowly situations by the lure of esteem and income possible in literature, however great the risk.[59]

This turn to authorship, out of necessity or choice, is reflected in the rising number of authors indexed in bibliographies of the period. In 1820 the *Bibliographie de la France* listed fewer than 1,700 living authors; in 1841, however, there were over 2,500. Moreover, the number of *hommes de lettres* among Parisians paying 300 francs or more in taxes rose from only one in 1820, to eight in 1828, and twenty-four in 1842. Similarly, the average voting author in Paris who paid 552 francs in annual taxes in 1828 paid 1,304 in 1842, a period of stable currency.[60] It appears, then, that the

56. For the legal status of the French author in the period, see F. A. Pic, *Code des imprimeurs, libraires, écrivains et artistes...* (Paris: Corby, 1827), vol. 2.

57. For discussion of the problem of overcrowding in socially acceptable professions in the first half of the nineteenth century, see Lenore O'Boyle, "The Problem of an Excess of Educated Men in Western Europe, 1800–1850," *Journal of Modern History* 42(1970), esp. 487–91.

58. Gautier, *Les Jeunes-France*, p. xiii.

59. Du Camp, *Souvenirs*, 1:36–37.

60. Département de la Seine, *Liste des électeurs formants le collège électoral du département de la Seine* (Paris: Affiches Universelles, 1820); *Listes électorales et du jury du département de la Seine* (Paris: n.p., 1828); and *Listes électorales et du jury du département de la Seine* (Paris: n.p., 1842).

profession of letters in the elite *philosophe* tradition was more than honorable; it attracted large numbers of men and women as well by the substantial money to be made as a writer. With alternatives limited, the literary market grew, given the apparent potential for esteem—and profit.

Consequently, the popular image of the Icarus-like poet, far removed from the dirty tricks of the book trade, obscured the commercial skills of successful nineteenth-century writers. Among authors sampled from the *Bibliographie*, full-time authorship became increasingly common. Supplemental occupations apparently proved less and less necessary even in the romantic period (see Table 3.3). The list of writers who

TABLE 3.3
Occupations of Sampled Living Authors, by Percentage, 1820–1841

	1820	1827	1834	1841
Propriétaires	7%	6%	6%	5%
Clergy	5	5	4	3
Military, Retired and Active	11	9	9	3
Liberal Professions	7	14	9	6
Industry, Commerce, Banking	7	6	9	7
Diplomacy, Administration, Honorary Sinecures	24	17	10	13
Employés, Teachers, Librarians	28	27	21	27
Journalists, Men of Letters, Dramatists	10	16	32	36

Source: See fn. 32, p. 82.

earned remarkable incomes from the sales of their work begins with P.-J. de Béranger, Eugène Sue, Alphonse de Lamartine, George Sand, Alexandre Dumas, among others. The publication of pot-boilers became more deliberate as the trade expanded and adopted new, more profitable means of production and distribution, especially the four-sous newspaper that paid up to 100,000 francs for a *roman-feuilleton*—when the average *journalier* was fortunate to make 750 a year.[61] As early as 1839 Sainte-Beuve criticized the *littérature industrielle* subsequently made infamous by Dumas' writers' "factory" in which he and seventy-three assistants reputedly specialized in the composition of adventure stories for popular consumption.[62]

61. See César Graña, "The New Literary Market," *Modernity and its Discontents: French Society and the French Man of Letters in the Nineteenth Century* (New York: Harper and Row, 1967), pp. 29–36.

62. Sainte-Beuve, "De la littérature industrielle," *Revue des deux mondes* 19(1839), 3:675–91. Knowledge of Dumas's work was common among contemporaries after a number of exposés written by jealous rivals were published. His actual mode of composition is detailed in the *Gazette des tribunaux*, January 21, 1858, when Maquet sued Dumas for former royalties.

Moreover, authors and their publishers became increasingly assertive. Hugo regularly wrote acclaims of his works that he had his publishers place in the daily newspapers.[63] Even the notoriety of young authors—their wild dress, their personal conflicts, their eccentric behavior—served the sometimes intended purpose of publicizing their works to a wider circle of readers in Paris.[64] Authors were now conscious of the need to protect their interests and founded a professional organization in 1838, the *Société des Gens de Lettres*, to petition the regime for a better law safeguarding literary property from Belgian *contrefaçons*.[65] Hence, the image of the noble poet untouched by commercial considerations, like Géricault's portrait of Jamar in his studio, was hardly an accurate picture of the literary entrepreneur who became increasingly prominent in the first half of the nineteenth century.

One such figure living well by his pen was Charles Paul de Kock (1793–1871), the popular novelist on the periphery of the romantic movement (see Illustration 6). His career exemplifies the response of minor literati to their new commercial context.[66] Born in Passy on the outskirts of Paris, Kock grew up in modest circumstances and spent five years during the Empire as a bank clerk at 200 francs a month before he turned to writing. His first novel, *L'enfant de ma femme*, was refused by more than fifteen different publishers. He bore the printing costs himself, 800 francs for 500 copies, but less than 100 were sold when the novel appeared in 1813. Discouraged, Kock turned to writing melodramas for the Ambigu Comique where his talents were better rewarded. Barba paid up to 300 francs for one act plays, a reliable source of ready income that Kock drew on occasionally for the rest of his life.

Finally in 1819 Kock published *Georgette, ou la nièce du tabellion*, the first of his many slightly salacious works that established his reputa-

63. See letters from Hugo to Renduel, his publisher, in Adolphe Jullien, "Le romantisme et l'éditeur Renduel," *Revue des deux mondes* 132(1895),4:655–66.

64. Dérôme claims that authors first developed the use of literary propaganda in the romantic period. See his *Causeries d'un ami des livres*, 1:29. See also the relevant discussion in Marsan, *La bohème romantique, documents inédits* (Paris: Cahiers Libres, 1929).

65. See Edouard Montagne, *Histoire de la société des gens de lettres* (Paris: Librairie Mondaine, 1889). For accounts of government attempts to establish literary property against Belgian *contrefaçons*, see A.N.F¹⁸2359 "Propriété littéraire et dépôt légal. Projets de loi, 1827–1876."

66. Paul de Kock, *Mémoires de Charles Paul de Kock, écrits par lui-même* (Paris: Dentu, 1873), translated into English in 1899. Kock's life serves as a remarkable contrast to the careers of earlier writers, equally minor, living in very different commercial circumstances. See Darnton's account of Grub Street authors before the Revolution in "The High Enlightenment and the Low Life of Literature in Prerevolutionary France," *Past and Present* 51(1971),81–115.

6. "Paul de Kock" (ca. 1838). Lithograph by Benjamin Roubaud (1811–1847). *Courtesy of the Boston Public Library, Print Department.*

tion and guaranteed his prosperity. "This was my first success as a novelist, the book which brought me out of obscurity," he noted later in his memoirs.[67] Accordingly, his publisher Hubert pressed him to write more such blends of adventure, comedy, and titillation. In time Kock commanded better offers, and in 1826 Baudry paid him 20,000 francs for L'amant de la lune. Wrote Kock somewhat bitterly about his early dealing with publishers, "He was the first to pay me for my works prices proportionate to the profits he anticipated from them."[68] From the subsequent sale of more than 200 plays and 400 volumes of novels, Kock managed a comfortable, bourgeois standard of living at his apartment in Paris and his country houses in Passy and in Romanville where he died in 1871.

Paul de Kock's example illustrates how important the literary marketplace was to the minor nineteenth-century author. Like nearly all writers in the period, Kock depended upon his clerical position to survive his first years as a novelist. But once his reputation was established, his understanding of circumstances enabled Kock to profit by his writing, however poorly rewarded he considered his talents. In fact, Kock's successful literary career owed not only to his talent as a writer, but also to his acceptance of the risks inherent in the market for books. "I'm greedy and I admit it," he stated baldly in his memoirs.[69] It may well be that the image of the grasping merchant of verse, satirized so fiercely in the period, was derived from such an open recognition among many authors, like Kock, who secured their "due share from all the literary millings."[70]

Conversely, the more popular image of the priestly Icarus may be traced to those authors who refused to accept the new socioeconomic context of writing.[71] Like Alfred de Vigny, a much better known writer, the young man in search of an honorable career often eschewed commercial values; they were bourgeois in the pejorative sense. Educated to an aristocratic view of the world, Vigny himself sought to establish his name in the salon tradition of the *philosophes* who had developed a kind of nobility far removed from the vulgarity of business. "The man of thought should esteem his work only by how little popular success it has," he

67. Kock, Memoirs, p. 135.

68. Ibid., p. 166.

69. Ibid., p. 160.

70. Ibid.

71. A similar analysis is developed in Graña, Modernity, pp. 37–59, that emphasizes the psychological consequences of the new literary market. Note the discussion of the apparent lack of conflict between the successful writer and his social context, in Roger L. Brown, "The Creative Process in the Popular Arts," International Social Science Journal 20(1968),4:613–24; and Duncan, Language and Literature in Society, pp. 58–74.

stated in his *Journal*.[72] Such an attitude was predicated upon patronage, not the literary market. Hence, Vigny the esoteric poet unwilling to compromise his esthetic values to popular taste condemned himself to martyrdom in the new conditions of authorship. "The true god, the strongest god is the god of ideas," the socially alienated poet incarnate vowed.[73] And in 1835 Vigny captured this image, ironically in his best known and most successful play, *Chatterton*. Evidently the clashing perceptions of the romantic modern man of letters, either as a promethean visionary like Vigny or as a vain mercenary like Kock, may be seen in this contrast in attitudes towards literature as commodity.

In such a system, how did most romantic authors fare? Were writers who adopted the new fashion more successful than those who did not? Answers to such questions would explain much about the origins of the conflicting images and the nature of the movement. Unfortunately, without publishers' records, success in the Parisian book trade is very difficult to assess.[74] But the literary evidence available does indicate that these writers followed an ambivalent pattern common among all authors in the period: success depended on the name.

Perhaps the most phenomenal romantic was Victor Hugo. From an obscure poet on a 3,200 franc pension in 1823, he rose to such wealth and prominence that he was accorded a chair at the Académie française in 1841.[75] "In 28 years I have earned with my pen about 550,000 francs," Hugo boasted in 1845. "Today, of these 550,000 francs, only 300,000 remain. [But] I have invested these 300,000 francs. With this revenue I live, I work as always, with what accrues in interest."[76] By then Hugo preferred to list himself in the tax rolls not as *homme de lettres*, but as *propriétaire*. Such a feat, of course, resulted in part from a lifetime of shrewd business dealing with publishers, moving from one to another, demanding more in turn from each. Despite the failure of his last play in 1843 and the other more profitable sources of income, Hugo still commanded more than 10,000 francs for manuscripts he had written and published many times before.[77]

72. Vigny, *Oeuvres complètes*, 2:895.

73. *Ibid.*, 1:215.

74. For discussion of problems in research on the Paris book trade, see Nicole Felkay, "Les libraires de l'époque romantique d'après les documents inédits," *Revue française d'histoire du livre* 5(1975),3:31–86.

75. See Boussel and Dubois, *De quoi vivait Victor Hugo?*, Chpt. 1.

76. Hugo, "Au rédacteur de *Phare de la Loire*," *Correspondance* (Paris: Calmann Lévy, 1898),2:74.

77. See account of Hugo's dealings with his publisher in an article on his legal dispute over *Les orientales* in *Gazette des tribunaux*, October 2, 1831.

At the other extreme were the lesser lights of the movement whose bargaining position with publishers lacked the strength of better known authors. The uncompromising poets of the *petit cénacle* earned little money from their work: O'Neddy, Borel, and Gautier all paid *libraires* to publish their first volumes of poetry.[78] Gérard de Nerval constantly overspent his monthly 250 franc wage from *La presse* and paid his running debts by timely sales of articles and stories to other Parisian journals, all the while complaining of "this tyranny of the pen in service to the stomach."[79] Although he did not exactly die penniless, Stendhal was never able to live by his fiction, a genre in which many others had exploited more profitably, if not more eloquently. In fact, this novelist admired by later generations rarely had editions larger than 1,000 copies, most of which sold with difficulty to the lending libraries.

But this evidence is far from complete. It fails to detail the success of all authors using the romantic conventions. However well or poorly known, many writers in the new fashion were certainly aware of their need to appeal to an audience if they were to sell their work. Indeed, it was to melodramatic plays and gothic novels that Hugo and his entrepreneurial peers, Balzac and Dumas, added romantic forms and feelings in some of their early efforts.[80] From evidence in Interior Ministry records and biographical dictionaries, this must have been common practice among other romantics as well. Randomly sampled writers publishing more than 10 titles, with at least one run larger than 1,500 impressions, included a significant share of men using romantic conventions.[81] Their percentage among these quasi-professionals rose from 25 percent in 1820, and 36 percent in 1827, to more than 44 percent in 1834.

The movement's triumph around 1830, then, not only coincided with the height of the fashion among the titles in the *Bibliographie*; it also marked the relatively widespread success of its authors. Apparently, the romantics did share in the rising production and profit of an expanding

78. Houssaye, *Les confessions,* 1:306.

79. Clément Borgal, *De quoi vivait Gérard de Nerval?* (Paris: Deux Rives, 1950), p. 52.

80. For discussion of popular elements of romantic literature, see Hauser, *Social History,* 3:197–207; George, *French Romanticism,* pp. 91–118; and Houston, *The Demonic Imagination,* pp. 46–47.

81. Data on edition sizes may be found in printers' declarations recorded in A.N.F.[18]II*7 "L'année 1820;" A.N.F.[18]II*14 "L'année 1827;" A.N.F.[18]II*24 "L'année 1834;" and A.N.F.[18]II*29 "L'année 1841." These volumes of the Interior Ministry list the title, the printer, the edition format, its number of volumes, as well as the size of its run. It is from these sources that nearly every title's edition size can be found. Moreover, this record serves as a good check for errors in the *Bibliographie de la France.* The remaining information about the authors may be found in the biographical dictionaries listed in note 32.

book trade that made room for young men to earn a livelihood from writing. Not only were their many works published in larger editions, but they earned sufficient profit and esteem to claim the status of *homme de lettres*: nearly 42 percent of the sampled writers identified as "romantic" devoted their professional energies to literature in the period (see Table 3.4). From this evidence authors adopting romantic devices appear to have made more of a reputation, if not a living, from the forms appropriate to a larger readership. Whatever the enormous variations evident in literary accounts of their relative successes and failures, the romantics were more popularly diffused and "professional" than others in the same period (see Appendix B).

TABLE 3.4
Occupations of Sampled Living Romantic Authors in France, 1820–1841

	Total	Percentage
Propriétaires, Rentiers	9	12.3%
Military, Retired and Active	3	4.1
Liberal Professions	3	4.1
Industry, Commerce, Banking	6	8.2
Diplomacy, Administration, Honorary Sinecures	9	12.3
Employés, Teachers, Librarians	12	16.4
Journalists, Men of Letters, Dramatists, Translators	31	42.5
Total	73	99.9

Source: Appendix B. 1820, 1827, 1834, and 1841 authors only; foreign authors not residing in France excluded.

This apparent sensitivity to prevailing market trends is also reflected in the temporary success of romantic writers. Their fortunes follow the same rise and fall of the movement's conventions in the *Bibliographie*. The number of successful authors adopting the vogue of the new literature, like the appearance of their titles in trade catalogs, rose and fell from 1820 to 1840. By 1841 their portion among the most published authors had dropped to only 28 percent from a high of 44 percent in 1834. After 1840 writers most aware of readership demand employed other forms and conventions. Despite its use of emotional moods, freer versification, concrete imagery, dramatic events, and more complex characters—elements that contributed to the new literature's initial popularity—the movement did not remain as profitable to its authors as it had been from 1827 to 1834.

The mean runs of romantic works by "professional" authors clearly detail this trend.[82] From 1,667 copies per edition in 1820, they were published in numbers averaging 2,611 in 1834, well above the mean and the median for all works published that year. But in 1841 their mean edition size declined again to nearly the average for all titles, 2,253 copies. From this and other evidence on the samples, the romantic authors' success seemed to have come and gone with the mode they adopted. Even though some writers faithfully continued the recently outmoded fashion, the rest either abandoned the mode or were overwhelmed by a new wave of authors interested in creating a literature more appropriate to an even larger audience. Like the movement itself, romantic authors enjoyed only a temporary vogue; like Dumas, Sand, and Balzac, they may well have changed the way they wrote in response to new market conditions from 1820 to 1840.

Obviously, then, the image of the romantic man of letters as a youthful idealist needs to be modified in light of all the evidence available. On the one hand, demographic data indicate that the romantics belonged in fact to a "cohort" of younger writers—and were even younger as a group at the height of the movement. One popular notion of the romantics, apparently, was correct. On the other hand, biographical and literary evidence shows that the stereotypical portrait of the romantic author, martyred for his uncompromising esthetic, was misleading. From publication records he appears a much more commercially minded figure, sensitive to the trends of supply and demand; after 1834 either he developed a new set of literary conventions or he lost his opportunity to become a "professional" author.

Thus contemporary accounts of a young romantic generation merit credence, but their views of the romantic author as an uncompromising visionary do not. Authors in the new movement adopted its forms and conventions as much from necessity as from literary tradition. Even the most idealistic writers could not escape completely their demographic and commercial situation in the early nineteenth century. Not that their works were determined by such conditions, but the range of choices writers enjoyed was certainly limited by significant age and economic

82. The conception of professional writer here as one who realizes a significant return on the time he invests in writing does not actually qualify as a social scientific category defined by sociological theorists. See Talcott Parsons, "Professions," in David L. Sills, ed. *International Encyclopedia of the Social Sciences* (New York: Macmillan and the Free Press, 1968), 12:536–47. Note also the small population sizes of the quasi-professional romantic authors: N=5 (1820), N=7 (1827), N=9 (1834), and N=9 (1841). Their mean edition sizes calculated here can be taken only as very crude indications of publishing patterns in the period.

considerations. In this context romantics were apparently both younger and more worldly than most, a conclusion suggested by aggregate data on all writers, despite the many exceptions among prominent romantics, whatever their esthetic, social, or political pretensions still remembered today.

Thus the clash of images between the idealist and the philistine may well lie in the ambivalent nature of authorship in the romantic period— one of the youth in search of an honorable career in the literary market- place, in spite of the inevitable social compromises such a quest entailed. Of course, the romantic *angst* and idealism, indebted as they were to insatiable yearnings, owed little to this conflict. Most of the sampled authors did not express a deeply felt *mal de siècle* in their works analyzed in Chapter 2. Yet even these popular literati could not remain indifferent to the clash between social aspirations and economic actualities of the younger generation. Such a conflict was the fate of many romantic authors in early nineteenth-century Paris. In these circumstances, younger authors shared in the popularity of the movement, profiting by its brief vogue, while growing older and more experienced not only in literary creation, but also in appealing to an audience eager for distraction. In- deed, popular romanticism may well have reached a broader cross section of the Parisian population from 1820 to 1840 as a consequence of this shrewd generation of younger, more professional authors.

❦4❧

THE ROMANTIC BOOK TRADE

❦N *Illusions perdues* MAY BE FOUND THE PORTRAIT of perhaps the first modern publisher in French fiction: Dauriat, owner of a weekly newspaper as well as bookseller, openly speculated in literature, investing thousands of francs in advertising and friendly reviews for each book he published.[1] "I do not find it amusing to risk 2,000 francs on publishing a book [only] in the hope of recovering my investment. . . . With my influence and the articles that I secure, I handle affairs worth 500,000 francs, not little volumes worth 2,000."[2] Each year he received more than a thousand manuscripts for his consideration, a task that necessitated a filing department and an editorial staff in his office at the Palais-Royal. With his capital and organization Dauriat claimed he could literally create the success of his authors. "I have made three great men in the last year," he boasted, despite the risks inherent in such a business.[3]

Like his numerous colleagues in the Wooden Galleries, famed for their fashionable bookstores, this sophisticated Parisian publisher specialized in the "New Literature."[4] Busts of Byron and Goethe adorned his shop, the ostensible symbols of Dauriat's success as well as the portraits of important romantic authors. Evidently, Dauriat welcomed romanticism, for it meant more than an intellectual movement; it was a commercial venture as well, rewarding shrewd booksellers even in genres doomed to publishing losses, like poetry. "There may be immortal poets in the world, . . . but for the publishing business, young man," he told Lucien, an aspiring young author, "there are only four poets:

1. Dauriat was a fictional portrait of an active publisher and bookseller in the romantic period, Charles Ladvocat, according to Roland Chollet, "Introduction," *Illusions perdues* in Balzac, *La comédie humaine,* 5:54.

2. Balzac, *La comédie humaine,* 5:367.

3. *Ibid.,* p. 365.

4. *Ibid.,* p. 355.

Béranger, Casimir Delavigne, Lamartine, and Victor Hugo."[5] Of these successful names in the Paris book trade, only Béranger was not closely associated with the romantic movement.

However exaggerated, Balzac's portrait of this enterprising *libraire* speculating on romantic *nouveautés* marks an important point in French publishing history, a significant confluence of major literary and economic developments.[6] In the hands of businessmen like Dauriat, the book trade moved from a traditional artisanal craft to a more modern industry in consumer goods by the middle of the nineteenth century. The trade no longer published cautiously for a fixed and known audience of wealthy subscribers. Rather, it invested heavily in producing cheap titles for a larger, faceless readership. The number of titles increased, their prices dropped, and their sales climbed, as entrepreneurs sought new means and modes of production and distribution. Printers adopted stereotyped plates and mechanical presses that permitted the mass production of classical and popular titles well before 1850. Similarly, publishers attempted to stimulate the market for books by publishing in less expensive formats and more attractive book designs. And *libraires* learned to advertise effectively in newspapers and wall posters. It was largely as a consequence of these developments that authors could earn a living from their writing in the romantic period, generally an impossibility only fifty years earlier.

But innovation did not stop with the book, it also required a new content. Many publishers like Balzac's Dauriat considered new manuscripts from well-known romantic authors as a way to interest more readers and increase demand for their products. With the rapid expansion in the book trade in a relatively restricted literate market, publishers turned increasingly to such new titles, a concern that coincided with the appearance of popular as well as elite romanticism.[7] Literature in the movement appealed not only because it represented new work of interest to old readers, but also because it was so easily adapted to the tastes of new, even more naive readers. As seen in Chapter 2, romantic forms pervaded the *chansonniers*, melodramas, and romances intended for a plebeian audience, even though the vogue did not last. In time as a less sophisticated audience grew with higher literacy rates, and as this readership sought a literature more appropriate to its thirst for distraction, *libraires* emphasized other popular works without the overlay of romantic convention

5. *Ibid.*, p. 369.

6. For discussion of more general concurrent literary and economic developments in the period, see Hauser, *Social History*, 4:3–25; George, *French Romanticism*, pp. 3–66; and Neret, *Histoire illustrée*, pp. 110–98.

7. See George, *French Romanticism*, esp. pp. 3–66.

to meet the new demand. Romantic extravagance, apparently, did not satisfy many for very long, and publishers were quick in turning to more successful sentimental songs, stormy dramas, and adventure stories by 1840.

In this way the growing sophistication of the trade facilitated the diffusion of new popular literary innovations, of which romanticism was one of the earliest and most important. It was no accident that popular romanticism briefly changed the face of French literature just when the book trade was becoming a more modern industry sensitive to changing market conditions. Such a coincidence of literary and publishing innovation promoted the development of both in a way that deserves closer examination. The romantic "revolution" appeared in the book as well as in its contents from 1820 to 1840. How it did so will be considered in this chapter.

FROM CRAFT TO INDUSTRY

To be sure, the Parisian book trade did not actually evolve into a genuine industry by 1840—no more than the popular romantics effected a true intellectual revolution in their lifetime. Much of the trade in the period remained the bastion of unimaginative men retaining many of the traditional marketing practices of the eighteenth century.[8] After publication of classical authors had saturated the buying public in the Restoration, creating a temporary dislocation among marginal producers, more substantial *libraires* attempted to stimulate demand by acquiring the manuscripts of "living" classics, the great authors whose names seemed to insure publishing success. The lesser lights were not considered worth the risk. Firmin Didot, for example, refused to publish Lamartine's first volume of poetry because it was not what Didot considered marketable literature, like that of Delille and Parny. He surely regretted this judgement after the *Méditations poétiques* reached its ninth printing in less than three years.[9]

Similarly, many booksellers employed a very restricted commercial network that rarely extended beyond a few locations in Paris. Most booksellers did not cultivate the worldwide business interests of Martin Bos-

8. For similar analysis of the Paris book trade, see Chollet, "Un épisode inconnu de l'histoire de la librairie: la société d'abonnement général," *Revue des sciences humaines* 36(1971), 141:55–84, esp.

9. Cited in Neret, *Histoire illustrée*, p. 143.

sange;[10] nearly every title in the 1820 *Bibliographie de la France* noted only one retailer. Of course, the fear of speculation moved more cautious *bouquinistes* not to advertise at all, while keeping prices beyond the means of most readers, in their devotion to a luxury trade.[11] Forcing a book did not mean its promotion to consumers. Rather, it involved an elaborate system of rebates to other booksellers who accepted the title on credit. Such a discount did not affect the retail price, since *libraires* often paid off their notes within eighteen months or less. They needed a quick return, a concern that led many after a year to remainder their unsold copies to *étalagistes* on the quays.[12] Thus for the older booksellers, business meant the tried-and-true practices, however unprofitable, of a conservative trade even after 1830.

This attitude also perpetuated tradition in book production. Since *libraires* often feared the loss of quality and profit, first publications rarely exceeded 500 copies. When the first edition sold out, another slightly larger edition was produced, and so on until the final edition had to be remaindered. The expense of successive editions, however, kept per unit costs high: materials may have cost only 1 fr. 50, but all other expenses pushed it to over three francs per volume.[13] Moreover, titles often ran to many volumes of blanched pages because the lending libraries preferred them: *cabinets de lecture* rented books by the volume, the more volumes the better. Only there were fewer than 500 *cabinets* in the city, and very few of the relatively vast literate public could afford these multivolumed books at 7 fr. 50 per volume. Three-volume titles sold for 22 fr. 50, more than a day-laborer's weekly wage.[14]

Booksellers blamed the problem on the lack of available credit. The

10. See discussion of this major figure in nineteenth-century French publishing, in Henry Lauzac, *Galerie historique et critique du dix-neuvième siècle. Martin Bossange* (Paris: "Galerie Historique," 1865); and J.-M. Quérard, *Quelques mots sur M. Bossange père, doyen des imprimeurs et des libraires de Paris* (Paris: Imp. Lainé and Havard, 1863).

11. E.g., see discussion of such a view of the luxury trade in Paul Dupont, *Histoire de l'imprimerie* (Paris: Dupont, 1854), 2 vols., detailing the great books printed but rarely marketed.

12. See the perceptive commentary on the anachronistic pricing system discussed in the introductions to the successive volumes of Alexandre Pigoreau, *Petite bibliographie biographico-romancière, ou dictionnaire des romanciers...* (Paris: Pigoreau, 1821-28), 3 vols.

13. See the sample budget of costs of printing books, A. T. Scott de Martinville, *Lettres à M. Plassan, ancien imprimeur, sur les intérêts matériels de la typographie* (Paris: Imp. Bachelier, [1838]).

14. See Victor Fouque, *De quelques abus en librairie et des moyens de les combattre* (Chalon-sur-Saône: Fouque, 1841), p. 7; and insightful discussion of similar abuses in Emile de Girardin, "De l'invention des ouvrages de littérature, de science et d'art," *Etudes politiques*, 1st ser. (Paris: Mairet and Fournier, 1842), p. 324.

haute banque refused to lend money to *libraires*, believing like Balzac that unsold books were literally not worth the paper they bound; the print ruined what might have been a resaleable commodity.[15] Similarly, numerous bankruptcies gave booksellers the image of bad credit risks. What credit they did get cost more than 15 percent per annum from local money changers. Nevertheless, even wealthy booksellers preferred to save their money for early retirement to a house in the countryside rather than put it back into the business. When they could, most men bought properties whose rents they could live on instead of expanding their commercial ventures, a pattern common among French businessmen generally in the early nineteenth century.[16] Thus it was not credit that limited innovation, but the *libraires'* cautious attitudes. With such a vision of business, the book trade remained largely a craft in Paris late into the period.

This conservatism may well have been the decisive factor in the disastrous years from 1828 to 1833. Earlier in the Restoration, the political climate had encouraged the publication of Enlightenment authors. Complete editions of Montesquieu and Rousseau, among others, not only passed the relatively lax censors, but they attracted the interest of liberals and republicans in open or covert opposition to the regime. One Restoration *libraire*, Touquet, sold more than 1.6 million volumes of Voltaire and Rousseau in less than seven years.[17] These mammoth editions were made possible by Louis-Etienne Herhan's *clichés* that permitted the printing of standardized copies in the tens of thousands without tying up all a printer's type. Although some deliberate attempts were made to reach a larger audience with these titles in cheaper formats, most booksellers had yet to discover the popular reader during the Restoration.[18]

Given a market marked by inelastic demand above a few francs per book, and given traditional, luxury trade commercial practices, the result was a glut. By 1828 the wealthy buying public, like Balzac's César Birotteau, had already purchased complete sets of the classics; the rest of the literate public never had the money for them.[19] Sudden remainders to

15. Balzac, "L'état actuel de la librairie," *Oeuvres diverses*, 1:363.

16. See discussion of this common French business practice in the nineteenth century, in David S. Landes, "French Entrepreneurship and Industrial Growth in the Nineteenth Century," *Journal of Economic History* 9(1949),45–61.

17. Paul Salvan, "Un moment de la diffusion du livre: livres et lectures en 1825," *Humanisme actif: mélanges d'art et de littérature offerts à Julien Cain* (Paris: Hermann, 1968),2:173–74.

18. Note, however, Debra Perry's work devoted to this problem in the Restoration book trade, "Publishers, Politics, and the Discovery of the Popular Reader," unpublished doctoral dissertation (in progress), Yale University, under the direction of Peter Gay.

19. Balzac, *La comédie humaine*, 6:166.

colporteurs and *étalagistes* ruined those booksellers who still held unsold copies at three or four times the price offered on the street. Consequently, bankruptcies among marginal producers, and even some major ones, soared from five in 1827, to thirty-two in 1830,[20] while other *libraires* sought less painful solutions to the crisis in overproduction. Some even resorted to lotteries and unscrupulous subscription schemes. With the July revolution, demand in the luxury trade nearly disappeared entirely, forcing many to request loans from the new regime they felt was more responsive to business interests.[21] The problem, of course, was not politics but producing and marketing appropriate to the readers in the city at the time.

In these desperate circumstances, more enterprising publishers realized that survival meant more sweeping innovation: the solution was not to limit losses, as many men in the trade did with varying degrees of success; rather, the answer was to stimulate demand among new readers, as many others learned to their profit. The most venturesome adopted new production and distribution practices, cutting costs and prices, promoting sales of more attractive products to a largely untapped public. This involved not only new books, but also new authors and a new literature like the romantic movement. The inexpensive *nouveauté*, in both format and content, insured the salvation of the entrepreneurs' fortunes in a period of serious economic dislocation from 1828 to 1833. Thus publishers, and the advances in the book trade they promoted, fostered the new popular romantic literature and its younger, commercially minded creators.

Now it would be truly presumptuous to argue that publishers and booksellers determined literary taste. On the contrary, the trade was actually responding to the demand of new readers in the city, whose tastes were informed by many more complex influences than new, sophisticated marketing techniques.[22] *Editeurs* and *libraires* were not "tastemakers." But they did encourage existing trends; they exploited shrewdly

20. See the records of bankruptcies kept in Archives du Département de la Seine et de la Ville de Paris D 10 U3. "Dossiers des faillites, 1828–1830;" A.D.S.V.P. D 11 U3. "Registres d'inscription des faillites, 1831."

21. See review of reasons for requests for help from the government in Martin Bossange père, *A messieurs les membres de la Chambre des Députés* (au sujet du prêt fait en 1830 par le Trésor au commerce de la librairie) (Paris: Imp. Bourgogne and Martinet, 1830). See also discussion of crisis in the book trade before and after 1830 in pp. 192–94 of this study.

22. See discussion of the complexity of defining taste in Zeldin, *France, 1848–1945*, 2:349–762. And for discussion of the importance of entrepreneurship in nineteenth-century French industrialization and economic growth, see Edward C. Carter II, Robert Forster, and Joseph N. Moody, eds. *Enterprise and Entrepreneurs in Nineteenth- and Twentieth-Century France* (Baltimore: Johns Hopkins University Press, 1976), pp. 87–136.

the interests and habits of their audience by bringing to light the vogue of popular romanticism, among readers both high and low, when the market for other literary trends seemed to disappear. In this function, the book trade did indeed nurture the movement, making it more possible for the new literature to flourish when it became good business, especially after 1828.

Perhaps the most obvious exploitation of the romantics' commercial possibilities appeared in illustration and book design. The movement's conventions attracted publishers to romantic lithographs and engravings that graced the volumes of many titles, whether or not they expressed the appropriate sensibility.[23] Prior to 1826, generally only special, heavily subsidized editions featured illustrations: the Didots' *Racine* printed during the Empire was considered a rare masterpiece.[24] At the height of the romantic movement, however, elaborate engravings were common features in the *belles lettres*. For instance, Goethe's *Faust*, in 1826, was published with illustrations by Delacroix, while Nodier's *Histoire du roi de Bohème* carried fifty vignettes designed by Tony Johannot. Many romantic artists, like Célestin Nanteuil and the Devéria brothers, first achieved renown for their etchings in books.[25] Thanks to such pioneers, book illustrations by 1840 became standard in popular titles, from the fancy keepsakes sold by installment to the seemingly endless serial novels in the newspapers.

Moreover, type-founders cast fantastic characters more appropriate to the movement than the austere classical type commonly used since the eighteenth century.[26] Complemented by elaborate frontispieces, title pages now employed gothic letters reminiscent of medieval script and vignettes with comparable romantic motifs, such as moonlit castles and misty-eyed maidens playing the lyre. Such designs were not limited to the bound pages; many front covers revealed equally attractive devices— just as back covers were now devoted to advertising other titles available from the same bookseller. Obviously, the romantic period marked an

23. See Girard "Le livre, l'illustration, et le reliure à l'époque romantique"; Carteret, *Le trésor du bibliophile romantique et moderne*; Dérôme, *Causeries d'un ami des livres*; and Fleury, *Les vignettes romantiques*.

24. See discussion of the art of bookprinting in Robert Brun, *Le livre français* (Paris: Larousse, 1945).

25. See discussion of Nanteuil and the Devérias' work in Gautier, *Histoire du romantisme*, pp. 52–61, 218–23. See also Charles Asselineau, *Bibliographie romantique. Catalogue anecdotique et pittoresque des éditions originales...* (Paris: Rouquette, 1872), and *Mélanges tirés d'une petite bibliographie romantique...* (Paris: Pincebourde, 1867).

26. See discussion of romantic type faces in Maurice Audin, *Histoire de l'imprimerie* (Paris: Ricard, 1972), pp. 240–47.

opportunity for *libraires* to promote sales by illustration and book design in keeping with the publicity of the new movement in literature, in many cases for reasons that had less to do with the romantic mood than they did with its audience appeal.

Much of the movement's renown was also closely tied to the development of advertising by its publishers and booksellers. Earlier in the period, the only notices of new books appeared in the *Bibliographie de la France* where, in a few lines, the title, its author, printer, and publisher were simply announced. Overt publicity lowered the reputation of not only the work, but also the bookseller.[27] The overproduction crisis promptly led many to break this taboo. New titles were no longer discreetly listed once in the catalogs: they received larger and more numerous notices in the *Journal de la librairie*, appended to the *Bibliographie de la France*, and on pages of the daily and weekly newspapers devoted to *les annonces anglaises*. By 1835 newspaper ads had ballooned to nearly a third of the page, sometimes next to the notices of clothiers and chocolate manufacturers, as books became less a luxury and more a consumer item within the modest means of a growing literate audience.[28]

Similarly, Charles Ladvocat, a flamboyant publisher of the romantics, mounted street posters using "fantastic letters, bizarre colors, vignettes, and later lithographs that often made the notice a poem for the eyes and a deception for the unsuspecting reader."[29] Slower selling titles earned the "puff" of successive editions or reappeared under a false title to encourage prospective readers.[30] More sophisticated use was also made of critical reviews in the newspapers, a subtle form of advertising that publishers often secured by lavishly entertaining the right critics. Martin Bossange actually offered Stendhal fifty copies of a book for generous treatment in the *Journal des débats*.[31] It was becoming increasingly common practice among *libraires* at the Palais-Royal to permit browsing in shops that once were practically storerooms closed to the curious. By such means, more and more booksellers were learning to promote sales in the romantic period.

But publicity did not insure a romantic title's purchase if it was too

27. E.g., "Que disait aujourd'hui le philosophe s'il voyait les produits de la librairie exposés jusque dans des boutiques d'épiciers?" J. Hébrard, *De la librairie, son ancienne prospérité, son état actuel...* (Paris: Hébrard, 1847), p. 23. See also Dérôme, *Causeries d'un ami des livres*, 1:29.

28. E.g., see the ad announcing the termination of Napoléon Landais' dictionary in the June 27, 1835, edition of the *Journal de débats*.

29. Balzac, *La comédie humaine*, 5:449.

30. Fouque, *De quelques abus en librairie*, pp. 9, 12.

31. Stendhal, *Souvenirs d'égotisme*, p. 1436.

expensive. Consequently, booksellers also began lowering their prices from the standard 7 fr. 50 per volume during the Restoration. In fact, book prices dropped more than 50 percent in the period, even though only the prices of select titles dipped before 1830 since many *libraires* feared a loss in quality.[32] Individual classics published in the tens of thousands sometimes cost less than 3 francs. But the simpler formats of other books also cut production costs—one printer estimated that an in-32 pocket edition could be sold at a third the price of an in-12 or in-8 copy without loss of profit.[33] Realizing the limited market for multi-volumed titles published especially for the *cabinets de lecture*, many booksellers turned to these cheaper formats to reach a larger clientele. In 1838 Gervais Charpentier offered the first standardized in-18 editions of romantic authors at only 3 fr. 50, a veritable commercial revolution in the book trade.[34]

As booksellers learned to market "opinion as a merchandise," a wider range of printed material in Paris became cheaper.[35] After 1830 enterprising publishers employed the system of selling books by installment. Not all titles lent themselves to this treatment, but serialized novels, grand illustrateds, and collections of stories and essays were easily cut into magazinelike *livraisons* costing as little as two sous.[36] Rising competition among booksellers in a limited market naturally forced many out of business, their entire stock often sold by their creditors at prices competitive with *colporteurs* and *étalagistes*.[37] Although this was hardly a shrewd marketing "strategy," it did provide books well within the means of more ordinary Parisians. During the Restoration, Agricol Perdiguier regularly bought copies of Voltaire and Racine on the quays for 20 sous or less. Only fifteen years later the romantics like Victor Hugo could be purchased there for the same price.

32. Note the drop in the price index calculated by Tihomir J. Markovitch in the cost of books and newspapers, from 1059.0 in 1803–12, to 347.6 in 1835–44 (Base 1905–13 = 100). See Table 5 in his *Industrie française de 1789 à 1964* (Paris: Institut de science economique appliquée, 1966),3:Appendix.

33. J.-M. Mosse, *Du commerce de la librairie, des moyens de le rendre plus florissant et de déjouer les contrefacteurs étrangers* (Paris: Imp. Goetschy, 1824), pp. 12–14.

34. See list of published works selling for 3 fr. 50 advertised in the frontispieces of Charpentier's editions after 1838, e.g., Dante Alighieri, *La divine comédie* (Paris: Charpentier, 1841).

35. Alexandre Baudouin, *Anecdotes historiques du temps de la Restauration, suivies de recherches sur l'origine de la presse, son développement...* (Paris: F. Didot frères, 1853), p. 104.

36. E.g., Lachevardière's *Le magasin pittoresque* that first appeared in 1833.

37. E.g., see prices in J.-N. Barba, Cour des Fontaines, No. 7, *Rabais considérables, par suite de cessation de commerce* (Paris: Barba, 1827).

The entrepreneurial spirit among Parisian *libraires* led to more than new commercial practices. Besides illustrations, advertising, and price cuts, romantic booksellers often sought new means and modes of production. The most important producers, of course, were authors, and publishers went to great lengths to secure their manuscripts.[38] Louis-Désiré Véron established a morning routine of visiting prospective writers at their homes, at times before they awoke, to be ahead of other publishers with equally attractive offers.[39] Payments for works by well-known authors were exceptionally high from 1828 to 1833, largely as a consequence of the competition among *libraires* for new titles to stimulate the lagging demand for still expensive books. Edmond Werdet actually compared the problem of getting copy from reluctant authors to the extraction of oil from the ground, "the most difficult task I know of."[40] In fact, the prominent writer often held the upper hand in the negotiations: witness Hugo's condescending letters to Eugène Renduel.

The traditional paternalism of the bookseller was rapidly giving way to a more distant exchange relationship in which each party openly bargained in his self-interest.[41] As booksellers became increasingly anxious about publishing *nouveautés* to survive the trade crisis, even relatively unknown writers could extort advances on books that were never written, a fairly common practice for the penniless adherents to Gautier's *petit cénacle*.[42] Thus if an *éditeur* wanted to profit in his trade, he had to be more aggressive and shrewder in his acquisition of manuscripts, even soliciting works in some genres. More professional authors like the romantics must have learned to benefit from this situation, however far removed it was from their expectations of an income, both reliable and honorable, from their publishers.

In response to this demand for the titles of new, often romantic authors, printers also began to adopt new means of production, especially important given the legal limitation on the number of printers in Paris.[43]

38. Neret, *Histoire illustrée*, p. 152.

39. Louis-Désiré Véron, *Mémoires d'un bourgeois de Paris* (Paris: Librairie Nouvelle, 1856),3:52.

40. Edmond Werdet, *De la librairie française, son passé, son présent, son avenir...* (Paris: Dentu, 1860), p. 92.

41. See account of the open battle between author and publisher in Elias Regnault, "L'éditeur," in Curmer, ed. *Les Français*, 4:323.

42. Note the letters requesting advances written by Pétrus Borel and Théophile Gautier, in Jullien, *Le romantisme et l'éditeur Renduel, souvenirs et documents sur les écrivains de l'école romantique...* (Paris: Fesquelles, 1897), pp. 144, 234.

43. For good accounts of developments in printing, see G.-A. Crapelet, *Etudes pratiques et littéraires sur la typographie,* (Paris: Crapelet, 1837); Audin, *Histoire de l'imprimerie*; James Moran, *Printing Presses: History and Development...* (Berkeley: University

In 1798 Nicolas-Louis Robert had developed the first papermaking machine that was used by the Didot family mills in Sorel (Somme) by 1814. At least four machines manufacturing paper on continuous rolls were in operation in 1827, and eight more in 1833. Industrial production of printers' ink was initiated in 1808 by Pierre Lorilleux at the Imprimerie Impériale, and by 1827 there were eleven such establishments in Paris. Before 1800 Herhan had perfected the stereotyping process bought by the Didots during the Restoration. But the most important inventions occurred in the printing press. Although eighteenth-century modifications to the hand press made traditional printing more efficient, they did not affect production as radically as the mechanical press built first by William Nicolson, the inventor of the rubber ink roller in 1790. The best hand presses produced only 250 impressions an hour, the slowest *presses mécaniques* more than 1,000 (see Illustrations 7 and 8). Ferdinand Koenig considerably improved Nicolson's model which Philippe Taylor refined in 1834 to print simultaneously on both sides of the page. Parisian printers could now make up to 3,600 impressions an hour, permitting not only larger but also cheaper editions. By 1836 such technical changes in printing enabled the industry to profit romantic authors and their booksellers.

Moreover, the diffusion of these innovations was rapid. Within four years of its introduction in 1823, there were twelve Nicolson presses in Paris.[44] In August 1830, A. A. Renouard, the mayor of the eleventh *arrondissement*, suggested to the Interior Ministry that the mechanical presses of no fewer than twenty printers were sabotaged during the July revolution.[45] Although most printers used their new presses only for job printing, some began using them to print books despite initially high production costs and damage done to the type. "One can still cite the works printed by Rignoux with the old process that maintain a competitive price against those works coming off the mechanical presses of Lacheverdière [sic]," wrote Charles Ladvocat, the prominent romantic *libraire*, to the Minister of the Interior in September 1830.[46] In 1833, 34 of Paris' 80 printers had 56 mechanical and 819 hand presses. In 1841, 34 of 40 printers surveyed by the prefect of the police had 79 new presses.[47]

Only half of the printers were mentioned in the latter report, but the apparent ratio of new to old presses was already capable producing

of California Press, 1973); and especially on the mechanical press, Théodore Goebel, *Frédéric Koenig et l'invention de la presse mécanique*, Paul Schmidt, trans. (Paris: Schmidt, 1885).

44. Moran, *Printing Presses*, p. 140.
45. A.N.F^{18}567 "Affaires diverses, 1815–1854," dossier 262 bis.
46. *Ibid.*
47. *Ibid.*, dossier 314.

7. Late Wooden Hand-Press (ca. 1819). Print from *Ree's Encyclopedia* in James Moran, *Printing Presses: History and Development* (1973). *Courtesy of the University of California Press, Berkeley, and Faber and Faber, London.*

more than two-thirds of the city's total output of printed material. Moreover, in time these mechanical presses cost less, facilitating their diffusion. The initial price declined from 36,000 francs in 1815 for a clumsy Nicolson press, to 12,000 francs in 1848 for a more efficient Koenig model.[48] Thus by 1844 Firmin Didot noted that only such widespread technical advances had enabled printers to keep up with the incredible flow of words from authors' pens.[49] With the spread of these innovations and the corresponding increase in productive capacity, the printing industry actually made possible some selective growth in the book trade, despite the depression between 1828 and 1833 near the height of the romantic movement.

48. Pierre-Emile Levasseur, *Histoire des classes ouvrières en France depuis 1789 jusqu'à nos jours* (Paris: Hachette, 1867),2:124.

49. Firmin Didot, *L'exposition de 1844* (Paris: Didot, 1845),3:168–69.

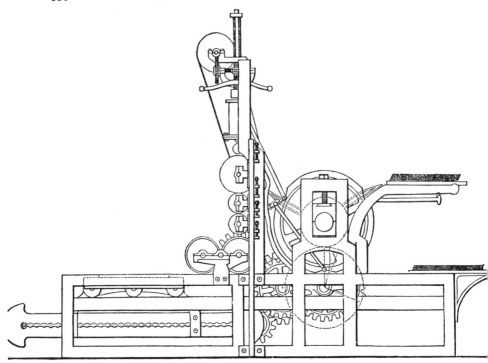

8. Diagram of Ferdinand Koenig's First Cylinder Machine (ca. 1811). Print from Theodore Goebel's biography of Koenig in James Moran, *Printing Presses: History and Development* (1973). *Courtesy of the University of California Press, Berkeley, and Faber and Faber, London.*

The impact of these developments on romantic production is implied in the increased production of all books. Under the *ancien régime* the copies of a title rarely exceeded 1,000; but by the July Monarchy, publication runs were often over 2,500.[50] Apparently Voltaire's *boutade* about the limited audience of even a pleasant book was no longer so amusing. Rising production of printed works impressed less witty observers like the comte Daru and the baron Dupin in 1827, when the latter estimated that the last 12 years had seen more impressions than the previous 375 years in printing history.[51] The *Bibliographie de la France*

50. Lucien Febvre and Henri-Jean Martin, *L'apparition du livre* (Paris: Albin Michel, 1971), pp. 307–13; A.N.F[18]II*6–29. "Déclarations de Imprimeurs."

51. Dupin, *Situation progressive des forces de la France depuis 1814* (Bruxelles: Tencé frères, 1827), p. 44; Pierre A. N. B. Daru, *Notions statistiques sur la librairie, pour servir à la discussion des lois sur la presse* (Paris: F. Didot, 1827).

recorded 3,357 titles in 1815, and 8,272 in 1826, the highest level in the first half of the nineteenth century. Repeated titles and stricter administrative surveillance accounted for much of this rise; so that in the 1830s, under a new regime and when other organs were used for advertising, the number of titles averaged only 6,500 a year. But this was still nearly twice the annual average for the early Restoration.

A more accurate indication of growth, the number of copies per title, corroborates this evidence of rising production. In 1820 editions in the *belles lettres* and history averaged 1,130 copies; in 1841, a comparable economic year, they averaged 2,253 (see Table 4.1). The most dramatic jump occurred in poetry, from 688 to 2,570 copies, largely as a consequence of the new vogue of popular songs after the 1830 revolution. Less impressively, the editions of drama and history doubled, while those of fiction rose by more than 20 percent in the same period. (The medians generally followed the same pattern as the means.) Overall, these averages reflect the rise in production calculated for the industry by T. J. Markovitch who based his figures on the manufacture of paper for print.[52] At 5.9 percent annual growth, the book trade compared favorably with the global trends studied by other recent French economic historians.[53] Although the industry was not a prime element in the 5.6 percent annual economic growth during the July Monarchy, it did reflect this impressive rise in national production coincident with the romantic movement in literature. As the economy expanded, so too did the capacity for the book trade to produce and market new books.

ENTREPRENEURS: ROMANTIC AND NONROMANTIC

Expansion of the Parisian trade owed much to the flood of new men entering the profession. With the dissolution of the book guild during the Revolution, large numbers of them rushed into business, protected from

52. See Line XIX, Table 1. "Indices de la Production," in Markovitch, *Industrie française*, 3:Appendix. The actual editions sizes of titles after 1840, and hence the real growth in the book trade, may actually have been much larger than indicated here using the A.N.F^{18}II* series data. It was common practice among printers using stereotype plates to report to the Interior Ministry a succession of smaller printings instead of the total edition size of the work they were contracted to print. Thus, a printer would declare not one edition of 5,000 copies, but ten editions of 500; the calculation of the apparent mean edition size would then be much smaller than it actually was. But, for the period under discussion in this study (1820–40), multiple editions were not yet a major problem. See Bellos, "Le marché du livre à l'époque romantique," pp. 652–53, for a brief discussion of the A.N.F^{18}II* series.

53. Marczewski, "Some Aspects of the Economic Growth of France;" Lévy-Leboyer, "Croissance économique en France au XIXe siècle"; and Crouzet, "Essai de construction d'un indice annuel de production industrielle française au XIXe siècle."

TABLE 4.1
Mean and Median Edition Sizes of

Year	Poetry			Drama		
	Mean	N	Median	Mean	N	Median
1820	688	25	500	1,028	25	1,000
1827	670	20	500	889	22	1,000
1834	2,037	23	800	1,628	30	2,000
1841	2,570	23	1,000	2,234	27	2,000

Source: Random samples from the genre indexes of the *Bibliographie de la France*; edition sizes were approximately equal (plus or minus 10 percent) to the averages, indicating a wide dispersion

restriction by the law of 19 July 1793 and encouraged by intense political activity. Over 500 *libraires*, some of whom were even illiterate, opened shops in Paris within fifteen years, alarming many older men in the trade who petitioned Napoleon to reinstate the ancient corporation of booksellers.[54] Less to grant this request than to check the possibility of sedition among so many booksellers, the Emperor required each *libraire* to be licensed, subject to certification of his "upstanding life and morals, and his attachment to country and sovereign." This system established in 1810 was retained in its essentials by the decree of 14 October 1814 and subsequent laws during the Restoration and July Monarchies.[55]

Despite this close surveillance, the actual number of booksellers in Paris continued to grow rapidly, from 373 in 1815, to 945 in 1845, at a rate 50 percent faster than the rise in the city's population.[56] In 1839 one *libraire* actually complained that "the honor of the trade" was jeopardized by this mass of booksellers, "to which should be added a comparable number of publishers and keepers of rental libraries, for a total twenty times greater than the number in 1791."[57] Similarly, the number of printers grew. Even though they had been limited to eighty by decree in 1811, larger printing operations routinely contracted out much of their work to smaller shops without licenses. By 1835 nearly a fourth of the city's printers had *succursales* in Paris, and an unknown number in the provinces, to boost the effective number of shops to well over 105.[58] More-

54. J.-R. Plassan, *Mémoire à M. le comte de Montalivet, Ministre de l'Intérieur, sur l'imprimerie et sur la librairie* (Paris: Imp. Terzuolo, 1839), p. 9.

55. For the legal status of booksellers and printers throughout the period, see Pic, *Code des imprimeurs, libraires, écrivains et artistes*, vol. 1.

56. See Perry, "Publishers, Politics, and the Discovery of the Popular Reader," Chpt. 2.

57. Plassan, *Mémoire*, p. 9.

58. A.N.F^{18}567. "Affaires diverses." Dossier 314.

Sampled Titles, by Genre, 1820-1841

Fiction			History			Total		
Mean	N	Median	Mean	N	Median	Mean	N	Median
1,322	30	1,000	1,421	27	1,000	1,130	107	1,000
1,223	20	1,000	1,388	22	1,000	1,047	84	1,000
1,620	23	1,000	2,600	19	3,000	1,919	95	1,500
1,627	29	1,500	2,773	22	2,000	2,253	101	1,750

from the Archives Nationales F¹⁸ II*7, 14, 24, 29. "Déclarations des Imprimeurs," Standard deviations in nearly all cases around the means.

over, printing operations also increased in size. According to an 1848 Chamber of Commerce survey, 84 percent of the city's printers employed more than ten workers, including their illicit subsidiaries; less than 11 percent of all industries in Paris employed that many workers.[59]

Besides such remarkable growth, the trade also specialized more. At the turn of the century, distinctions were drawn only between *libraires anciens et modernes*; by the Restoration booksellers began selling books mainly in certain fields, like J.-N. Barba who specialized in drama and Louis Hachette who concentrated on textbooks.[60] Others focused on even smaller aspects of production and distribution. *Editeurs, marchands, commissionnaires,* and keepers of *cabinets de lecture* adopted entirely new functions or others formerly undifferentiated in the age-old *imprimeur-libraire,* a tradition well represented by the famous Didot family.[61] In 1820 Edmond Werdet became one of the first *commis-voyageurs* in bookselling, though he was soon joined by a dozen others at the end of the Restoration.[62] By the July Monarchy the commercial traveller had become a familiar figure in provincial cities as Parisian firms attempted to establish a more truly national commercial network.

59. Chambre de commerce et d'industrie, *Statistique de l'industrie à Paris...pour les années 1847-1848* (Paris: Guillaumin, 1851), p. 36. For a sense of the publisher's scale of operations in the period, see the various roles assigned 241 people involved in the publication of a single book, by C. L. F. Panckoucke, *Budget statistique d'un éditeur* (Paris: Panckoucke, 1837).

60. J.-N. Barba, *Souvenirs de Jean-Nicolas Barba, ancien libraire de Palais-Royal* (Paris: Ledoyen and Giret, 1846); Jean Mistler, *La librairie Hachette de 1826 à nos jours* (Paris: Hachette, [1964]), pp. 3-26.

61. Werdet, *Etudes bibliographiques sur la famille des Didots...1713-1864* (Paris: Dentu, 1864). See also an account of specialization even among publishers in Regnault, "L'éditeur," in Curmer, ed. *Les Français,* 4:322-34.

62. See Werdet, *De la librairie française,* Chpt. 1.

Similar developments occurred among printers who acquired equipment designed specifically for certain kinds of production. Herhan used stereotyped *clichés* to print the classics, Lachevardière employed mechanical presses to print newspapers, and the Imprimerie Royale bought a steam engine to power its presses for the *Bulletin des lois*. The parallel between *libraires* and *imprimeurs* extended as well to their professional organizations. After a decade of ad hoc commissions aimed at moving the regime to halt book smuggling, Paris booksellers founded the *Cercle de la Librairie*, officially recognized in 1847 to promote the larger interests of the trade.[63] Printers, too, formed a typographical association in 1839, largely in response to their workers who were among the most active in Paris.[64] Given these developments in expansion and sophistication of the book trade, among booksellers and printers alike, the romantic movement could not help but benefit. Certainly such new industrial conditions made it possible for many authors, especially those in the new fashion, to survive by their writings.

But what portion of this remarkable expansion in the Paris book trade is owed to publishers primarily of romantic works? What kind of men promoted *nouveautés* in the period? The limited literary evidence available strongly suggests their entrepreneurial reputation as younger, more aggressive men who earned the admiration and ire of contemporary observers.[65] In 1841, Elias Regnault called the romantic publisher a brave *parvenu*.

He gathered all the audacious poets, the byronic geniuses, the dishevelled glories. A bold speculator and adventurous spirit, he gave the book trade an impulsion that had, like all temerities, something enormous about it. Romantic in his dealings as in his publications, he opened the doors of industry to larger avenues where others ventured with less imprudence and more success, profiting from his lesson and even his faults.[66]

In many ways the *éditeur* of the new literature represented an anomaly in nineteenth-century French industry: the businessman who eschewed the

63. See account of Parisian *libraires'* organization attempts in Hébrard, *De la librairie*.

64. See Louis Radiguer, *Maîtres imprimeurs et ouvriers typographes, 1470–1903* (Paris: Société Nouvelle, 1903), pp. 209–18, 236–47; and Jean Vidalenc, "L'imprimerie," *La société française de 1815 à 1848* (Paris: Marcel Rivière, 1973),2:206–14.

65. See review of literary evidence in Alfred Humblot, *L'édition littéraire au XIXe siècle* (Paris: Evreux, [1911]); and Edmond Biré, *Dernières causeries historiques et littéraires* (Paris: Vitte, 1898), pp. 105–123.

66. Regnault, "L'éditeur," in Curmer, ed. *Les Français*, 4:328–29.

safety, continuity, and privacy symbolized by the family firm. He appeared to slight the aristocratic social values that inhibited investment and commitment to innovation and expansion.[67] Not only did he pay his authors well, according to Regnault, but he also openly applied "the commercial principle of augmenting the number of consumers by reducing prices," claimed Alexandre Baudouin, himself a romantic publisher.[68]

To others, however, this was only a blatant form of immorality that encouraged the proliferation of new titles and thus the ruin of the time-honored *bouquiniste* devoted to the "antique." Especially during the crisis before and after the July revolution, many petitions and addresses accused the new men of exploiting "the public credulity" by speculating in "the multiplicity of business . . . solely in quest of a shameful profit."[69] Publishers of the new literature evidently posed the same kind of threat to cautious, established *libraires* that the romantic authors did the neo-classicists. This conflict between the audacious *éditeur* and the conservative *libraire* recurs in numerous accounts of the trade at the height of the new literature. Much of this clash, of course, owed to the rise of an entirely new aspect of the business: the exclusive publication of living authors.[70] That many of them were romantic in this period is evident not just in the coincidence of literary and economic innovation. It also appears in the testimony of men proud to have recognized the movement's commercial and esthetic value.

One of Balzac's early publishers, for example, Werdet actually claimed to have promoted the book trade's interest in new works. "The renaissance in the commerce of books is itself only the dawn of the renaissance in literature," he wrote in his partially autobiographical account of the trade.[71] After working seven years as a commercial traveller for J.-J. Lefèvre, Werdet refused an increase in his commission to set up business

67. Note that this tendency was a crucial element in the economic development of Europe as well as France. See Landes, *The Unbound Prometheus: Technological Change and Industrial Development in Western Europe from 1750 to the Present* (Cambridge: Cambridge University Press, 1969), pp. 124–92.

68. Baudouin, *Anecdotes historiques*, p. 104.

69. Plassan, *Mémoire*, p. 4. See appeals to the regimes for restriction of the number of men legally permitted in the book trade, citing the flood of new, often "unscrupulous" *libraires* speculating in literature, e.g., Levacher-Duplessis, *Requête au Roi et mémoire sur la nécessité de rétablir les corps de marchands et les communautés des arts et métiers...* (Paris: Imp. Smith, 1817); Ducessois, *Notes sur la proposition de M. Benjamin Constant relative aux imprimeurs...* (Paris: Ducessois, [1830]); and "La commission de recherches les moyens de soutenir la librairie française contre la contrefaçon belge," *Comte rendu* (Paris: Panckoucke, 1837).

70. Neret, *Histoire illustrée*, p. 132.

71. Werdet, *De la librairie française*, p. 92.

for himself. In 1827 he bought out Lequien père for 280,000 francs and then purchased the rights to publish the *Répertoire du Théâtre français* for another 40,000. Like other new *libraires-éditeurs*, he borrowed his money from discounters, who charged him 0.75 percent each month, to turn out cheap editions of the seventeenth- and eighteenth-century French masters. But Werdet did not reprint the classics for long. Twice he was undersold by more ruthless publishers who produced Voltaire's works 120 francs cheaper and a collection of eighteenth-century novels at less than half his price. Just after the 1830 revolution, Werdet turned instead to the novels and light literature of living authors. Profits from his *nouveautés* thus enabled him to survive the trade crisis, pay off his outstanding debts, and retire to a rural retreat after forty successful years in the book trade.

Werdet was acutely aware of this new specialization in publishing. He recounted two different approaches to the trade embodied in "Ladvocat and Lefèvre, publishers par excellence in the period: the first for authors just acquiring fame, the second for writers with already established reputations."[72] It was obvious that Werdet most admired Charles Ladvocat, the first "man of modern publishing. . . . He knew how to give to the book trade, to literature itself . . . an impulsion, a lift, a life that could have come without him no doubt, but only much later."[73] Ladvocat's apparent success owed as much to others' perceptions of him as it did to his shrewd business dealings. Balzac was among the first to lionize him in *Illusions perdues*. Later Jules Janin recalled his name: "Ladvocat! It seems to me that I can still see that prophetic name shining in a huge sign at the Palais-Royal, a name precious to all the glories of the century," a legend in his own time.[74]

Balzac and Janin greatly exaggerated the publisher's "incendiary" reputation. But in more judicious moods, they pointed out that this *libraire extraordinaire* was among the first to recognize the romantics during the Restoration.[75] Whether or not he actually "chased after the manuscripts of *les jeunes gens*," as Janin claimed, Ladvocat did develop a flamboyant career for himself and the men he published: Byron, Goethe, Schiller, Chateaubriand, Hugo, Sainte-Beuve, among others closely associated with the romantic movement in France. "Nearly all the famous literati from the first quarter of the century began under the auspices of

72. *Ibid.*

73. *Ibid.*

74. Jules Janin, "Histoire d'un libraire (Ladvocat)," *Critique. Portraits et caractères contemporains* (Paris: Hachette, [1859]), p. 223.

75. *Ibid.*, p. 229.

this god whose golden figure became the symbol of successful publishing," wrote Augustin Thierry appreciatively in 1854.[76] Beyond the expense of his sartorial trappings that added to his renown, Ladvocat paid authors generously enough to make them among the first to live grandly by their pens. The sums he offered to Chateaubriand (550,000 fr.) and Vidocq (200,000 fr.) for their memoirs represent the true triumph of the *nouveautés* over neo-classical works.[77]

A less foolhardy figure in romantic publishing was Eugène Renduel.[78] He too was something of a *parvenu* in the trade, beginning as a *notaire's* clerk before coming to Paris to work for Touquet, the liberal publisher of the *philosophes* during the Restoration. In 1821 Renduel established his own shop to publish many of the same Enlightenment authors that made the brief fortunes of so many *libraires* before 1828. Only after the revolution, when the romantic movement moved into its second phase, did Renduel replace Ladvocat as its best known publisher. He paid Victor Hugo 2,000 francs in 1831 for the rights to print 1,100 copies of *Marion Delorme*. Although Hugo demanded more with each contract, Renduel realized sufficient profits to continue publishing him until 1837 when, in a declining market for romantic works, he refused to buy *Ruy Blas* for 10,000 francs.

By then, Renduel had already made a minor fortune on nearly every other figure in the movement: Charles Nodier, Alexandre Dumas, Pétrus Borel, Paul and Alfred de Musset, Théophile Gautier, Gérard de Nerval, and a host of lesser romantic lights. Paul Lacroix's translations of Walter Scott and E. T. A. Hoffmann contributed significantly to the publisher's success. Thanks also to Renduel's orchestration, the abbé de Lamennais' *Paroles d'un croyant* sold more than 35,000 copies in 1834, the largest single publication by a living author in the first half of the nineteenth century.[79] (It saw innumerable Belgian *contrefaçons* as well as long lines of readers waiting to read a copy at the lending libraries.) Much of this *libraire's* fortune owed not to his devotion to traditional publishing practices. Rather, it was a consequence of his single-minded promotion of the new literature, his exclusive concern until its decline and his retirement in 1840.

There were many other publishers like Werdet, Ladvocat, and Ren-

76. Augustin Thierry, *Le moniteur*, September 12, 1854.

77. Marie Jeanne Durry, *La vieillesse de Chateaubriand, 1830–1848* (Paris: Le Divan, 1933), 1:361; Neret, *Histoire illustrée*, p. 143.

78. For accounts of Renduel's publishing activities, see Jullien, *Le romantisme et l'éditeur Renduel*; Biré, *Dernières causeries*, pp. 105–123; and Marius Gérin, *Eugène Renduel, 1798–1874, éditeur romantique* (Nevers: Imp. Lebel, 1929).

79. Neret, *Histoire illustrée*, p. 151.

duel who made much of romanticism's success.[80] Besides this, the most immediate consequence of their entrepreneurial activities was to help raise the book trade from its depression. The mean production run of all books dropped steadily from 1827 to 1830, when it reached a low of only 1,310 copies; but by 1834 it had risen again to a new high of 2,936. Apparently, the efforts of these aggressive publishers were rewarded during a brief new heyday in the book trade from 1833 to 1836.[81] For authors, too, this was a comparatively good period. The percentage of living authors published moved from only 70 percent in 1827, to nearly 80 percent in 1834, for an increase of 14 percent in only seven years. And as seen in Chapter 3, younger, more worldly romantic writers were entering the market as never before. The new movement in literature surely benefited from these developments, not only influencing the literary conventions used by popular authors, but also enabling them to reach a larger readership, thanks largely to those publishers who realized romanticism's commercial possibilities.

This diffusion meant more than profits for authors and their promoters. It also implied a special attention to the marketable aspects of the movement. Such a concern contributed to the almost exclusive adoption of the movement's forms by authors, properly speaking, more popular than romantic. Writers in the movement proper sometimes prided themselves on their obscurity as a way to spite the clarity and order of French classicism. But for this they paid a price: a smaller audience capable of understanding their work. On the other hand, their new iconoclastic conventions were much more accessible and amusing to significantly more readers anxious for distraction. As a commodity, popular romanticism became one means for an enterprising publisher to profit from an expanding urban culture, a development that alarmed even the leaders of the new literature who saw their more exclusive sensibility bastardized in the marketplace.

Despite the elite romantics, the movement influenced plebeian literature the way it did perhaps because the new men in the book trade sought out authors who wrote in the most fashionable vogue, whether or not they expressed the romantic mood that Baudelaire characterized in 1846. For the publishing entrepreneurs before and after 1830, romanti-

80. See M. Cloche, "Un grand éditeur du XIXe siècle, Léon Curmer," *Arts et métiers graphiques* 33(1933),28–36; A. Parménie and C. Bonnier de la Chapelle, *Histoire d'un éditeur et de ses auteurs: P.-J. Hetzel (Stahl)* (Paris: Albin Michel, [1953]); E. F. A. Rosseeuw Saint-Hilaire, *Notice sur Charles Furne* (Paris: Imp. Claye, 1860); Eugène Plon, *Notre livre intime de famille* (Paris: Imp. Plon, Nourrit, et cie., 1893); and Alphonse Alkan aîné, *Notice sur L. C. Silvestre, ancien libraire-éditeur...* (Paris: Aubry, 1868).

81. See runs listed in A.N. F^18II*9–26. "Déclarations des Imprimeurs."

cism did appear to be a profitable, popular literary venture, and the actual movement's more refined view of the world probably meant less to them than its attractiveness in the market.

But this state of affairs did not remain for very long. With the overproduction crisis past, the book trade now faced fierce new competition from the cheap newspaper.[82] In 1836 Emile de Girardin and Armand Dutacq both founded newspapers that no longer derived their incomes primarily from subscriptions. Instead, they profited from paid advertisements. *La presse* and *Le siècle* accordingly cut subscription rates in half, from 80 to 40 francs a year, to stimulate larger circulations, while they charged as much as 500 francs per page for ads. But cheaper newspapers, first at six then four sous before 1848, needed copy appropriate to their new audience to boost circulation and profit from advertisements. The solution was the serial novel started at the same time as the new formats in 1836 when *La presse* ran the first installment of *Lazarillo de Tormes*. Although romantics were among the first to write *romans-feuilletons*, the newspapers cultivated a much more popular convention of mystery and adventure stories without the overlay of romantic devices, attracting tens of thousands of new readers in only a few weeks.[83]

The sudden and enormous success of the newspapers running the serial novels, however, spelled the doom of the romantic book trade, despite the standardized books Charpentier published after 1838. Titles in the new literature, even at half price, could not compete with the four-sous newspaper. Developments in the book trade simply did not keep pace with those in the press; by 1842, popular romantic books had become a temporary fashion of the past. Entrepreneurs turned to ever more popular and more profitable ventures in literature and publishing, even though earlier they had promoted the remarkable diffusion of an elite culture to a more plebeian audience. The basic formulas remained what they had been since the turn of the century, only literature no longer retained romantic conventions since they no longer appealed as they had in recent times past.

In these developments after 1836, Emile de Girardin perhaps exemplifies the news publishers even more enterprising than those in the book trade.[84] After a few years as an unpaid assistant inspector of fine arts,

82. For a good account of the competition between the press and the book trade, see Pierre Orecchioni, "Presse, livre et littérature au XIXe siècle," *Revue française d'histoire du livre* 4(1974),33–44. For good account of these developments in the press, see Claude Bellanger et al., *Histoire générale de la presse française* (Paris: Presses Universitaires de France, 1971),2:114–23.

83. See Nora Atkinson, *Eugène Sue et le roman-feuilleton* (Nemours: Imp. Lesot, 1929), pp. 12–16.

84. See amusing cameo of Girardin in Zeldin, *France, 1848–1945*, 2:494–97.

he abandoned the safe paths of bureaucracy to make a living in journalism and literature. He was aware as early as 1828 that the route to fortune demanded close attention to popular taste: "Health, Prosperity, and Knowledge" became the motto of the *Journal des connaissances utiles,* sold at half the price of other newspapers at the time. His *Musée des familles, La mode, Le voleur,* and a host of other popular periodicals with circulations in the tens of thousands, even in this early period, made him one of the most important publishers after 1830. He never had to rely on the romantic movement to promote his sales.

"When the people is sovereign," he wrote in Véron's *Revue de Paris,* "it is crucial that the sovereign learn to read. With six sous I can give him an education."[85] So in 1836 *La presse* cost only six sous in a deliberate attempt to reach the largest possible audience not only for its benefit, but also for the publisher's profit. Realizing the success of his formula, Girardin criticized the book trade for its short-sightedness. "The works selling with great difficulty and risk at 1,000 copies would move much more easily, certainly more rapidly at 10, 20, or 50,000 copies or more, that is, if the trade allows the reduction of the price of books in proportion to their cost."[86] He implemented this shrewd principle in his brief interest in the trade, producing popular books in *livraison* well before the idea became widespread after 1835. But his main concern remained the press whose profits earned him 8 million francs by the time he died during the Third Republic.

Other entrepreneurial spirits besides Girardin promoted the success of the press and popular literature at the expense of the book trade and romanticism.[87] In fact, other influential *éditeurs* after 1835 like Girardin turned to keepsakes and *étrennes* sold by installment, a valiant attempt to counter the erosion of demand for books in the face of a growing newspaper audience. Léon Curmer and P.-J. Hetzel were in the forefront of the trend towards grand illustrateds in the 1840s. This search for cheaper, more attractive books continued among other booksellers, men essentially unable to compete on equal terms with the new vogue of the press and the serial novels it featured: Charpentier's mass-produced, in-18 titles after 1838 reflected this desperate response of the book trade to meet the commercial threat of newspapers in Paris. His success was limited, as was the growth of the trade until the revolutionary events of 1848.

85. Emile de Girardin, "La littérature à six sous," *Revue de Paris,* August, 1834.

86. Girardin, *Etudes politiques,* pp. 307–308.

87. E.g., Véron, *Mémoires d'un bourgeois de Paris,* vol. 3; Jacques Boulenger, *Sous Louis-Philippe. Les dandys* (Paris: Ollendorff, 1907), pp. 130–35; Du Camp, *Souvenirs,* 1:400–425; and Mistler, *La librairie Hachette.*

Such practices helped displace older traditions in the trade and older conventions in literature. Expensive, multivolumed historical novels produced for the rental libraries could not compete with serialized adventure stories in the press. Given the new world of publishing after 1836, traditional *cabinets de lecture* that featured only books passed with their literary contemporary, the romantic movement, thanks in part to men even shrewder than earlier leaders in the literary market.[88]

With the fall of romanticism and its promoters, the more sophisticated business of publishing in Paris brought to a logical conclusion its contribution to the development of literature in the period. Recent improvements in printing during the Restoration had promoted the remarkable growth in the publication of *philosophes* and classical authors whose overproduction created a commercial crisis by 1828. To survive this depression deepened by political upheaval, more imaginative *libraires* sought out authors in the new literature to publish in cheaper, more attractive editions. Further, they stimulated demand by adopting new modes of distribution, soon matched by even newer means of industrial production. The result helped create a temporary revival of the trade and the commercial success of romanticism. But after 1836 the advent of the penny press, developed by equally profit-minded men, undermined the book trade and its promotion of romantic works. The newly tapped audience encouraged, instead, the publication of *romans-feuilletons* and similar popular titles that no longer shared in the romantic movement in only a few years.

Thus what had led to the extensive diffusion of new literary conventions, briefly breaking down the cultural distinctions between the middle classes and the *menu peuple*, gave way to purer popular forms and promoted a literature for an even larger audience. Such developments were surely fostered during the constitutional monarchies by ever more enterprising booksellers and publishers in Paris who, in time, came to resemble Balzac's remarkable Dauriat, at first the boon and then the bane of the popular romantic movement in France.

88. Neret, *Histoire illustrée*, pp. 175–91.

❧ 5 ❧

THE PRODUCTION AND DISTRIBUTION
OF ROMANTIC WORKS

MUCH OF THE EVIDENCE here on the relative success of the romantic fashion, its authors and publishers from 1820 to 1840 indicates that the movement's works were generally produced and distributed in larger numbers than nonromantic titles. Despite a major recession in the book trade before and after the July revolution, romanticism prospered with important developments in publishing, especially in stereotyped plates, mechanical presses, simpler formats, and more attractive book designs. The vogue of the romantic *nouveauté* appeared in a new Parisian literary market which until the July Monarchy devoted more than 30 percent of its production to nonliving authors. By 1834 this had dropped to approximately 20 percent with the influx of younger, more professional, often romantic authors.[1] Moreover, the actual movement appeared to blur with popular literature as it evolved in Paris from the eighteenth century. Even if its sensibility was not, romantic conventions were appropriated by *chansonniers*, melodramas, romances, and national histories, to the profit of authors and publishers alike. But romanticism was soon the victim of its own success; its works were rapidly displaced by other products of a greatly expanded literary market. Cheaper standardized titles, particularly in the press, appeared without any apparent romantic influence as the demand of a larger, more naive readership grew for simpler, less bizarre literary conventions in the *belles lettres* by 1840.

The importance of the romantic fashion to larger cultural developments, as well as to *libraires* and authors in the period, owes much to the larger, more sophisticated publishing industry in Paris. Just how important this growth of a new book trade was to the movement, however, must be examined in more detail. The pervasiveness of the new literature's conventions among titles listed in the *Bibliographie de la France*

---

1. According to randomly sampled authors listed in the *Bibliographie de la France* in 1827, 1830, and 1834.

126

actually indicated their impact more on authors than on readers. That writers changed forms in apparent response to readership demand was certainly due to their social and economic context limiting their range of choices in literary creation, yet just how much more attractive the new fashion was in the period remains unclear. Similarly, enterprising *libraires-éditeurs* adopted new marketing practices that tended to favor romantic works, but not all of them enjoyed the same success: Ladvocat actually went bankrupt in 1831. Consequently, more documentation is needed of the production and distribution of romantic titles from 1820 to 1840 before the previous discussion of the new literature's debt to authorship and publishing can be verified, and more importantly, before the movement's impact on popular taste can be assessed more accurately.

MAKING AND SELLING BOOKS

Despite temporary lulls, the Paris book trade grew enormously after 1814. Contemporary observers were amazed by the increase in the production of printed material. Paul Dupont, a notable printer in the period, cited technical advances in printing, from type-casting to ink production, that tripled the number of sheets printed for non-periodicals between 1814 and 1826; he went on to estimate that nearly 360 million books were produced during the July Monarchy.[2] To this must be added the flood of periodicals in Paris whose number jumped tenfold within fifteen years of Waterloo.[3] In 1827 the comte Daru also tried to document and explain this explosion. He counted in Paris alone 367 paper manufacturers, 24 type founders, 7 makers of industrial ink, 870 presses, and more than 4,500 press workers.[4] "However extensive, however rapid have been the development of our physical activities and the rise in our material wealth, the development of our intellectual activity and the increase in our literary wealth have been even more extensive and rapid," claimed another writer who calculated a 9.25 percent annual increase in print production during the Restoration, the highest of any other economic sector.[5]

This rise naturally coincided with the relative prosperity of the

2. Dupont, *Histoire de l'imprimerie*, 1:320–25.

3. Calculated from Eugène-Louis Hatin, *Bibliographie historique et critique de la presse périodique française...* (Paris: Firmin-Didot frères, 1866).

4. Daru, *Notions statistiques sur la librairie*, pp. 29–30.

5. Dupin, *Forces productives et commerciales*, pp. xvi–xvii.

French economy in the same period that saw a steady expansion in the social surplus accruing to bourgeois property owners.[6] Although there was no actual "take off" into sustained industrial growth, the long term, regular growth in total French production was as evident during the constitutional monarchies as during any other period between 1700 and 1945. This global expansion fostered a comparable development in the production of books, including its various subsidiaries in the manufacture of ink and paper as well as printing and bookbinding. Increase in the consumption of paper for printing, for example, rose from 4.1 percent to 5.9 percent annually from 1820 to 1840.[7] In such a remarkable context, the romantic book trade loomed considerably larger than that of the eighteenth-century Enlightenment, tied as the latter was to a more anachronistic economy.

Examination of the number of titles published each year indicates to what extent the book trade shared in this general trend during the early nineteenth century.[8] Between the Empire and the Second Republic the number of new books listed in the *Bibliographie de la France* doubled, despite important fluctuations around 1830, 1839, and 1847, years of serious economic difficulties. The largest increase occurred during the Restoration, from only 2,547 titles in 1814, to 8,273 in 1826, the peak for the entire first half of the century. Some of this growth, to be sure, owed to the frequent practice among *libraires* of announcing each volume of

6. See the good synthesis of issues in the economic history of nineteenth-century France by Tom Kemp, *Economic Forces in French History* (London: Dobson, [1971]), pp. 106–141.

7. Markovitch, *Industrie française de 1789 à 1964*, 4:71–72.

8. The numbers of new titles listed in the *Bibliographie de la France* are as follows:

1814: 2,547	1823: 5,893	1832 6,478	1841: 6,300
1815: 3,357	1824: 6,974	1833: 7,011	1842: 6,445
1816: 3,763	1825: 7,605	1834: 7,125	1843: 6,176
1817: 4,046	1826: 8,273	1835: 6,700	1844: 6,577
1818: 4,837	1827: 8,198	1836: 6,632	1845: 6,521
1819: 4,568	1828: 7,616	1837: 6,417	1846: 5,916
1820: 4,881	1829: 7,823	1838: 6,603	1847: 5,530
1821: 5,499	1830: 6,739	1839: 6,186	1848: 7,234
1822: 5,824	1831: 6,180	1840: 6,369	

See also the graphs indicating publishing growth in the nineteenth century, in Zoltowski, "Les cycles de la création intellectuelle et artistique," p. 192; and Julien Cain et al., *Le livre français: hier, aujourd'hui, demain* (Paris: Imprimerie Nationale, 1972), pp. 58–59.

Note should be made of the variations in the numbers of titles listed as a consequence of uneven enforcement of the press laws. The total for 1826 may be too high, while that for 1830 may be too low, more because of politics than because of the economy. See Bellos, "Le marché du livre à l'époque romantique," pp. 648–51.

multivolumed titles as separate books and of advertising false re-editions of slow selling titles.[9] But as a crude indicator of growth, assuming that such deceit was constant over time and that lapses in administrative surveillance were important only in 1830, the number of books published annually shows clearly a rapid rise to the end of the Restoration and then a halting pace during the Orleanist Monarchy when sharp competition with the press limited the appearance of new titles (see Figure 5.1).[10]

FIGURE 5.1

The Numbers of New Titles Published in France, 1814–1848

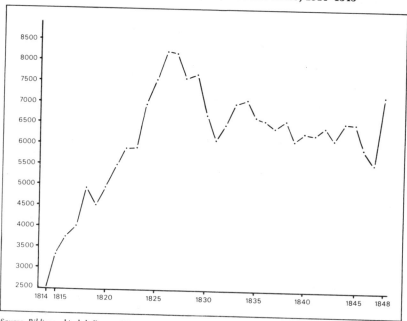

Source: *Bibliographie de la France,* 1814–1848.

Moreover, it is interesting to note the brief recuperation after the July revolution at the height of the romantic movement—a comparable development does not occur until the politically charged atmosphere of 1848. Romanticism thus shared in both a relative and an absolute increase

9. Fouque, *De quelques abus en librairie,* pp. 9, 12, 21.

10. For discussion of the competition between the press and the book, see Orecchioni, "Presse, livre et littérature au XIXe siècle." See also the corresponding rise in the production runs of newspapers in Charles Ledré, *La presse à l'assaut de la monarchie,* 1815–1848 (Paris: Colin, [1960]), pp. 242–45.

in titles published before 1827 and after 1833 during significant economic resurgences nationally.

Nevertheless, the total number of books published annually from 1814 to 1848 can only be an approximate measure of an expanding book trade.[11] Such undiscriminating figures fail to show the important variations among the genres that contemporaries were quick to note in their numerous accounts of literary production. During the Restoration these observers were proud to note the relative sophistication of readers' habits. The baron Dupin, for one, praised not only the increase in intellectual activity measured by the number of titles, but also the rise in their apparent quality.[12] There was a new interest in history, he noted, whose proportion among the total number of titles rose from less than 13 percent in 1812, to more than 46 percent in 1826. "All aspects of human knowledge are studied more today," the baron remarked in another glowing account of the positive influence of a renewed economy after the disastrous years during the Empire.[13] He concluded that the relative relaxation of political preoccupations conjoined with industrial growth to make possible this sophisticated intellectual activity.

Similar observations were made by less statistically minded writers. Edgar Quinet the romantic philosopher described the revived intellectual climate in the first years of the Restoration as "a sort of intoxication of reawakened thought, an unappeased thirst of the soul after years in the desert of the Empire. All of this combined with a consuming desire to produce, to create, to accomplish something in the midst of a still empty world."[14] It was no accident that this serious creative spirit coincided with the number of new titles and the literary tolerance of the new regime. In the year 1825, perhaps the culmination of the Bourbon Restoration, politically and economically, E.-J. Delécluze also noted that "the taste of readers, the fervor which preceded even the new literature, exploded in all their vivacity."[15] Such marked the enthusiasm with which many writers greeted the broader range of creative expression possible in the romantic period.

Much of the renewed intellectual endeavor, especially the politically sensitive, stemmed directly from a censorship relatively lax compared to that of the Empire. The Restoration thus permitted massive

11. Bellos, "The *Bibliographie de la France* and its Sources"; and "Le marché du livre à l'époque romantique," p. 651.

12. Dupin, *Forces productives et commerciales*, p. xvii.

13. Dupin, *Situation progressive des forces de la France depuis 1814*, p. 60.

14. Edgar Quinet, *Histoire de mes idées, autobiographie. Documents inédits* (Paris: Germer-Baillière, [1878]), p. 241.

15. Delécluze, *Souvenirs de soixante années*, p. 279.

editions of Enlightenment authors, published more as political state-
ments against the regime than as affirmations of reawakened thought
among serious writers.[16] Where authors of similarly liberal views during
the Napoleonic Empire had been harried out of the country, like Madame
de Staël, they could now live, write, and publish their contrary opinion in
France, at least covertly like Paul-Louis Courier. Its unpredictability
aside, the political atmosphere after the Empire surely stimulated many
authors to share in the expanding book trade, however much of it was still
given over to classical works for a relatively enlightened audience. This
new climate and the economic growth that accompanied it would benefit
writers and their publishers even more after 1830 when the romantic
movement was prominent.

Such serious tastes did not last; other commentaries remarked a
contrary development among the titles produced in the period. The new
vogue of the popular novel posed a genuine challenge to more respectable
literary works as early as the Restoration.[17] Alexandre Pigoreau, an important bookseller to lending libraries in the city, lamented the rapid
rise in fiction with the publication of his first catalog in 1821: "We must
carry popular novels, if I may express myself thus, since people wish to
read novels . . . especially the current novels, the most insipid productions."[18] Another Paris bookseller, C.-L. Lesur stated that a new era
of prose fiction was replacing the golden age of poetry, for the *roman noir*
enjoyed more public favor than the elegy.[19] Poetry production, he noted,
peaked in 1827; verse accounted for 537 titles, the novel only 295. From
then on, poetry slid so quickly that by 1831, the classically minded Lesur
complained that only two branches of literature remained in Paris: the
theater and the novel. As for the latter, it flourished to a degree "no man
can explain and no society can stand."[20]

The genre indexes in the back of annual editions of the *Bibliographie de la France* show this trend clearly. A new popular genre by the
standards of the early nineteenth century, the novel rose irregularly from
only 210 titles in 1820, to more than 400 in 1838, its highest point in the
romantic book trade. This was a significant increase from 4.3 to 5.9 per-

16. See Salvan, "Un moment de la diffusion du livre," pp. 173–74.

17. See discussion of the growth in prose fiction in George, *French Romanticism*,
pp. 37–58.

18. Pigoreau, *Petite bibliographie biographico-romancière*, 2:iii–iv. Also note this
bookseller's recognition of a growing trend in the trade, esp. in Supplements 7–10, July 20,
1824–August 30, 1825.

19. C.-L. Lesur, *Annuaire historique universel pour 1825...* (Paris: Thoisnier-
Desplaces, 1826), p. 863.

20. Lesur, *Annuaire historique universel pour 1831*, p. 333.

cent of all titles published in the same period. Moreover, in 1836 the vogue of the *roman-feuilleton* in the newspapers arrived and began to divert even more attention away from "respectable" literature in books to popular prose fiction in the press. Similar trends in the other genres occurred as well; without their former neo-classical constraints, poetry turned more anecdotal, while drama became more melodramatic. A new popular taste was inexorably affecting production in the book trade. *Libraires* accommodated ever larger numbers of less sophisticated readers in the romantic period, though book publishing appeared a bastion of elite culture again in the 1840s thanks to the extraordinary success of the press.[21] By then, however, the drift of published titles available in all forms had moved toward not only more numerous, but also less serious literature, one suited to a whole new audience as shown in Chapter 2.

What role did the romantic movement play in this apparent growth in more popular literature? Did romanticism necessarily foster such a development? Whether or not it did, literary and social critics then were quick to identify the new literature with these trends. Commented one in the *Globe*, "The romantics, in all the brashness of youth, in all the proud security of a growing success, see themselves multiplied every day in all the formats."[22] In 1845 Charles Louandre remarked that all the great romantic poets, "those who inhabited the peaks of the mythological mountain, have realized that they wish to descend, and we find nearly all of them tracing their furrows in the humble fields of prose."[23] Unfortunately, their more prosaic productions failed to maintain the high standards of their poetry, Louandre complained, since the world of fiction invariably encouraged authors to write a marketable commodity instead of a work of art.[24] The movement viewed in this way laid it open to the neo-classicist's accusations that it was debasing the exalted world of letters by making it a republic for writers and readers alike.

This was true not only for the *roman-feuilleton*, but also for the older gothic novel whose reputation often blended with that of romantic works. The popularity of the historical novel *à la* Walter Scott during the Restoration rivaled that of the ghoulish *roman noir*. Combining the gothic with the historical, one anonymous novel in 1826 was actually entitled, *Les ombres sanglantes, galerie funèbre des prodiges, événemens* [sic]

21. See Charles Louandre, "Statistique littéraire de la production intellectuelle en France depuis quinze ans," *Revue des deux mondes* 20(1847),5:257–58; and chart of novel production in Marguerite Iknayan, *The Idea of the Novel in France: The Critical Reaction, 1815–1848* (Geneva: Droz, 1961), p. 185.

22. Cited in Salvan, "Un moment de la diffusion du livre," p. 173.

23. Louandre, "Statistique littéraire," p. 677.

24. *Ibid.*, pp. 687–88.

merveilleux, apparitions nocturnes, songes épouvantables, délits mystérieux, phénomènes terribles, forfaits historiques . . . . The romantics' melodramatic success at the boulevard theaters certainly did not improve their reputation for creating and indeed promoting the publication of such popular *nouveautés*. With their reputed vulgarity, the authors in the new literature were believed to have published more and more broadly than the neo-classical creators of serious works; the apparent contrast in the nature of their achievements was evidence enough for many contemporaries.[25]

This may well be true. Besides the pervasiveness of the romantic vogue in the *Bibliographie de la France*—a good indication of its diffusion among authors—random samples sharing in the new movement were very likely to be printed in editions larger than nonromantic titles. Only the production figures indicate a slight variation in time and genre that reveals a pattern more complex than the linear growth in the overall means and medians of the sampled titles (see Table 5.1). The romantics by this evidence achieved a bright but brief moment of glory. In the number of copies printed of each title, the height of romanticism's success arrived in 1827, seven years earlier than that of their diffusion in the catalogs. By 1827 the mean edition size of romantic titles exceeded that of nonromantic works in all genres, except poetry where the fashion never seems to have surpassed the production of popular *chansonniers* and political verse. Romantic fiction and history, on the other hand, were all published very early. In 1820 they were more likely to be printed in editions larger than other works, indicating that the historical novels and dramatic histories of the Middle Ages were of interest earlier than the *drame* and freer verse. (This may have been because the neo-classical rules were more firmly established in poetry and drama.)

But when the fashion reached its peak in the theater in 1834, the movement as a whole was already facing severe competition from popular titles in poetry, fiction, and history no longer using its conventions. By 1841 editions in the movement were eclipsed in all genres but history which continued to maintain interest in its easily popularized accounts of Napoleon and the Middle Ages. Undoubtedly the rapid growth of the Napoleonic legend during the 1840s, from the return of the Emperor's ashes to the election of his nephew, fostered one strand of romantic history well past the movement's demise as a whole. Nevertheless, the production figures still show the same relative rise and decline that made popular romanticism a temporary mode. It lost an increasing portion of an expanding market, after 1834, to essentially nonromantic

25. See such a view of the work by Victor Hugo in Alfred Nettement, *Etudes critiques sur le feuilleton roman* (Paris: Perrodil, 1845), 1:10–11.

TABLE 5.1
Mean and Median Edition Sizes of Sampled

Year		Poetry			Drama		
		Mean	N	Median	Mean	N	Median
1820	Romantic	—	0	—	1,000	1	1,000
	Nonromantic	688	25	500	1,030	24	1,000
1827	Romantic	500	3	300	1,000	4	1,000
	Nonromantic	700	17	500	871	19	500
1834	Romantic	1,094	7	700	1,895	12	2,000
	Nonromantic	2,540	16	900	1,392	18	2,000
1841	Romantic	700	3	1,000	2,000	2	2,000
	Nonromantic	2,850	20	1,000	2,259	25	2,000

Source: A.N.F.[18] II*7, 14, 24, 29. "Déclarations des Imprimeurs," for edition sizes of titles sampled from the *Bibliographie* equal to the averages (plus or minus 10 percent), indicating a wide dispersion around the means.

works whose editions seemed to grow at the expense of the no longer "new" literature.

Thus the brief romantic reputation as popular *nouveauté* appears to be justified by these publication figures. They confirm what was strongly suggested by the samples from the *Bibliographie de la France* and other evidence on their authors and publishers, namely, the temporary but significant vogue of romanticism in France. As impressive as these data appear, however, they do not exhaust all the sources available on the movement's impact on the literary world of Paris during the constitutional monarchies. Moreover, production only implies distribution; a title printed does not necessarily mean a title bought. *Libraires* were unable to sell nearly 20 percent of all new books they received each year.[26] Nor did *libraires, nouveauté* retailers, *cabinets de lecture, étalagistes,* and *colporteurs*—the city's primarily agents of literary distribution—all offer the same titles. These considerations require a closer look at the problem of distribution to qualify the remarkable pattern of evidence on the production of romantic works.

Bookselling, for one, appears to remain generally devoted to elite literature throughout this period. Examination of the few privately printed catalogs extant shows that a surprisingly high percentage of their holdings was given over to serious titles at the usual high prices. For example, Firmin Didot listed more than 2,000 titles at 7 fr. 50 in 1830,

26. Daru, *Notions statistiques sur la librairie*, p. 29.

Romantic and Nonromantic Titles, by Genre, 1820–1841

Fiction			History			Total		
Mean	N	Median	Mean	N	Median	Mean	N	Median
1,600	5	1,500	3,000	1	3,000	1,429	7	1,250
1,319	25	1,000	1,360	26	1,000	1,100	100	1,000
1,313	8	1,000	1,870	5	1,000	1,270	20	1,000
1,150	13	1,000	1,246	17	1,000	979	66	750
1,665	10	1,000	2,583	6	3,000	1,778	35	1,500
1,585	13	750	2,608	13	2,500	1,983	60	1,450
1,883	6	1,500	2,975	8	2,000	2,168	19	1,750
2,032	23	1,500	2,657	14	2,000	2,465	82	1,750

de la France and classified by romantic influence (Appendix A). Standard deviations in nearly all cases were approximately

more than twice an average *journalier's* daily wage.[27] (Of these, only 32, more than half of which were Scott's historical novels, could be considered at all influenced by romanticism.) His vast range of offerings resembled the more erudite sections of the *Bibliographie de la France* where titles were represented in nearly every subject, from theology to history, of interest to a very limited audience. Moreover, most *libraires* were concentrated in only three of the city's twelve *arrondissements*—near the universities on the left bank and in the Palais-Royal on the right. Their businesses there catered to clientele, living in the Faubourgs Saint-Germain and Saint-Honoré, far wealthier and more sophisticated than elsewhere in the city.[28] As Alphonse Karr noted in 1835, "older booksellers were those who assured their landlords the most certain and regular rents."[29]

27. Firmin Didot frères, *Catalogue* (Paris: F. Didot frères, 1830). See also *Recueil des catalogues et des prospectus des libraires de Paris, 1806–1831* (Paris: Bibliothèque Nationale, [n.d.]); Barois, *Catalogue...* (Paris: Silvestre, 1838); LeNormant, *Livres d'assortement...* (Paris: LeNormant, [n.d.]); and J. Techener, *Bulletin du bibliophile* (Paris: Techener, 1834–). Nearly all these various catalogs reveal collections similar to the Didots'.

28. See Sébastien Bottin, *Almanach du commerce de Paris...* (Paris: Bottin, 1819–38) for extensive though incomplete listings of Paris *libraires* and their addresses in the period.

29. Alphonse Karr, "Imprimeurs, libraires, bouquinistes, cabinets de lecture," in *Nouveau tableau de Paris au XIXᵉ siècle* (Paris: Mme. Vve. Charles Bechet et al., 1835),5:67.

Nevertheless, rising competition and specialization among Parisian *libraires* made them increasingly less secure in their growing dependence upon a more diverse readership. Not only did the growth in the number of booksellers keep ahead of the expansion in the city's population, but they were found more frequently in plebeian areas of Paris, especially in the form of *nouveauté* retailers, small shopkeepers selling like colporters much more than books in nearly every *arrondissement* in the city.[30] These less reputable "booksellers" often shared their poor public esteem with licensed *libraires* in the Palais-Royal who sold many of the same literary works by new authors, major and minor. And their simpler formats and cheaper prices discredited their promoters in the eyes of the older, more established *libraires* dealing in the luxury trade.[31] But without more complete lists of the books offered by booksellers, old and new, it is difficult to ascertain with any certainty the influence of romanticism on their trade or the movement's diffusion among different kinds of readers. Too few of their catalogs are extant for systematic analysis.

Another approach to the literary market may be found in an examination of the wills left by those who bought enough books to leave records of their purchases. Many members of the middle classes detailed their private libraries in the city's notarial records. The Parisian bourgeoisie, perhaps 20 percent of the population by one estimate, maintained substantial collections. Analysis of these libraries by Adeline Daumard indicates, however, that while well over half of the middle classes in the city bought complete collections of the seventeenth- and eighteenth-century classics during the Restoration, very few of them risked money on "new" authors (see Table 5.2). Only 14 percent of the private libraries that Daumard studied contained works by Chateaubriand, while Madame de Staël and Béranger appeared in less than 4 percent. Only a wealthy elite paying more than 500 francs in taxes had titles by living authors in significant numbers.[32] The romantics do not seem to have reached most of the middle classes, probably because the new literature was not perceived to be respectable enough to an increasingly class-conscious elite.

30. *Ibid.*, pp. 73–74. See also the account of the Palais-Royal as a center for disreputable *nouveautés* in Balzac, *La comédie ʾhumaine*, 5:356–61; A. and W. Galignani, *Galignani's Paris Guide* (Paris: Galignani, 1822), p. 19; and Perry, "Publishers, Politics, and the Discovery of the Popular Reader," for a fuller discussion of this phenomenon.

31. Most older *libraires* calling for renewed regulation of the trade were actually referring to these *nouveauté* retailers who posed a threat to their business. See discussion of this conflict between old and new men in the trade in Chapter 4, pp. 118–19.

32. Daumard, *La bourgeoisie parisienne de 1815 à 1848* (Paris: S.E.V.P.E.N., 1963), pp. 353–54.

TABLE 5.2
Percentages of Middle-Class Occupational Groups
Owning Books, 1815–1848

Occupation	With Libraries	With Some Books
Boutiquiers	6.3%	2.7%
Négociants	35.5	4.9
Professions libérales	60.4	—
Employés diverses	15.9	—
Employés d'Etat	36.9	2.7
Fonctionnaires	51.1	—

Source: Adeline Daumard, *Les bourgeois de Paris au XIXe siècle* (Paris: Flammarion, 1970), p. 75. Based on a survey of "Inventaires après décès" in Paris.

These figures are unfortunately obscured by *notaires'* frequent failures to itemize in the wills. For reasons of apparent value, books were grouped by format and binding, not by author and title. Many books were excluded completely, since relatives with different tastes often thought them worthless. However revealing in some ways, studies of *notaires'* inventories do not give a full picture of the book market, much less the diffusion of romantic titles among the vast majority of readers. In the period most were too poor to leave very much for family survivors; some 80 percent of Paris had to be buried at public expense.[33] Not only do notarial records omit details about the titles held by will-making Parisians, but they also overemphasize the wealthiest portion of the population, one far from representative in its literary tastes.

Perhaps a better approach to discovering what kinds of books Parisians purchased from their *libraires* lies in the catalogs of book auctions.[34] Many private libraries were sold when the head of the family passed away, and their contents are detailed in thousands of lists printed to inform prospective buyers of the sale. But in 22 randomly selected catalogs totaling over 13,000 titles auctioned between 1824 and 1830, a trend similar to that evident in the wills appears; nearly 20 percent were classical titles in both Greek and Latin as well as in French translation. Less than 3 percent were by recognizable romantic authors. Although most of these works were purchased before romanticism's notoriety, they

33. Daumard, "Le peuple dans la société française à l'époque romantique," p. 25.

34. See the uncatalogued △ series at the Bibliothèque Nationale, containing thousands of book auction catalogs from the eighteenth to the twentieth centuries in Paris. This is the same series used by Daniel Mornet in his assessment of the diffusion of Enlightenment titles in the eighteenth century. See his "Les enseignements des bibliothèques privées, 1750–1780," for discussion of their value and contents.

were resold in the early romantic period and thus constituted a part of the city's literary market.

Even after 1830 the percentages were not significantly different. Of 35 catalogs printed from 1831 to 1838, notable romantic titles still made up less than 4 percent of 9,089 items listed for sale, even though the proportion of Greek and Latin classics declined to only 12 percent. Serious literature remained paramount. The *belles lettres* rose less than 2 percent among the listings in the later catalogs; history claimed well over a third of the collections (see Table 5.3). Most books in the large private

TABLE 5.3
Percentages of Titles in Auctioned Libraries,
By Subject, 1824–1838

Subject	1824–1830	1831–1838
Theology and Jurisprudence	13.4%	6.2%
Sciences and Arts	22.6	25.9
Belles Lettres	27.6	29.1
History	36.4	38.8

Source: Fifty-seven randomly sampled catalogs of libraries auctioned in Paris, 1824–1838, △ series, Bibliothèque Nationale.

libraries during the constitutional monarchies reflected the same range of titles available in the *Bibliographie de la France* and the elite bookstores. As the *libraires'* best individual customers, these wealthy men and women remained unmoved by the promotion of romantic works by more enterprising publishers before and after the July revolution, perhaps for the same reasons that the notarial records indicate the same classical and neo-classical preference for expensive and well-bound books: class status.

Such evidence of the elite nature of Parisian booksellers, however, still poses the problem of representativeness. It would, in fact, be wrong to conclude from an analysis of the book collections of such a very special minority what the book trade sold in the romantic period. Not all booksellers catered to the interests of the wealthy, classically educated middle classes in Paris. As noted in Chapter 4, the differences between older *libraires* and newer retailers of *nouveautés* were immense.[35] As contemporary observers also noted, the book trade spanned widely divergent interests, tastes, and clientele, from the respectable academic market on the left bank to the less reputable merchandising on the right.[36] More-

35. See discussion of various merchandise by *libraires* in Chapter 4, pp. 117–18.

36. See contemporary accounts of this diversity in the Paris book trade summarized acerbically in Rossignol Passe-Partout (Auguste Imbert), *Voyage autour du pont-neuf, et promenade sur le quai aux fleurs* (Paris: Imbert, 1824), pp. 3–44.

over, these private libraries actually reflected trends of a much earlier period, that is, when the deceased originally purchased his books at the turn of the century, well before their resale during the Restoration and Orleanist monarchies. The very fact that the titles had to be auctioned to the general public indicates what little value these collections had for Parisian *libraires*.

Even as literature, the books from private libraries do not always provide an accurate indication of their owners' tastes, since many like Balzac's César Birotteau probably never read the books in their possession.[37] Impressive, well-bound volumes served the dual purpose of interior decoration as expensive knick-knacks for empty shelves, and of status symbols for socially aspiring *arrivistes* to the middle classes. The mania to buy books for the sake of collecting existed then as it does today even among scholars. Consequently, the image of a book trade in Paris given exclusively to serious classical works for an urban elite, reflected in these catalogs, is misleading. More information about the owners, their interests, their motives, their occupations, and their social status, as well as the *libraires* from whom they acquired their books is needed before any further conclusions may be drawn about the literary marketplace in the romantic period.[38]

RENTING AND HAWKING BOOKS

Actually the *libraire*'s most important customer at the time was not the individual but the *cabinet de lecture*. Lending libraries constituted not only the book trade's most regular clientele for old and new titles, but also the public's most accessible source of books.[39] In the early nineteenth century, when public libraries remained the bastion of exclusive interests, the cabinets rented books "by the month, by the year, by the sitting, by the volume, or by the day" for nominal fees, often as little as 10

37. Balzac, *La comédie humaine*, 5:166.

38. See Mornet, "Les enseignements des bibliothèques privées, 1750–1780," pp. 449–53; and the more intensive study of Parisian booksellers and their market in Perry, "Publishers, Politics, and the Discovery of the Popular Reader."

39. Important studies of the *cabinets de lecture* are M. Tirol, "Les cabinets de lecture en France, 1800–1850," *Revue des bibliothèques* 33(1926),77–98, 198–224, 401–423; 34(1927),13–25; Claude Pichois, "Pour une sociologie des faits littéraires. Les cabinets de lecture à Paris durant la première moitié du XIX e siècle," *Annales: E.S.C.* 14(1959),3:521–34; H. E. Whitmore, "The *Cabinets de Lecture* in France, 1800–1850"; and Françoise Parent, "Les cabinets de lecture dans Paris: pratiques culturelles et espace social sous la Restauration," *Annales: E.S.C.* 34(1979),5:1016–38.

centimes per title.[40] This made access to books during the Restoration cheaper than a kilo loaf of bread, well within the means of the Parisian day-laborer who normally earned more than two francs a day. This was also well before booksellers dropped their prices and trimmed the number volumes per title, especially after Charpentier offered the first *nouveauté* for 3 fr. 50 in 1838.[41] Despite the many multivolumed novels published exclusively for the cabinets that rented not by the title but by the volume, cabinets served as an important cultural intermediary, making available to a large audience anxious for reading material the many books offered by booksellers who were still overpricing their products.

Parisian cabinets were even more modest and numerous than bookstores. Since no *brevet* and little capital were required, widows and retired officers on half pay frequently set up business when their fortunes turned for the worse, according to police records.[42] In one 1829 report to the Ministry of the Interior, seven petitioners for permission to operate cabinets in Paris included an artillery officer's widow, a wigmaker, a retired captain of the Hussars, and other equally modest middleclass figures of "good reputation" whose "morals, politics, even religion" appealed to the authorities.[43] Official reports in Sébastien Bottin's *Almanach du commerce de Paris* indicate that there were only 32 cabinets in 1820, 150 in 1830, 189 in 1840, and 226 in 1850, after which date they declined in number as rapidly as they had appeared. Other sources were more sensitive to the many unregistered operations throughout the city, a problem recognized by the police. The actual number before mid-century was much higher: one recent historian identified and documented 463 for the Restoration alone.[44] Although most, like the bookstores, were located near the Palais-Royal and the universities, they existed primarily on the east-west, north-south thoroughfares in Paris to create, by such a distribution, an even greater impact than absolute numbers imply (see Figure 5.2).

40. Joseph Pain "Les cabinets de lecture," *Nouveaux tableaux de Paris, ou observations sur les moeurs et usages des parisiens au commencement du XIX*e *siècle...* (Paris: Pillet ainé, 1828),1:69. See also amusing accounts of public libraries in Paul Lacroix, dit Jacob le bibliophile, *Dissertation sur quelques points curieux de l'histoire de France: sur les bibliotheques de Paris* (Paris: Techener, 1840); and Louandre, "La bibliothèque royale et les bibliothèques publiques," *Revue des deux mondes* 13(1846),3:1045-67.

41. Note the drop in the price index calculated by Markovitch in the cost of books and newspapers from 1,059.0 in 1803–12, to 347.6 in 1835–44 (Base 1905–1913=100). See Table 5 in the appendix to *Industrie française*, vol. 3.

42. See A.N.F[18]2162 bis "Cabinets de Lecture. Demandes d'Autorisation, 1816–1850," in which such cases are found.

43. *Ibid.*

44. Parent, "Les cabinets de lecture dans Paris," p. 1021.

FIGURE 5.2

The Distribution of 463 Lending Libraries in Paris, 1815–1830

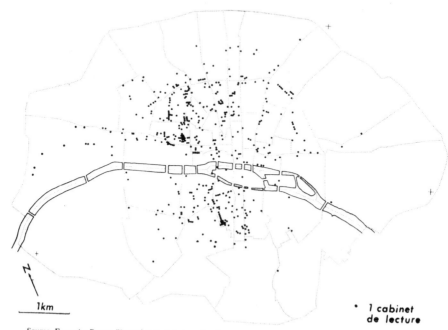

1km

• 1 cabinet
de lecture

Source: Françoise Parent, "Les cabinets de lecture dans Paris: pratiques culturelles et espace social sous la Restauration," *Annales: E.S.C.* 34,5(1979): 1020.

Few lending libraries attained the prestige of Madame Cardinal on the rue des Canettes, perhaps the best known cabinet of the period that maintained a substantial collection of over 20,000 well-chosen titles.[45] (Her valuable collection of first editions, including the romantics, eventually was bought for the library at the University of Louvain, unfortunately lost during World War II.) Most cabinets in the early nineteenth century offered only 5,000 titles in one or two rooms furnished with "a table, a stuffed chair, a fire, . . . some pens, paper, and ink, and tobacco in the neighboring shops . . . each *habitué* with his own seat."[46] Many cabinets, in fact, were even less elaborate, providing books or newspapers only and no place to read them. Some set up operations in parks and near cafés with little more than a few crudely constructed shelves and the titles

45. See Claire Girou de Buzareingues, "Les cabinets de lecture et les débuts de l'époque romantique," *Bulletin de la librairie ancienne et moderne* 140(1971),220–25.

46. Karr, "Imprimeurs, libraires, bouquinistes, cabinets de lecture," pp. 71–72. An amusing account is a novel, Mathurin-Joseph Brisset, *Le cabinet de lecture* (Paris: Magen, 1843), 2 vols.

for rent by the hour. Such modest circumstances must have invited a wide circle of readers from nearly every social class in the city, a fact attested to by the various satires of the cabinet clientele written as early as the First Empire.[47] One lithograph (ca. 1840) by Félix Regamey detailed a worker in his smock and a domestic with her apron, besides better-heeled borrowers, waiting to return or take out books in a lending library.

Lending libraries generally specialized in one genre: the *nouveauté*, whose reputation frequently blurred with that of the romantics according to many observers.[48] For Alexandre Pigoreau the *libraire*, the most successful rental collection was at least two-thirds romance, nearly all by comparatively recent authors. Yet relatively few of his recommendations early in the romantic period included recognizable leaders in the new literature. Rather, Pigoreau's formula for a successful *boutique à lire* called for titles by

> Richardson, Fielding, Cervantes, LeSage, Prévost, LaPlace; Mme Guénard, Mme de Bon, Mme Voïard [*sic*] (esteemed for their translations); Mme Brayer de Saint-Léon (besides her novels, she has given us excellent translations); Ducray-Duminil, Florian, Montjoie [*sic*], Pigault-Lebrun, Legay, Auguste Lafontaine, Walter Scott, Lord Byron (these three authors are novelists [*sic*] now in fashion); Mmes Ann Radcliffe, Maria Roche, Bennett, Edgeworth, Helme, Jane Porter, Maria Porter, etc.[49]

Only the translations of Scott and Byron represented romantic literature in Pigoreau's suggestions, and were far from defining a literary "movement" in the lending libraries.

In 1821, then, when Pigoreau was writing, the movement was not a major factor in the cabinets. But much later in the Third Republic, Armand de Pontmartin noted in his memoirs how one keeper, Malvina Vermot on the place de l'Odéon during the July Monarchy, "represented the most refined example of a species long extinct today: the mistress of the lending library, living on equal footing with her clientele and discussing the merits of *Claire d'Albe*, of *Delphine*, of *Dernier jour d'un condamné*, of *Bug Jargal*," among the many important romantic titles

47. See the diverse social mixture of cabinet frequenters in Robert (Louis Solvet), *Le cabinet de lecture*, pièce satirique (Paris: Imp. Egron, 1808); and Brisset, *Le cabinet de lecture*, vol. 1., chpt. 1. See a review of the literary evidence on this problem in Whitmore, "Readers, Writers, and Literary Taste in the Early 1830s: The *Cabinet de Lecture* as Focal Point," *Journal of Library History* 13(1978),2:119–30.

48. E.g., see Louandre's judgement of Hugo's *Cromwell* in "Statistique littéraire," p. 691.

49. Pigoreau, *Petite bibliographie biographico-romancière*, 3:iv–v.

maintained in her collection.[50] According to contemporary accounts many such cabinets became centers for the romantic literature, entertaining its authors as well as stocking their latest books, in much the same way Madame Cardinal threw open her doors to the leaders of the movement.[51] Given the neo-classical exclusiveness of many salons, academies, and booksellers in the period, the more accessible lending libraries naturally served the romantics, albeit on a much more modest scale.

How well were romantic works actually represented in the lending libraries? Did the movement prevail any more there than it did in the bookstores or in private collections? In the printed catalogs extant from the constitutional monarchies, romantic authors were indeed prominently featured.[52] Of 16 catalogs dated between 1826 and 1831, works by Nodier appeared in 15; Chateaubriand, 13; Hugo and Scott, 12; de Staël and Byron, 10; Vigny, 9; Schiller, 7; Mérimée, 5; Lamartine, 4; among others representative of the new conventions. After 1830 works from the literary movement appear even more prominently. In 26 catalogs printed before 1842, all had pieces by Hugo, Balzac and Scott; 25 by Nodier, 23 by Mérimée, Sand, and de Staël, and 22 by Chateaubriand and Stendhal (whose name was often misspelled). The movement found its home in the lending libraries of Paris.

Although popular novels far outweighed those by the romantics, the cabinets were open to the new trend in literature in numbers entirely disproportionate to their share of the book trade. Romantic poetry, especially, appeared in catalogs much more frequently than expected from their dismally small editions. Pétrus Borel was listed in 9 of the catalogs dated after 1831, Desbordes-Valmore 13, even though their works rarely exceeded 300 copies. But romantics were generally represented less by poetry or drama than by fiction. Historical novels appeared in catalogs as often as popular novels, despite their editions that were little larger than the average for the genre. Thus the romantic fashion was perhaps better known by its contemporaries than studies of the book trade proper suggest. The romantics formed an important part of the holdings of Parisian cabinets; in light of their number, diversity, and accessibility to a socially

50. A. A. J. M. de Pontmartin, Mes mémoires, enfance et jeunesse (Paris: Calmann Lévy, 1886),2:111–12.

51. Girou de Buzareingues, "Les cabinets de lecture et les débuts de l'époque romantique," pp. 244–25.

52. Bibliothèque Nationale series Q²⁸. "Catalogues des Cabinets de Lecture." Approximately thirty boxes of catalogs, dating from the eighteenth to the twentieth centuries, are available but uncataloged at the Bibliothèque. Unfortunately, of the seventy-five or so catalogs of lending libraires in Paris dated between 1826 and 1843, many are supplements to nonexistent catalogs which seriously handicap a detailed investigation of their collections.

heterogeneous clientele, the movement must have reached a broad and large audience after all.

But only briefly, for the percentage of other *nouveautés* available in the lending libraries began to rise after 1838. The supplements issued subsequently contained fewer and fewer recognizable romantic titles. As literary tastes changed, keepers of rental libraries added new titles to stay abreast of the new demand for works no longer so obviously influenced by romanticism. One *libraire*, for example, Piltan on the rue des Saints Pères, offered a collection nearly 5 percent of which consisted of titles by leading romantic writers in 1832. In 1838 these rose to 8 percent.[53] But his collection was still 8 percent romantic two years later after a substantial addition to his stock; by 1840, this proportion in Piltan's catalog, like those of his many colleagues, gave way to titles far removed from the movement's influence. Meanwhile, the vogue of *romans-feuilletons* not reflected in the catalog hit the cabinets and diverted public attention away from the books to the newspapers.[54]

Clientele now came not so much to rent books, but to read the latest installment of the serial novels. On some days when Eugène Sue's *Les mystères de Paris* was being carried by the *Journal des débats*, "it was necessary to rent the newspaper several hours in advance" to anticipate the crowd clamoring for the same issue, according to one observer.[55] The consequences of a cheaper, more entertaining press for the movement promoted by the cabinets are obvious: romanticism enjoyed the reputation of popular *nouveauté* only before the 1840s when its vogue was greatest during the heyday of the lending libraries. And its apparent life there, like that of the cabinets themselves, was short—less than twenty years, thanks to the six-sous press and cheaper titles in the book trade. Essentially the same social and economic context that made for the demise of romanticism also forced the lending libraries to close their doors soon after mid-century.[56]

The romantic movement did achieve, however, a wide distribution both in Paris and in the provincial cities where lending libraries were also found. Titles in the new literature quickly reached the shelves of cabinets

---

53. Piltan, *Catalogue des livres du cabinet de lecture*... (Paris: Piltan, 1832), 203 pages; and *Catalogue* (1838), 268 pages.

54. Piltan, *Supplément du catalogue*... (1840), 23 pages.

55. Cited in "Un anglais à Paris," in Charles Simond, *La vie parisienne à travers le XIX e siècle: Paris de 1800 à 1900 d'après les estampes et les mémoires du temps*... (Paris: Plon, Nourrit et cie., 1900–1901), 2:221–22.

56. See reasons for the demise of lending libraries detailed more fully in Whitmore, "The *Cabinets de Lecture* in France, 1800–1850," pp. 135–40.

as far away from Paris as Avignon and Narbonne.[57] In 1832 readers there clamored for romantic *nouveautés*—Byron's poetry, Scott's novels, histories of Napoleon and the Middle Ages—just as they did in Paris. Although the movement's actual leaders proved to be less prominent in the provincial lending libraries than their local imitators, the impact of the romantic *nouveauté*, however late or muted, was felt throughout France as the commercial network slowly reached national proportions, especially when the railroads extended further from Paris.

As Alfred de Musset noted in 1836, the cabinets provided cheap and easy access to a remarkably high percentage of fashionable romantic titles for a wide range of urban readers, both high and low.[58] Here the intellectual values of elites filtered downward to perhaps the most plebeian audience ever reached by a movement in ideas in France, not only influencing the literary usages of other authors, but also promoting a new popular literature for broad public consumption. Lending libraries, in Paris and elsewhere, fulfilled an important function as the primary agents for the distribution of a new literary culture to a large and diverse audience. From the literary and other evidence available, modest shopkeepers, artisans, prosperous journeymen, domestics, as well as financiers, *rentiers,* and their families came to borrow books from the cabinets.[59] Moreover, lending libraries encouraged new and more regular reading habits among such a clientele anxious more for distraction than instruction. Indeed, their literary tastes moved increasingly toward new literary conventions, even at the expense of the romantic movement. Sensitive to the demands of its socially heterogeneous borrowers, the *cabinets de lecture* promoted the development of a new popular literature—of which romanticism was one of its earliest and most significant forms in the nineteenth century.

This is not to say that older, more traditional cultural patterns disappeared completely in the period. *Colporteurs,* for example, still existed in Paris during the constitutional monarchies despite close police surveillance to guard against sedition and pornography.[60] They continued to ply their trade in and out of the cities, selling images, ribbons, mirrors,

---

57. See Pierre Lelièvre, "Livres et libraires en Avignon à l'époque romantique," *Mélanges d'histoire littéraire et de bibliographie offerts à Jean Bonnerot* (Paris: Nizet, 1954), pp. 269–75; and Pierre Jourda, "Un cabinet de prêt en province en 1832," *Revue d'histoire littéraire de la France* 44(1937),540–50.

58. Musset, "Lettres de Dupuis et Cotonet," p. 860.

59. Parent, "Les cabinets de lecture dans Paris," pp. 1035–36.

60. See police reports on *colporteurs, étalagistes,* and *canard* criers in A.N.F¹⁸551 "Bouquinistes et colporteurs. Renseignements généraux, 1818–1850;" and A.N.F.¹⁸554 "Commission de colportage. Circulaires aux préfets, 1822–1862."

and pins besides titles in the *bibliothèque bleue*. In the romantic period, however, colporters and their eighteenth-century literary wares began disappearing from Paris where they enjoyed an increasingly limited market. With a host of other urban distractions in an older cultural tradition—street musicians, acrobats, sword swallowers, dancers, jugglers, magicians, and the like—they competed with a new popular literature in a new social and economic context that would eventually prevail in Paris; by mid-century the penny press and inexpensive fiction attracted nearly enough attention to displace a much older literary world.

Etalagistes faced a similar fate. Booksellers frequently remaindered their unmarketable titles to keepers of stalls on the quays where books normally sold for a franc or less. So long as the Paris book trade retained eighteenth-century production and commercial practices, the *étalagistes* could count on a livelihood, however meager. But the shift to cheaper *nouveautés* and serial novels also made this book trade in the street more and more difficult.[61] *Canards,* on the other hand, represented an early forerunner of the newstabloid and survived longer than other traditional literary forms. Balzac defined them as "a fact with an air of truth, though it was invented to enliven details of a palid city life," an old convention developed in the street sheets relating sensational events to a credulous public.[62] Stories of multiple murders, natural catastrophes, political assassinations, and public executions, these *nouvelles à un sou pièce* provided distraction for urban working classes well into the nineteenth century.[63] And yet the same type of news soon appeared in equally cheap newspapers published after 1860. Eventually the *canards,* like colporters and booksellers in stalls, suffered significantly with the development, production, and distribution of a new popular literature.

How far the romantic movement may have extended into this older, rapidly declining popular milieu cannot be determined with any certainty. Literary evidence indicates that the new literature occasionally appeared in the traditional popular literary world. As a child, Agricol Perdiguier bought saints' lives and adventure stories from itinerant colporters, and as a young man he purchased plays of Voltaire and Racine from *étalagistes* in Bordeaux, Lyon, and Paris. When he was more established in his literary interests, however, he acquired titles by Sophie Gay and Jules Michelet from booksellers in the street.[64] In 1838 when Gosselin, one of Hugo's publishers, went out of business, copies of *Notre*

61. See the list of remaindered classics surrendered to the government as collateral on loans to *libraires* after 1830 in Bossange, *Nouvelles observations...relatives au prêt fait à la librairie...* (Paris: F. Didot frères, 1833).

62. Balzac, *La comédie humaine*, 5:437.

63. Seguin, *Nouvelles à sensation*, Introduction.

64. Perdiguier, *Mémoires d'un compagnon*, pp. 137–38. Note also Jules Michelet's

Dame de Paris were sold by *étalagistes* for one franc per volume.[65] More strikingly, Martin Nadaud the stonemason reported perhaps the widest diffusion of a major romantic work; in 1834 Lamennais' *Paroles d'un croyant* sold for 20 sous throughout Paris and was read avidly by the workers in Nadaud's impromptu school, even though this success was exceptional.[66] Usually the romantics were neither remaindered nor sold cheaply enough to reach such a huge audience.

Similarly, a few *canards* evinced signs of romantic influence. One published during the July Monarchy related a romantically inspired double suicide of a Saint-Simonian couple. The young man declared that "he was at the point of putting an end to the melodrama of his young life, like [Victor] Escousse and his companion [Auguste Labraz] whose courage and virtue he exalted," before shooting himself and his lover in frustration over his failing career as a writer—Escousse and Labraz had done the same when their play *Raymond* failed in 1832 (see Illustration 9). However much in keeping with the movement's most popular conventions, such situations were still far removed from the essence of the new literature. Apparently, romanticism's immediate impact in traditional popular culture appeared but very faintly, tied as the latter was to a rival, illiterate world, dependent on face-to-face collective life, whose values differed widely from those of a lettered, urban elite.

This remote romantic influence can also be seen in studies of titles frequently found in colporter baskets. In 1854 Charles Nisard published the findings of a government commission on popular books peddled primarily in the countryside, though some were also sold in the cities. He found an increasing proportion of the novels enjoyed by the *habitués* of the *cabinets de lecture*: eighteenth-century sentimental and gothic tales as well as a few obvious take-offs on romantic subjects. *Atala et Musacop* (based on Chateaubriand's *Atala* and *René*) and *Mystères de la nouvelle tour de Nesle* (in the vogue of Alexandre Dumas' *La tour de Nesle*) appeared in Nisard's account of colporter fiction.[67] Just as remainders from the Paris book trade began to reach a wider rural audience in the romantic period, more enterprising *libraires* produced new titles especially for the colporters. Nisard cited five publishers in this newer trade, three of whom also regularly published romantic works: Gosselin, Mame, and Levavasseur. This is probably only a coincidence.[68]

---

readings of Walter Scott's novels listed in his *Journal de mes idées*, cited in Maigron, *Le roman historique à l'époque romantique*, p. 413, n. 1.

65. Jullien, *Le romantisme et l'éditeur Renduel*, p. 102.

66. Martin Nadaud, *Les mémoires de Léonard, ancien garçon maçon...* (Paris: Delagrave, [1912]), pp. 106–107.

67. Nisard, *Histoire des livres populaires*, 2:579–81.

68. *Ibid.*, p. 581.

Commis par un Saint-Simonien et une Saint-Simonienne, qui se sont tués tous deux en se tirant un coup de pistolet à bout portant, samedi soir, rue Folie-Méricourt, n° 9, à Paris. Autres détails sur leur fatale résolution, sur les pompes et funérailles qui auront lieu demain au cimetière du Père-Lachaise, à l'occasion de leur inhumation. Discours prononcé par le père Enfantin sur la tombe de ces deux malheureuses victimes de l'amour et de la jalousie. Chants funèbres des Saints-Simoniens, etc. Conversation intéressante entre eux. Lettres extraordinaires qui ont été trouvées sur la table à côté de leur lit.

M. Perret des Isserts, âgé de 22 ans, natif de Saint-Nazaire, près Grenoble, et madame Claire Demart connue par plusieurs publications saint-simoniennes, se sont simultanément suicidés. M. le commissaire de police du quartier, appelé ce matin pour constater les faits, les a trouvés tous deux sur le lit qu'ils partageaient et ne manquent où ils se sont donnés la mort avec un pistolet. Ils avaient pris la précaution d'allumer du charbon au réchaud qui étaient au milieu de l'appartement, afin sans doute que ce moyen ne leur manqua pas, si le premier ne réussissait pas.

Quelques papiers trouvés dans les habits du jeune Perret, peuvent donner une idée de l'exaltation de l'esprit de cet infortuné : dans une lettre adressée à M. Gérin, curé de Saint-Nazaire, il énumère avec une sorte de colère sardonique les reproches qu'il se croyait en droit de faire à la société. Il se plaint du peu de succès de quelques publications dont il était l'auteur, et finit par déclarer qu'il est sur le point de mettre à une fin au drame de sa jeune vie, comme à une fin. Madame Claire Démar était déjà arrivée à cette époque à la vie où les femmes renoncent à plaire et à briller dans le monde; elle était saint-simonienne, et à soutenue par plusieurs écrits que le mariage était une PROSTITUTION.

LES SAINTS-SIMONIENS.
Air du vaudeville des deux Edmonds.

CHARLATANS, adroits hypocrites,
Parés du surnom de Jésuites,
Croyez-moi, pour porter vos coups,
Déguisez-vous;
Mais vous, de Simon gais convives,
Qui riez jusqu'aux sombres rives,
Quand vous donnez un grands repas,
Ne vous déguisez pas.

Vous qui paraissez en justice,
Avec des cœurs nés pour le vice,
Et qui redoutez son courroux,
Déguisez-vous;
Mais vous qu'Enfantin en bon père,
Guide, défend, protège, éclaire,
Dans vos discours, dans vos débats,
Ne vous déguisez pas.

Coquettes qu'on voit, à la ronde,
Tour-à-tour, tromper tout la monde,
Sans en excepter vos époux,
Déguisez-vous;
Mais vous, Sainte Simoniennes,
Qui savez être femmes humaines,
A chacun livrer vos appas,
Ne vous déguisez pas.

Coupables que l'erreur acquitte,
Et dont on vante le mérite,
Quand d'autres sont sous les verroux,
Déguisez-vous;
Mais vous, dont Thémis, qu'on encense,
N'a pas reconnu l'innocence,
Pour mieux cacher votre embarras,
Ne vous déguisez pas.

Simoniens, si votre affaire
Au public ne paraît pas claire,
Que vous soyez sages ou fous,
Déguisez-vous;
Mais si le mal escroquerie,
Chez vous n'est pas de la partie,
Pour amasser force ducats,
Ne vous déguisez pas.

CARACTÈRE DES SAINTS-SIMONIENS.

Air : *Les Gueux.*

Les Saint-Simons
Sont des bons lurons,
Et c'est avec eux
Quon est joyeux.

C'est pour le bonheur du monde
Qu'ils parlent de liberté,
Et qu'ils trinquent, à la ronde,
Avec nous tous, sans fierté.

Les Saint-Simons, etc.

Dans les cafés, les guinguettes,
Quant ils entrent sans façon,
Ils chantent la chansonnelle,
Et pincent le rigodon.

Lorsque l'on se met en route,
Pour revoir un bon parent,
Le chemin de fer, sans doute,
Vous y conduit promptement.

Si notre mère éloignée
Nous appelle de là-bas,
Prenons la route ferrée,
Nous volerons dans ses bras.

Lorsqu'il était à l'école,
Celui qu'on nomme Enfantin,
Sous notre drapeau d'Arcola
S'est battu comme un lutin.

Quand Paris, dans les alarmes,
Vit approcher l'étranger,
Plusieurs d'eux prirent les armes,
Courant au lieu du danger.

On les a vus à l'ouvrage
Travailler soir et matin,
La sueur sur le visage,
Des durillons à la main.

Si des doux fruits de la vigne
Vous avalez sans façon,
Vous pourrez le faire signe,
Ils en boiront un canon.

Ils ne veulent plus de guerre.
Pourquoi tuer nos voisins?
Cela fait pleurer des mères;
Il vaut mieux être cousins.

À Paris, chez GARSON, Fabricant d'Images, rue de la Huchette, n° 25. (*Affranchir.*)

9. "Détails sur un Double Suicide" (ca. 1835). *Canard* from the Bibliothèque Nationale, Paris, in Jean-Pierre Seguin, *Canards du siècle passé* (1969). *Courtesy of Editions Pierre-Horay, Paris.*

Slowly traditional cultural patterns in the countryside were beginning to change. With the growing interest of urban *libraires* in the largely
unexploited rural literary market, new popular titles appeared among the
peasantry for the first time. Long before Louis Hachette purchased the
right to sell his books at train stations during the Second Empire, a
distinctly urban literature, possibly influenced by romantic usages, appealed to ever larger numbers of plebeian readers nearly everywhere in
France.[69] But without a more systematic analysis of colporter literature
in the period, such a conclusion is simply speculative. This impression
rests solely on the coincidence of the romantic movement with the very
slow and halting expansion of the Parisian book trade in rivalry with the
bibliothèque bleue of Epinal and Troyes.[70]

From all the available evidence on the production and distribution
of books in Paris, however, romanticism did indeed participate in the
growth of publishing and its development of a literature aimed at a more
ordinary audience. The movement's extensive diffusion in the period may
have even promoted this remarkable expansion in the industry. Very
early titles borrowing romantic conventions, especially in drama and
fiction, were published in editions generally larger than those that did
not. The brevity of this apparent advantage in production suggests the
commercial nature of the fashion that was used by enterprising *libraires*
to stimulate demand in a depressed market for books before and after
1830. Moreover, romanticism achieved its greatest vogue in the lending
libraries patronized by a broad spectrum of readers anxious for distraction
and attracted by the low cost of acquiring the latest *nouveautés*. Too little
evidence exists to show an equal impact among *libraires, étalagistes,* and
colporteurs, even though the movement's conventions pervaded the titles
reaching readers on nearly all social levels in the cabinets, the most
important distribution agency in Paris in the first half of the nineteenth
century.

Thus the fashion of romanticism played a temporary but significant
role in the Paris book trade, in the livelihoods of younger, more professional authors, but even more in the rapid evolution of a new popular
literature. The expansion and redirection of literary interests, encouraged
by the growth of the city's more sophisticated publishing industry, meant
not only new tastes in the *belles lettres* and history, but also a break in the
cultural barriers between urban social classes. The extensive production

69. Darmon, *Le colportage de librairie en France sous le second empire,* pp. 158–
76; Mandrou, *De la culture populaire,* pp. 184–87; and A. Morin, *Catalogue descriptif de la
bibliothèque bleue de Troyes* (Geneva: Droz, 1974).

70. See Perry, "Publishers, Politics, and the Discovery of the Popular Reader," on
the slow and incomplete national book trade network in the Restoration.

and distribution of romantic works reached the hands of ever larger numbers of readers at a crucial period in the rise of a mass culture that would engulf middle and working classes alike nearly everywhere in France by the end of the century.

In this widespread acculturation, the promotion of the romantic movement made a brief but important contribution; it prepared a socially diverse audience for a more genuine literature for mass consumption. Although the new literature was disappearing by 1840, its impact on cultural patterns lingered on in the new tastes of readers for years afterward as the commercialization of literature, its production and distribution became even more extensive.

With other advances in the world of books, such an evolution in popular taste might have occurred even if the romantic movement had never appeared. The development of mass culture did not depend upon just one element, however apparent. Younger, more professional authors in search of careers in literature, enterprising *libraires* in quest of profit in new market conditions, rising literacy among Parisians anxious for distraction as well as instruction all played important roles. But the growth of new public tastes was also promoted by the timely appearance of the romantic vogue. With such a broad appeal it helped tear elites from their neo-classical canon and raise the *menu peuple* from their street literature. The movement marked a transition from traditional to modern cultural patterns. In this way popular romanticism moved, with changes in reading, writing, and publishing, its broad audience toward a new popular culture in the nineteenth century.

ᘒ6ᘒ

ROMANTIC READERSHIP

ᘒ Y THE EARLY YEARS of the July Monarchy, social and literary critics had long become alarmed by the extent of literacy among the lower orders. "The fact exists, the people know how to read," worried one observer sharing this fear often expressed by middle-class writers.[1] The political and social consequences of literate workers were obvious to most conservatives; they were less docile and more ambitious. Just how restive a plebeian audience could become, according to a much earlier and more generous observer like Sébastien Mercier, was exemplified by the active political role of the literate *sans-culottes* during the 1789 revolution: "Nearly all the social orders can read—so much the better . . . . The nation that reads carries in its bosom a happy and singular force."[2] If not everyone agreed with his politics, many noted the same widespread habit of reading in the early nineteenth century.

This was not all. For some commentators a lettered *menu peuple* also influenced the literary world, especially by its demands for distraction rather than instruction. Its very presence encouraged acquiescence from writers anxious to live by their pens. "Instead of being a mission, the career of letters has become an industry," complained Alfred Nettement in 1845 when the impact of larger numbers of naive readers promoted the *roman-feuilleton*.[3] Apparently, widespread literacy meant vulgarity in the literary market. A less sophisticated readership demanded a less serious literature in books and newspapers alike, and encouraged their authors to produce what the audience wanted. As Sainte-Beuve feared, "the products of fatuity combined with cupidity" catered to the lowest tastes, largely in response to this new readership.[4]

1. Karr, "Imprimeurs, libraires, bouquinistes, cabinets de lecture," p. 64.

2. Sébastien Mercier, *Tableau de Paris*, cited in Tirol, "Les cabinets de lecture en France, 1800–1850," 33(1926),78.

3. Nettement, *Etudes critiques sur le feuilleton roman*, 1:45.

4. Sainte-Beuve, "Quelques vérités," p. 13.

Implicit in these observations and fears is the important demand romanticism temporarily enjoyed with a growing body of uneducated readers and their influence on literary production. Initially the romantics benefited by a larger readership seeking a literature more appealing than that of the neo-classicists; a new, more numerous audience may well have been attracted by the movement's innovations. Romanticism's rise, in part, owed to changes in readership demand that facilitated the new literature's extensive though brief diffusion. The movement's expanding audience encouraged its vogue among younger, more professional authors and its promotion in the hands of enterprising publishers, while the *cabinets de lecture* stocked romantic works for their socially diverse clientele.

But the movement actually shared much of its notoriety and favor with a new urban, popular literature, one that had evolved its own standardized conventions by the early 1840s without the influence of romanticism. The movement's fall, in turn, resulted from further expansion in the number of undiscriminating readers clamoring for a literature even more deliberate in its appeal than romanticism. Perhaps because of this and its limited esthetic, its bizarre extravagance, and its relative sophistication, the romantic mode did not interest many readers, old or new, for very long.

These assumptions about a growing body of "tasteless" readers affecting the course of literature need to be examined in more detail. The actual growth of a romantic audience must be measured more precisely before its impact on literary production can be fairly assessed. Just how many and what kinds of readers were there in the romantic period? Can specific audiences be defined? Answers to these questions promise to explain much of the demand for the romantics, and then for other popular authors, in the rise of a new urban culture in the first half of the nineteenth century.

Study of a romantic readership unfortunately poses problems.[5] First, what does it mean to read? Is simple literacy enough? Or must a reader be educated to the habit of books? Levels of comprehension ranged from semi-literates unable to sign their names to intellectual elites writing as well as reading the most current literature. Certain minimum

5. See discussions of the problem of defining readership in Escarpit, Robine, and Orecchioni, "La lecture," *La vie populaire en France du moyen âge à nos jours* (Paris: Editions Diderot, 1965),2:279–356; Carlo M. Cipolla, *Literacy and Development in the West* (Baltimore: Penguin, 1969), pp. 11–37; Furet and Ozouf, *Lire et écrire: l'alphabétisation des français de Calvin à Jules Ferry* (Paris: Editions de Minuit, 1977),1:13–58; and Harvey J. Graff, *The Literacy Myth: Literacy and Social Structure in the Nineteenth-Century City* (New York: Academic Press, 1979), pp. 10–17.

standards need to be established. Second, what kinds of audiences were there? Surely not everyone read all the titles listed in the *Bibliographie de la France* each year. Not only would it have been physically impossible, but the diversity of books available would not have appealed to the fairly narrow tastes of most readers. Reading interests were often specialized according to social class, educational attainment, standard of living, as well as level of literacy. In any definition of readership, both literacy and audience must be specified, despite the difficulties inherent in such a task. Functional illiteracy and overlapping readerships pose difficulties here that can only be resolved by careful conjecture.

Such problems are complicated even further by the absence of adequate sources. Few records exist suggesting answers to questions about literacy in the period. Ordinary readers simply did not leave accounts of their literary activities. Nor were schools sufficiently widespread to justify official interest in testing educational attainment, a development that had to wait until the Second Empire. Consequently, we must rely upon a wide variety of imperfect sources, from signatures on marriage and military records to contemporary statistics on the number of students and schools. Although no single document appears conclusive or entirely reliable, patterns of evidence do suggest tentative generalizations, especially about the size and nature of readership in the romantic period. However indefinite and difficult to generalize, such evidence throws light on the socioeconomic context of romanticism, its diffusion, and its adoption by authors and booksellers in the development of a new popular literature. A social history of the romantic movement cannot ignore an attempt to define its readership more precisely.

LITERACY IN PARIS, 1815–1848

This venture is made easier by numerous contemporary observers claiming that reading had become a new leisure activity on nearly every social level in Paris. In 1829 one writer in the *Universel* complained,

> The rage to read has invaded everywhere: I learned this fact recently before the door to my kitchen and the lodgings of my doorman where I threatened twenty times, without issue, to hang the culprits if they did not bring my dinner. Reading has now reached the blacksmith's shop, the quarries, the sheds of wood-joiners' apprentices, and the stonemason's closet under the stairs.[6]

6. *Universel*, June 6, 1829.

Literary accounts often poked fun at the innocent domestic lost among the books in a *cabinet de lecture*. One working girl's preference for "something good, with castles, secret passages, old villains, and lovers who marry in the end" was mocked in one satirical novel set in a lending library.[7] Ever sensitive to his customers' wants, Alexandre Pigoreau noted that cabinets existed for all social classes, "one for my doorman and another for my fruit seller," because "everyone wants to write, everyone wants to read."[8] A similar phenomenon was described in Edmond Werdet's study of the book trade in which he stated that all of France appeared to be "an immense reading room."[9] In the provincial cities one English traveller claimed how books were "familiar to the middling and lower orders of society," a fact evident from "almost every lounge you take in the streets" of Rouen in the first years of the Restoration.[10] Similar observations were common throughout the romantic period and suggest a huge potential audience for popular literature in and out of Paris, the heart of the French literary world.

This literary evidence clearly exaggerates. However sweeping the claims, contemporary observers could not specify just how many people in the city could actually read. Unfortunately, systematic literacy figures for the city do not exist. Only reasonably reliable studies of the departments are available, and it is from these that literacy rates for Paris must be inferred.[11] In Louis Maggiolo's survey of signatures on marriage registers in 15,928 communes, literacy for both men and women was highest in departments where conscripts consistently declared the highest reading abilities: Doubs, Marne, Haute-Marne, Moselle, and Meuse. Although Paris was not among the communes whose signatures were studied, the conscripts in the Seine claimed literacy often enough in 1827, 1833, and 1856 to place the department second, sixth, and tenth

7. Brisset, *Le cabinet de lecture*, 1:13–14.

8. Pigoreau, *Petite bibliographie biographico-romancière*, 2:iv.

9. Werdet, *De la librairie française*, p. 118.

10. Thomas Frognall Dibdin, *A Bibliographical, Antiquarian and Picturesque Tour in France and Germany* (London: Shakespeare Press, 1821), 1:137.

11. In Ministère de l'Instruction Publique, *Statistique de l'enseignement primaire*, Tome II: *Statistique comparée de l'enseignement primaire, 1829–1877* (Paris: Imprimerie Nationale, 1880), pp. clxvi–clxxiv. The value of this document in measuring the fair reading comprehension of those able to sign their names has been studied by Michel Fleury and Pierre Valmary, "Le progrès de l'instruction élémentaire de Louis XIV à Napoleon III," *Population* 12(1957),71–92; and Furet and Sachs, "La croissance de l'alphabétisation en France, XVIII e–XIX e siècles," *Annales: E.S.C.* 29(1974),714–37. According to the later study, Maggiolo's survey of signatures in 1686–90, 1786–90, 1816–20, and 1860 measures the ability to read fluently, a level probably sufficient for potential interest in books.

nationally.[12] Moreover, Paris enjoyed some distinct advantages; literacy rates are known to be highest in urban areas, among migrants largely from the north of France, and in the artisanal trades concentrated in the city.[13] It would seem safe, then, to place the Seine among the ten most literate departments. Thus Paris may have had a literacy rate in 1816–1820 comparable to that of the Marne calculated by Maggiolo's survey, i.e., 84 percent of the men. Similarly, 60 percent of the Parisian women should have been able to read, the figure prevailing in the Eure. By these conjectures, 85 percent of the men and 60 percent of the women in Paris could sign their names at the beginning of the romantic period.

These figures for Paris during the Restoration are also corroborated by other sources, both earlier and later. In 1959 George Rudé listed the percentage of literate *émeutiers* documented in the remaining archival materials on the revolutionary *journées* from 1787 to 1795. He found that more than 78 percent of all participants residing in Paris were able to sign their names at official investigations after the events.[14] Although most of those examined were men, a large number of women signed a petition circulated immediately before the massacre at the Champs de Mars in July 1791, but no count was ever taken before the document was destroyed in 1871.[15] Similarly, in a survey of industries in Paris taken during the 1848 revolution, a comparably high percentage of workers claimed abilities to read and write. The Paris Chamber of Commerce study stated that 87 percent of the *ouvriers* and 79 percent of the *ouvrières* were completely literate in 1848.[16] From this evidence relatively high literacy rates among men rose only slowly between the two revolutions, while those among women climbed dramatically in the same period.[17]

12. Conscripts declaring abilities to read and write correlate highly (+0.91) with signatures according to Furet and Sachs, "La croissance de l'alphabétisation," pp. 720–21. Departments most consistent in recording highest percentages of conscripts reading and writing from 1827–29 and 1856–60 are listed in Ministère de l'Instruction Publique, *Statistique de l'enseignement primaire*, pp. cliv and clvi; and for 1830–33, in Adolphe d'Angeville, *Essai sur la statistique de la population française, considérée sous quelques-uns de ses rapports physiques et moraux...* (Bourg: Dufour, 1836), pp. 330–31.

13. See discussion of variables by region and trade in Cipolla, *Literacy*, pp. 75–76.

14. Georges Rudé, *The Crowd in the French Revolution* (New York: Oxford University Press, 1959), p. 249.

15. P. J. B. Buchez and P. C. Roux, *Histoire parlementaire de la révolution française, ou journal des assemblées nationales, depuis 1789 jusqu'en 1815...* (Paris: Paulin, 1834–1838), 11:112–13.

16. Chambre de commerce et d'industrie, *Statistique de l'industrie à Paris*, p. 68.

17. Literacy among women increased more rapidly than it did among men in this period, which accounts for the significant rise in female rates from 1820 to 1848 in Paris. See Furet and Sachs, "La croissance de l'alphabétisation," pp. 730–31.

Statistics such as these, of course, are open to various interpretations. Skeptics may even doubt the significance of the marriage register signature as a fair indicator of literacy: How many people were able to sign without ever learning to read or write? How reliable is a signature a measure of one's ability to read and write? And even if its reliability is accepted, what level of literacy does a signature signify? Found in unintentional sources whose original purpose was not to determine literacy rates but to legitimate religious or legal documents, this evidence is open to serious challenge. Or at least the conclusions drawn from it should be, unless the meaning of the signature as a measure of the abilities to read and write in the early nineteenth century is considered. Consequently, the arguments advanced by most historians of literacy posit that signing one's name meant more in this period than it does today, in the sense of the educational achievement that it represents. They argue this for three reasons:

1. There was a higher regard for the written word prior to the twentieth century. Literate skills were revered more by the common people before the advent of mass media and free, compulsory, public education; such skills were social status symbols, the tools of the middle classes, the elements of *la civilisation*. Commentators like Jules Michelet believed this mystery of the word held a fascination for many ordinary men and women in the past. This innate urge to read is simply less intense today, largely as a consequence of audio and visual media unknown in the nineteenth century.[18]

2. A signature meant that one had already learned to read. Elementary skills were taught in a set order according to classical and plebeian educational practice; one learned to read first—that was important to master primarily for religious reasons. Salvation for French Catholics in the period was tied to reading and understanding the catechism and the liturgy. Then, after mastering that skill, one learned writing, then ciphering, then Latin and rhetoric if one stayed in school long enough. This curious practice was not changed in France until the educational reforms of the Third Republic when the three "r's" were taught simultaneously, making the ability to write less of an educational accomplishment than it had been formerly.[19]

18. Michelet cited in Escarpit, Robine, and Orecchioni, "La lecture," p. 318. See also Marshall MacLuhan, *Understanding Media: The Extensions of Man* (New York: McGraw-Hill, 1964), pp. 81–84, and a similar idea developed by an anthropologist, Jack Goody, "Introduction," *Literacy in Traditional Societies* (Cambridge: Cambridge University Press, 1968), pp. 1–26. Note also the relatively high regard for reading among French workers even in the twentieth century, documented in René Kaës, *Les ouvriers français et la culture: l'enquête 1958–1961* (Paris: Institut de Travail, 1962), pp. 161–76.

19. This argument was advanced first and most persuasively by Roger Schofield,

3. Signatures also represented an expense beyond that required for learning to read. Itinerant tutors in the countryside and informal schoolmasters in the cities, for most people their only contacts with schooling, often charged one rate for teaching people to read, another higher rate for writing, and even higher rates for arithmetic, grammar, and Latin—if they could teach them, which not all teachers could. Moreover, writing tools were still expensive then; ink, quills, desks, chairs, and the like were not always within the modest means of ordinary people. To learn to write one's name was thus an expensive as well as advanced educational achievement.[20]

Given these considerations—respect for the written word, order of learning reading and writing skills, and their relative expense—scholars argue that a signature in the nineteenth century represented a reasonable ability to read, though a rather poor ability to write. This has been confirmed by social historians since Roger Schofield's 1968 essay on the problem. Nearly 97 percent of everyone who signed his name could read at a fair level of comprehension, according to François Furet and Wladimir Sachs' comparison of a detailed 1866 educational survey with marriage register signatures and military conscripts' declarations about their abilities to read and write in the same year.[21] On the basis of this careful work and the arguments they have advanced verifying the significance of signatures, one may feel confident that nearly everyone who signed a name before the Ferry Laws of the 1880s could read "fluently at a fair level of comprehension" a message of 200 words in simple language. This was probably more true then than it is today.[22]

The evidence of comparable levels of literacy by the end of the July Monarchy is confirmed by other archival sources. In 1829 the War Ministry directed local authorities to ask young men, when they registered for the military lottery, whether or not they could read and write. Although the actual records are extant for only three *arrondissements* in Paris, they show a general rise in literacy among men from 1830 to 1845.[23] This is especially true in one of the poorest districts, the eighth *arrondissement* (see Table 6.1). Here only 72 percent claimed they could read

"The Measurement of Literacy in Pre-Industrial England," in Goody, ed. *Literacy in Traditional Societies*, pp. 311–25.

20. This is well documented in Furet and Ozouf, *Lire et écrire*, 1:131.

21. Furet and Sachs, "La croissance de l'alphabétisation."

22. See this level of literacy discussed in historical perspective in Daniel P. Resnick and Lauren B. Resnick, "The Nature of Literacy: An Historical Exploration," *Harvard Educational Review* 47(1977),370–85.

23. Archives du Département de la Seine et de la Ville de Paris DR^{1}26–57 "Tables de Recensement" and "Listes de Tirage" (1829–45) provide the annual conscript records of all men registered in the first, eighth, and tenth *arrondissements*. The records contain between 300 and 500 entries per *arrondissement* each year.

TABLE 6.1
Percentages of Paris Conscripts Claiming to
Read and Write, by *Arrondissement*,
1829–1845

Year	Arr. 1	Arr. 8	Arr. 10	City-Wide
1829	—	72.0	86.4	79.5
1830	89.5	75.6	92.6	
1831	95.1	73.1	92.3	
1832	92.9	72.4	90.5	
1833	95.5	79.9	93.2	
1834	90.9	80.2	90.9	
1835	94.3	79.3	90.0	84.7*
1836	94.9	79.7	91.9	
1837	94.9	77.0	91.3	
1838	93.1	80.3	95.4	
1839	93.8	82.0	93.9	
1840	95.2	82.9	94.2	87.1*
1841	92.0	83.3	94.9	
1842	94.6	83.7	94.7	
1843	96.7	84.2	95.6	
1844	97.0	85.5	96.7	
1845	95.3	85.3	96.1	86.5*

* Average for previous five years.

Source: A.D.S.V.P. DR¹ 26–57. "Tables de Recensement" and "Listes de Tirage" 1829–1845; Ministère de l'Instruction Publique, *Statistique de l'enseignement primaire*, Tome II: *Statistique comparée de l'enseignement primaire, 1829–1877* (Paris: Imprimerie Nationale, 1880), Table LXXXI. Between 300 and 400 entries were recorded for each *arrondissement* annually.

and write in 1829; fifteen years later more than 85 percent did so, an increase of 13 percentage points despite continued poverty and increased overcrowding in the Faubourg Saint-Antoine and Popincourt. Evidently even the lowest social strata recorded the ability to read and write at rates roughly comparable to those determined by marriage registers and surveys of the industrial classes for the entire city.

Similar rises in male literacy were registered in the prosperous first and tenth *arrondissements*, including the Champs-Elysées and the Faubourg Saint-Germain, respectively. A higher percentage of young men from wealthy middle-class families improved the figures here, since they too were forced to register whether or not they later hired a substitute or secured an exemption from military service.[24] And if the total number of

24. Furet and Ozouf, *Lire et écrire*, 1:30.

conscripts claiming to read is considered, literacy among all men of military age in Paris was remarkable very early in the century; 79 percent of all conscripts in Paris declared the ability to read in 1829, only eight percentage points fewer than in 1840, according to the Ministry of Public Instruction survey.[25]

Thus the simple ability to read in early nineteenth-century Paris must have been a widespread one, even if the ability to write was not. This is certainly not contradicted by the very low percentage of conscripts, less than 2 percent, who claimed only to write; had they learned writing before reading, the figure would have been much higher.[26] Moreover, the declaration compares closely with the signature as a literacy indicator. Although the likelihood of deliberate deception in conscript declarations was limited by the possible consequences to which lying might lead if detected, authorities soon felt compelled to test the accuracy of the declarations. After 1850 they demanded signatures of the men during registration. Not surprisingly, less than 3 percent could not sign their names after claiming that they could read and write (see Table 6.2). It appears that the reading sophistication among those actually signing or declaring their abilities to read and write was reflected in the records. Such a fluency even indicates a potential interest in printed material whose production increased accordingly.

To this large, relatively accomplished readership were major exceptions that must be pointed out. Omitted from the marriage registers were illiterate couples cohabitating without legal or religious sanction. The problem of concubinage was recognized by many contemporary observers and historians since then.[27] Similarly, city records surely overlooked recent migrants to Paris who were probably less literate than most. It could be that the shiftless and uneducated drifted to Paris in large numbers in the nineteenth century. Women, too, generally did not share in written culture to the same extent as men, just as certain trades required few literate skills, particularly in the rapidly industrializing textile industry on the outskirts of the city. The suburban areas like Saint Denis and Belleville outside the city limits swelled with the poor and unskilled recently arrived in search of employment. The apparent consequences of these unrecorded illiterate additions to the urban popu-

25. Ministère de l'Instruction Publique, *Statistique de l'enseignement primaire*, pp. 342–43.

26. See A.D.S.V.P. DR¹26–57 "Tables de Recensement" and "Listes de Tirage," 1829–45.

27. E.g., Chevalier, *Classes laborieuses et classes dangereuses...* (Paris: Plon, 1959), p. 389.

TABLE 6.2
Percentages of Paris Conscripts Signing and Percentages of
Paris Conscripts Claiming to Read and Write Who Signed,
by *Arrondissement*, 1850–1854

Percent	Year	Arr. 1	Arr. 8	Arr. 10	Total
Signing	1850	96	74	93	85
Claiming		100	94	100	97
Signing	1851	97	81	93	88
Claiming		100	97	100	98
Signing	1852	97	81	96	89
Claiming		99	99	100	99
Signing	1853	96	85	94	90
Claiming		100	98	100	99
Signing	1854	95	82	95	89
Claiming		100	98	99	98

Phi Coefficient $=$ Chi^2/N $= 0.68$

Source: A.D.S.V.P. DR^{1}67–77 "Tables de Recensement" and "Listes de Tirage" for Paris *arrondissements* 1, 8, and 10. Between 400 and 500 entries were recorded for each *arrondissement* annually.

lation was to undermine the high percentage of readers shown in official documents.

Yet their actual influence on literacy levels appears to have been minimal. Cohabitating couples openly flouting bourgeois morality were a decided minority of the population and frequently made their unions legal upon the arrival of children to insure their rights to inheritance. According to a recent study by Michel Frey, no correlation exists between illiteracy and the trades most given to concubinage in the Paris of 1848.[28] Moreover, recent immigrants were not significantly less literate than those native to the city. Most came from the relatively lettered northeastern and eastern departments and upon examination for conscription, declared abilities to read and write at nearly the same rates as those born in Paris (90.6 percent province-born versus 90.8 percent Paris-born).[29] Although female literacy remained lower than that of males, women learned to read in larger numbers generally in France during the

28. Michel Frey, "Du mariage et du concubinage dans les classes populaires à Paris (1846–47)," *Annales: E.S.C.* 33(1978),3:801–826.

29. See Chevalier, *La formation de la population parisienne*, pp. 58–59; Pouthas, *La population française*, pp. 168–69; and A.D.S.V.P. DR^{1}26–57 "Tables de Recensement" and "Listes de Tirage" (1829–45).

nineteenth century. While those for men rose only 33 percent, female rates jumped 44 percent from 1790 to 1870.[30] Besides witnessing rapid industrialization of only a few trades, Paris was fortunate in remaining the major administrative and financial center in France where the middle classes set a conspicuously literate example for many among the *menu peuple* to follow.[31] Even literacy rates in the *banlieue* do not seem to have declined radically in the period, according to the Maggiolo figures for the department of the Seine after 1853.[32]

Consequently, the number of potential readers in Paris more than likely grew from 1820 to 1840 at a rate faster than the expansion of the city's burgeoning population. In these conditions, could not the new vogue in literature have reaped its remarkable gains? As Paris grew, largely from changes in migration patterns, so did its body of readers who provided the demand necessary for a corresponding growth in the romantic book trade. Of course, a portion of the increased flow of printed material owed to the new wealth and leisure of the classically educated bourgeoisie who derived a disproportionate share of the city's relative economic prosperity.[33] But this sizable new demand for literature can not be explained solely by the increased consumption of so small a minority in the city. More published material, much of it using romantic conventions after 1830, must have reached the hands of a swelling proportion of new, less sophisticated readers among the lower orders demanding an appropriate literature for distraction. Rising literacy rates of the uneducated and growing production of popular works coincided in the romantic period as the city's population expanded from less than 800,000 to more than one million in only twenty years. This fact surely benefited the authors and publishers of romantic titles aimed at an audience more plebeian than that reached by the neo-classicists.

The trend towards a larger, popular readership meant a growing demand for even less serious works, such as those sold by *étalagistes*, *colporteurs*, and peddlars of broadsheets in the streets. This literature prospered, too, from the rising literate population in Paris. Contemporary observers often complained of the appearance of the many *mauvais*

---

30. Ministère de l'Instruction Publique, *Statistique de l'enseignement primaire*, pp. clxiv–clxvi.

31. Note the differences in literacy rates among the trades registered in the Chambre de commerce et d'industrie, *Statistique de l'industrie à Paris*, nearly all with rates high enough to offset those of factory operatives also included in the survey. See also Daumard, "Le peuple dans la société française à l'époque romantique," p. 28.

32. See Maggiolo's literacy rates for the Seine after 1853 in Ministère de l'Instruction Publique, *Statistique de l'enseignement primaire*, Tables LXXXV and LXXXVI.

33. Daumard, *Les bourgeois de Paris au XIXe siècle*, pp. 363–65.

livres offered at lower prices in the shops of less scrupulous *libraires* and *nouveauté* retailers. Stated one writer indignantly, "It is shameful, indeed scandalous to see the sermons of Père Lenfant side by side with the tales of conjugal love" often demanded in a bookseller's boutique by a diverse clientele, including members of the fair sex.[34] The new popular culture, despite the rise in literacy, remained what it had been since the 1789 revolution, only now its audience had grown sufficiently to alarm middle-class critics. Informally taught, untrained in finer discrimination, most of these readers remained unsophisticated in their tastes and limited in their interests.[35]

This does not necessarily mean that new readers aspired only to the crudest literary culture. Since the eighteenth century there had been a lively interest in education on nearly all social levels in France.[36] As François Guizot quipped later, the 1789 revolution marked no real turning point in the persistent desire for letters; it resulted only in a flood of words.[37] An enduring demand for schools was reflected in the locally run and financed *petites écoles*, supervised by the Church during the *ancien régime*, then by the State after 1789. Although they intended to inculcate religious fear and political obedience, these schools made a lasting contribution to the general literacy of rural migrants to the city, testified by Maggiolo's survey that registered better than a 75 percent increase in signature rates in the provinces after 1690. In fact, despite the administrative failures and financial shortcomings of successive regimes, literacy rates rose even faster in the early nineteenth century. And this occurred in local schools using the same inadequate facilities and antiquated books left from the *ancien régime*.[38] The widespread thirst for literacy was simply

34. M***(Painparré) *Le petit diable boiteux, ou guide anecdotique des étrangers à Paris...* (Paris: Painparré, 1823), p. 175.

35. For discussion of changes in popular literature in the first half of the nineteenth century, see Chapter 1, pp. 29–34.

36. See Furet and Ozouf, *Lire et écrire*, 1:69–176. Contemporary accounts of primary education are numerous for this period. See useful collection of documents in Pierre Chevallier and Bernard Grosperin, eds. *L'enseignement français de la révolution à nos jours* (La Haye: Mouton, 1971), vol. 2; and excellent survey of primary education in Paris, M. Fosseyeux, "Les écoles de chartié à Paris sous l'ancien régime et dans la première moitié du XIX⁰ siècle," *Mémoires de la Société de l'Histoire de Paris et de l'Ile de France* 39(1912),225–367.

37. Cited in Matthew Arnold, *The Popular Education of France...* (London: Longman et al., 1861), p. 29. See also Furet and Ozouf, *Lire et écrire*, 1:69; and Maurice Gontard, *L'enseignement primaire en France de la révolution à la loi Guizot (1789–1833): des petites écoles de la monarchie d'ancien régime aux écoles primaires de la monarchie bourgeoise* (Paris: Belles Lettres, 1959), pp. 546–47.

38. See revealing surveys of educational facilities in C.-P. Collard de Martigny, *Coup-d'oeil sur l'état de l'instruction publique en France et sur les développemens* [sic]

10. "L'Ecole Chrétienne" (ca. 1828). Lithograph by Nicolas Charlet (1792–1845). *Courtesy of the Boston Public Library, Print Department.*

irrepressible, and largely unrecorded. Explained Jules Michelet, the world of books "was an enchanted circle for which the lower orders strived without the upper classes ever knowing."[39]

Official interest also recognized the need for a broader effort to educate the masses, despite the timeless controversy that raged over the actual purposes of schooling.[40] While the ultra-royalists and doctrinaires argued, congregationalists and supporters of mutual instruction created dozens of new schools during the Restoration. Scenes of children lining up to enter school, like that depicted by Nicolas Charlet, became increasingly frequent from the Restoration onward (see Illustration 10). By 1835 there were more than 100 elementary schools in Paris alone, a net increase of over 100 percent since the Napoleonic Empire.[41] Moreover, the revolutionary origins of the Orleanist regime implied a commitment to

qu'elle exige (Paris: Levrault, 1835); and Paul Lorain, *Tableau de l'instruction primaire en France, d'après des documents authentiques...* (Paris: Hachette, 1837).

39. Cited in Escarpit, Robine, and Orecchioni, "La lecture," 2:318.

40. See the chapter on the Restoration in Gontard, *L'enseignement primaire en France*, pp. 273–96.

41. Emile Levasseur, *L'enseignement primaire dans les pays civilisés* (Paris: Berger-Levrault, 1897–1903), 1:94.

public education that was finally realized in Guizot's law of June 28, 1833, "the constitutional charter of primary instruction in France."[42]

Attendance at schools rose remarkably. In Paris the number of primary students per 1,000 inhabitants moved from 21.7 in 1826, to 77.8 in 1867 when the city's literacy rate was nearly universal (see Table 6.3).[43] Government expenditure on education rose accordingly from less than 50,000 francs in 1827, to more than 1.5 million in 1834.[44] Such an improvement in public instruction, however modest by present-day standards, came in response to a widespread demand, not only from social conservatives anxious to keep the people obedient and from liberals interested in better workers. It also derived from the popular classes themselves in quest of personal dignity, social position, and political power. Although much of this effort to improve primary instruction came too late for the romantic generation of readers—little more than children during the Empire—attempts were made to teach older men and women in adult classes, and even more effectively, in military schools established especially to educate illiterate recruits.[45]

Literary evidence further indicates that these official figures ignored the private instruction offered by self-proclaimed tutors among the working classes. Martin Nadaud reported "a general movement towards popular education in France" during the early years of the July Monarchy that inspired a dozen workers to attend night classes in his sixth floor garret. Here their interests soon rose above the *canards* and *complaintes* sold in the streets to Lamennais' *Paroles d'un croyant*.[46] Other workers like Agricol Perdiguier, a frequent customer of *étalagistes* and *colporteurs*, expressed a lively interest in reading and writing. "My friends also read my plays and, like me, they were enchanted," he wrote in 1844 about other wood-joiners like himself.[47]

42. *Ibid.*, 1:51.

43. See figures on the national growth in the number of schools and students featured in Antoine Prost, *Histoire de l'enseignement en France, 1800–1967* (Paris: Colin, 1968), p. 108. Figures in text calculated from Dupin, *Forces productives et commerciales,* 1:Map Insert; and Ministère de l'Instruction Publique, *Statistique de l'enseignement primaire,* p. 57.

44. Arnold, *The Popular Education of France,* pp. 254–55.

45. Benigno Cacérès, *Histoire de l'éducation populaire,* (Paris: Editions du Seuil, [1964]), pp. 18–27.

46. Nadaud, *Les mémoires de Léonard,* p. 102. Note also Nadaud's and Agricol Perdiguier's accounts of their education that show, despite the miserable conditions of schools and the incompetence of their instructors, the possibilities of education in France of the early nineteenth century. *Ibid.*, pp. 35–44, 102–107; and Perdiguier, *Mémoires d'un compagnon,* pp. 8–20.

47. Perdiguier, *Mémoires d'un compagnon,* p. 137.

TABLE 6.3

Primary Schools and Students in the Department of the Seine, 1814–1850

	1814	1821	1828[d]	1837	1850
General Population	(800,000)	822,171	(850,000)	1,105,891	1,422,065
No. of Primary School Students		27,148[c]	25,582	54,874	82,205
No. of Primary School Students Per 10,000 Inhabitants		330[c]	294	496	586
No. of Primary School Students Attending Free	6,807[a]	9,209[b]	15,601	15,449[e]	44,084
Percentage of Primary School Students Attending Free			60.9%		53.6%
No. of Primary Schools	50[b]	369	403	870	990
No. of Primary School Teachers			489	1,227	1,243
No. of Primary Schools for Adults and Apprentices				28	66
No. Attending Primary Schools for Adults and Apprentices				2,252	4,443

( ) = approximations.

[a] Students in the *écoles de charité* of Paris (1814), according to Pastoret, *Rapport sur l'état des hôpitaux, hospices, secours, de 1804 à 1814* (Paris: n.p., 1816), p. 360.

[b] *Ecoles de charités* in Paris (1814) and their students (1821), according to M. Fosseyeux, "Les écoles de charités à Paris sous l'ancien régime et dans la première moitié du XIX[e] siècle," *Mémoires de la Société de l'Histoire de Paris et de l'Ile de France* 39(1912): 318.

[c] Figure from Louis-François Benoiston de Chateauneuf, *Recherches sur les consommations de tout genre de la ville de Paris* (Paris: Martinet, 1821), p. 40.

[d] Figures for 1828 from le comte de Chabrol, *Recueil publié d'après les ordres du préfet, comte de Chabrol* (Paris: Imprimerie Royale, 1829), Table 98.

[e] Students in the *écoles de charité* in Paris (1835), according to J. M. de Gérando, *De la bienfaisance publique* (Paris: Renouard, 1839), 2:476.

Source: Ministre de l'Instruction Publique, *Statistique de l'enseignement primaire*, Tome II: *Statistique comparée de l'enseignement primaire, 1829–1877* (Paris: Imprimerie Nationale, 1880), Tables I ff., except where noted.

Besides Nadaud and Perdiguier, the working classes received most of their instruction from itinerant teachers who charged nominal fees to teach reading and a little more for writing and ciphering.[48] Such a tradition was deplored by more respectable educators worried about the spread of seditious ideas, but the popular desire for learning defied their efforts to suppress these clandestine schools active since the seventeenth century. Where both public and private instruction was unavailable, many turned to religious schools, even though these were reserved primarily for the religious instruction of women that rarely went beyond the reading of catechisms and litanies. The rising literacy rates in the early nineteenth century indicate a growing interest in the written word among the lower orders who often resorted to informal schooling and even self-instruction in their quest to read and write (see Illustration 11).[49]

READING IN THE CITY

Widespread literacy among the popular classes marked a significant break with a long standing oral tradition.[50] Instead of relying upon a closed cultural network of face-to-face relationships, the common people looked to a larger written world. Indeed, interest in a new urban literature, in form and content different from that sold by itinerant colporters, grew with this awakening to another, more varied literate culture. It could well be that the well-documented vogue of romantic literature, especially its sentimental and gothic variations, owed to this rapid influx of naive readers in Paris. Popular tastes among peasants migrating to urban centers must have shifted from the traditional almanacs and saints' lives circulating in the countryside to many of the romantic *nouveautés* available at the *cabinets de lecture* and on the quays in the cities. Shrewd *libraires* like Pigoreau provided these works in the new fashion "for the artisan in his shop, for the little seamstress in her humble garret, for the second-hand clothes dealer in her basement. One must carry them all for the common people."[51] We will probably never know why this massive influx of new readers in Paris preferred the romantic fashion

48. Furet and Ozouf, *Lire et écrire*, 1:131.

49. *Ibid.*, 1:306, in which it is estimated that 20 percent of French literacy owed to self-instruction.

50. Mandrou, *De la culture populaire*, pp. 182–95; Weber, *Peasants into Frenchmen*, pp. 452–70.

51. Pigoreau, *Petite bibliographie biographico-romancière*, 3:iv.

11. "A! B! C!" (ca. 1828). Lithograph by Nicolas Charlet (1792–1845). *Courtesy of the Boston Public Library, Print Department.*

as it did; it could be that the movement struck a particularly sensitive nerve in the period, as suggested at the end of Chapter 2. But this element in the history of taste, literary or otherwise, remains for more intensive consideration.

Nevertheless, while the romantic book trade benefited briefly from this demographic and cultural movement, in the end cheap newspapers and the *roman-feuilleton* without romantic conventions surely attracted more attention from these new readers. Complete strangers to the literary world knew all the characters in *Les mystères de Paris* serialized in 1843, claimed Théophile Gautier: "Nearly all of France was occupied for more than a year with the adventures of Prince Rodolphe before going about its work."[52] Taking full advantage of suspense to encourage purchase of the next issue, Eugène Sue in *Le juif errant* in the *Journal des débats* and Alexandre Dumas in *Capitaine Paul* in the *Constitutionnel* more than doubled the circulation of their newspapers.[53] Stories of pure adventure and mystery developed by such masters of the serial novel form drew many to the four-sous newspaper in the 1840s, largely at the expense of the book trade and the romantics. Although romanticism by its deliberate violation of neo-classical proprieties prepared readers high and low for this popular literature, it could not compete with prose fiction even more deliberate in its appeal to a new, more plebeian audience.

Literacy alone did not create such a readership; material standards of living were equally important to its existence. If Parisians lacked sufficient disposable income and enough leisure time to read, they were not likely to put their literacy skills to much use, even for distraction. Readers like spectators need an environment conducive to their leisure activities. What, then, were the living conditions in Paris during the first half of the nineteenth century?[54] L.-F. Benoiston de Chateauneuf reported in 1821 that "in the first city of France . . . misery in all forms stood side by side with luxury. . . . The working class, that which especially needed restoring nourishment, a hearty stew, a good soup, was

---

52. Gautier, *Histoire de l'art dramatique en France depuis vingt-cinq ans* (Paris: Magnin, Blanchard et cie., 1858–59),3:161.

53. René Guise, "Le roman-feuilleton et la vulgarisation des idées politiques et sociales sous la monarchie de juillet," *Romantisme et politique, 1815–1851*, pp. 316–24.

54. Literary accounts of the extent of poverty in Paris are scattered throughout the classic studies of a national problem: J.-P. Alban de Villeneuve, *Economie politique chrétienne, ou recherches sur la nature et les causes du paupérisme en France et en Europe...* (Paris: Paulin, 1834), 3 vols.; Eugène Buret, *De la misère des classes laborieuses en Angleterre et en France...* (Paris: Paulin, 1840), 2 vols.; and Louis-René Villermé, *Tableau de l'état physique et moral des ouvriers employés dans les manufactures de coton, de laine et de soie...* (Paris: Renouard, 1840), 2 vols.

nearly always deprived of it."[55] In 1848 the situation was no better according to Charles Marchal: "The worker is unable to live by his work. . . . He is obliged to deprive himself of basic necessities."[56] Undoubtedly life for most Parisians was close to subsistence even in the best of years.

In such conditions few were likely to read. Work, when available, demanded twelve to fifteen hard hours a day. Mortality was generally higher in the city, and even higher in working-class districts like la Cité and Popincourt where cholera killed 55 in every 1,000 people in 1832.[57] Crowded, unsanitary housing certainly contributed to this misery that drew no fine line between the laboring classes and the indigent on relief.[58] Income was so low that nearly 80 percent of Paris, like Balzac's Père Goriot, left no money to be buried privately.[59] In light of the few data available on wages and prices, material standards of living stagnated in the thirty years before 1848. In only fifteen of these years a stonemason's nominal wages exceeded the cost of living (see Figure 6.1).[60] Only men in similar traditional trades may well have had the sous and hours necessary to use the *cabinets de lecture* or read the *romans-feuilletons* in the few good years between 1820 and 1840.

The general stagnation in popular standards of living, however, did not necessarily preclude large numbers of new readers from enjoying literature as a leisure activity. Relative prosperity permitted select artisanal groups, the so-called "aristocracy of labor," money and time to read between 1822 and 1827, 1833 and 1837, and 1841 and 1846. Similarly, individual workers enjoyed certain periods in their lives of above-subsistence income and leisure time. In 1840 L.-R. Villermé noted that

55. L.-F. Benoiston de Chateauneuf, *Recherches sur les consommations de tout genre de la ville de Paris en 1817...*, 2ᵉ éd. (Paris: Martinet, 1821), pp. 45–46.

56. Charles Marchal, *Du pain au peuple* (Paris: Desloges, 1848), p. 27.

57. Département de la Seine, *Recherches statistiques sur la ville de Paris et le département de la Seine* (Paris: Imprimerie Royale, etc., 1821–60),6:457.

58. M. Vée, "Du paupérisme et les secours publics dans la ville de Paris," *Journal des économistes* 10(1845),224–71.

59. A. Cochut, "Mouvement de la population de Paris," *Revue des deux mondes* 10(1845),1:725.

60. For wages in the construction trades from 1789 to 1848, see François Simiand, *Le salaire, l'évolution sociale et la monnaie; essai de théorie expérimentale du salaire, introduction et étude globale* (Paris: Alcan, 1932), esp. tables in vol. 1; Alexandre Chabert, *Essai sur les mouvements des prix et des revenues en France de 1789 à 1820* (Paris: Librairie de Medicis, 1945–49),2:242–44; Statistique générale, *Statistique de la France...*, 2ᵉ série. Tome XII: *Prix et salaires à diverses époques* (Strasbourg: Berger-Levrault, 1863), pp. xiii, 192; Chambre de commerce et d'industrie, *Statistique de l'industrie à Paris*, pp. 49–50. For prices in the same period, see Gustave Bienaymé, *Prix des principaux objets de consommation à Paris depuis deux siècles environ...* (Paris: Imprimerie Nationale, 1898), p. 101; and Jeanne Singer-Kérel, *Le coût de vie à Paris de 1840 à 1954* (Paris: Colin, [1961]).

FIGURE 6.1

Nominal Wages and the Cost of Living for a Stonemason Living in Paris, 1817–1847

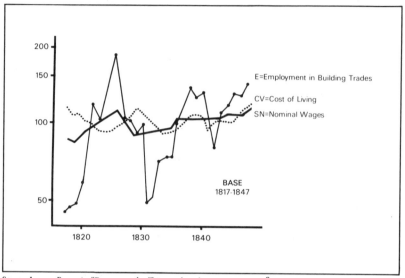

Source: Jacques Rougerie, "Remarques dur l'histoire des salaires à Paris au XIX ͤ siècle," *Mouvement social* 63(1968): 106.

workers realized the little comfort they were ever likely to know as working youths living at home with relatives (ages 15–30) and as parents of older children contributing to the family income (ages 45–60).[61] Although the rest of their lives were spent in dire poverty, workers with nominal family responsibilities managed a higher standard of living.

Such time made nonproductive pursuits possible and encouraged the quest for distraction among the common people of Paris. Life in the city offered a number of opportunities for inexpensive escapes into the world of fantasy. When the occasion arose, the working classes surely sought the entertaining possibilities of cafés, street players, even books and newspapers. By 1846 newspaper circulation, for example, had risen to more than 200,000 readers, many of whom were workers, when the vogue of the serial novel had reached its peak.[62] Whether or not they

61. Villermé, *Tableau de l'état*, 2:387–88. See also discussion of cyclical standards of living patterns among the working classes analyzed in B. Seebohm Rowntree, *Poverty and Progress: A Second Social Survey of York* (London: Longmans, 1941), pp. 55–71; and Gillis, *Youth and History*, pp. 118–21.

62. René Johannet, *L'évolution du roman social au XIX ͤ siècle* (Reims: Action populaire, [1910]), p. 37.

actually engaged in reading as a leisure-time activity, a large body of workers in the romantic period obviously read when conditions were right. Some may have done so in spite of their poverty as a release from the drudgery of their lives, though this would be nearly impossible to document.

The actual size of this readership, so important to the demand for romantic and popular works, requires more precision. Given the data available, one may estimate a *potential* audience, one defined by literacy, sex, age, as well as social class and material conditions. These calculations must be very crude; but figures on the bourgeoisie, laboring poor, age and sex structures of the population, and illiterates make assessments of Parisian readership possible (see Table 6.4).[63]

TABLE 6.4
Estimated Number of Potential Readers in Paris, 1817–1846

Year	Total Pop.	Pop. Older than 14	Literate Pop.	Upper-Class Readers	Working-Class Readers	Total	% of Pop.
817	713,966	485,662	350,199	52,530	—	52,530	7%
831	785,866	540,847	404,781	60,717	—	60,717	8
836	899,313	623,674	479,231	86,262	165,866	252,128	28
841	936,261	651,253	520,733	104,147	173,130	277,277	30
846	1,053,897	735,250	606,477	121,295	203,294	324,589	33

ource: See fn. 63, p. 171.

The results in the table involved a number of assumptions that should be made explicit. First, everyone under age 15 or on public relief was excluded because he was not part of the statistical population used to determine literacy rates in Paris. Children were too young and the indigent too unlikely to appear in the marriage registers or the military records, and so they were not included in the number of literate people in the city.

63. Data for Paris population (column 2) taken from Département de la Seine, *Recherches statistiques sur la ville de Paris*, vols. 1–6; on percentage of population older than 14 (column 3), Bourgeois-Pichat, "The General Development of the Population of France Since the Eighteenth Century," p. 498; on percentage of literate population (column 4), Ministère de l'Instruction Publique, *Statistique de l'enseignement primaire*, pp. clxvi–clxxiv; for the number of upper-class readers (column 5), all literate members of the bourgeoisie were taken—15 percent of literate Paris in 1817 and 1831, 18 percent in 1836, and 20 percent in 1841 and 1846, according to Daumard, *La bourgeoisie parisienne de 1815 à 1848*, p. 17; the number of working-class readers in 1836, 1841, and 1846, years of relative prosperity (column 6) was calculated by subtracting the number of bourgeois and the number on relief (official figures times three) from the total Parisian population. From the remainder was eliminated the percentage between ages thirty and forty-five and older than sixty, on the assumption that these groups were the least likely to have disposable income or

Second, men were more consistently literate than women and their portion of the literate population had to be calculated separately. Thus 85 percent of the men throughout the period were considered literate; but only 60 percent of the women in 1817, 65 percent in 1831, 70 percent in 1836, 75 percent in 1841, and 80 percent in 1846 were included. Third, all upper class Parisians, those paying more than 200 francs in taxes for the vote—from the aristocracy of finance to prosperous greengrocers—probably lived in circumstances comfortable enough to read as a leisure activity. To these elements of the middle class, however, must be added all those whose jobs required literate skills but paid too poorly to qualify their holders for the vote: liberal professions, *employés,* and functionaries, swelling the bourgeoisie to roughly 15 percent of the city and nearly 20 percent in periods of economic health. Fourth, the calculations of nonindigent working-class readers assumed that the economic conjuncture favored their participation in the literate world. The good years between 1822 and 1827, 1833 and 1837, and 1841 and 1846 may have been the only periods when employed workers could afford the time and money for reading. And fifth, the table assumes that these workers were likely to read only at certain periods of their lives, especially when family responsibilities were minimal, between ages 15 and 30 (before marriage and children) and between 45 and 60 (when children were contributing their wages to the family economy).

Consequently, between 5 and 35 percent of the Parisian populace *could* have read a book between 1817 and 1846, providing the demand necessary to support expansion in the romantic book trade. This body probably contracted to the relative comfort of the middle classes in bad years (1817 and 1831) and expanded to select portions of the working classes in good ones (1836, 1841, and 1846). It is this demand, rising gradually with the city's literate population and leaping higher in years of economic health, that provided the incentive for publishers to innovate and increase their production and distribution of popular romantic works.

With the general growth in bourgeois readership before the July Monarchy, the romantic movement enjoyed its initial vogue. Clearly the middle classes made up the movement's basic readership during the economic crisis between 1828 and 1833, even though some artisanal elements participated as a consequence of new publishing and marketing practices. But the addition of a huge body of new, unsophisticated readers later in the July Monarchy delivered a decisive blow to the demand

leisure time for reading. The remaining number of workers was then adjusted for literacy. Data on poverty and the indigent were taken from Jacques Rougerie, "Remarques sur l'histoire des salaires à Paris au XIXe siècle," *Mouvement social* 63(1968),71–108; Buret, *De la misère,* 1:259–74; and Chevalier, *Laboring Classes and Dangerous Classes,* pp. 350–55.

for romantic titles popular only a few years earlier among a smaller, more discriminating audience. Thus the brief vogue of popular romanticism appeared with rapid changes in readership size and composition that initially made, then undermined its success in the market.

This fluctuation in readership may have also influenced the development of romanticism itself. After 1830 many well-known romantics adopted new social and political commitments heavily influenced by Saint-Simonian socialist ideas;[64] Victor Hugo elaborated the Napoleonic myth in laudatory verse, Lamartine ran for public office even before the revelations of his trip to the Holy Lands, and George Sand took an interest in the welfare of the popular classes celebrated in her peasant novels. For the romantics, this actually marked only an apparent shift in emphasis, since their literary visions during the Restoration evinced an equally profound awareness of their historical moment.[65] Yet changes in the composition of their audience may well have encouraged them in this direction after the July revolution.

The new readership pressure may have been even more influential among other romantics who developed entirely new modes of expression by the end of the period. While Balzac's novels of manners and mores grew increasingly pessimistic, Dumas openly embraced the popular serial novel. Both expressed in very different ways their responses to a growing readership, the former as despairing as the latter was cynical. Indeed, the apparent shifts among authors using romantic conventions after 1840, studied in Chapter 3, indicate a relatively common movement away from the new literature toward other popular forms, a new emphasis that meant the effective demise of the romantic fashion.[66] However inconclusive, the role played by the new audience in these developments is certainly suggestive.

Without established reading habits, a working-class reader was unlikely to buy a newspaper, much less rent a book from a *cabinet de lecture*. But that did not necessarily exclude him from the literary world. Perhaps even more significant than the expansion in potential readership were other social agencies, such as the family and the shop, that promoted interest in entertaining literature.

64. See David Owen Evans, *Social Romanticism in France, 1830–1848* (Oxford: Oxford University Press, 1951), pp. 1–105; Jean Hervé Donnard, *Balzac. Les réalités économiques et sociales dans La comédie humaine* (Paris: Colin, 1961), pp. 61–85; and Herbert J. Hunt, *Le socialisme et le romantisme en France: étude de la presse socialiste de 1830 à 1848* (Oxford: Clarendon Press, 1935).

65. See George Boas, "Il Faut être de son Temps," *Journal of Aesthetics and Art Criticism* 1(1941), 1:52–65.

66. See Chapter 3, pp. 98–100.

Reading was not a completely solitary experience in the nineteenth century. Oral readings in family settings provided even the illiterate and the poor access to written culture. Although working-class domesticity developed only slowly in the nineteenth century, it did adopt traits of the bourgeois household in which reading aloud was a treasured activity.[67] Book collections existed among middle-class families, as did literature aimed at their children.[68] Among workers, domestics were the most likely to share in these gatherings around the middle-class hearth.[69] But an instance of this among lower social strata was reported in Frédéric Leplay's 1848 account of a *chiffonnier* who frequently enjoyed "reading with his family the Bible and other religious books of which he formed a small library."[70] As socially aspiring members of the *menu peuple* increasingly followed the bourgeois model, these familial activities became more common and brought the experiences of entertaining popular literature to illiterate relatives, old and young alike.

Similarly, informal social gatherings among the working classes also brought printed literature into the lives of non-readers in Paris. Henri Monnier's "Le roman chez la portière" (1830) depicted a group of six women of the *menu peuple* who gathered each evening to hear Ducray-Duminil's *Coelina.*[71] Such an urban version of the rural *veillée* was even portrayed in lithographs from the period.[72] More importantly, literary evidence also suggests readings at the shop. Charles de Rémusat mentioned tailors who, "informed by the readings they heard while at their sedentary labor, have in general progressive opinions," like many other workers forced indoors during the winter months.[73] And Jules Michelet remarked the practice of a weaver reading at his loom.[74]

67. See A. D. Tolédano, *La vie de famille sous la restauration et la monarchie de juillet* (Paris: Albin Michel, [1943]); Priscilla Robertson, "Home as Nest: Middle-Class Childhood in Nineteenth-Century Europe," *The History of Childhood*, Lloyd deMause, ed. (New York: Harper and Row, 1975), pp. 407–431; Ariès, *Centuries of Childhood*, pp. 339–407; and Daumard, *Les bourgeois de Paris au XIXe siècle*, pp. 167–82.

68. Daumard, *La bourgeoisie parisienne de 1815 à 1848*, pp. 137–38. See for examples of children's literature in the period, the *Journal des enfants* (1832–44); F.-G. Ducray-Duminil's *Les fêtes des enfants, ou recueil des petits moraux* (1818); and Louis Desnoyers', *Les aventures de Jean-Paul Choppart* (1834).

69. See amusing account of a housekeeper reading to her master in Kock, "Lecture d'une gouvernante," *Petits tableaux de moeurs, ou macédoine critique et littéraire* (Paris: Dupont, 1829),2:191–200.

70. Frédéric Leplay, *Les ouvriers européens...* (Tours: Mame et fils, 1877–79),6:259.

71. In Monnier, *Scènes populaires*.

72. See illustrations in Escarpit, Robine, and Orecchioni, "La lecture."

73. Charles de Rémusat, *Mémoires de ma vie*, Charles Pouthas, ed. (Paris: Plon, 1958–67),3:420.

74. Michelet, *Le peuple*, p. 118.

Like the cafés that generated interest in radical politics, the collective behavior of the Parisian working classes surely facilitated the diffusion of new literary forms, however many workers already could afford the luxury of reading by themselves.[75] But this diffusion of things literary by an oral tradition may have actually worked against the romantics as more entertaining stories became available and as the working classes turned increasingly collective and assertive; the socially concerned romantics and their imitators were not likely to have appealed as well to those in need of personal distraction or political action in the 1840s.

The fact of a working-class audience in Paris was confirmed by more than satirical middle-class accounts of its untutored literary enthusiasms or its apparent demand for reading or hearing the latest *nouveauté*. It also appeared in the recent efforts of writers with artisanal backgrounds in the flood of newspapers often aimed specifically at urban workers.[76] The best known journals, *La ruche populaire* and *L'atelier* whose staffs were almost entirely from the *menu peuple*, began publication by 1840. Similar ventures succeeded despite the regime's repressive September 1835 laws that had put an end to dozens of radical political journals attempting to rally republican sympathies in the wake of the July revolution. Moreover, established authors assisted "proletarian" writers after their first attempts in the *belles lettres* became known. George Sand wrote glowing articles on the poetry of Jean Reboul, Savinien Lapointe, and Charles Poncy in the expectation of adopting these prodigies worthy of her encouragement.[77] Although their achievements were frequently pallid imitations of middle-class forms and conventions, they did mark an expanding interest among the lower orders in reading and writing their own literature. This indigenous literary movement coincided with the larger phenomenon of a new working-class consciousness manifested in the political protest and strike activities of the 1840s.[78] As workers developed a sense of their own presence and power, their literary interests evolved as well and helped create a demand for popular literature no longer using the slightly more sophisticated romantic conventions.

75. See discussion of working class interest in a literature of its own in Newman, "L'Arme du Siècle, C'est la Plume."

76. See Hatin, *Histoire politique et littéraire de la presse en France...* (Paris: Poulet-Malassis et de Broise, 1859–61),8:547–68.

77. See George, *French Romanticism*, pp. 91–118; and Newman, "L'Arme du Siècle, C'est la Plume."

78. See, for example, Bernard H. Moss, *The Origins of the French Labor Movement: The Socialism of Skilled Workers* (Berkeley: University of California Press, 1976), pp. 31–41; Peter N. Stearns, "Patterns of Industrial Strike Activity in France during the July Monarchy," *American Historical Review* 70(1965),2:371–94; and Georges Duveau, *1848: The Making of a Revolution*, Anne Carter, trans. (New York: Vintage, 1967), pp. 161–81.

Thus the rise of these growing naive and politicized readerships spelled the doom of the romantic movement. The new interest in popular entertainment and political action must have come at the expense of the literary sensibilities of romantic authors, however remote even these were from the insight and introspection of romanticism proper.

This does not mean that the movement with its passing had no lasting effect on its audience. On the contrary, popular romanticism reached a diverse cross section of the Paris population to prepare it for subsequent literary developments. While traditional rural folkways had fostered fatalism, superstition, and fear, the new urban culture promoted a more active, rational, and assertive mentality.[79] For many peasants come to Paris, the timeless attitudes appropriate to the countryside, expressed in colporter literature, gave way to new ones more suited to life in the nineteenth-century city. Social ambitions and political aspirations spread with a frequently romantic literature aimed at a mass audience, one composed of the *menu peuple* as well as the middle classes. In this break with traditional attitudes in the city, marked by a new popular culture, romanticism shared a large measure of responsibility. It advanced forms and conventions appealing to a rapidly growing, more diverse readership. Although the movement was eventually undermined by the further evolution of this new sociocultural context, it did contribute, however briefly, to the displacement of traditional *mentalités* among the working classes in Paris.

Similarly, romanticism influenced its upper-class audience as well. The Parisian bourgeoisie already had a well-established literary interest, thanks largely to its greater opportunities for education and access to books. Its preference for a more erudite literature provided an audience for major intellectual and literary movements since the Renaissance. Yet by the early nineteenth century, the middle classes had grown sufficiently large and diverse enough to develop broader interests. In fact, many of the sentimental and gothic novels were written for and by middle-class women, even though these also appealed to socially aspiring members of the *menu peuple*. The weaning of the upper classes from serious literature occurred even more rapidly with the appearance of romanticism that stood between neo-classical works on the one hand and vulgar popular titles on the other.

Romanticism thus carried popular forms into the literature of the classically educated, facilitating a change in the tastes of elites besides those of the lower orders. In its widespread appeal, the movement participated in the development of a new mass culture early in the nine-

79. Mandrou, *De la culture populaire*, pp. 182–95.

teenth century. It drew the attention of both middle and working classes by its deliberate violation of neo-classical proprieties and its veritable celebration of distraction as an acceptable alternative to instruction. At its height romanticism marked a true watershed in the rise of popular literature for high and low readers alike.

ぶ7ゟ

ROMANTICISM AND REVOLUTION

𝒞RADITIONALLY THE YEAR 1830 has marked something of a minor historical watershed.[1] Early historians like François Guizot and Louis Blanc characterized the "three glorious days" as the completion of a self-consciously middle-class revolution that had its origins in 1789. For forty-one years it had been frustrated by a succession of regimes—republican, oligarchical, imperial, and royalist. But July brought about at last the political triumph of established commercial and financial elites embodied in the citizen-king Louis-Philippe. By the new electoral law of April 19, 1831, franchised citizens were required to pay 200 francs or more in taxes to guarantee the social and political stability of a regime empowered by popular revolution, even though less than 5 percent of the adult male population could vote in the revised *monarchie censitaire*. It was soon called for the *monarchie bourgeoise* possibly for good reason.

Perhaps of equal importance, this apparent middle-class victory in 1830 coincided with another sudden change, one in the French intellectual climate. As Jules Sandeau remarked, "Like the smell of gunpowder . . . revolt was in the air and unrest everywhere: in the streets, in books, and at the theaters."[2] This same year saw the climactic conclusion of the literary battle between the romantics and the neo-classicists: Victor Hugo's *Hernani*, a true romantic *drame*, finally appeared amidst the cheers of supporters and the jeers of opponents at the Théâtre français, long a bastion

---

1. The historiography of the 1830 revolution is sizable. Some representative works expressing the accepted view of the completed middle-class revolution include Guizot, *Mémoires pour servir à l'histoire de mon temps* (Paris: Michel Lévy frères, 1858–68),2:1–179; and Louis Blanc, *Révolution française, 1830, histoire de dix ans, règne de Louis-Philippe* (Paris: F.-H. Jeanmaire, 1882),1:7–201. More recent studies reassessing this interpretation of the revolution are Sherman Kent, *Electoral Procedure under Louis-Philippe* (New Haven: Yale University Press, 1937); and Pinkney, *The French Revolution of 1830.*

2. Jules Sandeau, *Marianna* (Paris: Charpentier, 1871 [1839]), p. 70.

of neo-classicism.[3] Moreover, Alphonse de Lamartine was installed in the Académie française, an explicit admission of romanticism to the ranks of literary respectability, an intellectual revolution comparable to the political "coup" staged by the plutocrats in July. Wrote George Sand in 1831, "Literature is in the same chaos as politics," an observation common among her contemporaries.[4] In such an atmosphere the romantics represented to the *belles lettres* what the middle classes were to politics: the apparent organizers of revolution in 1830.

This remarkable coincidence of political and literary upheaval suggests some interesting questions: What impact did the 1830 revolution have on romantic literature, its authors, publishers, and readers? How did rapid politicization of the Parisian populace, at the heart of important social and economic developments, affect the movement through its social and cultural context? The changing world of writing, publishing, and reading contributed to the brief romantic mode, as shown in earlier chapters. But the recently radicalized men and women in the political conflict of 1830 also helped inform this world, and hence that of the new literature.

This factor in the history of romanticism deserves more attention than it has received in the past. Most historians have regarded the 1789 revolution as more important to the movement, since the *angst* and melancholy of the displaced aristocrat like Chateaubriand were easily recognized and documented. Yet the great upheaval in 1789 affected the extraliterary milieu of literature in 1830 much less immediately than did the July revolution. Consequently, the present chapter focuses on the latter event and its impact on the production, distribution, and consumption of literature as a way to examine more closely the intriguing relationship between revolution and romanticism.

Other questions, of course, may be posed about events in 1830. In lieu of the revolution, could not romanticism have been an independent actor, one exerting a force of its own in political conflict? What impact did the movement's dynamic, egalitarian, even utopian tendencies among elites have on the social groups that carried out the July revolution? To what extent did the new literature move the middle classes and the *menu peuple* to revolt? Such connections between political action and intellectual discourse are equally intriguing, but nearly impossible to trace. Outside the words and deeds of public figures like Lamartine and Dumas, for example, study of the place that their ideas had in the minds and activities

---

3. See amusing contemporary account of the battle for *Hernani* in Gautier, *Histoire du romantisme*, pp. 109–114.

4. Sand, "Lettre à Jules Boucoiran. Paris, le 7 mars 1831," *Correspondance*, Georges Lubin, ed. (Paris: Garnier, 1964), 1:825.

of the anonymous masses, those people who actually made the revolution in 1830, simply cannot be documented with the few and inconclusive sources available.[5]

Investigation of the active role played by romanticism in 1830 is handicapped by more than a paucity of sources; it suffers as well from the emphases of recent social history predicated upon the study of data beyond the realm of individual consciousness. To be sure, census material, police records, parish registers, and the like tell us about ordinary men and women in earlier centuries in a way that literary sources cannot. One consequence of this, however, has been a focus on material forces in historical research since the middle of the nineteenth century, partly because of a misplaced concreteness in the study of the evidence available, partly because of a widely accepted behaviorism in historical explanation.[6] A new "wisdom" is found in the way economic factors shape human behavior beyond the power of personal ideals and aspirations. Thus the older histories that discussed events like the 1830 revolution as one step in a national striving for political liberty and democracy have long been disavowed for more functionalist, if not explicitly materialist examinations of the past.

Without wishing to return to a Whig interpretation of history, the present study takes vigorous exception to this latter trend in historiography. The interaction between the "superstructure" of ideas and the "infrastructure" of material reality presumably underlying it remains far more complex than some social scientists and Marxists have posited.[7] The fact that historians do not have as complete a set of documents from the past as they would like does not absolve them of the responsibility of exploring men's dreams and the significance they may have had. This approach is at the heart of the historical study of popular culture, both

5. Despite all the ambiguities of such a task, one attempt to assess the political role of the romantics is Manuèle D. Wasserman, "The Engaged Romantic Artist: One Aspect of Political Elitism in Nineteenth-Century France," Paper presented at the Twenty-Sixth Annual Conference of the Society for French Historical Studies, March 21–22, 1980, Washington, D.C. See also Newman's attempt to discover, "What the Crowd Wanted in the French Revolution of 1830."

6. See the interesting discussion of and challenge to such historical writing in Michael Zuckerman, "Dreams That Men Dare to Dream: The Role of Ideas in Western Modernization," *Social Science History* 2(1978),332–45; James Henretta, "Social History as Lived and Written," *American Historical Review* 84(1979),5:1293–322; and Lawrence Stone, "The Revival of Narrative: Reflections on a New Old History," *Past and Present* 85(1979):3–24.

7. See the imposing theoretical discussion of the larger historical role played by culture in Pitirim Sorokin, *Society, Culture and Personality: Their Structure and Dynamics. A System of General Sociology* (New York: Harper and Brothers, [1947]).

here and abroad, that attempts to recreate by a cautious exercise of the historical imagination the early mental life of ordinary men and women. Fortunately for the romantic period, a wide range of sources is available, enabling the historian to consider the profound dialectic between the intellect and its informing social and economic context. While the literary movement's contribution to political conflict may never be understood, the impact of the revolution on romanticism is much less inscrutable. On one level at least, it lies in the sudden, widespread, and indigenous interest in politics that moved both history and literature in 1830. Just how this popular politicization affected literature in particular will be suggested here more fully.

POLITICS AND ROMANTICISM

Romanticism and the revolution shared a common historical climate that partially explains their remarkable confluence in 1830.[8] The national mood of revolt, political and literary, owed much to major economic and social developments after Waterloo. Most of the Restoration had been relatively prosperous; nearly all sectors of the economy were developing more sophisticated means of production and modes of distribution. The baron Dupin and other liberal economists described in detailed volumes the steady growth in population, industry, and commerce evident since the disastrous years during the Empire. Except for the brief crisis of 1817–1818, due mostly to bad harvests and cheaper British goods, the Restoration prospered well enough to raise the capital and to extend the commercial networks necessary for later industrialization.[9] Until 1827 most middle-class elements benefiting by this remarkable expansion, perhaps the last bloom of a preindustrial economy, remained loyal to the Restoration, despite the reactionary policies of Charles X and his ultraroyalist ministers.[10]

But this liberal optimism was soon shaken by other developments, especially after 1827. Grain production lagged and wheat prices soared

8. See Eric Hobsbawm, *The Age of Revolution, 1789–1848* (New York: The American Library, [1962]), pp. 299–326, in which the romantic arts are placed into a European historical context of social and political revolution.

9. See Arthur Lewis Dunham, *The Industrial Revolution in France, 1815–1848* (New York: Exposition Press, 1955), pp. 432–35; and Claude Fohlen, "The Industrial Revolution in France," in Rondo Cameron, ed. *Essays in French Economic History* (Homewood, Ill.: Richard D. Irwin, 1970), pp. 201–226.

10. Bertier de Sauvigny, *The Bourbon Restoration*, pp. 355–58.

with the autumn's poor harvest. In 1828 the *haute banque* turned over less than half the business it did the previous year, while coal mining concerns faced sharply declining profits, as the crisis quickly spread to industry and trade.[11] Still other contradictions, social and political as well as economic, inherent in the anachronistic regime began to undermine much of its loyal middle-class support. The erratic politics of those who had "neither learned nor forgot" since the 1789 revolution promoted widespread demands for a revised charter from the Chamber of Deputies, including the 221 liberals elected in 1827. Although the political crisis did not come to a head until the spring of 1830, the growing disaffection of worker and bourgeois alike in the wake of economic depression contributed to the overthrow of the Restoration.

The more conservative romantics, of course, shared in the regime's brief economic development and social optimism. They benefited as well by the opportunities to develop a new literature in a growing book trade that encouraged the publication of their initial royalism, born of a disaffection with the social and political failures of the 1789 revolution and its Napoleonic aftermath. Most writers in the new fashion implicitly supported the regime for essentially the same reasons as the political liberals: it afforded them the chance to participate in the political stability and economic growth during the 1820s. The glowing accounts of romantic intellectual revival, marked by the end of the Empire, coincided with the many others on the economic growth that began in the same years.[12]

The romantics were also affected by the developments toward the end of the regime, and their writings soon turned from their former ardent royalism to a more progressive liberalism. In contrast to his early introspective melancholy, for example, Lamartine wrote later, "It is poetry that surveys and judges and, showing man the vulgarity of his work, calls him ceasely forward, pointing out to him utopias."[13] Most romantics like him participated in this general movement among middle-class elements against the Restoration. Moreover, the regime's reactionary politics touched them as authors personally; the gerontocracy seemed to limit further opportunities for young men in search of an honorable career. The sudden decline in the economy and the glaring political ineptitude of Charles X helped push this resentment into overt opposition.[14]

11. Paul Gonnet, "Esquisse de la crise économique en France de 1827 à 1832," *Revue d'histoire économique et sociale* 33(1955),264–89.

12. See Chapter 5, pp. 127, 130.

13. Lamartine, "Destinées de la poésie," *Revue de deux mondes* (1834),1:690.

14. See similar argument in Barbéris, "Le mal du siècle, ou d'un romantisme de droit à un romantisme de gauche."

However shaped by the same social and economic forces that fostered the revolution, the politics of literature did not suit all the well-known romantics. A number of obvious exceptions stand out; despite 1830 Balzac and Dumas maintained their entrepreneurial attitudes, Vigny and Musset their asocial estheticism. But the July days did mark, for most, a noticeable shift in a movement towards a more socially conscious literature.[15] In the first phase during the Restoration, romanticism was more individualistic and lyrical. It apotheosized feeling in all forms, and it set up the individual against society. Almost as if the relative wellbeing of the regime had reenforced the censorship, especially after 1820, most romantics avoided politics in lieu of the development of their very personal esthetic.

In its second phase during the July Monarchy, however, romanticism adopted the doctrine of progress and perfectability, just as it also espoused the cause of social reform. Even Alfred de Vigny, the most socially aloof of the writers in the new fashion, remarked in his journal that "the improvement of the most numerous class and the agreement between labor and property [were] essential issues."[16] Much of this new spirit owed to the orphic mission that many romantics defined for themselves in their reaction against not only the aristocratic royalists, but also the bourgeois Orleanists. Whatever the social oppositions that engendered it, the humanitarian notion of universal love evolved clearly after 1830. Hugo's *Contemplations*, Lamartine's *Jocelyn*, George Sand's *Le compagnon du tour de France*, among many others, represented this romantic assertion of a social conscience well after the July revolution.

Despite the persuasive historical circumstances, the role of revolutionary politics in this literary development is not perfectly clear. But the change in regimes certainly meant for all literati, romantic or not, a new legal context.[17] Although press laws were generally a bane to journalists more than they were to other authors during the Restoration, they affected writers in all fields, including the *belles lettres* and history. Four times before 1830, P. J. de Béranger and his publisher were fined and sentenced to prison for the apparent sedition of his songs.[18] Similarly,

15. See discussion of shift in the romantic movement to a more social commitment in Clement, *Romanticism in France*, pp. 249–64; and Evans, *Social Romanticism in France*, pp. 1–104.

16. Vigny, *Oeuvres complètes*, 2:968.

17. Besides the appropriate chapters in Irene Collins, *The Government and the Newspaper Press, 1814–1881* (London: Oxford University Press, 1959) pp. 36–52, 60–81, see Bellanger et al., *Histoire générale de la presse française*, 2:99–110.

18. P.-J. de Béranger, *Ma biographie; ouvrage posthume...* (Paris: Perrotin, 1857), pp. 199–207.

seven members of the Académie française objected to Hugo's characterization of Louis XIII in *Marion Delorme* (1829). The play's staging was delayed until the July Monarchy when Hugo convinced the Interior Ministry that no insult was intended.[19] In 1826 alone, thirty-two books in Paris were prosecuted for various offenses, from attacks against government officials to outrages against public and religious morality. Twenty-five of the books were condemned and sixty men jailed or fined for their part in the publication.[20]

Government restriction on the book trade, of course, was much less severe than it was in the press: licenses, regulations, deposits, fines, and sentences were all less burdensome, because books with their smaller, more "responsible" audience posed less of a threat to the regime than newspapers. Often journalists, like Paul-Louis Courier, published their articles as pamphlets to avoid the stringent press laws under the Restoration.[21] Still the book trade remained closely surveilled by the authorities who had the power to revoke a bookseller's or a printer's *brevet* for a long list of petty offenses. The failure to deposit with the Interior Ministry the requisite copies of a new work was one of the regime's favorite ruses to put a politically suspect printer out of business.[22]

After 1830 the legal context eased considerably for both journalists and authors. Article 7 of the new charter stated clearly that "censorship can never be established," and the law of October 8, 1830, instituted trials by jury for all libel cases and press offenses.[23] Not until Giuseppe Fieschi's spectacular attempt to assassinate Louis-Philippe in 1835 did the regime create a new press law as repressive as those during the Restoration, even though authorities resorted to prosecution to shut down overtly revolutionary newspapers.[24] Nevertheless, the political press flourished, however ephemerally, while the number of books condemned declined. During the Restoration, an average of twenty-six books a year were prosecuted successfully; during the July Monarchy twenty-three were annually brought to trial. Moreover, the new regime confis-

19. Frederick B. Artz, *France Under the Bourbon Restoration* (Cambridge: Harvard University Press, 1931), p. 340.

20. Département de la Seine, *Recherches statistiques sur la ville de Paris*, 4: Table 80.

21. Bellanger et al., *Histoire génénrale de la presse française*, 2:88.

22. See government cases against *libraires* for precisely this administrative offense in A.N.F[18]566–568 "Affaires diverses, 1815–1854."

23. J.-B. Duvergier, ed. *Collection complète des lois, décrets, ordonnances, règlemens* [sic] *et avis du Conseil d'Etat...de 1788 à 1845*, 2ᵉ éd. (Paris: Imprimerie Nationale, 1834–45),30:81,103.

24. Bellanger et al., *Histoire générale de la presse française*, 2:111–14.

cated titles apparently more for pornography than for political offenses, especially after 1840.[25]

This change in legal context was reflected in the principles expressed by the Interior Ministers responsible for enforcing the press laws under the two regimes. In 1829 François de La Bourdonnaye instructed the *préfets* that "religion, good morals, public or private life of the citizens, and legitimate authority must be preserved by you from all attacks, direct or indirect, for all fiction or allusion may injure: that is what constitutes the national honor and the State."[26] Only two years later the Orleanist Minister of the Interior Marthe de Montalivet directed the prefects only to monitor the daily activities of the press and to answer unfair charges against the regime.[27] The literate world operated with relatively more freedom during the July Monarchy, thanks to the regime's self-imposed constraints and juries' reluctance to convict, despite the maintenance of many Restoration laws aimed at the press and bookselling.

The change in regimes and their press laws may well have influenced the development of romanticism.[28] Under the Restoration, the charged political atmosphere was suppressed, leaving writers few legal avenues to express their opposition to the regime. For more creative spirits, the constraints against sedition in politics only made esthetic revolt more attractive, ironically the one avenue that Julien Sorel did not consider in *Le rouge et le noir*. For others romanticism was partly an appropriate literary response to a repressive political context. "Romanticism, in its essence, is nothing but liberalism in literature," enunciated Victor Hugo in 1830.[29] Many like Chateaubriand after 1824 used the romantic movement as a natural vehicle for their opposition to the Restoration. Although few carried their rebellion so far, Alexandre Dumas actually took to the barricades during the revolution.[30] Even the aristocratically inclined Alfred de Musset was not sorry to see the Restoration Monarchy fall.

With the recently sought freedom of expression, especially in the first years of the Orleanist regime, writers in the new fashion adopted

25. See list of censored titles in Fernand Drujon, *Catalogue des ouvrages écrits et dessins de toute nature poursuivis, supprimés ou condamnés depuis le 21 octobre 1814 jusqu'au 31 juillet 1877* (Paris: Rouveyre, 1879).

26. François de La Bourdonnaye, "Circulaire No. 40, Ministre Secrétaire d'Etat de l'Intérieur, De la Bourdonnaye aux préfets (le 8 septembre 1829)," A.N.F[18]2 "Imprimerie et Librairie. Circulaires, 1814–1850."

27. Marthe de Montalivet, August 29, 1832, *Ibid.*

28. A similar argument is developed in Milner, *Le romantisme*, p. 55.

29. Hugo, "Préface de *Hernani*," *Oeuvres complètes: théâtre*, 1:523.

30. Dumas, *Mes mémoires*, 3:175–426, esp.

new social and political commitments impossible before the revolution. In fact, the movement's writings became more diffuse and less concerned exclusively with literary issues. Hugo now published his more politicized poetry written during the Restoration, while he also experimented less in his newer verse: *Les feuilles d'automne* (1832) was not only more political, but also less iconoclastic than *Les orientales* (1829). Much of what the Restoration had prevented, the July Monarchy now permitted, facilitating the expression of new verities, political as well as literary. These shifts in focus among authors like Hugo owed much to the generally less restrained intellectual climate in the July Monarchy, a legal context whose loopholes even helped bring down the regime in 1848.[31]

The politicization of literature in general, and romanticism in particular, appears clearly in 120 random samplings from the genre indexes in the back of the 1830 *Bibliographie de la France* (see Appendix A). Romantic influence on the production of poetry, for example, continued to grow; 17 percent of the titles evinced some influence of the movement, a rise of more than 15 percent since 1827. That the new fashion became increasingly respectable was reflected in poetry obviously intended for an elite audience, such as that for Juste Olivier's *Poèmes suisses* and Edouard Alletz' *La nouvelle messiade*. But what was most significant about the sampled titles was the remarkable rise in political poetry using romantic conventions. While all poems in 1820 recounting the assassination of the duc de Berri followed neo-classical models, the verse arising from the revolution showed much more flexibility in meter and rhyme. One piece on the arrival of the duc d'Orléans in Paris in July broke a monotonous series of alexandrine couplets to refrain, "Chantons, célébrons sa sagesse;/ Les vertus dont it est doté,/ Dans les travaux de sa jeunesse,/ Décèlent leur maturité."[32] Amidst numerous popular patriotic pieces, in a genre whose form and content were usually irrelevant to developments in the new literature, appeared other imitations of the romantics. Despite his open

31. On the new legal context and its impact on the press' role in 1848 see Guise, "Le roman-feuilleton et la vulgarisation des idées politiques et sociales."

32. Jean Sarazin, *Cantate sur le retour de S.A.R. Mgr le duc d'Orléans à Paris* (Paris: Imp. Porthmann, 1830), p. 2.

Note the consistently conservative political nature of the sampled 1830 titles. One reason for this is the noticeable underrepresentation of political works in general, and of radically republican works in particular, in the *Bibliographie* and the A.N.F[18]II* series. Many printers of political tracts during the year simply did not report them to the Interior Ministry; they probably knew that the regimes, both the old and the new, could not administer the press laws effectively at the height of the violent upheavals of July and August. Consequently, the sampled works here can not be considered truly representative of the politics of 1830, even though they are likely to be much more useful in discussion of developments in the more strictly literary genres.

satire of Hugo's verse—"Ah! c'est bien là vraiment le langage des Dieux,/ Car nul mortel ne peut l'entendre"—J.-J. Lesergent's *Le troubadour français* borrowed many of the movement's freer ballad and lyrical forms in celebration of liberal interests after the revolution.[33]

A similar development occurred in drama, though hardly to the same extent as poetry. While the percentage of titles reflecting romantic influence doubled in only three years, many more popular political plays participated in the fashionable violation of the neo-classical proprieties. Clairville ainé's *Quatorze ans de la vie de Napoléon*, presented at the Théâtre du Luxembourg in November 1830, deliberately ignored both the unities of time and place; its four acts were set in Berlin, Paris, Waterloo, and Saint Helena, spanning nearly the entire course of the First Empire. Similarly, an anonymous piece sympathetic to the plight of the Bourbons in July followed their entourage from the splendors of the court to the humility of a provincial *auberge*. Subtitled *parades historiques*, the two acts of *Scènes de cour et de cabaret* dramatized the quiet dignity of the royal family despite their ignominious peasant disguises. The drama of 1830 not only incorporated the subjects appropriate to a politically charged atmosphere; they also adopted the popular usages of the romantic movement. But this development in the theater was much less marked than in poetry. Less than 10 percent of the sampled drama reflected the explicit impact of the July revolution, even though more than 26 percent evinced positive signs of romanticism. While verse was often used to express political opinion, plays were not, perhaps because the purer conventions of melodrama, comedy-vaudeville, comedy, and tragedy were so well established. The romantic influence continued in the choice of medieval subjects and the violation of the three unities, but politics appeared largely the butt of satire.

Because they took more time to write, most of the sampled novels continued earlier trends in the publication of popular historical fiction, whose share now reached a third of all the novels examined. Most works, begun well before the July revolution, did not adopt any of the political themes or subjects most evident in poetry. Rather, they remained largely sentimental and gothic tales set in the Middle Ages, the standard fare of the Restoration. Titles like Louise Lemercier's *Victor Amédée, ou le siège de Turin* and K. F. van der Velde's *La conquête du Mexique* were little different from the popular romantic vogue of Walter Scott's Waverly novels. Only Adam Mickiewicz's *Konrad Wallenrod* reflected the romantic interest in popular national aspirations: "Like Goethe, like Byron, like Lamartine," stated the preface, "Mickiewicz also has his detractors;

---

33. J.-J. Lesergent, *Le troubadour français, chansons philosophiques, politiques, satiriques, érotiques et badines* (Paris: Ladvocat, 1830), p. 227.

they avow nevertheless that he has no equal when he paints the tortures of unhappy love, when he describes the agonies of a patriotic soul."[34] Such a sentiment blending romantic longing with nationalistic feeling may well have fired the souls of the French in July, though it appeared among novels less frequently than it did among poems published in 1830.

This relative continuity in fiction was largely offset by the nearly total political preoccupation of titles in history, like poetry the genre most easily adapted to topics of contemporary interest. A flood of tracts more or less disguised as historical works appeared among the samples. Accounts of heroic acts during the revolution, praises of the virtuous populace, and favorable biographical sketches of Louis-Philippe took up nearly 50 percent of the titles, e.g., *Le reveil du lion, ou Paris dans les immortelles journées*; *Esquisse du mouvement héroïque du peuple français*; and *Philippe 1er, Roi des Français*. The dramatic treatment of important national events, of course, indicated less interest in romantic convention than in political polemic, but their treatment did reflect some literary concerns of the movement's colorful histories of the Middle Ages. Although it was hardly touched by the July revolution, E. Gauttier d'Arc's *Histoire des conquêtes des Normands en Italie, en Sicilie, et en Grèce* was a striking elaboration of Augustin Thierry's earlier study of the Normands appropriate as much to political as to literary revolution, as seen in Chapter 1. The present-mindedness of medieval histories was perfectly evident in E.-M. Masse's *Histoire du pape Alexandre VI et de César Borgia*: "It is by no motive to detract, for no hostile end that we have written this history," the author announced in the preface. "We have sought to understand the pontificate of Alexander VI, as in all other periods where we will have tried to find some lesson for the present."[35] This romantic trend in historical writing constituted a fifth of all the titles sampled in the genre.

Evidently, then, the 1830 revolution did influence popular romantic titles that as a consequence became increasingly politicized. This is also evident in the larger production of *belles lettres* and history. Despite a drop in the total number of titles, from 7,823 in 1829, to 6,739 in 1830, the number of titles in genres often given to political polemic actually rose; of those listed in the *Bibliographie de la France*, there were 518 new works in political economy, 416 in the history of France, and 665 in poetry, the vast majority of which was short pieces celebrating or decrying the events of July. On the other hand, genres more resistant to

34. Adam Mickiewicz, *Konrad Wallenrod, récit historique* (Paris: Gagniard, 1830), p. ix.

35. E.-M. Masse, *Histoire du pape Alexandre VI et de César Borgia* (Paris: Lefebvre, 1830), p. i.

contemporary issues, the drama and the novel, actually declined more than 10 percent from what they had been in 1827, to 299 and 264 respectively. This trend favoring easily politicized titles also appeared in the mean and median edition sizes of the random samples taken in poetry, drama, fiction, and history. While the overall mean in history and the *belles lettres* dropped to only 1,161 copies per edition, the means in poetry actually increased by more than 15 percent over those in 1827.

In the publication of all literary genres affected by the revolution, however, the romantic movement in particular enjoyed a decided advantage. In 1830 the mean and median edition sizes of titles in the new literature were generally larger than those of titles reflecting little or none of its influence (see Table 7.1). Romantic poetry benefited most from political developments: its vogue exceeded that of nonromantic titles in the same genre by a substantial margin for the only time between 1820 and 1840. Fiction in the new vogue, on the other hand, seems to have suffered slightly during the political turmoil that saw the publication of the Enlightenment authors at the expense of less polemical historical novelists. Nevertheless, the evidence available indicates that the intense politics of 1830 promoted rather than deterred the production of romantic titles, especially those easily adapted to topical polemical issues. Romantic authors moved by the revolution did see a greater demand for their works than most authors at the same time, despite a major crisis in the book trade, perhaps because they were willing to accommodate new content as well as new forms in their writing.

POLITICS AND ROMANTICISM'S CONTEXT

The atmosphere of 1830 was likely to touch nearly all writers in Paris eventually, since the patterns of conflict leading to July involved much more than politics. They reflected social developments as well, such as the problem of revolutionary generations that contemporaries often noted. Guizot, for one, viewed the revolution in terms of a new generation of moderate middle-class revolutionaries, on the English model, even though most other observers saw the revolution's leading edge in students on the barricades. "They came forth in a body, particularly the young men of the Polytechnic School . . . instantly gaining the confidence of the people," claimed Caleb Cushing in an eyewitness account of the events in Paris.[36] The extreme youth of the revolutionaries, be-

36. Cushing, *Review, Historical and Political, of the Late Revolution in France,* 1:159–60. See also Guizot, *Trois générations: 1789–1814–1848* (Paris: Michel Lévy frères, 1863).

TABLE 7.1
Mean and Median Edition Sizes of Sampled

Year		Poetry			Drama		
		Mean	N	Median	Mean	N	Median
1827	Romantic	500	3	300	1,000	4	1,000
	Nonromantic	700	17	500	871	19	500
1830	Romantic	1,375	4	1,000	760	5	500
	Nonromantic	823	18	500	510	17	500
1834	Romantic	1,094	7	700	1,895	12	2,000
	Nonromantic	2,540	16	900	1,392	18	2,000

Source: A. N. F^{18} II* 14, 19, 24. "Déclarations des Imprimeurs," for edition sizes of titles sampled from the *Bibliographie* equal to the averages (plus or minus 10 percent), indicating a wide dispersion around the means.

sides the romanticism of authors in 1830, was a frequent observation long after the July days.

But the three glorious days owed to more than bourgeois youth; they offered an opportunity to the young of all social ranks. Opined Frances Trollope, "There is scarcely a boy so insignificant as to doubt his having the power and the right to instruct the world."[37] Recent historical work has shown that most of the relatively young men on the barricades came from the many artisanal crafts in the city.[38] Moreover, the revolution mobilized the energies of such diverse social commitment in literature as well as politics. Sainte-Beuve noted how the July revolution brought a more idealistic spirit to the literary world in which younger writers developed new social themes in their creations. "Liberal in fact and by inclination, even when their opinions tend to conservatism, men of spirit and independence had in them a sympathy in tune with the future movement of society."[39]

With established reputations as youthful political and literary revolutionaries, the romantics earned their share of responsibility for events in 1830, whether or not they deserved it. Indeed, some contemporaries were acutely conscious of the coincidence of romanticism and revolution. "At the very hour when the *émeutier* with a violent hand tore from the constitution of this country those pages which displeased him," Jules Janin stated later, "the writer . . . also freed himself from the accepted

37. Trollope, *Paris and the Parisians*, p. 53.

38. Pinkney, *The French Revolution of 1830*, pp. 252–73.

39. Sainte-Beuve, "Espoir et voeu du mouvement littéraire et poétique après la révolution de 1830," *Premiers lundis* (Paris: Calmann Lévy, 1886), 1:403, originally published on October 11, 1830.

Romantic and Nonromantic Titles, by Genre, 1827–1834

Fiction			History			Total		
Mean	N	Median	Mean	N	Median	Mean	N	Median
1,313	8	1,000	1,870	5	1,000	1,270	20	1,000
1,150	13	1,000	1,246	17	1,000	979	66	750
1,350	8	2,000	1,370	3	1,000	1,190	20	1,000
1,712	16	1,500	1,120	13	1,000	1,040	62	750
1,665	10	1,000	2,583	6	3,000	1,778	35	1,500
1,585	13	750	2,608	13	2,500	1,983	60	1,450

de la France and classified by romantic influence (Appendix A). Standard deviations in nearly all cases were approximately

rules, broke the yoke which weighed upon him, and in his own world of prose or poetry, of the drama or the novel . . . accomplished his own little July revolution."[40] The new generation of writers, apparently, effected upheavals in both literature and politics in July.

Did such a generation actually appear in 1830? Demographic data in that year do show a marked regeneration of authorship that surely must have contributed to political and literary enthusiasms. The mean age of writers sampled from the *Bibliographie de la France* dropped from 46.6 in 1827, to 41.3 in 1830, the youngest average age of authors in the entire period (see Table 3.1). More than 51 percent of authors were under age 40, as the age structure of Parisian literati changed to accommodate larger numbers of more youthful writers (see Figure 3.2). Moreover, the mean and median ages of men and women borrowing romantic conventions sank even lower than those of all authors: 37.5 and 32 compared to 41.3 and 36, respectively. Although there is too little evidence of a romantic generation per se, younger people did join the ranks of writers in the new fashion at the height of the political conflict. Why they should have done so must be attributed, in part at least, to the revolutionary climate that encouraged youthful energies in a wide range of endeavors.

The impact of the July revolution on romantic authorship is equally apparent in the literary market. As Charles Ladvocat claimed, the change in regimes brought an end to many marginal businesses already hard pressed by the economic depression since 1828.[41] Bankruptcies climbed to 32, while both the number of titles published and the average size of

40. Janin, *Histoire de la littérature dramatique* (Paris: Michel Lévy frères, 1853–58), 1:154.

41. Ladvocat cited in Biré, *Dernières causeries historiques et littéraires*, p. 107.

first editions dropped in 1830 to their lowest levels in the period, reflecting the immediate influence of the revolution on the book trade in Paris.[42] Preoccupation with politics was distraction enough for readers buying and borrowing books. "Literature did not escape the evil influence of circumstances," wrote C.-L. Lesur, a prominent *libraire* lamenting the sudden intrusion of revolution in the literary market.[43] He was joined in this sentiment by Alexandre Dumas who also witnessed the dangers of political upheaval to literary production.[44] In such conditions only the shrewdest author like Dumas survived.

Consequently, romantic authors published in 1830 were markedly more professional: approximately 40 percent of all sampled writers adopting the romantic fashion devoted their energies to publishing more than any other occupation (see Appendix B). The contracted market for books made it more difficult for amateurs to place their manuscripts before many readers unless they turned to the new literature, a fact also apparent from the production figures of titles published in 1830. This not only marked the triumph of romanticism among fulltime writers whose numbers continued to grow to nearly 27 percent of all sampled authors in 1830. But it also encouraged the movement's publication and distribution by *libraires* in quest of marketable books to survive a disastrous year for the Paris book trade. Completely new authors not at the heart of popular romanticism in 1830 could not have chosen a worse time to break into print; their frustrations must have contributed to the disaffection of literati in the early years of the July Monarchy, despite the marked trend favoring younger, more worldly writers.[45]

The revolution also meant a disruption of production even more immediate than the loss of a market and the disillusionment of less cynical authors, romantic or no. Workers in the printing trade were among the most literate and best organized in Paris.[46] Their active opposition to the Restoration began the first day the July Ordinances were issued when the imposition of stringent press censorship put them out of work. Thus they were the first in the streets to organize armed resistance and build barricades.[47] In the short run the loss of such workers during

---

42. See A.D.S.V.P. D10 U3 "Dossiers des faillites, 1830"; and A.N. F[18]II*19 "Déclarations des Imprimeurs," 1830.

43. Lesur, *Annuaire historique universel* (1831), p. 285.

44. See Dumas, *Mes mémoires*, 4:338–39, on the incompatibility of radical politics and literature.

45. See discussion of important shift in the attitudes of romantic literati after 1830 in Barbéris, *Balzac et le mal du siècle*, 1:31–139.

46. See Paul Chauvet, *Les ouvriers du livre en France, de 1789 à la constitution de la Fédération du livre* (Paris: Marcel Rivière, 1956), pp. 90–113.

47. Pinkney, *The French Revolution of 1830*, pp. 260–62.

the revolution meant a halt to all production for the duration of the conflict; in the longer run it meant the sabotage of mechanical presses for twenty of the most important printers in the city.[48] Fears that replacements would displace jobs encouraged workers to join forces to petition the Chamber of Deputies and the King.[49] They wanted the new regime to prevent the further installation of new presses not only in the Imprimerie Royale, but also in the large private printing firms of Paris. Although it violated laws against working-class organization, circulars were sent to the 5,000 men working in the trade urging them to stop the repairs on the damaged presses. Meetings on August 15 and September 2 drew more than 2,000 workers affected by the new machines.[50] Only in 1831, after they had been convinced that mechanical presses did not actually displace workers, but, rather, speeded production to meet the new growing demand for printed matter, press men and compositors accepted this stage of mechanization.

The revolutionary spirit limited production for a full year after the revolution. But it contributed primarily to difficult structural problems already facing the book trade. The overproduction of the classics during the Restoration had exhausted an inelastic demand for expensive books and forced many *libraires* to precipitous remainders, unscrupulous practices, and even bankruptcies. The year 1830 actually intensified a well-established trend, so the sudden contraction of demand for books in the wake of the revolution only forced an earlier but nearly inevitable ruin for many traditional booksellers. For more conservative men the answer to the crisis lay in immediate governmental intervention.[51] Fifty-nine booksellers petitioned the new regime for massive loans provided by the laws of 17, 18, and 26 October 1830 at low or no interest, payable within two or three years in installments at three or six month intervals.[52] In this way more than 1,886,000 francs reached the hands of desperate *libraires* especially given to older trade practices. Nearly all the titles they left with the regime as collateral for the loans were serious, neo-classical and classical works of little market value in 1830, despite Martin Bossange's claim to

48. A.N.F¹⁸567 "Affaires diverses, 1815–1854," dossier 262 bis. See the letter of A. A. Renouard, mayor of the eleventh *arrondissement*, to the Minister of the Interior, August 1830.

49. See petition of printers' workers in *Le constitutionnel*, August 19, 1830; and in *La gazette des tribunaux*, September 6, 1830.

50. See account of the trial in *La gazette des tribunaux*, September 15, 1830.

51. E.g., even before the intensification of the trade crisis in 1830, *libraires* turned to the regime for help. See Commission d'enquête de la librairie de Paris, *Requête présentée à LL. EE. MM. les ministres du Roi* (Paris: F. Didot, [1829]).

52. See Ministère des finances, *Compte général de l'administration des finances, rendu pour l'année 1830* (Paris: Imprimerie Royale, 1831), pp. 280–311.

the contrary.[53] When *libraires* began to default, Bossange proposed to the Chambers a national library system, one that would use the titles of delinquent booksellers.[54]

Not all *libraires* responded to the crisis in the same fashion. While many turned to the new regime, others adopted new means and modes of production and distribution to market cheaper, more attractive titles for a larger, less sophisticated audience. As officials in the Interior Ministry well knew, many more new men after the revolution started printing and selling books without authorization.[55] The rapid influx of new men into the trade, more than half of whom were provincial-born, transformed the book business by the early years of the July Monarchy. Although part of a much older trend, its consequences became most evident only after 1830 whose events swept aside so many of the trade's anachronisms. In the face of such fierce competition, many *libraires* old and new adopted new commercial practices, especially the shift to current writers, on a much larger scale in order to survive.[56]

One shrewd observer in particular, Edmond Werdet, noted this movement to the publication of novels by living authors in popular formats. "Next to this rage for novels that had invaded all of France, the old classics of good literature, those faithful friends to the youth of all well-educated men, those masterpieces that will make the eternal glory of our country, were shoved aside and nearly forgotten in the book stalls."[57] However much he claimed to regret this development, Werdet himself began to publish more fashionable works, including Balzac's fiction. Entrepreneurs in the trade responded to the crisis, not in appeals to the new regime for cheap credit, but in new products for a larger, less sophisticated audience to stimulate demand for books. The revolution ruined the weaker, less imaginative *libraires* but provided others an opportunity to prosper even more once the national economic depression had eased.

In this revolutionary climate, in the book trade as well as in politics and literature, the romantics received a significant boost. As authors of *nouveautés* in vogue, they were promoted on an unprecedented scale.

53. Bossange, *Courtes observations de M. Bossange père à MM. les membres de la Chambre des Députés, relatives au prêt sur nantissement fait à la librairie par le gouvernement* (Paris: Imp. Dupont et Laguionie, [n.d.]), p. 7.

54. Bossange, *Nouvelles observations...relatives au prêt fait à la librairie, suivies du catalogue des livres donnés en nantissement.*

55. See letter from Minister of the Interior to the *Procureur* of the King, dated December 4, 1827 in A.N.F¹⁸568 "Affaires diverses, 1815–1854," dossier 406.

56. See discussion in Neret, *Histoire illustrée*, pp. 156–58.

57. Werdet, *De la librairie française*, p. 114.

More entrepreneurial spirits used them to survive as much as to profit in a particularly bad market for books, especially classics, in the immediate aftermath of the revolution. Political conflict gave romanticism a major impetus—albeit a more politicized one—among younger, more professionally minded authors in a rapidly changing market for books. The events of 1830 provided a new extraliterary context for the new fashion in literature that reflected many of the intense political interests of the moment. In this way, the revolution fostered romanticism and prepared its climax in the first years of the July Monarchy.

Clearly, sudden changes in the Paris readership also facilitated this temporary politicization that benefited the movement in 1830. From contemporary observers and indirect evidence, whatever the difficulties of more thorough documentation, there appeared to be a growing, politically conscious audience. The memory of 1789 and Napoleonic victories combined with a strong desire for self-improvement and direct action to make this consciousness widespread. One writer remarked the trend among the lower orders early in the Restoration: "The love of study is the true spirit of the century, this is the dominant passion that has won all walks of life, all classes, all conditions. One would take your streets and boulevards for the doors to the Académie."[58] Jules Michelet worried about the cultural pretensions of the people,[59] the same concern that Lady Morgan celebrated in 1830: "There is scarcely a porter, a water carrier, or a commissionaire, running the streets of Paris, who is not more learned and more enlightened, than this royal patron of letters of the Augustan age [Louis XV]."[60] She even noted the artisan's thirst for knowledge evident in his attendance to itinerant professors of physics in the Champs-Elysées.

Although this extensive curiosity was neither peculiar to 1830 nor antipathetic to entertainment, it became more politicized with the revolution. Even the illiterate heard about the July Ordinances in the Paris cafés where opposition newspapers were read aloud.[61] Action in the streets testified to this attention, indeed commitment to political passions

58. Hippolyte Mazier du Heaume, *Voyage d'un jeune Grec à Paris* (Paris: F. Louis, 1824), 1:143–44.

59. Michelet, *Le peuple*, pp. 119–20.

60. Morgan, *France in 1829–1830*, 1:383. Note the discussions of the politicization of the Parisian laboring poor in the essays presented in Roger Price, ed. *Revolution and Reaction: 1848 and the Second French Republic* (London: Croom Helm, 1975), pp. 73–132, 170–209.

61. Pinkney, *The French Revolution of 1830*, pp. 81–82. See also the brief account of café life as the center of political and social mixing in Galignani, *Galignani's Paris Guide*, p. xciv; and Nadaud, *Les mémoires de Léonard*, p. 90.

in 1830. The intense climate of opinion encouraged many workers to follow the course of events in various literary accounts, since standards of living remained too low for most Parisians to read simply for distraction. Few of them would want to afford books or newspapers in the middle of a depression. By 1830 the price of a kilo loaf of bread had climbed to over 60 centimes, nearly a third the daily wage of an unskilled laborer. Unemployment was high and the number on relief jumped to more than a third of the city.[62] After the severe winter of 1829, very few workers were likely to be interested in reading, except for some compelling reason, when even basic necessities were lacking.

But the revolution surely drew the attention of many readers, however hard pressed they must have been: nearly all journals saw a 10 percent rise in subscriptions after July. According to the prefect of police in a letter to the Président du Conseil, the circulation of the city's leading newspapers climbed to more than 61,000 readers in the course of 1830.[63] The demand for books and newspaper certainly could not have maintained the level it did, given the marginal living conditions of most Parisians, without a highly charged political atmosphere to promote the dissemination of written forms appropriate to revolutionary activity. As Auguste Raffet's frontispiece shows, politics marketed properly could actually be good business (see Illustration 12).

Even if the book trade suffered, there was a significant increase in the number of newspapers, especially those aimed at a self-respecting plebeian audience.[64] Besides the high percentage of popular books devoted to politics, more than twenty-eight new popular journals appeared from July to December 1830, largely as a consequence of more relaxed enforcement of press laws and greater readership demand. In the last two weeks of September alone, three newspapers in Paris began publication for an audience among the *menu peuple*: the *Journal des ouvriers* (September 19), *L'artisan* (September 26), and *Le peuple, journal général des ouvriers* (September 30). Popular journals appealed deliberately to the proud, literate artisan seeking to better his condition economically, socially, and politically.

This assertiveness among the lower orders, of course, alarmed many conservatives during the revolution and long afterward. Frances

62. Gonnet, "Equisse de la crise," pp. 285–90.

63. Bellanger et al., *Histoire générale de la presse française*, 2:100. See the April 8, 1831 letter from the prefect of police to Casimir Périer in A.N.F[18]2162 bis "Cabinets de lecture. Demandes d'autorisation, 1816–1850."

64. Hatin, *Bibliographie historique et critique de la presse périodique française*, pp. 373–435. See also the discussion of these journals in George, *French Romanticism*, pp. 91–96; and Guise, "Le roman-feuilleton et la vulgarisation des idées politiques et sociales."

12. "Paillasse" (ca. 1831). Frontispiece by Auguste Raffet (1804–1860). *Courtesy of the Boston Public Library, Print Department.*

Trollope noted their presence in the Tuilleries gardens and the Louvre, formerly the bastions of more respectable classes. "Till the fresh dirt (not the fresh gloss) of the Three Days' labour be worn off, dingy jackets, uncomely casquettes, ragged blouses, and ill-favored round-caps, that look like they did duty night and day, must be tolerated; and in this toleration appears to consist, at present, the principal external proof of the increased liberty of the Parisian mob."[65] She might have added that their presence also indicated a more confident and consciously aggressive attitude that surely must have encouraged many to read for instruction and even action in 1830, as Martin Nadaud noted in his memoirs.[66]

This revolutionary spirit touched all social levels in the city. Just as the *menu peuple* expressed their dissatisfaction in the streets with the regime, both Restoration and Orleanist, they also shared in a general reawakening to their conditions reported in a flood of investigations on "the social question."[67] In September *L'artisan* called for studies on the problems in individual trades, although only one article, on printing, ever appeared. Middle-class conservatives, however, were more prolific: Bigot de Morogues, Gérando, the Paris Chambre de commerce et d'industrie, among others, published their findings soon after the revolution in the hopes of shedding light on insistent poverty and crime in rapidly growing cities.[68] The particularly empoverished condition of the working classes combined with a greater sensitivity to their plight within a larger literate context. This milieu was derived, in part at least, from a renewed revolutionary consciousness after 1830, a widespread spirit reflected in the rise in literacy rates in poorer districts of the city, as military records show.[69]

More importantly, the public political concerns fostered the demand, despite low standards of living, for a literature appealing directly to the most immediate interests of the populace. In 1830 this contributed to the politicization of literature, including titles in the romantic fashion. The revolution marked an important stage in this evolution of a plebeian

---

65. Trollope, *Paris and the Parisians*, p. 39.

66. Nadaud, *Les mémoires de Léonard*, pp. 102–103.

67. See review of contemporary studies in Villermé, *Tableau de l'état*, 2:27–33; Hilde Regaudes-Weiss, *Les enquêtes ouvrières en France entre 1830 et 1848* (Paris: Alcan, 1936); and Chevalier, *Laboring Classes and Dangerous Classes*, pp. 135–39.

68. E.g., P. M. S. Bigot de Morogues, *De la misère des ouvriers...* (Paris: Imp. Huzard, 1832); J. M. de Gérando, *De la bienfaisance publique...* (Paris: Renouard, 1839); and Chambre de commerce et d'industrie, *Enquête relative à diverses prohibitions...* (Paris: Imprimerie Royale, 1835); and titles listed in Chapter 6, n. 54, p. 168.

69. A.D.S.V.P. DR¹26,28,33 "Tables de Recensement," Arrondissements 1,8, and 10, 1830. See Table 6.1.

audience and shaped the course of the literary movement whose popularity was to peak in the first years of the July Monarchy. In this the revolution and the new literature were intimately linked to ordinary men and women, politically charged, who collectively helped shape romanticism in a readily discernible way. Of course, these ties between politics and culture did not reflect the adaptation of modern republicanism to traditional folklore, as happened frequently in the provinces, according to Maurice Agulhon and others.[70] Rather, the impact of rapid and intense politicization on romanticism resembled more an interaction typical of a new popular culture, one sensitive to intellectual currents among elites and the demands of the lower orders for distraction, or in this case, political action.

In conclusion, this chapter should note that recent social historians of 1830 are probably correct to deny romantic ideas a major role in July.[71] Working-class victims of the street fighting reported to authorities how they fought for political rather than literary liberty. The memory of 1789 weighed more in their actions on the barricades than the melancholy and introspection of the romantic sensibility. The cries for greater literary freedom, by Hugo and others, meant little to men and women in the streets, sharing a common rage against the Restoration's glaring social and political anachronisms.

On the other hand, the revolution did exert a powerful influence on the romantic movement. In the short run it drew romantic authors to express their political opinions in *belles lettres* as well as history. Many young, more professional writers joined the ranks of older authors to air their revolutionary political and literary enthusiasms. Similarly, innovative publishers attempted to recover from a disastrous market for the classics by turning to these new men and women. Publication of living authors, frequently romantic, stimulated a book trade suffering from the structural problems left from the Restoration. The immediate interests of the Parisian populace in things revolutionary certainly encouraged authors and *libraires* alike to join the polemical swirl. Despite low material standards of living, 1830 facilitated by its success a consciousness among the lower orders who sought to better their conditions by reading *and* by political action.

70. Agulhon, *La république au village: les populations du Var de la Révolution à la IIᵉ République* (Paris: Plon, 1970), pp. 265–66; and *1848, ou l'apprentissage de la république* (Paris: Editions du Seuil, 1973), p. 109. See also Robert Bezucha, "Masks of Revolution: A Study of Popular Culture during the Second French Republic," in Price, ed. *Revolution and Reaction*, pp. 236–53; and Peter McPhee, "Popular Culture, Symbolism, and Rural Radicalism in Nineteenth-Century France," *Journal of Peasant Studies* 5(1978):238–53.

71. Pinkney, *The French Revolution of 1830*, pp. 252–73; and Newman, "What the Crowd Wanted in the French Revolution of 1830."

Still, in the long run, the revolution affected romanticism in a more profound way. New social themes, young committed authors, more enterprising publishers, expansion in the literary market, and a growing plebeian audience—all fostered by the revolution—would push the movement to its peak in 1834. Ironically enough, these same factors would then begin to undermine the movement's popularity, insuring its demise by the 1840s. With further developments in writing, reading, and publishing, the movement faded from popular literature aimed at the largest possible audience. In this larger development of a proto-mass culture, the revolution of 1830 was only a step, however important, in the march of popular romanticism that appealed to a diverse cross section of Paris, moved to varying degrees by an intense political climate. Such a revolutionary spirit made possible a much broader diffusion of romantic forms and conventions in a rapidly changing extraliterary context that made for their temporary success during the July Monarchy. In these ways the 1830 revolution undoubtedly helped shape the course of French romanticism, perhaps even more than the more famous revolution of 1789 and its Napoleonic aftermath.

THE LEGACIES OF FRENCH ROMANTICISM

𝓛ITERARY CRITICS BY 1840 claimed to witness a neo-classical resurgence in Parisian taste. "After having been completely abandoned for ten years, the tragedies of Corneille and Racine suddenly appeared and returned to favor," Alfred de Musset wrote in 1838. "*Horace, Mithridate, Cinna* are heard religiously and applauded with enthusiasm. Tears flow for *Andromaque* and *Tancrède*."[1] The near coincidence of François Ponsard's success and Victor Hugo's failure in 1843 seemed to mark the end to the romantic movement in France. Crowds disgusted with the movement's indulgences flocked to *Lucrèce* at the Odéon almost in relief after the *Burgraves* closed at the Théâtre français. After only a month of sparsely attended performances, Hugo's play was withdrawn, symbolically the very day Ponsard's production, starring the entrancing Mademoiselle Rachel, began its startling success. "In religion, politics, art, fashion, and custom," mused Sainte-Beuve, "there was a reaction everywhere."[2]

From such contemporary accounts, the romantic movement's decline apparently owed to esthetic extravagance. Literary excess, most observers agreed, soon lost romanticism public favor.[3] The chaos and bathos of many romantic works ceased to appeal to a large audience, perhaps because the movement had already served its creative purpose to free literature from classical proprieties: the point had been made many times over. Or it could be that too many corpses were strewn across the stage, too many verses failed to rhyme, too many medieval costumes cluttered the pages of novels to sustain interest in romanticism for very long.

1. Musset, "De la tragédie, à propos des débuts de Mlle Rachel," *Revue des deux mondes* 16(1838),4:348.

2. Sainte-Beuve, "Quelque vérités," p. 19.

3. See the traditional discussion of the movement's decline in Milner, *Le romantisme*, pp. 67–70.

When she first arrived in Paris, George Sand saw "every evening an execution, a hanging, a suicide, or at least a poisoning accompanied by cries, convulsions, and agony" at the theater.[4] In much the same way Agricol Perdiguier described the fright of one journeyman who had taken such theatrical action for real.[5] Like them the young Gustave Flaubert had grown annoyed with the sloppiness of the romantic creations he read. His own work reflected instead a scrupulous attention to *le mot juste*, to the careful crafting of his novels that in contrast to the prolific romantics took years to produce.[6] The apparent shift in taste among authors and readers alike in the 1840s suggested to many a sane return to cartesian rationality, the true spirit of French literature, after twenty years of emotional and esthetic indulgence.[7]

But was this the actual reason for romanticism's unenduring influence in France? Did the powerful classical tradition, re-enforced by the European prominence of enlightenment, revolution, and empire, necessarily undermine the impact and significance of French romanticism? In light of the movement's popular manifestations, one must not generalize about all of romanticism on the basis of its place among elites. Indeed, plebeian romanticism in France came and went for other reasons; its legacies to the nineteenth century differed considerably. As part of the new popular literature that grew rapidly after 1800, the movement owed much of its brief existence to a new cultural context, just as its debts and contributions to the period were tied closely to its large and remarkably heterogeneous readership. To understand the importance of French romanticism in Paris, in the period and later, demands a closer examination of other reasons for the movement's passing, its participation in popular taste and consciousness, its political and social bases, and its involvement in larger historical developments—at least as far as such speculations are possible with the evidence available. In this way the meaning of romanticism to ordinary men and women in past times will become clearer and perhaps the significance of the movement even more impressive.

4. Sand, "Lettre à Casimir Dudevant, (Paris) dimanche (le 9 mai 1830)." *Correspondence*, 1:640.

5. Perdiguier, *Mémoires d'un compagnon*, p. 291.

6. Benjamin F. Bart, *Flaubert* (Syracuse: Syracuse University Press, 1967), pp. 69–79.

7. See such an argument advanced recently in Nicholas V. Riasanovsky, "On Lamennais, Chaadaev and the Romantic Revolt in France and Russia," *American Historical Review* 82(1977),5:1165–86.

ROMANTICISM'S DECLINE AND
THE EVOLUTION OF LITERARY TASTE

Whatever the reasons for the movement's demise among elites, excess had very little to do with its passing among the vast body of readers in Paris. While elite tastes may have returned to more conservative literary values, most readers continued to favor a literature more popular than that of either romanticism or neo-classicism. The new literature in fact passed despite the popularity of serial novels every bit as extravagant as romanticism. With its gothic darkness and suspense, Eugène Sue's *Les mystères de Paris* reflected nothing of the deliberately ordered creations of a new generation that was reputed to have displaced the movement after 1840.[8] Elements of the new literature disappeared from nearly all the popular titles; in a way, popular romanticism passed because it was not excessive enough.

Of course, not all critics were blind to other reasons for the decline of the romantic fashion. Musset was among the first to mock the contradictions, exaggerations, and vagaries of works often associated with the movement; his provincial men of letters, Dupuis and Cotonet, were unable to define romanticism in 1837 because its various manifestations were too diffuse.[9] Similarly, in 1838 Sainte-Beuve recognized that a flood of new titles was overwhelming all serious literature. "The public has been so abused, books so inflated and surfeited, the old so taken for the new, vanity so hidden beneath the insipid and flat, that the public has become a cadaver to the world of letters."[10] With such a proliferation of pale imitations, the critic wondered where the life of romantic literature had gone.[11] On the same question William Makepeace Thackeray was more cynical: books like boots have their vogue, he said, and *les jeunes gens* had simply been carried off by another literary enthusiasm. Their romanticism was lost in the rush to a new fad in the world of rapidly changing literary fashions.[12]

The movement ironically seemed to prepare its own decline. Edmond Werdet noted that after 1830 "a new literary future more in keep-

8. See Atkinson, *Eugène Sue et le roman-feuilleton*, pp. 12–16.

9. Musset, "Lettres de Dupuis et Cotonet," p. 820.

10. Sainte-Beuve, "De la littérature industrielle," p. 684.

11. Sainte-Beuve, "Dix ans après en littérature," *Revue des deux mondes* 21(1840), 1:697.

12. William Makepeace Thackeray, *The Paris Sketch Book* (New York: F. M. Lipton, 1840), pp. 178–80.

ing with circumstances was avidly sought. Lamennais with his *Paroles d'un croyant,* Paul Lacroix with his *Soirées de Walter Scott* which had obtained a brilliant success, opened new avenues to the new generation, one in philosophy, the other in the novel. New horizons were discovered to the numberless crowd of rising literati" who went on to create freely for a larger, less serious audience.[13] By appealing deliberately to a more popular readership, romanticism planted the seeds of its own demise. New authors took this tendency to its logical conclusion and wrote other works when the movement no longer appealed to a larger audience.

But the old formula for success remained much of what it had been. The literary market was given less and less to romantic as well as elite works, a development that Louis Reybaud characterized by his cynical recipe for literary success.

> You take for example, sir, a young woman who is unhappy and persecuted. You add to her a bloody and brutal tyrant, a sensible and virtuous hero, and a sly and perfidious friend. When you have all these characters in hand, mix them vigorously in six, eight, ten or more installments and serve hot.[14]

More than a suitable mixture of characters and action was necessary; the successful author of serial novels also had to know how to use suspense to maintain reader interest from one installment to the next. "Each number must end well," Reybaud continued. "Tie it to the next issue by a sort of umbilical cord that calls, that creates the desire, indeed the impatience to read on. Speak of art today, well there it is. The art is to make it wanted, to make it anxiously awaited."[15] Thus what actually marked the end to the romantic movement was more than elite revulsion. It declined despite the continued rise of formulaic popular literature, one that no longer needed the romantic veneer to succeed.

Precisely why popular romanticism passed, however, remains something of a mystery.[16] Changes in public literary taste are much more easily documented than explained. According to the titles sampled from the *Bibliographie de la France,* authors no longer wrote, publishers no

---

13. Werdet, *De la librairie française,* p. 116. See similar analysis in Dérôme, *Causeries d'un ami des livres,* 1:xvi.

14. Reybaud, *Jérôme Paturot à la recherche d'une position sociale,* p. 60.

15. *Ibid.*

16. See discussion of French taste in Zeldin, *France, 1848–1945,* 2:349–762; and in the intriguing though poorly substantiated ideas in the last part of Arthur Mitzman, "The Unstrung Orpheus: Flaubert's Youth and the Psycho-Social Origins of Art for Art's Sake," *Psychohistory Review* 6(1977),1:1–16.

longer published, and readers no longer bought the new literature as much after 1840. Although the ultimate reasons for this widespread shift in preference may elude the historian until new sources or methodologies are discovered, more immediate reasons for the change in taste are less difficult to grasp. The brief romantic fashion owed much to the social and economic constraints imposed by a new extraliterary context. New modes of production, distribution, and consumption of books did not determine, but they did foster the evolution of literature in the period. The new style's failure in the 1840s occurred among many of the same factors that had made for its success earlier: the professionalization of authorship, the sophistication of production and distribution in the book trade, the expansion of readership in the city, and the revolutionary impulsion provided by the events of July 1830.

What had attracted authors, publishers, and readers to the romantic fashion? Why did they not prefer works expressing the sentiment that literary historians have characterized as the enduring essence of formal romanticism? It may well be that the widespread fascination with romanticism, at least among ordinary readers in the period, was not derived from an intellectual or esthetic rebellion so much as it was derived from the remarkable adaptability of the movement's conventions to the new formula literature evolving since 1800.[17] Popular songs certainly benefited from the flexibility of versification encouraged by elite romantics, just as melodramas did from violent action on the stage, gothic romances from medieval settings, and national histories from effective dramatization and local color. The elite and popular elements were conveniently complementary; the separate tradition among the lower middle classes borrowed easily the more attractive romantic devices. Although this does not explain essentially why the popular vogue came and went as it did, the façade of romantic trappings at least re-enforced the impact of many works intended for a plebeian audience and made their temporary adoption all the easier.

Many readers, like Emma Bovary, discovered romanticism through novels whose stock characters and plots were established forms well before the movement began to influence either elite or popular taste. The famous medieval figures resuscitated by authors in the *cénacles* appeared in gothic romances little different from those ordinarily there. Flaubert points out how closely Emma's infatuation with medieval romantic heroines like Marie Stuart, Jeanne d'Arc, and Agnes Sorel resembled her response to the fair virgins persecuted in earlier novels she had read.[18]

17. See discussion of examples in Chapter 1, pp. 34–44.
18. Gustave Flaubert, *Madame Bovary* in *Oeuvres*, A. Thibaudet and R. Dumesnil, eds. (Paris: Gallimard, 1951), 1:323–27.

Thus romantic elements strengthened the popular literary formulas in all their titillation and nostalgia, and for that reason, could be used to heighten the effects sought by authors and readers alike without imparting romanticism's more profound vision of the world and the self. Perhaps for the same reason, popular romanticism could have been discarded once its usefulness to plebeian literature and its enjoyment had faded when authors sought new variations in their formulas to maintain reader interest.

The decline of romanticism as fashion owed to these social and economic circumstances just as its rise had also benefited from them. For the arrival and departure of popular romanticism meant, in effect, the increasing commercialization of literature. Few aspects of nineteenth-century literature remained untouched by the growing intrusion of the market in artistic creation. The new urban culture was affected pervasively by new ways of writing, publishing, and reading in the period. No longer interested in the *bibliothèque bleue*, large numbers of readers experienced the productions of more professionally minded authors, enterprising publishers, mechanized printers, and sophisticated booksellers instead. Though these men did not decide what people read, sensitive as they were to predictable changes in demand, they did nourish new literary trends by making titles without romantic conventions readily and cheaply available after 1840, as Daumier's 1846 lithograph suggests (see Illustration 13).

Unfortunately, this analysis of the popular fortunes of French romanticism cannot resolve such an issue in the complicated history of popular taste. The motivations of literary creation and pleasure are far more complex. To be sure they must have resisted in part the market pressures of supply and demand. The student of history would be naive to claim that such literary developments were economically determined. That romanticism shared an important portion of the production, distribution, and consumption of books does not mean that a generation of more professional writers was likely to be moved by the new style solely for the material advantages of appealing to a new, large and unsophisticated audience. Other considerations, literary and psychological among authors and readers both, were also at work. The phenomenon of romanticism can only be understood after a much larger consideration of the social and cultural milieu of France in the early nineteenth century.[19] If

19. Note the attempt to discuss literary taste during the Second Empire in Mitzman, "Roads, Vulgarity, Rebellion, and Pure Art: The Inner Space in Flaubert and French Culture," *Journal of Modern History* 51(1979),3:504–524, even though Mitzman fails to discern the important development of a new popular culture, one very different from what he characterizes in his article.

13. "Quand le journal est trop intéressant" (ca. 1846). Lithograph by Honoré Daumier (1808–1879). *Courtesty of the Boston Public Library, Print Department.*

romanticism was so superficial and unenduring, more so among plebeian than more discriminating audiences, could it have been primarily a manifestation of the growing commercialization of modern popular culture? This question cannot be answered here, and will be left for other scholars to consider at greater length.[20]

Beyond the reasons for its brevity and apparent superficiality, however puzzling its sources, the romantic fashion implied different kinds of literary change. Elite and popular literatures appear to have evolved in the period. While the romantics were changing the form and content of works read by the well-lettered, popular authors incorporated many of their new devices in works appropriate to a less educated audience. New themes, characters, and settings in all genres can be found on all levels of literary achievement. And yet, the patterns of apparent romantic influence clouded the true nature of cultural continuity and change evident in the romantic movement.

The most significant transformation actually occurred in the elite literature in what intellectual historians fondly term the "romantic revolution," the new vision and the self and nature that marked something of a watershed in the history of western ideas. The new popular literature, on the other hand, hardly changed at all, despite its adoption of romantic conventions. Behind all the ostensible experimentation in poetry, drama, fiction, and history, most works remained largely what they had been since 1800: merry songs, stormy melodramas, sentimental tales, and political polemic, in a new trend of commercially standardized literature only borrowing the most superficial aspects of the movement. Most observers failed to make the distinction between the *romantic* mood, an exclusive phenomenon, and the "romantic" mode, a widespread experimentation in form. But with a careful examination of the titles themselves, this valuable discrimination between romanticisms high and low can be documented to show the remarkable evolution of elite sensibilities and the greater stability of the new popular cultural expressions in the period.[21]

Thus romanticism's revolution was more than a new vision of man and the world, the source of the modern ego in literature—this much is evident in works by major French romantic literati still read and studied today. Rather, the upheaval was also a series of new forms and conventions shared by authors writing for readers on much lower levels of society. The *chansonniers*, the comedy-vaudevilles, the gothic novels,

20. See alternative approaches to similar problems in Brooks, *The Melodramatic Imagination*, pp. 1–80; and Cawelti, *Adventure, Mystery, and Romance*, pp. 20–36.

21. See discussion of cultural developments from the eighteenth to the twentieth centuries in Crubellier, *Histoire culturelle*, pp. 9–18.

and the dramatic histories, all the popular literary genres using the movement's devices reached a huge, socially heterogeneous audience, from
the prissy salons in the Faubourg Saint-Germain down to the modest
lending libraries in the Marais. Elements of the new literature filtered
downward to be adapted by plebeian literary genres, reflecting an influence of elites unequalled by that of popular values on more sophisticated
literature in the period. Whatever the broad social interests of romantics
like George Sand, for instance, the banality of romanticism among the
most popular authors sampled from the *Bibliographie* was much more remarkable. By its very diffusion, popular romanticism must have appealed
to the tastes of many in the *menu peuple* as well as the middle classes and
promoted the convergence of formerly disparate tastes.[22]

The movement's significance, then, goes beyond its literary revolt
against the rationality, universality, and secularism of the eighteenth-
century Enlightenment. It marked as well the first blending of social class
interest in the development of a new literature for popular consumption
evolving since the turn of the century. Well before overtly hostile relations with the newer industrial classes developed during the 1848 revolution, important elements of both middle and small propertied classes
shared a wide range of cultural values. The humanitarian bourgeois set
the example for the socially aspiring master artisan, and during the romantic period they may have read the same books, or at least witnessed
the same devices and conventions in the books they read or heard.[23] Of
course, this social and cultural convergence was challenged by class conscious workers and by frightened middle-class proprietors, just as many
urban elites and rural peasants retained their traditional, preromantic
mentalities; the social prejudices of classes high and low, the cartesian
rationality of French classicism, and the suspicious fears of common folklore lingered well into the twentieth century. But the romantic contribution to popular verse, melodrama, fiction, and history drew a large, diverse urban readership to create a new literature aimed at all classes,
however brief its apparent success.

What romanticism in fact meant to the evolution of literature in
France may be seen more clearly in the diversity of tastes that have
evolved since the early nineteenth century. Elites enjoyed a much wider

22. See discussion of these forms and their diffusion in Chapter 2, p. 50–65.

23. See similar discussions in Daumard, "Le peuple dans la société française à
l'époque romantique"; and Agulhon, "Le problème de la culture populaire en France autour
de 1848." Note also Jules Michelet's fear of the cultural and social assimilation of the people
into the alien world of the bourgeoisie in *Le peuple*, pp. 118–21, while a similar fear is
expressed from an upper-class perspective by Tocqueville, *Democracy in America*,
2:71,73,93.

range of literary works in the wake of the romantic movement. The sophisticated reader did not have to limit himself to the production of either popular authors or the neo-classicists. There was now the elitist poetry of the Parnassians and the Symbolists, the well-crafted plays by Scribe, the naturalistic novels of Flaubert and Zola, and the professional histories of university-trained scholars by the end of the century. These titles attracted larger audiences than comparable genres in the eighteenth century, though they hardly compared in circulation to the penny press with subscribers in the hundreds of thousands. Yet in the face of the growing literature for mass consumption, elites developed more eclectic tastes, a diversity unequalled before romanticism. Essentially, the movement in its broad appeal and emphasis on freer creation marked the end to the bifurcation of literature high and low in the eighteenth century. And it fostered the beginning of the cultural variety enjoyed in the nineteenth and twentieth centuries.[24]

This is not to say that older cultural patterns disappeared entirely in France. There remained the immense gap in sensibility between the Paris intellectual and the rural peasant. As elites moved on to other literary forms, many readers in provincial areas still consumed titles in the timeless colporter baskets until World War I.[25] Similarly, the divergence in taste between avant-garde literati like Baudelaire composing poetry for a tiny circle of admirers and the shopkeeper relaxing with the latest edition of the illustrateds during the Second Empire curiously resembled the split between *philosophes* and readers of smuggled pornography during the Enlightenment. Even the growing presence of women readers, so important to writers of elite literature since the seventeenth century, was undermined by the relatively high levels of illiteracy among women in the lower orders well into the nineteenth century. Moreover, the realism of French novelists from Stendhal to Zola, that evolved despite the fancies of romantic writers, ran counter to the current of gothic romances and sentimental stories whose audience was nearly always much larger.

But these continuities were rapidly giving way to new pressures, a fact attested by the *Bibliographie de la France* and the Interior Ministry archives. Here lies evidence of the consistent growth of a new literature

24. See discussion of sharp distinctions between high and low culture in the eighteenth century in Ariès, *Centuries of Childhood*, pp. 62–99; and Burke, *Popular Culture in Early Modern Europe*, pp. 244–86. See also the discussion of changing literary values of elites and popular elements in Mandrou, *De la culture populaire*, pp. 185 ff.; and Clark, "The Beginnings of Mass Culture in France: Action and Reaction," *Social Research* 45(1978),2:277–91. On the larger theoretical framework, see Gans, *Popular Culture and High Culture*, pp. 56–58; and Lewis, "The Sociology of Popular Culture," p. 19.

25. See Weber, *Peasants into Frenchmen*, pp. 452–70.

intended for a mass audience.[26] The literate world no longer remained the exclusive preserve of the classically educated or the readers of the *bibliothèque bleue*. Instead it now shared an increasing portion of the literary market with another popular literary etiquette. Light poetry, sentimental songs, melodrama, simple but dramatic narrative histories, and the like began to displace both traditional elite and older popular literary forms. It was to this trend towards a new urban literature that romanticism contributed its notoriety and conventions.[27] The movement's freer verse, historical *drames*, medieval settings, and local color were quickly adopted and adapted on a large scale at its height in the first years of the July Monarchy. Although its impact was relatively brief and primarily a matter of form, romanticism helped foster the growth of a mass culture in the nineteenth century that saw not only a proliferation of smaller, more specialized elite audiences devoted to a variety of literary endeavors. But even more importantly, it encouraged a much larger, socially diverse audience for literary works intended for the broadest possible diffusion.

Apart from the profound changes it may have signified on various social levels, popular romanticism also had a more enduring and profound legacy, one difficult to discern even from a study of its widely read manifestations and the social context in which they flourished. For one, this literary world may well have represented a much larger intellectual development in the early nineteenth century. The remarkable adoption of elite conventions by poetry, drama, fiction, and history obviously intended for a plebeian audience suggests how responsive various elements of the movement were to a particular consciousness shared by nearly all readers, high and low. The very extent to which popular works borrowed from elite literature the precise forms they did implies more than the obvious workings of a new literary marketplace, filled as it was with brash young authors, daring publisher-entrepreneurs, and bands of undiscriminating readers. The patina of romantic devices actually represented a heightened historical awareness in Paris. The pervasiveness of romanticism in both elite and popular literature in the city does seem to place the movement's forms within a distinct mental structure in the period,[28] a consciousness that could well be what the movement meant to ordinary Parisians in times past.

26. See Table 2.2, p. 68.

27. See similar arguments made in George, *French Romanticism*, pp. 189–93.

28. It could be that the discovery of history among elites at the turn of the century discussed in Michel Foucault, *The Order of Things: An Archeology of the Human Sciences* (New York: Vintage, 1973), pp. 217–21, 367–73, finally penetrated the works of a more plebeian world, marking the beginning of a new *episteme* for the rest of France as well as the thinkers Foucault deals with.

Clearly the deep ambivalence signified by the most widespread devices—the melancholy poses, the nostalgia for the Middle Ages, and the pathetic fallacy on the one hand; the exuberant formal innovation, the admiration of Napoleon's dynamism, and the participation in historical drama on the other—implies a particular attitude toward the changes occurring generally in France since the revolution of 1789. By the Bourbon Restoration, not everyone had greeted the end of the *ancien régime* with unalloyed rejoicing; the widespread longing for the stability of medieval France portrayed in popular romantic fiction and history appealed to many contemporaries' desire for order and security in a rapidly changing world.[29] But not everyone appreciated the *monarchie censitaire* and its attempt to recreate elements of the old regime: the enthusiastic experimentation with new forms of popular literature suggested to many a contrary preference for renewal and reform in politics and society as well as literature.[30] In effect, the very elements of romanticism that reached most readers on all social levels could well have responded to their torn allegiances to the accomplishments and failures of the constitutional monarchies, and to these regimes' delicate balance between reaction and revolution, political and social, at the height of the movement's public favor.

On a purely symbolic level, the popular romantic façade reflected a pervasive mind frame on the verge of coming to terms, at long last, with revolution.[31] For the new literature in its elite and popular manifestations expressive of a deep quandry over the course of recent events—from the Restoration of 1815 to the revolution of 1830 and the return to a constitutional monarchy—did not remain before the public eye for very long. The movement passed, and presumably the historical consciousness it embodied did so as well. By the end of the romantic period, when the peculiar ambivalence of the movement's adoption by popular literature disappeared, authors and readers probably accepted the new world launched in 1789 and fashioned by subsequent economic and social developments. Although this did not mean a willingness to live with the July Monarchy, as 1848 would clearly show, the much less ambivalent literature of the 1840s represented a certain acceptance of literary and political change as a norm. The new plebeian fashion of adventure and mystery

29. This nostalgia for the Middle Ages, for example, is clearly apparent in the historical novels, like Joseph Quantin's *Le pâtre tirolien* (Paris: Locard, 1820), and in the historical dramas, like Charles Desnoyer and Alboize's *Caravage (1599)* (Paris: Barba, 1834).

30. Note the extravagant experimentation in such works as *Le chansonnier des grâces pour 1830* (Paris: Louis, 1830); and Rogeau, *Sardanapale*.

31. Note the discussion of this problem in Newman, "What the Crowd Wanted in the French Revolution of 1830."

in the serial novels, one without the overlay of romantic conventions, no longer implied the hesitant climate of opinion inherent in the popular literature only a few years earlier.[32] In fact this change in the historical climate may ultimately account for the brief vogue of popular French romanticism, a problem deserving far more and closer scrutiny.

POPULAR ROMANTICISM: VALUES AND SIGNIFICANCE

For all the apparent insignificant and unenduring character of a decidedly commercial literature, the romantic mode signified a pervasive attitude among Parisian readers and writers at a crucial point in French history. But the popular movement also had an even more prominent place in a series of new or sharply intensified historical rivalries. Romanticism's share in a contemporary *prise de conscience* was equally evident in the movement's political, social, and demographic bases whose profound differences outlived the literature that either spawned or nourished them. No account of the enduring ramifications of French romanticism can ignore its participation in the politics of the constitutional monarchies, in the redefinition and prominence of the middle classes, and in the growth of an identifiable subculture of youth in the first half of the nineteenth century in Paris. The new literature in many ways involved far more than a responsiveness to the *mentalités* of the period; it meant as well an intimate share in the nineteenth-century search for a stable form of government, a new social hierarchy, and a place for the young. Within the context of French romanticism, each of these involvements and their conflicts deserves at least some mention in a discussion of the movement's legacy to its own and later centuries.

The romantics clearly made no secret of their politics.[33] In light of the obvious anachronisms of the Restoration culminating in the 1830 revolution, leaders of the movement like Hugo shifted from an ardent royalism to an equally earnest liberalism; others like Dumas actually moved on to an open republicanism in opposition to the monarchy. The failures of the July Monarchy carried the movement even further to the left, encouraging Lamartine's brand of visionary socialism and his active revolutionary role during the 1848 revolution.[34] Underlying this political

32. See discussion of the new climate of opinion by mid-century in Chevalier, *Laboring Classes and Dangerous Classes*, pp. 359–417.

33. See insightful analysis of French romanticism's politics during the Restoration in Barbéris, "Le mal du siècle, ou d'un romantisme de droit à un romantisme de gauche."

34. See Hunt, *Le socialisme et le romantisme en France*; and Evans, *Social Romanticism in France, 1830–1848*.

transition, to be sure, was a more consistent antipathy for the French middle classes. In the Restoration this antibourgeois sentiment appeared in the widespread disaffection of most elite romantics with the effects of the 1789 revolution and those who had benefited by it.[35]

The romantics perceived the contradictions of bourgeois values, esthetic as well as political, throughout the constitutional monarchies that turned many of them against the Orleanist regime's clear plutocratic character.[36] The art for art's sake of Gautier's *cénacle* was as firmly antagonistic to the middle classes as "pure" art could possibly be. But this social and political belligerence also blurred with another they maintained for older age groups. The authors in the new literature were self-consciously younger, their age-consciousness part of a much more general assertion of youth in the early nineteenth century.[37] With its decidedly younger appeal and authorship, with its hostility to the established middle classes, their politics, and their taste, elite romanticism marked the appearance of a subculture whose ideals and behavior contrasted sharply with the world of the older bourgeois.

The long standing historical influence of elite romanticism—its political transition from right to left, its aversion to middle-class complacency, and its share in the lives of self-assertive youth—remain important to the course of the nineteenth century, as many social, intellectual, and literary historians have recognized. No discussion of romanticism's social history can ignore the movement's debt and contribution to political, social, and age-group conflict that were to plague Paris, if not all of France, long afterward.[38] Nevertheless, crucial distinctions must be drawn between the different historical bases of romantic literature, high and low. The popular movement's participation in its historical moment differed in important ways from that of the elites in the new literature, primarily because of their different cultural contexts. Not only did the plebeian romanticism enjoy a broader and socially less prominent audience, they also were more dependent on the literary marketplace that ensured the sensitivity of authors and publishers to the values and attitudes of their modest clientele. Romanticism on this level expressed another political, social, and demographic perspective much more in tune

35. See important study of the origins of this antibourgeois spirit in France in Bénichou, *Le sacre de l'écrivain*, pp. 346–52, despite the attempt to characterize the middle-class nature of European romanticism in Hauser, *Social History*, 3:163–227.

36. See Bénichou, *Le temps des prophètes: doctrines de l'âge romantique* (Paris: Gallimard, 1977), pp. 381–422.

37. See discussion of French romanticism's age-consciousness and its demographic foundation in Chapter 3, pp. 76–88. Gillis, *Youth and History*, pp. 37–93, provides useful European background to the generational conflict in the period.

with its different literary world, despite the marked similarities in their conventions and perhaps even their expression of a historical consciousness.

In politics, for example, the popular romantics took a path different from that taken by their esthetic "betters." The movement for a plebeian audience actually moved in the opposite direction. Throughout the constitutional monarchies, wherever glimmers of its politics appeared, popular literature espoused a consistently liberal spirit. While prominent early romantics openly embraced the Restoration royalists, popular romantics took a more revolutionary stand, portraying in their works the attacks of scheming nobles on the medieval monarchy, on the livelihood of the serfs, or on the personal virtue of modest middle-class heroines— all behind the façade of romantic conventions assumed by melodramas and gothic fiction especially.[39] Moreover, the July Monarchy saw the political opposition of the social romantic elites, far to the left of the old themes in popular romantic literature. If any shift in the politics of the latter occurred, it was to a more apolitical stance of a literary world anxious more to please and distract than to instruct and polemicize. Much of the Restoration vogue of Béranger's songs honoring the poor and dispossessed gave way during the Orleanist regime to *chansonniers* informing the humble family how to treat its guests on holidays.[40] The worker poets published after 1840 with a more radical vision did not enjoy the same favor that less politicized song writers realized in the same period.

Similarly, despite Vigny's disdain for his bourgeois readership—a disdain much in keeping with the movement's belief in its orphic mission—popular titles adopting elite conventions reflected another social spirit entirely. To the same extent that major romantics baited the bourgeoisie their plebeian imitators saw no threat in their largely middle-class audience.[41] From the tone of their work, they seemed anxious to flatter it as much from a genuine community of interest as from a hypocritical attempt to increase royalties. Compared with the *bibliothèque bleue* hawked by colporters in the eighteenth century, the popular literature in

38. See bibliography in Milner, *Le romantisme*, pp. 367–71, for works in this area.

39. Brooks makes a similar observation about the melodrama in his *The Melodramatic Imagination*, pp. 87–88, as does Georg Lukács about the novel in *The Historical Novel*, Hannah and Stanley Mitchell, trans. (Boston: Beacon Press, 1963), pp. 19–88.

40. E.g., A. Désaugiers, *Chansons et poésies diverses* (Paris: Delloye, 1834), 2 vols., which suggests songs for all family and social occasions. Despite this, there is need for an intensive study of the implicit politics of the new popular literature.

41. Contrast Pétrus Borel's rabid *Rhapsodies* (Paris: Levavasseur, 1832), with the socially complacent anonymous collection, *Le jardin d'enfance, de la jeunesse et de tous les âges* (Paris: Pigoreau, 1820).

the romantic period, whether or not it imitated the movement's forms, appealed to a distinctly urban, small propertied readership. The *chanson-niers*, melodramas, gothic novels, and nationalistic histories enjoyed the attention of artisans, prosperous journeymen, shopkeepers, and the lesser bourgeoisie of the city. Nearly all the dramatic interest of this literature focused on situations most likely to arise in or near their social milieu, such as the fair heroine, daughter to a man of modest means, pursued by a handsome man of slightly better social standing.[42] The popular romantic patina on this literature did little to alter the essentially middle-class values and attitudes expressed in it. The elite leaders of the movement imparted their devices, not their antibourgeois hostility, to plebeian literature.

Participation in the development of a separate and identifiable youth culture was also less evident in plebeian romanticism. Although this literature still shared in the demography of the period, it did not appear to depend on or encourage an awareness of sharp age differences. While upper middle-class youths were acclaiming their independence from their parents' generation, those of less impressive social status expressed more traditional values little different from their families. As late as the Third Republic, according to one survey of elementary school children, youthful occupational ideals largely mirrored parental expectations.[43] Recent social historians have documented similar reasons for many young women joining the work force in the nineteenth century, a participation in the economic world which re-enforced the family-economy and not the emancipation of the young,[44] as some historians have assumed from the revolt of the romantic generation and after. The youthful "counter culture" so evident among the movement's elites never actually existed among youth in the lower middle and working classes. Accordingly, the romantic literature aimed at this readership portrayed the conflict between age groups in tones much more muted than that aimed at elites: despite the opposition of parents to the love of their daughter, the suitor always turns out to be acceptable and the novel ends happily, the

42. As in la comtesse de Nardouet, *Vice et vertu*, in which Zélie Dolmon is seduced, abandoned, but finally married seven years later by the comte de Saint-Firmin, once more reconciled with virtue.

43. See discussion of Octave Gréard's 1876 survey in John W. Shaffer, "Family, Class, and Young Women: Occupational Expectations in Nineteenth-Century Paris," *Journal of Family History* 3(1978), 1:62–77.

44. Especially, Louise Tilly and Joan Scott, "Women's Work and the Family in Nineteenth-Century Europe," *Comparative Studies in Society and History* 17(1975), 1:36–64.

generations once more in accord.[45] Open conflict between generations was a facet of another kind of romanticism.

Evidently, then, the movement on the plebeian level revealed a place in French historical development that differed sharply from romanticism among elites. The jolly songs, the comedy-vaudevilles, the sentimental romances, and the dramatic histories expressed a more stable and moderate political outlook: where the elites first embraced royalism, liberalism, then socialism, the popular romantics tended to prefer liberalism if any politics at all, since in time their appeal was less in polemic than in deliberate entertainment, except of course during the 1830 revolution. Similarly, the plebeian movement did not bait its lower middle-class audience; it depended too precariously on its modest readership to antagonize it as the elite romantics often times did theirs. Among the clientele of the lending libraries, popular romanticism apparently sought to please as much as possible. And the youthful antics of the movement, as it is still studied by most scholars, were considerably moderated in the literature intended for a broad audience. Little evidence of a youthful subculture, in opposition to older people, appeared in popular works—certainly not to the same extent. There old age continued to be venerated despite the assertion of younger middle-class youth.

From these distinctions between two romanticisms, another view of the movement's historical role appears warranted, indeed necessary. Just as the waning of elite and plebeian romanticisms owed to different factors, their place in the political, social, and demographic developments of the early nineteenth century differed. The romanticism of Hugo, Vigny, Lamartine, and other literary masters shared in the major conflicts of their day. But the romanticism most likely to have reached the hands of ordinary men and women at the height of the movement signified little of the high romantics' vacillation between royalism and socialism, their antipathy for the bourgeoisie, or their youthful assertiveness. Rather, popular romanticism participated in the values and attitudes of its audience embracing political liberalism, lower-middle class social propriety, and sentimental relations between the generations. Here the popular romantic "bohemian" was hardly at odds with his lesser bourgeois environment. Given these remarkable distinctions between their audiences and their perspectives, the political, social, and demographic place of

45. As in Louise Lemercier, *Victor-Amédée II, ou le siège de Turin* (Paris: Gaudiot, 1830), for example, where Angela Mica falls in love with Seigneur Gaetano in spite of her father's reservations with the suitor's higher social standing. The generations are brought together by Victor-Amédée's bequest to Angela and her family so that the lovers could marry without a serious social *mésalliance*.

romanticisms in France was bound to reflect their different legacies to nineteenth-century Paris.

Thus distinctions, literary and historical, must be made in the literature published in the period. But careful study of these crucial discriminations points up two qualifications important to an understanding of the century's major historical developments. The first is the close tie between the literary and the intellectual. The widespread changes in the literature of the period paralleled, and represent one essential manifestation of, significant changes in the intellectual climate occurring not only in France but also in western Europe. As writers on philosophy, history, science, and society shifted from the rationalistic attitudes of the eighteenth century to the more organic metaphors in the nineteenth, for example, creative spirits in the arts, in literature especially, shared in a similar exploration. In many ways the French romantic mood in poetry, drama, and fiction from 1820 to 1840 reflected precisely this radical change in values among European intellectuals generally from 1760 to 1840. The literary sensibility, so crucial to the new literature at least among elites, marked a departure from the classical tradition of the Enlightenment and its emphasis on objectivity, universality, and rationality, just as other innovations in the nineteenth century emphasized imagination, particularity, emotion, and spontaneity. The most prominent romantic literati attempted to capture a deeply personal state of mind in their use of natural imagery, and thereby participated in a comparable development among intellectuals nearly everywhere in the West. To focus here on the literary changes taking place in the period, then, is in effect to single out one very important manifestation of this larger phenomenon in the history of ideas: for all its peculiarities literature was no less a part of this transition.

But the new insights among writers still read and appreciated today for their contribution to the modern temper were significant for other reasons. European romanticism endured, but it also pervaded. In France it reached a remarkably large audience in the devices and conventions adopted by popular works appearing on the shelves of the *cabinets de lecture*. The romantic mode in literature, however emptied of meaning in popular usage, actually reveals the lower reaches of this movement among ordinary men and women, albeit in a muted form and within a more prescribed period. Such a system of signs permits the social historian of ideas to document the influence of romanticism on the most plebeian level possible. While serious-minded authors and readers responded to changes in the intellectual climate, much of literate Paris felt their impact no less immediately in the freer verse, the historical dramas, the novels set in the Middle Ages, and the nationalistic histories widely available. The message may have been altered in the vulgarization, but the details of popular French literary creation—its authorship, publication, and readership—illustrate the precise mechanisms of diffusion in the history of the intellectual watershed known as romanticism.

From another perspective this relationship suggests another development marked by the literary evidence. Songs, melodramas, novels, and histories reflect not just a transition to new patterns of thought among intellectuals, they also mirror an equally crucial change in the mentalities of the lower orders in Paris, a shift in cultural paradigms much less discussed in intellectual histories, less because it is not perceived to be important than because it is not well understood.[46] The decline of old folkways among peasants migrating to the city in the nineteenth century may be seen in the growth of a new literature whose urban audience no longer clamored for titles in the *bibliothèque bleue.* Instead of gathering for evening *veillées* as they had in the country, the common people of Paris crowded the boulevard theaters to see the latest vaudeville. The production of a literature aimed at this readership gradually displaced that sold in the *colporteur* baskets limited increasingly to rural areas where their market lingered for perhaps another fifty years. If the literary creations examined here were closely tied to intellectual developments among elites, they were also linked to no less remarkable changes among more ordinary folk whose traditional superstition, fatalism, fear, and deference gave way in time to experience, optimism, empathy, and self-assertion, first primarily in the cities and then in the countryside. Popular romanticism participated in this transition, even if it did not originate it, in France to be sure and perhaps in other European countries as well.[47]

The second qualification underlying the present attempt at a social history of ideas is the historical linkage between the elite and the popular, a complex interaction only sketched in this study. Apparent in the samples taken from the *Bibliographie de la France* was a pervasive borrowing of elite romantic conventions by popular titles expressing a vision of the world rather different from the literary works still studied today. Because most of the *chansonniers,* comedy-vaudevilles, and sentimental fiction had established a tradition of their own in Paris from the end of the eighteenth century onward (or even earlier), their adoption of the new conventions originating in the more exclusive *cénacles* indicates a flow in influence

46. For discussion of this development, see Crubellier, *Histoire culturelle,* pp. 9–18; Weber, *Peasants into Frenchmen,* pp. 452–70; and Darmon, *Le colportage de librairie en France,* pp. 159–62.

47. See discussion of the important historical role of ideas in Zuckerman, "Dreams That Men Dare to Dream"; Henretta, "Social History as Lived and Written"; and Stone, "The Revival of Narrative."

from top to bottom, from the elite to the popular on a scale unknown in the previous century. Of course, major romantic writers dabbled in plebeian genres, bringing with them, in some cases, both the mood and the mode of the romantic movement. But it would appear from the present approach that romanticism reached a huge audience more in the works of hacks than in those of better known writers. Part of the intellectual world of elites filtered downward and encouraged a brief cultural interaction of a very particular sort between social classes high and low in early nineteenth-century Paris.

This marked a decidedly urban version of an important development noted by recent historians of rural France. Maurice Agulhon and his students, for instance, have documented a similar interaction between local notables and their peasants in which republican values were expressed in the guise of traditional fêtes. In the countryside the peasantry also adapted elements of a new political world, rather different from an older moral economy, to a well-established popular tradition.[48] But in Paris the older rural folklore was rapidly giving way to another popular culture whose relationship with elites, though similar in some ways, played a different historical role in the period. Here the range of literary values shared by readers high and low marked the emergence of a new urban, middling class as a force in the city's social and political structure: the new popular culture brought with it new power and class relationships.

For perhaps the first time in French cultural history since the seventeenth century, the middle classes and respectable artisans and shopkeepers shared a common literary activity—the new popular literature, much of it romantic in the period. Chansons, melodramas, novels, and history formed an important part of Parisian cultural life, if we are to believe contemporary observers in the nineteenth century. But this new "taste group" based on the relatively narrow range of values expressed in the new literature also suggests a new social grouping with other common interests, political as well as cultural.[49] For instance, historians have already noted the different rates of politicization among various social strata in modern France: the aristocratic and middle-class elites mobilized first and most pervasively in the eighteenth century, the menu peuple later and more violently in the nineteenth. The illiterate peasantry and laboring poor took longer to arrive at such a revolutionary consciousness.

48. See Agulhon, La république au village, pp. 265–66; Bezucha, "Mask of Revolution: A Study of Popular Culture during the Second French Republic"; and McPhee, "Popular Culture, Symbolism and Rural Radicalism in Nineteenth-Century France."

49. For theoretical discussion of social "taste groups" see Gans, Popular Culture and High Culture, pp. 65–118.

By the June days of 1848, however, the "awakening" of the marginal unpropertied classes of Paris was complete and marked a decisive shift in the sociopolitical structure of Paris. Consequently, the more "respectable" artisans and shopkeepers who had manned the barricades in times past increasingly identified now with the less revolutionary interests of the Parisian bourgeoisie, the *rentiers* and financiers, who attempted to contain the recently self-conscious proletariat. After 1848 a political reaction set in among the propertied and middling classes in opposition to the new working-class revolutionary threat.[50]

It is no accident, then, that this well-documented redefinition of social and political class interests in Paris coincided with the development of a more popular bourgeois culture in which romanticism played a prominent role. This also included the new literature aimed at a readership far broader than the audience of any elite or plebeian genre in the eighteenth century.[51] Widely available in the lending libraries and increasingly inexpensive in the bookstores, popular romantic works helped define a new middle-class audience participating in a common cultural activity that could not but re-enforce its political values—values distinct from those of the largely illiterate laboring poor who neither read nor shared in the political reaction of their social betters. The reading material of the *nouvelles couches sociales* as they evolved in the nineteenth century clearly distinguished its audience culturally by the end of the constitutional monarchies, well in advance of their more overt social and political roles during the Third Republic.

Thus popular romanticism participated in a major cultural change influencing, albeit indirectly, the class and power structure of Paris before mid-century. Although the precise share the movement had in the changing tastes and attitudes of Parisian readers remains obscure, it did promote the transition from an older literature expressive of a traditional folk *mentalité* to a newer literature embodying a more modern middle-class frame of mind. Moreover, its broad social appeal helped establish a new protomass culture, and its implicit values must have fostered the creation of a broadened middle class fashioned by recent financial and

50. For discussion of the different rates of political assertion among the social classes of France, see Georges Lefebvre, *The Coming of the French Revolution*, R. R. Palmer, trans. (Princeton: Princeton University Press, 1947), pp. 1–151; and Richard Cobb, "La Vie en Marge: Living on the Fringe of the Revolution," *Reactions to the French Revolution* (London: Oxford University Press, 1972), pp. 128–79.

On the shifting political alliances of the middling classes, see Lynn Lees and Charles Tilly, "Le peuple de juin 1848," *Annales: E.S.C.* 29(1974), 1061–91.

51. See Darnton, "Reading, Writing, and Publishing in Eighteenth-Century France."

industrial innovations.[52] Meanwhile, the laboring classes enjoyed something of a counter culture, after 1848 at least. Largely illiterate, dependent on face-to-face collective life at work and in the cafés, ever on the margin of romantic influence, the new proletariat was still defined by its lack of capital that set it off from the propertied classes. But the divergence in conscious attitudes and values—political, social, and literary—between the cultures of the middle and laboring classes in early nineteenth-century Paris owes much to the agency of the popular romantic revolution.

Other factors, social and economic, were at work in this development, to be sure. But the role of ideas and culture in the redefinition of classes and their conflicts in the period cannot be dismissed because literature is only part of the superstructure of history.[53] New class lines arose from the new literary tastes as well as the growth of new industry and economic relations, though this problem of defining sociocultural classes needs more study employing sources and methods more appropriate to its analysis. But romanticism's apparent participation in the development of a more modern popular culture and its contribution to the form and content of a broad public taste, at least among the middling classes of Paris between 1820 and 1840, define the immediate historical role of the movement. Although this perspective differs considerably from that of other histories of romanticism of and for elites, popular romanticism represented a significant consciousness of change, a moderate liberal political creed, a lower middle-class ethos, and a sentimental identification of intergenerational interests. Such an outlook, derived from romanticism's actual social context during the constitutional monarchies, embodied the movement's most likely meaning to ordinary men and women in Paris in the early nineteenth century, and perhaps ultimately its legacy to the cultural history of modern France. Apparently superficial and brief, popular romanticism was no less important for all that.

52. On the definition and redefinition of the Parisian bourgeoisie, see Daumard, *Les bourgeois de Paris au XIXe siècle*, pp. 93–101, 123–45, 319–27.

53. A similar interaction between cultural forms and social change is examined by Geertz, albeit in a very different milieu. He argues that "cultural structure and social structure are not mere reflexes of one another but independent, yet interdependent, variables," a finding based on his study of a Javanese funeral which failed to function properly as a traditional ritual in a new socioeconomic context. The sharp conflict he found in an Indonesian lower-class neighborhood was "not simply indicative of a loss of cultural consensus, but rather was indicative of a search, not yet entirely successful, for a new, more generalized and flexible pattern of belief and value." Similarly, the change in literary-cum-cultural forms in nineteenth-century Paris reflected much the same search for new patterns of belief and value among the middling classes in the process of redefinition. See Geertz, *The Interpretation of Cultures*, pp. 142–69.

CONCLUSION

*B*Y NOW BENJAMIN ROUBAUD'S satirical vision in "Le grand chemin de la postérité" should be more intelligible. This 1842 lithograph, whose description opened the present essay, posed a number of intriguing problems in the history of ideas: Who were all those authors in Hugo's wake? What relationship did they have to the romantic movement? Why were they so prolific? Evidently many of the men Roubaud portrayed created the popular romanticism that the social and cultural context of the period not only made possible but also encouraged. The diffusion of the elite romantics' new conventions among titles in a new popular literature— jolly *chansonniers,* melodramas and comedy-vaudevilles, gothic and sentimental novels, and dramatic nationalistic histories—coincided with remarkable developments in the production, distribution, and consumption of books: authors like those in Roubaud's lithograph were younger and more worldly in their response to the new literary marketplace, publishing entrepreneurs turned increasingly from the masterworks of the classical writers to the *nouveautés* composed by these new men, and many more, often naive readers anxiously awaited their work in the *cabinets de lecture.* The 1830 revolution intensified these trends, promoting a briefly politicized romanticism on the plebeian level; the July days helped make the movement of interest on nearly all social levels in Paris, but especially to the growing readership of the middling classes, small property owners, prosperous shopkeepers, and artisans.

The significance of Roubaud's lithograph sharpens focus in light of the rise of popular literature, one that would serve a truly mass audience by the end of the nineteenth century. Well before the differentiation of the upper bourgeoisie as a distinct cultural elite, so well portrayed in Marcel Proust's *A la recherche du temps perdu,* the middle, middling, and even some of the working classes enjoyed the same songs, drama, fiction, and history increasingly available for small fees. Such a literature began to appeal to a broad social spectrum in post–Napoleonic Paris where it developed a romantic fashion borrowed from the writers truly representative of this European intellectual movement. The freer versification, the melange of genres, the medieval mystique, and the use of strong local color, for example, pervaded nearly all urban literature at the height of romanticism's influence among elites. No doubt this blurring of social class interest in a singular cultural phenomenon resulted from both the commercialization of literature and the pervasiveness of romanticism among the works of popular authors similar to those portrayed by Roubaud. But it also suggests in its own right, by the brief and selective adoption of the romantic mode, the appearance of an ambivalent attitude toward historical change signified by the conventions, at once nostalgic and experimental in nature. The popular vogue of romanticism may even have fostered a "false consciousness" among the *menu peuple* that moved them to side with the established notables, most notably in the reaction of June 1848, against more radical workers including unskilled as well as many artisans.

In all this Roubaud represents insights not found in subsequent accounts of romanticism focusing solely on the relatively small circle of authors writing for an exclusive, elite audience. The close study of the movement's more popular manifestations actually leads to a new, though incomplete, interpretation of romanticism's expression of political, social and demographic change, an expression that differs considerably from that of the great masterworks in the period. The romantic literature that was so distinctly liberal, petty middle-class minded, and insensitive to generational conflict deserves more careful consideration, to be sure, to elucidate clearly the movement's place in the new popular culture and the contribution to its historical moment. Further investigation of the literary world of ordinary men and women in Paris in the romantic period is needed if the movement is ever to be understood as people then must have known it. The present venture, devoted primarily to the documentation and material circumstances of romanticism's more plebeian manifestations, has only been able to point out some of the areas for future study. Hopefully others will take up the suggestions left for them.

For one, this approach to romanticism deliberately invites more critical attention to a subject that has long been considered peripheral, even trivial by serious students of both history and literature, namely, the problem of modern popular culture.[1] Important studies of the intellectual

---

1. Increased scholarly attention to popular culture is reflected in the important syntheses by Crubellier, *Histoire culturelle*; Gans, *Popular Culture and High Culture*; and Lewis, "The Sociology of Popular Culture."

and esthetic lives of anonymous masses, past and present, are relatively few and handicapped by a number of serious theoretical problems still to be resolved. Most definitions of culture are difficult to apply in empirical research. Just what is popular culture and how do we go about studying it? Obviously it involves far more than surveys, published by enthusiastic antiquarians, of the little remembered literature intended for a broad audience years ago. Although anthropologists like Claude Lévi-Strauss and Clifford Geertz have posited some sophisticated conceptions, they have not proved of interest to many in social or literary history.[2]

Moreover, popular culture continues to be the victim of assumptions that seriously undermine its apparent significance.[3] Marxists see in art, literature, and music for the masses since the industrial revolution the ruling class' attempt to impose rational bourgeois work values, or to distract the proletariat from recognition of an exploitive economic system. For more conservative analysts, the popular arts are simply innocuous nonsense, distasteful imitations of true art among the educated elite, though some openly admit enjoying kitsch. In such a context the relevance of popular culture to modern history and social science is at best problematic. Much western scholarship has reduced culture to a more or less simple reflection of society that cannot effect change as powerfully as economic growth or political conflict.

There are at least two reasons for these problems leading to either the neglect or the outright dismissal of popular culture for scholarly consideration. The first and most obvious is the established tradition of intradisciplinary research that defines issues, sources, methods, and conclusions of interest within narrow fields. This logical development in the growth of professional scholarship and the specialization of knowledge since the nineteenth century has made possible significant advances in our understanding of the problems in the purview of well-prescribed areas of investigation.[4] But subjects like popular culture lying on the edge of disciplinary boundaries—between literature, art, music, anthropology, sociology, and history—are unfortunately left unexamined. Or they are

2. This exaggerates, of course. The remarkable range of Geertz' influence is well shown in Ronald G. Walters, "Signs of the Times: Clifford Geertz and Historians," *Social Research* (August 1980), forthcoming. See also the serious attempts to translate Lévi-Strauss's ideas into a usable analytic framework for modern popular culture, in Kress, "Structuralism and Popular Culture"; and White, "Structuralism and Popular Culture."

3. See discussion of the reasons for popular culture's scholarly disrepute, in Lewis, "The Sociology of Popular Culture," pp. 4–7.

4. See Laurence Veysey, "The Plural Organized Worlds of the Humanities," in Alexandra Oleson and John Voss, eds., *The Organization of Knowledge in Modern America, 1860–1920* (Baltimore: Johns Hopkins University Press, 1979), pp. 51–106.

taken up by journalists without the necessary conceptual tools and skills to elevate their examinations above polemic.[5]

A second and less admitted reason for the subject's disrepute lies in a social and cultural prejudice. The apparent lack of universality, profundity, and complexity in mass culture, for many people, bears no serious comparison with the great monuments of western artistic achievement which, by contrast, have nothing standard, homogeneous, or commercial about them. Only this reflects a genuine bias. By judging the popular by the same standards as the elite, in much the same way late nineteenth-century Europeans judged the "primitive" by the values of the "civilized," specialists often overlook or even demean the cultural differences within their own community. These differences demand as much fair-minded scrutiny as, for example, the distinctions between the art of various tribes in central Africa. The cultural tolerance of anthropologists has apparently not yet pervaded the disciplines of literary and intellectual history.[6]

Nevertheless, as a consequence of interdisciplinary work, particularly in France where early modern folk traditions have been studied extensively, popular culture represents a topic far more important than some scholars have thought. Besides explicit admissions of cultural relativism—the popular is just another esthetic form working within a set of constraints different from those of the elite—a recognition of the complex mental structures represented in popular culture has led to intriguing speculation about the role of ideas in past human behavior. For Robert Mandrou, Geneviève Bollème, Maurice Agulhon, E. P. Thompson, among others, the literary fare of common people reflects a structurally conceivable outlook, a *mentalité* whose importance to historical explanation has grown considerably within the last fifteen years.[7] Thanks to this new attention to what earlier scholars have shunned, our understanding of the interaction between culture and social change has become much more sophisticated. Even though there remains something tautological in

5. This obvious interdisciplinary weakness in the study of popular culture is reflected in the "serious" studies devoted to the subject since Bernard Rosenberg and David Manning White, eds., *Mass Culture: The Popular Arts in America* (New York: Free Press, 1957); and most recently, Daniel Bell, *The Cultural Contradictions of Capitalism* (New York: Basic Books, 1976), p. 3–30, esp.

6. With some notable exceptions, of course, e.g., Cawelti, *Adventure, Mystery, and Romance*; and Brooks, *The Melodramatic Imagination*.

7. See Mandrou, *Introduction to Modern France, 1500–1640*; Bollème, *Les almanachs populaires*; Agulhon, *La république au village*; and E. P. Thompson, "The Moral Economy of the English Crowd in the Eighteenth Century," *Past and Present* 50(1971),76–136. See Burke, *Popular Culture in Early Modern Europe*, pp. 166–204, for a survey of the rich historical literature on *mentalité*.

applying norms of behavior to explain historical events, especially when those norms are derived from observations of those events in the few sources available, the place of cultural custom in historical analysis is still a major contribution to the study of history. In this way plebeian literature takes on new significance as a subject in its own right and will continue to receive the examination it merits.

The present study of romanticism thus owes much to recent developments in French historical research. Historians of France, here and abroad, have given increasing attention to popular culture, in the early modern period primarily. (This may be because the significance of the oral tradition within a closed peasant community is most accessible using the insights of anthropologists.)[8] The repression of traditional manners and mores from the Counter-Reformation onward has been a major theme in accounts of the changing role of the Church, the evolution of new social structures, the growth of the state, and the development of a capitalist economy. Many monographs in French social history of the *ancien régime* now include discussion of traditional song, dance, and play as an integral part of every day life in times past.[9]

Despite all this attention to an earlier *culture populaire*, however, little work has been focused on what replaced folk customs. Exclusive consideration of the early modern has neglected the transition to a new mentality during the eighteenth and nineteenth centuries, and the historical ramifications of this momentous displacement.[10] To some extent the present study of romanticism is meant as a corrective. Admittedly, the problem is too complex to be treated adequately in a brief monograph, one devoted to such a narrow selection of many controversial issues in "modernization." More work on romanticism's share in the history of plebeian cultural life is certainly needed before both the movement and its popular context in Paris, as well as in the rest of France in the early nineteenth century, can begin to be understood more fully. This demands serious interdisciplinary approaches to a long neglected and difficult field of historical research.

8. See Robert Redfield, *The Little Community/Peasant Society and Culture* (Chicago: University of Chicago Press, 1963), and discussion of his insights in Burke, *Popular Culture in Early Modern Europe*, pp. 23–29. Impressive use of anthropological insights in historical study of popular culture is found in Natalie Z. Davis, *Society and Culture in Early Modern France* (Stanford: Stanford University Press, 1975), esp. 97–123, 227–67.

9. Many local studies recognize the importance of popular culture to the everyday life of a subsistence economy, e.g., Gérard Bouchard, *Le village immobile: Sonnely-en-Sologne au XVIIIe siècle* (Paris: Plon, 1972), in which cultural factors are characterized as refuge from an extremely harsh material reality.

10. Except Crubellier, *Histoire culturelle*; Darmon, *Le colportage de librairie*; and Weber, *Peasants into Frenchmen*.

Moreover, the present examination of French romanticism also invites more attention to the social and economic co..tribution to cultural developments. Attitudes and values existed in an informing extraliterary context whose influence has rarely been examined by literary and intellectual historians. Accounts of the Renaissance, the Reformation, the Scientific Revolution, the *fin de siècle* malaise, even the twentieth-century extremist movements have frequently focused on their debt to a strictly intellectual tradition to the exclusion of material factors.[11] Indeed, developments in printing are largely overlooked in the history of ideas after the Renaissance.[12] What attempts have been made to consider broader issues outside the isolated realm of intellectual discourse have attended to political and social conflicts on an equally abstract level of description.

Climates of opinion, class consciousness, and political and industrial revolutions undoubtedly contributed to the shape and course of man's understanding of himself and the world. But their analysis often fails to explain how ideas as books were produced, distributed, and consumed. Ideas did not exist in a vacuum; people wrote, published, and read in a milieu that must have informed the attitudes and values of a period in a discernible fashion. Although these elements did not determine the ideas themselves, such social and economic circumstances did make possible their diffusion and limited their variations over time.

Recent studies of the importance of the printing press as an agent of cultural change have underscored these insights in their study of intellectual developments in early modern Europe.[13] Lucien Febvre and Henri-Jean Martin focused on the production and distribution of the book from the Middle Ages to the eighteenth century, detailing the crucial events in the manufacture of paper, the "discovery" of printing with moveable type, the first legal and commercial networks of printed works, the evolution of the guilds, the early geography and agencies of diffusion, and

11. E.g., see a "traditional" intellectual history, however controversial or important it may be to scholars in the field, Thomas Kuhn, *The Structure of Scientific Revolutions* (Chicago: University of Chicago Press, 1970). Despite the significance of Kuhn's thesis to the history of science, he ignores the material factors necessary to the study of scientific phenomena. What becomes of the scientist today without access to an expensive laboratory?

12. See Elizabeth Eisenstein, "The Advent of Printing in Current Historical Literature: Notes and Comments on an Elusive Transformation," *American Historical Review* 75(1970),2:727–43.

13. See Febvre and Martin, *L'apparition du livre*; and Eisenstein, *The Printing Press as an Agent of Change: Communication and Cultural Transformation in Early Modern Europe* (Cambridge: Cambridge University Press, 1979), 2 vols., whose extensive bibliography cites nearly every source, primary and secondary, concerned with this problem.

finally the place of the book in Renaissance humanism, the Reformation, and the standardization of the vernacular. But the actual consequences of the shift from script to print and its promotion of relatively inexpensive editions of influential writers are discussed at greater length in Elizabeth Eisenstein's extensive synthesis of secondary studies. To assess the impact of early printed books, she characterizes the larger role of printing in the preservation and establishment of texts and the diverse effects over time of these texts on intellectual, religious, and scientific developments from the fifteenth to the eighteenth centuries. She also shows the particular role of printers and their workshops in fostering the values and attitudes of the authors they patronized, published, and sold. Like Caxton and the Estiennes, for example, many printers themselves became prominent humanists and established international cultural communication through their far-flung business contacts. The significance of this process in the history of ideas, of course, has been recognized by some intellectual historians, but never with the judicious and scrupulous attention of Eisenstein's study.

Another historian, Robert Darnton, has also developed this new approach to the history of ideas.[14] His publishing history of the *Encyclopédie* traces the specific influence of the "booty capitalism" in the eighteenth-century book trade on the message, format, and diffusion of a single book, albeit a very big and important one. By choosing one of the most representative titles in the French Enlightenment, Darnton documents the biography of not just a book but the century's ideas contained in it. The extensive records and correspondence of Panckoucke, Duplain, and the Société Typographique de Neuchâtel, publishers of the *Encyclopédie*'s successive editions, provide the author a first hand acquaintance with the material circumstances of nearly an entire intellectual movement. The business of enlightenment chose authors, changed the text, and provided the readers of eighteenth-century works in a ferocious brand of entrepreneurial piracy to effect something of a cultural revolution. Indeed the history of the *Encyclopédie* shows how the principles of 1789 "became expressed in print, disseminated in the social order, embodied in institutions, and incorporated in a new vision of the world" that cannot be understood in a discussion of Enlightenment ideas alone.[15] Here intellectual and social history converge to suggest the complex place external factors had in the world of the mind.

Similarly, the extraliterary milieu of early nineteenth-century Paris

14. Darnton, *The Business of Enlightenment*. See also his bibliographical discussion of this problem in the history of the Enlightenment in his "Reading, Writing and Publishing in Eighteenth-Century France," pp. 238–50.

15. Darnton, *The Business of Enlightenment*, p. 545.

had a definite impact on the shape and scope of romanticism, as the present venture has emphasized.[16] The social history of romanticism, still incomplete in its consideration of popular culture, clearly builds on the insights of Eisenstein, Darnton, and scholars at the Ecole des Hautes Etudes en Sciences Sociales into the historical context of ideas among authors, readers, and the book trade in early modern Europe. Unfortunately, these historians stopped short of postrevolutionary developments no less important to ideas and their tradition. Some aspects of romanticism, especially the profusion of its forms and conventions, are difficult to conceive without younger, more professional writers, an innovative publishing trade, and a larger audience in the first half of the nineteenth century in Paris where a new popular literature was taking hold. Were the records available, a publishing history of Walter Scott's works in France and the romantic sensibility they expressed, for example, would provide equally suggestive and even more concrete insights into the business of romanticism and its influence on the French intellectual world in the period. But other kinds of sources are available, and they deserve consideration on an appropriate level of description comparable to that given by scholars to much older documents.

What is true for the Renaissance, the Reformation, the Enlightenment, and the romantic movement may also be true for later intellectual movements. The material approach is applicable generally to the history of ideas in the nineteenth and twentieth centuries. As early as 1923 the German L. L. Schücking suggested a brand of literary sociology that would give a full account of "the process revealing [the] movement in taste . . . as a sociological current" among writers and readers.[17] More recently Robert Escarpit has promoted the sociology of literature in France, a field that has met with some success both overseas and here in the United States.[18] Apart from its debt to Schücking, Escarpit's central insight into the dual nature of literature, as both expression and artifact, rests on a long and well-established tradition in the history of literary theory.[19] By focusing on the "objective" *fait littéraire*, the discrete unit of

16. Pioneering work on the material context of writing in the romantic period is found in George, *French Romanticism*; Graña, *Modernity and its Discontents;* and Barbéris, *Balzac et le mal du siècle*—however different their perspectives, themes, sources, and analysis. An important theoretical basis for such an approach is suggested in Pierre Bourdieu, "Le marché des biens symboliques," *L'année sociologique* 21(1970),49–126.

17. Schücking, *The Sociology of Literary Taste*, pp. 32–33.

18. See Escarpit, *Sociologie de la littérature;* and his collection of essays, *Le littéraire et le social: éléments pour une sociologie de la littérature* (Paris: Flammarion, 1970).

19. E.g., see Austin Warren and René Wellek, *Theory of Literature* (New York: Harcourt, Brace, and World, 1956), pp. 73–135.

communication such as the book or the periodical, Escarpit has sketched a complex network of relationships of which literature is the center—the author, the publisher, the reader, the critic, and the social, economic, and cultural structures that affect the work, including academies, universities, public and private foundations. In this way literary creation can be situated within certain historical constraints, such that some genres and styles are simply inconceivable in another social milieu.

When these considerations of literature's material as well as cultural context are also applied to the history of ideas, past and present, the heuristic possibilities multiply. The narrowly disciplinary study of intellectual movements actually shades into social history and invites reassessment of many *idées forces* in western Europe—nationalism, liberalism, and socialism—as well as many more strictly literary developments that coincided with them—naturalism, symbolism, and surrealism. The results would surely elucidate the place such "isms" had in crucial periods of European history. As Marshall MacLuhan has suggested, the medium is almost as important as the message; artifacts of intellectual history require more attention on all levels of artistic creation, from the classical works of Greece and Rome to the contemporary romances of *True Confessions,* however heretical such a suggestion may sound in any field.[20]

As for the present analysis of French romanticism, however, a number of qualifications must still be made to anticipate the more specific objections that literary and intellectual historians are likely to raise, whatever the merits of the approach and its precedents. For one, the intellectual revolt against empiricism and rationality known as the romantic movement was hardly confined to a twenty-year period in the first half of the nineteenth century. Signs of a preromantic sensibility appear more than 100 years earlier: the growth of sentimentality in epistolary novels and *drames larmoyants* at the beginning of the eighteenth century does foreshadow important elements of romanticism. Jean-Jacques Rousseau's response to the emotional sterility of eighteenth-century writers encouraged the romantic return to primitive ideals captured in the rustic antics at Marie-Antoinette's *hameau* in Versailles. Mention, too, must be made of an earlier form of romanticism at the turn of the century among Madame de Staël, Senancoeur, and Chateaubriand, the so-called first generation of authors in the new literature. Despite the interruption of the revolutionary and Napoleonic neo-classicism, romanticism in France had a much longer history than its literary manifestations during the *monarchie censitaire.*[21]

20. See Marshall MacLuhan's exaggerated but interesting argument in *Understanding Media,* pp. 7–21.

21. Paul Hazard, *The European Mind, 1685–1715,* J. Lewis Day, trans. (Cleveland:

Nor did this intellectual revolt end with Hugo's failure at the Théâtre français as some contemporary observers claimed. An argument can be made for the lasting impact of romanticism, for better or worse, on the entire nineteenth century and even the modern mind since then.[22] The romantic tradition is clearly evident in the private, often obscure imagery of the symbolists Verlaine and Huysmans, for example. The dadaist and surrealist revolts in the wake of World War I resemble remarkably the youthful and esthetic antipathies of the romantic generation a century earlier. There is even something strikingly romantic about Jean-Paul Sartre's attempt to marry the subjectivity of existentialism to the objectivity of Marxism in the postwar period. And again the May 1968 events called for an artistic renewal that harks back to the literary manifestoes of the early nineteenth century. This much about the impact of romanticism is important and bears closer scrutiny. Such a history of romantic ideas in France from the seventeenth century onward, so controversial to serious students of literature and intellectual history, indeed promises knowledge of the origins of the modern sensibility.[23]

Similarly, the movement was hardly confined to literary forms: art saw equally impressive changes in the period that were obviously related to the romantic rebellion in literature.[24] Even though elements of the romantic and the classic are discernible in European painting long before and long after, a sharp division between the two appeared among artists from the middle of the eighteenth to the middle of the nineteenth centuries. Definitions of what constitutes romantic art, of course, are as difficult to make as those of the literature in the same period. But there was certainly an appeal to emotions by the choice of subject and the sensuous use of color that approximated the romantic sensibility in other creative endeavors. While the classicists believed that art should aim at noble simplicity and calm grandeur, the romantics declared that it should excite the emotions, particularly the emotion of fear which was the truest

---

World, 1964), pp. 335–434; Babbitt, *Rousseau and Romanticism*, pp. 220–39; and Barbéris, *Chateaubriand: une réaction au monde moderne* (Paris: Larousse, 1976).

22. See useful overview of French romanticism's extended history in Peyre, *Qu'est-ce que le romantisme?*

23. See Robert Wohl, *The Generation of 1914* (Cambridge: Harvard University Press, 1979), pp. 5–41; H. Stuart Hughes, *The Obstructed Path: French Thought in the Years of Desperation, 1930–1960* (New York: Harper and Row, 1968), pp. 170–89; and José Pierre, "Create!" in Charles Posner, ed., *Reflections on the Revolution in France: 1968* (Harmondsworth: Penguin, 1970), pp. 239–43.

24. See Kenneth Clark, *The Romantic Rebellion: Romantic versus Classic Art* (New York: Harper and Row, 1973), esp. pp. 19–20, 40–42; Hugh Honour, *Romanticism* (New York: Harper and Row, 1979); and more controversially, Donald Sutherland, *On, Romanticism* (New York: New York University Press, 1971), esp. pp. 3–63.

source of the sublime. Romanticism in art, as in literature, developed a new set of values in its rebellion against the static conformity of classicism. As Kenneth Clark and others have observed, the romanticism of the great tableaux in the early nineteenth century clearly reflected the sensibility of literati in the same period. The primacy of inspiration, emotion, and subjective judgment prevailed among painters as well as poets; the dramatic exoticism of Hugo's *Les orientales* is complemented by the paintings of Delacroix.

The romantic revolution did not stop here; it also invaded music, perhaps the most romantic of the arts.[25] Music's ordered sound and rhythm, so detached from the concrete world of objects, made possible the suggestions of impressions, thoughts, and feelings at the heart of the romantic mood. Similar tendencies had been in evidence among many composers: in Hayden's *Creation* may be found the romantics' pleasure in depicting the world of nature, in Mozart's *Don Giovanni* their preoccupation with the inner life of the individual, and in Beethoven's ninth symphony their faustian longings and heroic quest for the infinite. Program music, largely a romantic development, was not the movement's attempt to reduce the sublime to the mundane, but its response to the imaginative possibilities of music's association with poetic, descriptive, even narrative subject matter which ultimately were beyond the power of words to express. As in Hector Berlioz's *Symphonie fantastique*, the melody was elevated to central interest; picturesque episodes prevailed over a larger conceptual unity. The most remarkable romantic achievement in many other works besides Berlioz's lay in the development of harmony and color, the principle means by which nineteenth-century composers sought to express in music the romantic ideals of remoteness, ardor, and boundless longing.

Romanticism thus transcended many boundaries, between social classes and cultural tastes, indeed between all the arts.[26] The same may also be said about the movement's ability to penetrate the borders between countries as different from each other as Germany, Italy, Britain, and Russia where the romantic mood was expressed in literature, art, and music just as it was in France.[27] Despite its relatively late and unendur-

25. Useful surveys of romantic music are Alfred Einstein, *Music in the Romantic Era* (New York: Norton, 1947); Jacques Barzun, *Berlioz and the Romantic Century* (New York: Columbia University Press, 1969), 2 vols.; and Jean Chantavoine and Jean Gaudefroy-Demombynes, *Le romantisme dans la musique européenne* (Paris: Albin Michel, 1955), esp. pp. 351–95.

26. See Moreau, "Le romantisme et la 'fraternité' des arts," *Symposium* (Winter 1969), 319–24.

27. See Tieghem, *Le romantisme dans la littérature européenne*, pp. 221–343, and Mario Praz, *The Romantic Agony*, Angus Davidson, trans. (London: Oxford University Press, 1951), on the international characteristics of European romanticism.

ing quality, French romanticism was part of a European movement from the eighteenth to the nineteenth centuries that marked a radical departure in man's perception of himself and the world. Among other things, what French romantics shared with their English and German counterparts was a rejection of sterile and mechanistic modes of thought inherent in the rational, Newtonian conceptions of the universe, as well as a belief in the boundless power of the imagination to create a world of freedom, movement, passion, and endless yearning after impossible fulfillment. Similar conflicts between the artist and his audience, between nature and society, between the irrational and the scientific, between idealism and materialism, between the national and the cosmopolitan, between revolution and tradition all pervaded the romantic period throughout Europe, as many intellectual, literary, art, and music historians have pointed out for the past 150 years.

These "sins" of omission in a social history of romanticism may be forgiven, perhaps, but for other possible problems raised by the present approach. Can romanticism truly be defined on the plebeian level? Is not the distinction between the romantic mode and mood too artificial, contrived in such a way to "discover" what the study intended to find? Given the diversity of literature on all levels, did a popular romanticism actually exist where it may not have been consciously conceived by authors or perceived by their readers oblivious to the deeper implications of the movement? These questions closely resemble what nearly every historian must face in the world of the intellect, fraught as it is with subtleties and distinctions, especially in the history of literature. Difficulties enough arise from the exegesis of one author's work; to identify common characteristics in the work of a hundred with equal precision is more than enough for any one historian, however shrewd or productive. The three criteria used to define romanticism in Chapter 1 were derived largely from a reasonably close reading of recognized romantic masterworks and the closer study of critical surveys by prominent literary historians. Whether or not such an elite definition of romanticism is at all appropriate to the achievement of popular writers and their apparent imitations of the movement remains to be verified by other students in the field. What was obvious to one may not be obvious to others in the remarkable variety of popular literature published at the height of romanticism in France.[28]

But this study's research premises also pose difficulties specific to the field of social history. How do we know that such plebeian romantic

28. Note, however, a similar attempt to characterize romanticism in a variety of genres, to draw many of the same distinctions between the romantic mood and mode, and to discuss the nature of romanticism in the popular genres, in Tieghem, *Le romantisme dans la littérature européenne*, pp. 347–458, 221–98, and 274–78, respectively.

ideas, such as they were, ever reached readers in Paris? How does the documentation of romanticism's diffusion in the *Bibliographie de la France* and the *cabinets de lecture* prove that even the literate people in the city read or heard about the titles sampled? What were the specific audiences of romantic works, high and low? Obviously too much must not be inferred from the relative paucity of evidence at hand. Assuming public taste from the catalogs of auctioneers, booksellers, lending libraries, and colporters, without knowing precisely which books were bought, borrowed, or read by whom, can be dangerous speculation, even with the edition sizes declared by printers in the Interior Ministry archives. The documentation of relatively high literacy rates among the Parisian populace by marriage register signatures and conscript declarations does not locate the actual readers of books, no more than it identifies the readership of a particular author. The diaries kept by some people of their daily reading are too few to indicate anything more than the tastes of a very special, self-conscious minority. The place of romantic works and their conventions in the lives of ordinary people can only be inferred until new sources and methods are focused on the problem.

These qualifications about both the scope and the approach of the present study are important and must not be ignored. However general the discussion of the movement's cultural and material context in Paris from 1820 to 1840, it hardly does justice to the larger historical phenomenon of romanticism in western Europe. The long tradition of romantic ideas from the eighteenth century onward, the range of its manifestations in the different arts, and its European impact all have been neglected here, purposely. Such considerations are more than enough for others to study. This social history of French romanticism has deliberately selected instead a very particular view, though not out of irreverence for this major and well-studied development in elite culture. Its selective focus derives from a deference to the specificity of social historical research and, ironically, to the even broader significance of the cultural role played by the movement. What was so apparent in the popular literature and its context in the period has never seen a history and thus merits its almost exclusive consideration here.

Moreover, the problems of definition and inference in this study, serious objections in nearly all social history, have necessitated the openness with which the present methodology and sources are stated. However inelegant this "social scientific" attention to procedure, or however awkward the historian's fastidiousness about references, these "intrusions" in an essay on literature have not been capricious: large historical generalizations demand some documentation as well as qualification, especially in a field where few have ventured. Future attempts to elucidate the movement's popular diffusion must also define romanticism and draw on sources at best only suggestive. The questions posed may never be answered satisfactorily, whatever the approach. We can know for certain relatively little in social history; anonymous people in times past left few records of themselves or their activities, and preclude full, accurate knowledge of their attitudes and lives—contrary to diplomatic history, for example, whose documentation for many events is nearly perfect. For the social history of ideas, the means and manner of knowing must be more tentative, forcing the researcher to make the best case possible from the available evidence.[29] Although romantic ideas may not have reached the hands of ordinary men and women in the past, chances are good that with so many romantic titles readily and cheaply available to a diverse group of readers, the movement was experienced by many. And the audience most likely to have participated can be surmised from the social classes in a position to share in this cultural activity. But to glean more, given the indirectness of the study, would no longer be informed speculation.

Further work on popular literature and its politics promises many new insights into the world of common people in the nineteenth century. Recent research on the attempts of prominent bourgeois to use the growing book trade for social control during the Restoration has traced the origins of many successful titles.[30] Occupational guidebooks for women, religious tracts of the Société Catholique des Bons Livres for the working classes, how-to-books for artisans and journeymen in nearly every trade, and new rational almanacs intended to replace those in the *bibliothèque bleue* all enjoyed widespread circulation during the constitutional monarchies largely under the sponsorship of elites anxious to inform or tame the lower orders. Similarly, work on the songs and singing societies, the *goguettes* and *orphéons*, should portray clearly one important aspect of the cultural life shared by identifiable groups, in some cases from a single factory or regional industry.[31] In time, as many of the societies organized to compete for prizes and later for more explicit professional purposes, their politics moved from the revolutionary left to the nationalist right. What began as politically suspect café concerts during the July

29. See discussion of the various epistemological difficulties of social history in Henretta, "Social History as Lived and Written."

30. Note the forthcoming doctoral dissertation by Perry, "Publishers, Politics, and the Discovery of the Popular Reader in France"; as well as forthcoming study of the *cabinets de lecture* as a cultural, social, and political agency in the Restoration by Françoise Parent at the Ecole des Hautes Etudes en Sciences Sociales, Paris.

31. Note the forthcoming doctoral dissertation by Nathan Therien, "The Orphéons and the Failure of Amateurism," Harvard University, written under the direction of Patrice Higonnet.

Monarchy ended as government sponsored military choruses during the Third Republic. Like increasing attention to sociability and the performing arts, such accounts of the politics inherent in popular literary activities depict more fully the conflicts of literature and its development in nineteenth-century France.[32]

In the meantime, this work in the social history of French romanticism in Paris from 1820 to 1840 must suffice in suggesting one direction intellectual history may take. At least one may now claim with some confidence that if only a few experienced the romantic melancholy described by contemporary observers, a great many more witnessed significant changes in the literature they wrote, published, or read in the first half of the nineteenth century. Such marked the beginning of a new cultural world for the working classes as well as the bourgeoisie, particularly in the city of Paris. Popular romanticism accustomed both social groups to a more common literary interest that by mid-century would evolve into a literature for truly mass consumption, despite the elites and their retreat from popular culture in the wake of revolutionary conflicts, political, social, and intellectual. Similarly, the new popular literature first enjoyed by Parisians and other urbanites by the Second Empire would in time penetrate the rural recesses and backwaters by the end of the century, bringing the peasantry more fully into what was then nearly a national literary experience, especially when the Ferry Laws had finally established literacy in the French language throughout the country. Although the romantic movement surely did not effect all these subsequent cultural developments, it did participate in their early stages and may even have promoted them by its catholic appeal.

Consequently, the romantic movement takes on an even greater significance than earlier histories have assigned to it.[33] No doubt it marked a major watershed among intellectual elites sensitive to the limitations of eighteenth-century thought: the modern mind in its extraordinary self-consciousness owes much to those early nineteenth-century writers who explored the inner resources of the mind and its relationship to the conscious world, who conceived the possibilities of organic nature in the process of becoming, who revelled and agonized in the boundless

32. See Agulhon, *Le cercle dans la France bourgeoise, 1810–1848: étude d'une mutation de sociabilité* (Paris: Colin, 1977); and Conrad L. Donakowski, *A Muse for the Masses: Ritual and Music in an Age of Democratic Revolution, 1770–1870* (Chicago: University of Chicago Press, 1977), pp. 33–75.

33. Even though his discussion does not focus on either romanticism or popular culture, Foucault still recognizes an important watershed in the evolution of a new *episteme* at roughly the same time as the changes discussed in the present study. Perhaps the romantic cultural revolution has its origins in the discovery of literature and historicity that Foucault discusses in *The Order of Things*, pp. 294–300, 367–73.

imagination of man. Romanticism, as it has been studied, was all this and much more. But it was something of a watershed for other reasons as well: romanticism saw the beginning of a new literature, a new popular culture, and perhaps even a new mind-frame for many ordinary men and women, in Paris at least. After more than a century of living an older intellectual paradigm, one first abandoned by the aristocracy and the middle classes during the seventeenth and eighteenth centuries, the middling and lower classes shared values and attitudes far more in keeping with the self-assertion that made possible a new political and social system in the nineteenth century. Thus the romantic revolution shared in a much larger historical change than is evident in the masterworks still read and studied by scholars today, a change that is far more apparent in the reading matter of the *menu peuple* and the new cultural context in which they lived.

APPENDIX A

SAMPLED TITLES REFLECTING ROMANTIC INFLUENCE

1820

Poetry

Drama

J. C. F. von Schiller, *Marie Stuart*, tragédie, Henri Latouche, trans. (Barba)

Fiction

J. H. Bernardin de Saint-Pierre, *Paul et Virginie* (Lefèvre)

J. Q. (Joseph Quantin), *Le pâtre tirolien*, roman historique (Locard et Davi)

J. A. S. Collin de Plancy, *Mémoires d'un vilain du XIVe siècle*, traduit d'un manuscrit de 1369 (L'Huillier)

Charles Nodier, *Adèle* (Gide fils)

Anna Maria Porter, *Don Sébastien, Roi de Portugal*, roman historique traduit de l'anglais (F. Louis)

Walter Scott, *Ivanhoe, ou le retour du croisé*, A. J. B. Defauconpret, trans. (Nicolle)

History

M. G*** *Beautés de l'histoire des croisades et de différens* [sic] *ordres religieux et militaires* (Eymery)

239

1827

Poetry

Evariste Boulay-Paty, *Athéniennes* (Chaumerot jeune)

Augustin André, *Les étrennes du troubadour,* recueil de poésies diverses . . . (Rusand)

(Charles Malo, ed.), *Le chansonnier des dames pour 1827* (Janet)

Drama

M. E. G. M. Théaulon de Lambert, *Le paysan perverti, ou quinze ans de Paris,* drame en trois journées (Barba)

Le sieur Luc (H. A. Cavé et Dittmer), *Une commission de censure,* scènes non-historiques (Brière)

Ludavic Vitet, *Les Etats de Blois, ou la mort des MM. de Guise,* scènes historiques, décembre 1588 (Ponthieu)

William Shakespeare, *Othello, the Moor of Venice,* a Tragedy (Mme. Verge)

Fiction

Madame la baronne d'Ordre, *Les suisses sous Rodolphe de Habsbourg,* roman historique (Gosselin)

Stendhal (Henri Beyle), *Armance, ou quelques scènes d'un salon de Paris en 1827* (Canel)

A. H. de Kératry, *Frédéric Styndall, ou la fatale année* (Delaunay)

(Achille Roche), *Le fanatisme, extrait des mémoires d'un ligueur* (Chaigneau)

K. F. van der Velde, *Christine et sa cour,* F.A. Loève-Veimars, trans. (Gosselin)

Walter Scott, *Contes de mon hôte,* A. J. B. Defauconpret, trans. (Gosselin)

Thomas Moore, *The Epicurian,* a Tale (Galignani)

J. W. von Goethe, *Les souffrances du jeune Werther,* Henri La Bedoyère, trans. (Didot)

History

J. A. de Norvins, *Histoire de Napoléon* (Dupont)

(Anonymous), *Général Gourgaud et Sir Walter Scott* (Imp. Boucher)

L. F. J. de Bausset-Roquefort, *Mémoires anecdotiques sur l'intérieur du palais . . . pour servir à l'histoire de Napoléon* (Baudouin frères)

E.-Hyacinthe Langlois, *Essai historique et descriptif sur l'Abbaye de Fontenelle ou de Saint-Wandrille* (Tastu)

L. F. de Villeneuve, *Chapelle ducale de Nanci, ou notice historique sur les ducs de Lorraine* (Blaise)

1830

Poetry

Edouard Alletz, *La nouvelle messiade*, poème (Rusand)

Alphonse de Lamartine, *Oeuvres de A. de Lamartine* (Gagniard)

Théophile de M***, *Le quatorze juin. Stances sur Alger* (Dentu)

Juste Olivier, *Poèmes suisses: Julia Alpinula* [et] *La bataille de Grandson* (Delaunay)

(Anonymous), *Le chansonnier des grâces pour 1830* (F. Louis)

J.-J. Lesergent, *Le troubadour français*, chansons philosophiques, politiques, satiriques, érotiques et badines (Ladvocat)

Drama

(Anonymous), *François 1er à Chambord*, comédie (Charpentier-Méricourt)

J. A. P. F. Ancelot, *Un an, ou le mariage d'amour*, drame (Breauté et Barba)

C. F. J. B. Moreau de Commagny et d'Epagny, *L'auberge d'Auray*, drame lyrique (Vente)

(Théophile Lavallée), *Jean-Sans-Peur, duc de Bourgogne*, scènes historiques (Lecointe)

(C. M. Wieland), *Oberon*, opéra (Vinchon)

T. C., *Scènes de cour et de cabaret*, parades historiques (Levavasseur)

Henri Monnier, *Scènes populaires, dessinées à la plume* (Levavasseur)

L. F. N. Clairville, *Quatorze ans de la vie de Napoléon, ou Berlin, Potsdam, Paris, Waterloo, et Sainte-Hélène* (Barbier)

Fiction

E. Arthaud, *Jules, ou le fils adultérin*, roman historique et de moeurs du XIXe siècle (Lecointe et Pougin)

Honoré de Balzac, *Scènes de la vie privée* (Mame et Delaunay-Vallée)

E. Loyau de Lacy, *Le prêtre* (Igonette)

Fleury, *La nuit de sang*, roman historique (Lecointe)

Louise Lemercier, *Victor-Amédée II, ou le siège de Turin*, nouvelle historique (Gaudiot)

Walter Scott, *The Prose Works of Sir Walter Scott*, vol. 3: *The Abbot-Kenilworth-The Pirate—The Fortunes of Nigel-Quentin Durward* (Galignani)

Walter Scott, *Le vieillard des tombeaux, ou les Presbytériens d'Ecosse*, Albert de Montémont, trans. (Armand-Aubrée)

Walter Scott, *La jolie fille de Perth, ou le jour de Saint Valentin*, A. J. B. Defauconpret, trans. (Furne)

Adam Mickiewicz, *Konrad Wallenrod*, récit historique (Gagniard)

K. F. van der Velde, *La conquête du Mexique*, F. A. Loève-Veimars, trans. (Gosselin)

F. A. R. de Chateaubriand, *Génie du christianisme* (Lefèvre et Ladvocat)

History

E. M. Masse, *Histoire du pape Alexandre VI et de César Borgia* (Audin, Lefèvre et cie.)

Joseph Zielinski, *Histoire de Pologne* (Barbezat)

L. E. Gauttier du Lys d'Arc, *Histoire des conquêtes des Normands en Italie, en Sicilie et en Grèce* (L. de Bure)

(Anonymous), *Testament de Napoléon* (Mathiot)

(Anonymous), *Description du Château Biron* (Imp. Porthmann)

Jehan, sire de Joinville, *Histoire de Saint Loys, roi de France*, F. X. Michel, ed. (Bibliothèque choisie)

1834

Poetry

Gibert de Montreuil, *Roman de la violette ou Gérard de Nervers*, F. X. Michel, ed. (Silvestre)

Casimir Faucompré, *Poésies diverses, odes, épigrammes* (Imp. Sétier)

Antony Luirard, *A M. Alex. Dufieux* (Imp. Ayné)

(Anonymous), *Un bal*, poésies (Imp. Chassaignon)

(Anonymous), *La Fayette*, ode (Duvernois)

C. Léopold Curez, *Abeilard à Héloïse* (Babeuf)

J. C. Blumenfeld, *Les soupirs de la Pologne*, en sept psaumes (Mercklein)

Edouard Alletz, *Caractères poétiques* (Delaunay)

Favier, *Poésie. Jane Grey. Tableau de M. Delaroche* [sic] (Imp. Goetschy)

Ernest Legouvé, *Les vieillards* (Guyot)

Drama

Jacques Arago, *Un noviciat diplomatique*, comédie (Barba)

(Anonymous), *Les quatre âges*, moralité à III personnes (Techener)

J. F. C. Delavigne, *Théâtre de M. C. Delavigne* (Furne)

Julien de Mallian, *Les dernières scènes de la fronde*, drame (Marchant)

J. A. P. F. Ancelot, *Lord Byron à Venise*, drame (Marchant)

J. A. Havard, *Oeuvres dramatiques de Shakespeare et de Schiller* . . . (Havard)

M. E. G. M. Théaulon de Lambert, *Les quatre âges du Palais-Royal*, histoire dramatique en trois époques (Marchant)

Lockroy (J. P. S. Simon) et Anicet Bourgeois, *L'impératrice et la juive*, drame (Marchant)

Charles Desnoyer et J. E. Alboize du Pujot, *Caravage* (1599), drame (Barba)

R. C. G. de Pixérécourt et Anicet Bourgeois, *Latude, ou trente-cinq ans de captivité*, mélodrame historique (Marchant)

Alfred de Musset, *Un spectacle dans un fauteuil* (Renduel)

Fontaine de la Meuse, *Afgar le bérébère*, drame (Fontaine)

Fiction

Carl Spindler, *Soirées de Dresde*, M. Paquis, trans. (Dumont)

James Fenimore Cooper, *Le bourreau de Berne, ou l'abbaye des vignerons*, A. J. B. Defauconpret, trans. (Furne)

Leitch Ritchie, *Schinderhannes, ou le brigand du rhin*, A. J. B. Defauconpret, trans. (Gosselin)

J. H. Bernardin de Saint-Pierre, *Paul et Virginie* (Imp. Joly)

J. W. von Goethe, *Werther* (Ledentu)

Maurice de Viarz (A. E. R. de Serviez), *Neuf jours d'hymen, ou la cour en seize cent dix* (Lachapelle)

Amédée de Bast, *Le clocher de Saint-Jacques-la-Boucherie (ou Nicolas Flamel), histoire du XIVe siècle* (Lecointe)

Alfred Mousse (Arsène Housset), *De profundis* (Lecointe et Pougin)

A. C. Thibaudeau, *La bohême,* roman historique (Paulin)

Madame de Ranchoup, *Une châtelaine du XIIe siècle,* nouvelle (Aillaud)

Georges Touchard-Lafosse, *Les réverbères,* chroniques de nuit du vieux et du nouveau (Lachapelle)

Honoré de Balzac, *Etudes philosophiques* (Dentu)

(Anonymous), *Marie, ou la fille du croisé,* épisode du tems [sic] féodal (Gaume)

Jules Lacroix, *Corps sans âme* (Renduel)

History

(Anonymous), *Tableau de l'histoire générale de l'Europe depuis 1814* (Vimont)

Alexandre Barginet, *Chroniques impériales* (Laisné)

R. O. Spazier, *Histoire politique et militaire de la révolution polonaise . . .* 3e éd. (Spazier)

Augustin Thierry, *Dix ans d'études historiques* (Tessier)

J. C. F. de Ladoucette, *Histoire, topographie, antiquités, usages, dialectes des Hautes-Alpes* (Fantin)

(Anonymous), *Histoire du gouvernement représentatif en France . . .* (Imp. Crapelet)

C. Neilson (Léon Curmer) et A. R. Bouzenot, *Histoire nationale de la révolution française* (Breauté)

Adhelm Bernier, *Monumens* [sic] *inédits de l'histoire de France, 1400–1600* (Joubert)

1841

Poetry

(Anonymous), *Heures perdues* (Fain)

M. A. Corradini, *Chants du Danube* (Charpentier)

G. A. Bürger, *Lénore,* E. de Labédollière, trans. (Curmer)

Thomas Moore, *Chefs d'oeuvres poétiques de Thomas Moore,* Mme. Louise Belloc, trans. (Gosselin)

Drama

Victor Hugo, *Théâtre de Victor Hugo* (Charpentier)

Victor Hugo, *Cromwell*, drame (Charpentier)

Fiction

Victor Hugo, *Han d'Islande* (Charpentier)

Marcellin Pochet-Dassin, *Païda, ou la rage en amour* (Challamel)

Georges Touchard-Lafosse, *Hélène de Poitiers*, roman historique (XIVᵉ siècle) (Sandré)

Augustine Gottis, *Le Tasse et la princesse Eléonore d'Est* [sic], roman historique (Berquet et Pétion)

Walter Scott, *L'antiquaire*, M. d'Exauvillez, trans. (Société de Saint-Nicolas)

James Fenimore Cooper, *Mercédès de Castille*, histoire du temps de Christophe Columb, E. de Labédollière, trans. (Curmer)

Ernest Minard, *Robert d'Arbrissel*, roman historique (Desessart)

History

J. F. Michaud, *Histoire des croisades* (Furne)

J. H. Merle d'Aubigné, *Histoire de la reformation du XVIᵉ siècle*, vol. 3 (Didot)

F. P. G. Guizot, *Histoire de la révolution d'Angleterre* (Didier)

Mademoiselle Vauvilliers, *Histoire de Blanche de Castille, Reine des Français* (Paulin)

J. C. L. Simonde de Sismondi, *Histoire des républiques italiennes du moyen âge* (Truttel et Wurtz)

Charles Nodier, *Souvenirs, épisodes et portraits pour servir à l'histoire de la révolution et de l'empire* (Charpentier)

(Anonymous), *Histoire populaire de Napoléon* (Feret fils)

E. M. de Saint-Hilaire, *Les aides-de-camp de l'empereur, souvenirs intimes* (Magen et Comon)

Ferdinand Langlé (J. A. F. Langlois), ed. *Funérailles de l'empereur Napoléon, relation officielle de la translation de ses restes mortels depuis l'ile Sainte-Hélène* (Curmer)

A. P. B. de Barante, *Histoire des ducs de Bourgogne de la maison de Valois, 1364–1477* (Furne)

J. B. H. R. Capefigue, *Les cents jours* (Langlois et Leclerc)

APPENDIX B

SAMPLED LIVING AUTHORS INFLUENCED BY ROMANTICISM [a]

Author	Age	No. of Titles Published	Edition Size	Occupation
1820				
Henri Latouche[b]	35	1	1,000	Journalist
Joseph Quantin	—	2	750	—
J. A. S. Collin de Plancy	27	15+	—	Bookseller
Charles Nodier	37	15+	2,000	Librarian
Anna Maria Porter[c]	40	6	1,000	Novelist
Walter Scott[c]	49	15+	1,500	Man of Letters
A. J. B. Defauconpret[b]	53	15+	1,500	Translator
1827				
Evariste Boulay-Paty	22	2	200	Law Clerk
Augustin André	—	1	300	—
Charles Malo	37	6	1,000	Journalist
M. E. G. M. Théaulon de Lambert	40	15+	1,000	Dramatist
H. A. Cavé[d]	33	1	1,000	Employé
Ludavic Vitet	25	2	1,000	Man of Letters
Baronne d'Ordre[c]	—	3	1,000	Rentier
Henri Beyle	42	8	1,000	Diplomat
A. H. de Kératry	58	12	2,000	Politique
Achille Roche	24	6	1,000	Secrétaire
F. A. Loève-Veimars[b]	26	15+	1,000	Man of Letters
Walter Scott[c]	56	15+	1,500	Man of Letters
A. J. B. Defauconpret[b]	60	15+	1,500	Translator
Thomas Moore[c]	48	15+	2,000	Lawyer

Author	Age	No. of Titles Published	Edition Size	Occupation
J. W. von Goethe[c]	78	11	2,000	Man of Letters
Henri La Bedoyère[b]	45	15+	2,000	Rentier
J. A. de Norvins	58	13	2,000	Diplomat
E. H. Langlois	50	8	850	Commerce
L. F. de Villeneuve	43	3	500	Rentier
1830				
Edouard Alletz	32	5	—	Professor
Alphonse de Lamartine	40	15+	2,000	Man of Letters
Juste Olivier	23	2	1,000	—
J. J. Lesergent	—	2	1,000	—
J. A. P. F. Ancelot	36	15+	300	Librarian
C. F. J. B. Moreau de Commagny[d]	43	15+	500	Administration
Théophile Lavallée	26	1	1,500	—
Henri Monnier	25	5	1,000	Dramatist
L. F. N. Clairville	19	1	—	Dramatist
E. Arthaud	—	2	800	—
Honoré de Balzac	31	15+	—	Man of Letters
E. Loyau de Lacy	—	1	2,000	Military
Louise Lemercier	47	3	500	—
Walter Scott[cf]	59	15+	2,000	Novelist
Albert de Montémont[b]	42	15+	2,000	Man of Letters
A. J. B. Defauconpret[b]	63	15+	2,000	Translator
Adam Mickiewicz	32	3	500	Rentier
F. A. Loève-Veimars[b]	29	15+	—	Man of Letters
F. A. R. de Chateaubriand	61	15+	1,000	Rentier
E. M. Masse	52	12	—	—
Joseph Zielinski	—	3	1,000	Professor
L. E. Gauttier du Lys d'Arc	31	10	—	Diplomat
F. X. Michel	21	8	1,600	Professor
1834				
F. X. Michel	25	10	200	Professor
Casimir Faucompré	—	1	100	—
Edouard Alletz	36	6	700	Professor
Favier	55	1	250	Military

Author	Age	No. of Titles Published	Edition Size	Occupation
Ernest Legouvé	27	6	300	Man of Letters
Jacques Arago	35	13	2,000	Dramatist
J. F. C. Delavigne	40	15+	2,500	Pensionnaire
Julien de Mallian	29	15	2,000	Avocat
J. A. P. F. Ancelot	40	15+	3,500	Dramatist
J. A. Havard	—	1	2,000	Bookseller
M. E. G. M. Théaulon de Lambert	47	15+	1,000	Dramatist
J. P. S. Simon[d]	31	6	3,000	Employé
Charles Desnoyer[d]	28	15+	3,000	Dramatist
R. C. G. de Pixérécourt[d]	61	15+	2,000	Dramatist
Alfred de Musset	24	5	750	Rentier
Fontaine de la Meuse	—	1	3,000	—
James Fenimore Cooper[c]	45	15+	3,500	Rentier
A. J. B. Defauconpret[e]	67	15+	3,500 650	Translator
Leitch Ritchie[c]	34	4	650	Man of Letters
A. E. R. de Serviez	27	3	500	—
Amédée de Bast	39	15+	1,000	Military
Arsène Housset	26	1	—	Journalist
A. C. Thibaudeau	69	14	1,000	Administration
Georges Touchard-Lafosse	54	15+	—	Man of Letters
Honoré de Balzac	35	15+	900	Novelist
Jules Lacroix	25	1	—	—
Alexandre Barginet	36	15+	1,500	Employé
R. O. Spazier	31	1	3,000	Rentier
Augustin Thierry	39	12	1,000	Pensionnaire
J. C. F. de Ladoucette	64	1	—	—
Léon Curmer[d]	33	1	1,500	Bookseller
Adhelm Bernier	28	8	—	Avocat
1841				
M. A. Corradini	—	1	1,000	—
Emile de Labédollière[e]	29	15+	−/2,500	Man of Letters
Thomas Moore[c]	59	15+	1,000	Lawyer
Louise Belloc[b]	45	15+	1,000	Translator
Victor Hugo[f]	39	15+	2,000 2,000 3,500	Rentier
Marcellin Pochet-Dassin	—	1	500	—

Author	Age	No. of Titles Published	Edition Size	Occupation
Georges Touchard-Lafosse	61	15+	800	Man of Letters
Augustine Gottis	—	15+	1,000	Novelist
P. I. B. d'Exauvillez[b]	55	15+	3,000	Man of Letters
James Fenimore Cooper[c]	52	15+	2,500	Rentier
J. H. Merle d'Aubigné	47	15+	—	Professor
F. P. G. Guizot	54	15+	—	Politique
Mlle. Vauvilliers	—	4	1,000	—
J. C. L. Simonde de Sismondi[c]	68	15+	—	Administration
Charles Nodier	58	15+	3,000	Man of Letters
E. M. de Saint-Hilaire	62	15+	800	Rentier
J. A. F. Langlois	43	15+	2,000	Commerce
A. P. B. de Barante	59	10	2,000	Rentier
J. B. H. R. Capefigue	42	15+	1,000	Bookseller

[a] Only identifiable living authors are listed; those deceased or too obscure to be included in bibliographic or biographical references are excluded. Ages are cited for year of publication, as are numbers of titles published and occupations approximating the authors' major source of income. The edition sizes of the authors' work appearing in the samples (Appendix A) are also listed, where known. The mean and median editions of romantic works, calculated in Tables 5.1 and 7.1, are based on the *tirages* of all titles listed in Appendix A, some of which are not included here. But data on mean ages of romantic authors, p. 83, and on their occupations, Table 3.4, are taken from Appendix B.

[b] French translator of work by foreign author.

[c] Foreign author not residing in France but receiving royalties on sales of titles sold in Paris.

[d] First author of title written by two or more individuals; co-authors excluded.

[e] Translator listed more than once in sample year.

[f] Author listed more than once in sample year.

GLOSSARY*

Alexandrine: A verse line with twelve syllables, the standard neo-classical verse frequently rhymed in couplets. For example,

O France! O ma patrie! O séjour de douleurs,
Tes enfants malheureux recommencement leurs pleurs!

Arrondissement: A French administrative district. During the First Republic (1792–1799) Paris was organized into twelve *arrondissements* encompassing forty-eight *quartiers*, an organization retained until the Second Empire.

Belles Lettres: Literature, especially that body of writing comprising drama, poetry, fiction, criticism, and essays, recognized by its inherent imaginative and artistic rather than its scientific or intellectual qualities.

Bibliothèque bleue: Cheap, standardized almanacs, saints' lives, and simple tales published generally in Epinal and Troyes since the sixteenth century. They were generally sold by colporters in the provinces and covered in a coarse blue paper, varying little in format or content for more than three centuries.

Bouquiniste: A second-hand book dealer, generally in rare editions or incunabula.

Bourgeoisie: The middle classes, ranging from wealthy bankers and landowners to small greengrocers and master artisans. A complex, much debated social group in France, the bourgeoisie has often been defined in the nineteenth century as everyone without an aristocratic title who did not work with his hands, whether or not he owned any capital. Thus even a minor bureaucratic functionary or empoverished member of the liberal professions, earning less than a journeyman, could also be included among the middle classes.

Boutiquier: A petty shopkeeper offering a limited range of specialized goods for sale. Such a figure of narrow vision has long been a stereotype of the extremely cautious French commercial retailer.

Brevet: A license to operate a business, issued by the municipality, subject to the payment of an initial fee and the approval of local authorities. *Brevets* were often passed on to members of the family or sold with the business as a form of property, even though police could revoke them at any time.

---

* Definitions of literary terms adapted from William Flint Thrall and Addison Hibbard, *A Handbook to Literature*, ed. C. Hugh Holman (New York: Odyssey Press, 1960).

Cabinet de lecture: A rental or lending library. In the eighteenth and nineteenth centuries booksellers often rented multivolumed and expensive books for fees considerably cheaper than the retail price. More often the cabinet was a reading room or depository where books were rented exclusively.

Caesura: A pause or break in the metrical or rhythmical progress of a line or verse. Originally in classical literature, the caesura characteristically divided a line after the sixth syllable. The romantics often sought diversity of rhythmical effect by placing the caesura elsewhere in the line.

Canard: A broadside. Soon after the development of printing, ballads were published on folio sheets relating a wide variety of sensational subjects: accidents, dying words of criminals, miraculous events, religious and political harangues, often sold for only one sou.

Cénacle: A literary circle, often advocating a distinct set of values or ideas Like a romantic Christ surrounded by his disciples, Hugo held weekly meetings at his house during the Restoration, until a disaffected Sainte-Beuve mocked him and his followers by calling them a *cénacle*. Since then the term has been applied more generally to any literary salon.

Chansonnier: A book of popular, mostly sentimental songs.

Classicism: A body of doctrine which is thought to be derived from or to reflect the qualities the French valued in ancient Greek and Roman culture, enshrined for literature in Boileau's seventeenth-century poem, *L'art poétique*. Some of its values are suggested in the French understanding of what constitutes restraint, restricted scope, dominance of reason, sense of form, unity of design and aim, clarity, simplicity, balance, attention to structure and logical organization, chasteness in style, severity of outline, moderation, self-control, intellectualism, decorum, respect for tradition, imitation, conservatism, and good sense. Of course, not all neo-classicists lived up to these ideals, however much they may have espoused them.

Clichés: Stereotyped plates made from special wax molds imprinted by a sheet of type. A process invented in France by Louis-Etienne Herhan in 1798, such plates for a whole book could be prepared and used for 10,000 impressions without tying up or damaging a printer's valuable type.

Colporteur: An itinerant seller of chapbooks, images, combs, mirrors, pins, and the like to people of modest means during the early modern period. The colporter generally carried a basket of goods strapped around his neck, hence the term.

Comedy: A form of drama lighter than tragedy, aiming to amuse and ending happily. It differed from farce and burlesque in its more sustained plot, more weighty and subtle dialog, more natural characters and their less boisterous behavior. Generally less structured than the tragedy, the classical comedy still attempted to fulfill the three unities of time, place, and action.

Comedy-vaudeville: A comedy consisting of successive performances of often unrelated songs, dances, dramatic sketches, acrobatic feats, juggling, pantomimes, puppet-shows, and various stunts. By the nineteenth century it had become a convention to add only light songs to a low comic plot.

Commissionnaire: A retail or wholesale salesman on commission.

Commis-voyageur: A commercial traveller, generally working outside of Paris.

Complainte: A plaintive song or poem, written in the manner of the complaints of lovers to their mistresses. In the nineteenth century this lyric monologue had become a popular form of poetry printed in both *canards* and *chansonniers*.

Constitutional Monarchies: The Restoration Monarchy (1814–1830) and the Orleanist Monarchy (1830–1848). Both regimes were based on charters, one granted by Louis XVIII before the Hundred Days and another granted by Louis-Philippe in 1830, explicitly limiting the perogatives of the king and defining the powers of parliament. The lower house, the Chamber of Deputies, was elected by all citizens paying enough taxes to qualify them for the vote, a major source of popular dissatisfaction. The regimes were also termed the *monarchies censitaires* after the tax censuses employed to determine voter eligibility.

Contrefaçon: A counterfeit book. Before international copyright laws original editions of books were pirated to Belgium where they were reproduced exactly and sold in provincial cities in France, often well before Parisian booksellers could. Counterfeited editions of successful works even appeared in Paris, thus limiting the market for successful editions by the original publishers.

Drame: A form of play between tragedy and comedy originating in the eighteenth century, comparable to the modern serious, problem play. The romantics developed this type to flout the neo-classical integrity of tragic and comic forms.

Editeur: A publisher. Developed in the eighteenth century as a separate function in the book trade, publishers specialized in acquiring manuscripts, raising the capital to print them, distributing the books to booksellers, and advertising them by the appropriate means. Booksellers often acted as publishers early in the romantic period when the money and sophistication involved were still relatively little.

Elegy: A classical form, common to both Greek and Latin literatures, originally signifying almost any type of serious meditation of the poet's. In neo-classical writing, the subject was less important than its form: the couplet in twelve syllables.

Enjambement: A device used by many romantic poets to escape the monotonous rhythm of the regular alexandrine by running the sense and grammatical structure past the second line of a couplet. *Enjambement* occurs with the presence of the "run-on" line and offers a contrast to the rigid neo-classical "end-stopped" line.

Epic: A long narrative poem presenting characters of high position in a series of adventures which form an organic whole through their relations to a central figure of heroic proportions and through their development of episodes important to the development of a nation or a race. The neo-classical model was often Virgil's *Aeneid*.

Epistle: Theoretically any letter, but in practice a formal poetic composition written by an individual or group to a distant audience. It differed from the common letter not only in its serious subject, but also by its alexandrine verse.

Etalagiste: A street vendor operating from a more or less portable stall. Still in evidence in Paris today, *étalagistes* mounted their boxes of wares in public squares, and more frequently on the quays and bridges on the Seine.

Etrenne: An expensive, well-illustrated volume intended more for display than reading, sold at year's end to celebrate events of the previous twelve months.

Format: The size of a book based on the number of pages in a signature. A printed sheet often represents two or more pages in a book. Full sized books, measuring more than 14 by 17 inches, have only two pages to the signature, the front and back of one printed page. Folio volumes (in-2) have four pages to the signature, two printed pages on each side of one folded, printed sheet. Quarto volumes (in-4) have eight pages to the signature, four to each side of the printed sheet folded twice. A book's format, then, is determined by the number of pages printed on a single large sheet.

   Consequently, the terms in-8, in-12, in-18, etc., refer to the number of printed pages forming a signature, even though the actual size of the book varies according to the measurement of the original printed sheet before it is printed, folded, and cut. Of course, the larger the number of pages printed on each sheet, the cheaper the production cost of the book.

Generation: A demographic cohort generally born within a fifteen-year period and distinguished by a unique historical role. The progression of an individual's life from childhood (birth–age 15), young adulthood (ages 15–30), maturity (ages 30–45), dominance (ages 45–60), to decline (age 60–death) has often been taken by theorists as stages of a generation's rise and fall in historical influence. But individuals born within a relatively narrow time frame must identify themselves (or be identified by others) as a group being shaped by, and then shaping in turn their environment. The men and women born between 1795 and 1805 in France, for example, may have shared in the course of romantic literature in just this way.

Genre: A group or classification. In its literary sense, genre is employed to indicate style, medium, or manner of writing. The term is also used in the sense of literary type, such as the picaresque novel and the epic, whose definition and examples are often matters of study in literary history.

Gothicism: A literary form in which magic, mystery, and terror are the chief characteristics. Horrors abound; one may expect a cadaver suddenly to come alive, while ghosts, clanking chains, and cemeteries impart an uncanny atmosphere of terror. The emphasis is nearly always on the mood of the setting, unexpected twists in the plot, and characters appropriate to a sinister threat to virtue.

Historical Novel: A novel whose characters, setting, and action are drawn from the records of a locality, nation, or race, generally based loosely on events prior to the eighteenth century—an important romantic form developed in the first half of the nineteenth century.

Imprimeur: A printer.

Inelastic Demand: Technically, when the percentage change in demand for a commodity is less than the percentage change in its price. More colloquially, it means that the demand for a good does not change significantly with substantial changes in price above a certain level. Thus no matter how much fluctuation in the price of books above five francs (nearly twice a day laborer's daily wage in 1830), the demand for it was likely to remain constantly low.

Libraire: A bookseller who in the romantic period often published books or maintained a lending library, hence the broad significance of the term that covered a number of important functions in the trade.

Livraison: An installment.

Local Color: Writing which captures the speech, dress, mannerisms, habits of thought, and topography peculiar to a certain region or country. Of course, all fiction and history have a locale, but local color writing exists primarily for its portrayal of the people and life of a geographic or national setting.

Marchand: A retailer often specializing in a limited range of merchandise, sometimes including books.

Melodrama: A play based on a fantastic plot and developed sensationally, with little regard for convincing motivation and with constant appeal to the emotions of the audience. In the early nineteenth-century melodrama, music was an essential element, the action being accompanied by songs and instrumental music suggested by the situation. Most were characterized by action marked by circumstance, while stereotypical characters engaged in the battle between good and evil.

Menu peuple: Literally, the little people, the common men and women on the street with little or no property. More particularly, the term refers to the class of respectable, gainfully employed people in the retail trades and the artisanal crafts. As modest master craftsmen, prosperous journeymen, humble shopkeepers, and the like, the *menu peuple* were distinguished from the wealthier and more esteemed bourgeoisie above them and the unemployed and indigent below them. In fact, they were the most active, class-conscious, and socially aspiring elements who manned the barricades during the French revolutions.

Mode: A manner, way, or method of expression in a particular literary form. Among the popular romantics, it meant the adoption of the movement's conventions—characters, plots, settings, and stylistic changes—without necessarily expressing its ideas.

Monarchie censitaire: The constitutional monarchies.

Mood: A pervading impression on the reader's feelings conveyed in a literary work. For the romantics recognized by literary specialists, a particular frame of mind expressed in their creations was their distinguishing characteristic.

Neo-classicism: A term applied to the classicism of the late eighteenth and early
nineteenth centuries, partly because the movement was a "revival" of classicism, partly because its ideas were drawn largely from Boileau and the Roman
Horace rather than directly from the Greeks. What had been a more creative
set of literary principles during the seventeenth century became, by the early
nineteenth century, a rigid and stultifying force in French literature. It was
this spirit to which the romantics responded.

Nouveauté: A literary novelty, a new work often associated with lower popular
forms, since they were sold in shops selling other, nonliterary novelties, from
combs to caps.

Ode: Any strain of enthusiastic and exalted lyrical verse, directed to a fixed purpose and dealing progressively with one dignified theme. Such a flexible, less
defined lyric form was readily adopted by the romantics for their experiments
in versification.

Paradigm: A world view arising from a tradition of rules and assumptions based on
the work of earlier thinkers. Although Thomas Kuhn has used paradigm to
mean the model that a scientific community emulates in its research at any
one time, the term here signifies the epistemological vision shared by other
intellectuals at a specified period in the history of ideas, such as the classicists
in 1750. Thus paradigm, as the word is used in the present essay, is actually a
metonymy in which such reference to the work of influential writers means
the identifiable cultural mind-frame expressed by many subsequent authors
in the same field.

Petit cénacle: The group of young writers and artists in 1830 including Théophile
Gautier, Pétrus Borel, and Philothée O'Neddy. Their romantic vision differed
considerably from Hugo's group during the Restoration, and so they were
distinguished from the better known, more middle-class *cénacle*.

Picaresque: A chronicle, usually autobiographical, presenting the life story of a
rascal of low degree engaged in making his living more through his wits than
his industry. Episodic in nature, the picaresque novel is, in the usual sense of
the form, structureless. It presents little more than a series of thrilling incidents impossible to conceive ever happening in one life.

Popular romanticism: The romantic movement among popular titles, characterized by their exclusive adoption of its new conventions without expressing any
of its mood or sensibility. It is, in short, a superficial overlay of literary devices
onto an established tradition of popular poetry, melodrama, romance, and
national history in the romantic period.

Poème héroïque: A poem composed of alexandrines and rhymed in line pairs called
heroic couplets.

Romance: A fictitious narrative in prose whose scenes and incidents are very
remote from those of ordinary life. As distinguished from medieval stories in
verse, the modern romance is essentially the foil to the modern realistic
novel, ill-structured and fantastic.

Roman-feuilleton: A serial novel, frequently characterized by romancelike qualities, mysterious and sentimental.

Romanticism: The literary movement self-consciously characterized by a new sensibility and a new mode of expression in the late eighteenth and early nineteenth centuries in Europe. For the purpose of this study, it includes any work that (1) claims allegiance to the new literature; (2) expresses an appropriate mood in an attempt to bridge the gap between the self and the world; or (3) deliberately employs iconoclastic literary conventions.

"Romanticism": The literary movement's mode but not its corresponding mood.

Sentimentality: A term used in two senses important to the study of literature: (1) an overindulgence in emotion, especially the conscious effort to induce emotion in order to analyze or enjoy it—also the failure to restrain or evaluate emotion through the exercise of judgement; and (2) an optimistic overemphasis on the goodness of humanity, representing in part a rationalistic reaction against Jansenist theology which regarded human nature as depraved.

Social romanticism: The strain of French romanticism adopting wider social and political concerns, especially after 1830. Hugo's celebration of the Napoleonic myth, Lamartine's participation in politics, and George Sand's novels written for a peasant audience are good examples.

Stereotyped plates: *Clichés*.

Tragedy: A form of drama exciting the emotions of pity and fear. According to Aristotle and adapted by the French classicists, its action should be single and complete, presenting a reversal of fortune, involving persons renown and of superior attainments, and it should be written in poetry embellished with every kind of artistic expression. The three unities of action, time, and place were considered *de rigueur*.

Unities of Action, Time, and Place: Important elements of serious drama. The most important one and the only enjoined by Aristotle is that of action. He called a tragedy "an imitation of an action that is complete and whole, and of a certain magnitude; a whole should have a beginning, a middle, and an end, with causal relationships in the differential parts of the play." Inevitability and concentration result from adherence to the unity of action.

The unity of time was developed from Aristotle's simple and undogmatic statement concerning tragic usage: "tragedy endeavors as far as possible to confine itself to a single revolution of the sun, or but slightly to exceed this limit."

The unity of place, limiting the action to one place, was the last to emerge and was not mentioned by Aristotle. It followed quite naturally the requirement of limiting the action to a particular time, i.e., to one town or city. This unity was closely allied to that of time in the theory and practice of neo-classical writers.

Veillée: An evening working bee in rural French communities in the early modern period. During the long winter nights, families of neighboring farms would gather together in a barn or shed to save precious wood or fuel for heat and light, to repair clothes and tools, and to enjoy an important collective life, including dancing, singing, story telling, and sometimes readings from chapbooks bought from colporters.

BIBLIOGRAPHY

$\mathcal{B}$ECAUSE OF THE TENTATIVE nature of this investigation, the sources listed here are far from exhaustive; they are limited to the actual archival material and printed works used in this study. To point the way to more thorough research on the issues, however, titles are listed under various headings providing a range of information or insight important to the social history of French romanticism. A number of items span several categories, so their placement is inevitably somewhat arbitrary.

I. ARCHIVAL PRIMARY SOURCES
   A. Archives Nationales de France (A.N.)
   B. Archives du Département de la Seine et de la Ville de Paris (A.D.S.V.P.)

II. PRINTED PRIMARY SOURCES
   A. Statistical and Social Accounts
   B. Memoirs and Accounts of Travel and Literary Developments
   C. Literary Works
   D. Correspondence, Compilations, Bibliographies, and Catalogs
   E. Printing and Bookselling
   F. Newspapers and Other Periodicals

III. PRINTED SECONDARY SOURCES
   A. Methods and Theory
   B. History
   C. Romanticism
   D. Production, Distribution, and Consumption of Reading Matter

I. ARCHIVAL PRIMARY SOURCES

A. Archives Nationales de France

$F^{18}2$ "Imprimerie et librairie. Circulaires, 1814–1850."

$F^{18}551$ "Bouquinistes et colporteurs. Renseignements généraux. Demandes particulières, 1818–1844."

$F^{18}554$ "Commission de colportage. Circulaires aux préfets, 1822–1862."

$F^{18}566$–568 "Affaires diverses, 1815–1854."

$F^{18}2162$ bis "Cabinets de lecture. Demandes d'autorisation, 1816–1850."

$F^{18}2342$ "Direction de l'imprimerie et de la librairie. Circulaires, 1827–1876."

$F^{18}2359$ "Propriété littéraire et dépôt legal. Projets de loi, 1827–1876."

$F^{18}2368$ "Affaires diverses de toutes natures, 1820–1909."

$F^{18}2370$ "Imprimerie, librairie, presse."

$F^{18}2371$ "Imprimeries brevetées. Affaires diverses, 1811–1900."

$F^{18}2375$ "Affaires diverses de toutes natures, 1817–1874."

$F^{18}I*17$ "Enregistrement des brevets des libraires et imprimeurs de Paris, 1815–1864."

$F^{18}II*6$–29 "Déclarations des imprimeurs. Paris. Années 1819–1841."

B. Archives du Département de la Seine et de la Ville de Paris

D 10 U3 "Dossiers des faillites, 1820–1830, 1832–1843."

D 11 U3 "Registres d'inscription des faillites, 1831."

$DR^{1}26$–70 "Tables de recensement/Listes de tirage. Arrondissements 1, 8, et 10. 1829–1854."

II. PRINTED PRIMARY SOURCES

A. Statistical and Social Accounts

Angeville, Adolphe d'. *Essai sur la statistique de la population française, considérée sous quelques-uns de ses rapports physiques et moraux...* Bourg: Dufour, 1836.

Arnold, Matthew. *The Popular Education of France...* London: Longman et al., 1861.

Benoiston de Chateauneuf, L.-F. *Recherches sur les consommations de tout genre de la ville de Paris en 1817...*, 2e éd. Paris: Martinet, 1821.

Bigot de Morogues, P. M. S. *De la misère des ouvriers...* Paris: Imp. Huzard, 1832.

Blanc, Louis. *Révolution française, 1830, histoire de dix ans, règne de Louis-Philippe.* Paris: F.-H. Jeanmaire, 1882. 2 vols.

Buret, Eugène. *De la misère des classes laborieuses en Angleterre et en France...* Paris: Paulin, 1840. 2 vols.

Chambre de commerce et d'industrie. *Enquête relative à diverses prohibitions...* Paris: Imprimerie Royale, 1835. 3 vols.

————. *Statistique de l'industrie à Paris...pour les années 1847–1848*. Paris: Guillaumin et cie., 1851.

Collard de Martigny, C.-P. *Coup-d'oeil sur l'état de l'instruction publique en France et sur les développemens* [sic] *qu'elle exige*. Paris: Levrault, 1835.

Cushing, Caleb. *Review, Historical and Political, of the Late Revolution in France*. Boston: Carter, Hendee, 1833. 2 vols.

Département de la Seine. *Recherches statistiques sur la ville de Paris et le département de la Seine*. Paris: Imprimerie Royale, etc., 1821–1860. 6 vols.

Dupin, Charles. *Forces productives et commerciales*. Paris: Bachelier, 1827.

————. *Situation progressive des forces de la France depuis 1814*. Bruxelles: Tencé frères, 1827.

Fazy, James (Jean-Jacob). *De la gérontocratie, ou abus de la sagesse des vieillards dans le gouvernement de la France*. Paris: Delaforest, 1828.

Galignani, A. and W. *Galignani's Paris Guide*. Paris: Galignani, 1822.

Gérando, J. M. de. *De la bienfaisance publique*. Paris: Renouard, 1839.

Girardin, Emile de. *Etudes politiques*, 1ᵉʳ série. Paris: Mairet et Fournier, 1842.

Guizot, François. *Trois générations: 1789–1814–1848*. Paris: Michel Lévy frères, 1863.

Karr, Alphonse. *Nouveau tableau de Paris au XIXᵉ siècle*. Paris: Mme. Vve. Charles Bechet et al., 1835, 5 vols.

Kock, Charles Paul de. *Petits tableaux de moeurs, ou macédoine critique et littéraire*. Paris: Dupont, 1829, 2 vols.

Lacroix, Paul, dit Jacob le bibliophile. *Dissertation sur quelques points curieux de l'histoire de France: sur les bibliothèques de Paris*. Paris: Techener, 1840.

Lorain, P. *Tableau de l'instruction primaire en France, d'après des documents authentiques...* Paris: Hachette, 1837.

Marchal, Charles. *Du pain au peuple*. Paris: Desloges, 1848.

Mazier du Heaume, Hippolyte. *Voyage d'un jeune Grec à Paris*. Paris: F. Louis, 1824. 2 vols.

Michelet, Jules. *Le peuple*. Ed. Robert Casanova. Paris: Julliard, 1965 [1846].

Ministère des finances. *Compte général de l'administration des finances, rendu pour l'année 1830*. Paris: Imprimerie Royale, 1831.

Pain, Joseph. *Nouveaux tableaux de Paris, ou observations sur les moeurs et usages des parisiens au commencement du XIXᵉ siècle...* Paris: Pillet ainé, 1828. 2 vols.

M*** (Painparré). *Le petit diable boiteux, ou guide anecdotique des étrangers à Paris...* Paris: Painparré, 1823.

Rossignol Passe-Partout (Auguste Imbert). *Voyage autour du pont-neuf et promenade sur le quai aux fleurs*. Paris: Imbert, 1824.

Villeneuve, Alban de. *Economie politique chrétienne, ou recherches sur la nature et les causes du paupérisme en France et en Europe...* Paris: Paulin, 1834. 3 vols.

Villermé, Louis-René. *Tableau de l'état physique et morale des ouvriers employés dans les manufactures de coton, de laine et de soie...* Paris: Renouard, 1840. 2 vols.

B. Memoirs and Accounts of Travel and Literary Developments

Auger, Louis-Simon. *Discours sur le romantisme,* prononcé dans la séance annuelle des quatre académies du 24 avril 1824. Paris: F. Didot, 1824.

Azaïs, Hyacinthe, *Comment cela finira-t-il?* Paris: Vve. Cellis, 1819.

Barba, J.-N. *Souvenirs de Jean-Nicolas Barba, ancien libraire de Palais-Royal.* Paris: Ledoyen et Giret, 1846.

Baudouin, Alexandre. *Anecdotes historiques du temps de la Restauration, suivies de recherches sur l'origine de la presse, son développement...* Paris: F. Didot frères, 1853.

Béranger, P.-J. de. *Ma biographie, ouvrage posthume...* Paris: Perrotin, 1857.

Delécluze, Etienne-Jean. *Souvenirs de soixante années.* Paris: Michel Lévy frères, 1862.

Deschamps, Emile. *Un manifeste du romantisme.* Paris: Presses Françaises, 1923 [1825].

Dibdin, Thomas Frognall. *A Bibliographical, Antiquarian and Picturesque Tour in France and Germany.* London: Shakespeare Press, 1821. 2 vols.

Du Camp, Maxime. *Souvenirs littéraires.* Paris: Hachette, 1882–1883. 2 vols.

Dumas, Alexandre. *Mes mémoires.* Ed. Pierre Josserand. Paris: Gallimard, 1954–1968. 5 vols.

Gautier, Théophile. *Histoire de l'art dramatique en France depuis vingt-cinq ans.* Paris: Magnin, Blanchard et cie., 1858–1859. 6 vols.

———. *Histoire du romantisme...,* Paris: Charpentier, 1911.

Guizot, François. *Mémoires pour servir à l'histoire de mon temps.* Paris: Michel Lévy frères, 1858–1868. 8 vols.

Houssaye (Housset), Arsène. *Les confessions: souvenirs d'un demi-siècle, 1830–1880.* Paris: Dentu, 1885. Vol. 1.

Janin, Jules. *Critique. Portraits et caractères contemporains.* Paris: Hachette, [1859].

———. *Histoire de la littérature dramatique.* Paris: Michel Lévy frères, 1853–1858. 4 vols.

Jouffroy, Théodore. *Le cahier vert.* Ed. Pierre Poux. Paris: Presses Françaises, [n.d.; 1825].

Kock, Charles Paul de. *Mémoires de Charles Paul de Kock, écrits par lui-même.* Paris: Dentu, 1873.

Morgan, Lady Sydney. *France in 1829–1830.* London: Saunders and Otley, 1830. 2 vols.

Nadaud, Martin. *Les mémoires de Léonard, ancien garçon maçon...* Paris: Delagrave, [1912].

Nettement, Alfred. *Etudes critiques sur le feuilleton roman.* Paris: Perrodil, 1845. 2 vols.

Ordre, M. le baron d'. *Les classiques et les romantiques.* Paris: n.p., 1829.

Perdiguier, Agricol. *Mémoires d'un compagnon.* Paris: Librairie de Compagnonnage, 1964.

Pontmartin, A. A. J. M. de. *Mes mémoires, enfance et jeunesse.* Paris: Calmann Lévy, 1885–1886. 2 vols.

Quinet, Edgar. *Histoire de mes idées, autobiographie. Documents inédits.* Paris: Germer-Baillière, [1878].

Rémusat, Charles de. *Mémoires de ma vie.* Ed. Charles Pouthas. Paris: Plon, 1958–1967. 4 vols.

Sainte-Beuve, C.-A. *Causeries du lundi,* 4ᵉ éd. Paris: Garnier frères, [1883]. 15 vols.

———. *Premiers lundis.* Paris: Calmann Lévy, 1886. 3 vols.

Stendhal (Henri Beyle). *Oeuvres intimes.* Ed. Henri Martineau. Paris: Gallimard, 1955.

———. *Racine et Shakespeare.* London: Oxford University Press, 1907 [1823].

Thackeray, William Makepeace. *The Paris Sketch Book.* New York: F. M. Lipton, 1840.

Tocqueville, Alexis de. *Democracy in America,* 2nd ed. Trans. Henry Reeve. Ed. Francis Bowen. Cambridge, Mass.: Sever and Francis, 1863[1835–40]. 2 vols.

Trollope, Frances. *Paris and the Parisians in 1835.* New York: Harper and Brothers, 1836.

Véron, Louis-Désiré. *Mémoires d'un bourgeois de Paris.* Paris: Librairie Nouvelle, 1856. 5 vols.

C. Literary Works

Balzac, Honoré de. *La comédie humaine.* Ed. Pierre-Georges Castex. Paris: Gallimard, 1976–1979. 10 vols.

Baudelaire, Charles. *Oeuvres complètes.* Ed. Y.-G. LeDantec and Claude Pichois. Paris: Gallimard, 1961.

Borel, Pétrus. *Rhapsodies.* Paris: Levavasseur, 1832.

Brisset, Mathurin-Joseph. *Le cabinet de lecture.* Paris: Magen, 1843. 2 vols.

Désaugiers, A. *Chansons et poésies diverses.* Paris: Delloye, 1834. 2 vols.

Flaubert, Gustave. *Oeuvres.* Ed. A. Thibaudet and R. Dumesnil. Paris: Gallimard, 1951–1952. 2 vols.

Gautier, Théophile. *Les Jeunes-France, romans goguenards...* Paris: Champion, 1875.

Gauttier du Lys d'Arc, L. E. *Histoire des conquêtes des Normands, en Italie, en Sicilie, et en Grèce.* Paris: L. de Bure, 1830.

Guizot, François. "Introduction," *Oeuvres de Shakespeare.* Paris: Didier et cie., 1860. Vol. 1.

Hugo, Victor. *Oeuvres complètes.* Ed. Paul Meurice, Gustave Simon, and Cécile Daubray. Paris: Ollendorff et Albin Michel, 1904–1952. 44 vols.

Le jardin d'enfance, de la jeunesse et de tous les âges. Paris: Pigoreau, 1820.

Lamartine, Alphonse de. *Oeuvres poétiques complètes*. Ed. Marius-François Guyard. Paris: Gallimard, 1963.

Lemercier, Louise. *Victor-Amédée II, ou le siège de Turin*. Paris: Gaudiot, 1830.

Léroux de Lincy, A. J. V., ed. *Nouvelle bibliothèque bleue, ou légendes populaires en France*. Paris: Columb de Batine, 1842.

Monnier, Henri. *Scènes populaires, dessinées à la plume*. Paris: Levavasseur, 1830.

Musset, Alfred de. *Oeuvres complètes en prose*. Ed. Maurice Allem and Paul Courant. Paris: Gallimard, 1960.

Nardouet, Mme. la comtesse de (Ruault de la Haye). *Vice et vertu, ou l'heureuse séduction*. Paris: Brianchon, 1820. 3 vols.

Nerval, Gérard de (Gérard Labrunie), ed. *Chansons et ballades populaires du Valois*. Paris: Garnier frères, 1885.

————. *Oeuvres*. Ed. Albert Béguin and Jean Richer. Paris: Gallimard, 1960–1961. 2 vols.

Le rendez-vous, ou le moment d'amour. Chansonnier pour tous les âges. Paris: Tiger, 1820.

Reybaud, Louis. *Jérôme Paturot à la recherche d'une position sociale*. Paris: Michel Lévy frères, 1876 [1842].

Robert (L.-P. Solvet). *Le cabinet de lecture, pièce satirique*. Paris: Imp. Egron, 1808.

Rodrigues, Olinde, ed. *Poésies sociales des ouvriers*. Paris: Paulin, 1841.

Rogeau, Auguste. *Sardanapale, essais rétrogrades*. Paris: Imp. Delacombe, 1834.

Sand, George (Aurore Dupin). *Les légendes rustiques*. Paris: A. Morel, 1858.

Sandeau, Jules. *Marianna*. Paris: Charpentier, 1871 [1839].

Scribe, Eugène. *Le mariage d'argent, comédie*. Paris: Bezou, 1828.

Théaulon de Lambert, M. E. G. M. *Le paysan perverti, ou quinze ans de Paris, drame en trois journées*. Paris: Barba, 1827.

Viarz, Maurice de (A. E. R. de Serviez). *Neuf jours d'hymen, ou la cour en seize cent dix*. Paris: Lachapelle, 1834. 2 vols.

Vigny, Alfred de. *Oeuvres complètes*. Ed. Ferdinand Baldensperger. Paris: Gallimard, 1948–1950. 2 vols.

D. Correspondence, Compilations, Bibliographies, and Catalogs

Asselineau, Charles. *Bibliographie romantique. Catalogue anecdotique et pittoresque des éditions originales...* Paris: Rouquette, 1872.

————. *Mélanges tirés d'une petite bibliographie romantique...* Paris: Pincebourde, 1867.

Balteau, J. et al. *Dictionnaire de biographie française*. Paris: Letouzey et Ané, 1933–1970. 12 vols.

Balzac, Honoré de. *Oeuvres diverses*. Ed. Marcel Bouteron and Henri Longnon. Paris: Conrad, 1935–1940. 3 vols.

Barba, J.-N....*Rabais considérables, par suite de cessation de commerce*. Paris: Barba, 1827.

Barois. *Catalogue...* Paris: Silvestre, 1838.

Beuchet, A. J. Q., ed. *Bibliographie de la France, ou journal de l'imprimerie et de la librairie*. Paris: Pillet ainé, 1811–1847. 35 vols.

Bibliothèque Nationale. Q²⁸ série. "Catalogues des cabinets de lecture, 1700–1900."

Bibliothèque Nationale. △ série. "Catalogues des bibliothèques privées, 1700–1900."

Bibliothèque Nationale. *Recueil des catalogues et des prospectus des libraires de Paris, 1806–1831*. Paris: Bibliothèque Nationale, [n.d.].

Bottin, Sébastien. *Almanach du commerce de Paris...* Paris: Bottin, 1819–1838. 19 vols.

Curmer, Léon, ed. *Les Français peints par eux-mêmes*. Paris: Curmer, 1841. 4 vols.

Département de la Seine. *Liste des électeurs formants le collège électoral du département de la Seine*. Paris: Affiches Universelles, 1820.

————. *Listes électorales et du jury du département de la Seine en 1828*. Paris: Imp. Engelmann et Langlume, 1828.

————. *Listes électorales et du jury du département de la Seine en 1842*. Paris: Imp. Engelmann et Langlume, 1842.

Didot, Firmin, et frères. *Catalogue*. Paris: F. Didot frères, 1830.

Drujon, Fernand. *Catalogue des ouvrages écrits et dessins de toute nature poursuivis, supprimés, ou condamnés depuis le 21 octobre 1814 jusqu'au 31 juillet 1877*. Paris: Rouveyre, 1879.

Duvergier, J.-B. et al., eds. *Collection complète des lois, décrets, ordonnances, règlemens [sic], et avis du Conseil d'Etat...de 1789 à 1845*, 2ᵉ éd. Paris: Imprimerie Royale, 1834–1845. 68 vols.

Hatin, Eugène-Louis. *Bibliographie historique et critique de la presse périodique française...* Paris: F. Didot frères, 1866.

Hugo, Victor. *Correspondance*. Paris: Calmann Lévy, 1898. 2 vols.

Larousse, Pierre et al. *Grand dictionnaire universel du XIXᵉ siècle*. Paris: Larousse, 1865–1888. 22 vols.

LeNormant. *Livres d'assortement...* Paris: LeNormant, [n.d.].

Lesur, C.-L. *Annuaire historique universel...* Paris: Thoisnier-Desplaces, 1817–1832. 15 vols.

Ministère de l'Instruction Publique et des Beaux Arts. *Catalogue général des livres imprimés de la Bibliothèque Nationale: auteurs*. Paris: Imprimerie Nationale, 1897–1979. 228 vols.

Morin, A. *Catalogue descriptif de la bibliothèque bleue de Troyes*. Genève: Droz, 1974.

Pigoreau, Alexandre. *Petite bibliographie biographico-romancière, ou dictionnaire des romanciers...* Paris: Pigoreau, 1821–1828. 3 vols.

Piltan. *Catalogue des livres du cabinet de lecture...* Paris: Piltan, 1832 and 1838. 2 vols.

―――. *Supplément du catalogue des livres...* Paris: Piltan, 1840.

Quérard, Joseph-Marie et al. *La France littéraire, ou dictionnaire bibliographique des savants, historiens et gens de lettres de la France...* Paris: Didot frères, 1827–1839. 10 vols.

―――. *La littérature française contemporaine, 1827–1849.* Paris: Daguin et Delaroque, 1840–1857. 6 vols.

―――. *Les supercheries littéraires dévoillées...* Paris: Editeur, 1845–1853. 5 vols.

Sand, George (Aurore Dupin). *Correspondance.* Ed. Georges Lubin. Paris: Garnier, 1964. Vol. 1.

Simond, Charles (Paul A. Vancleemputte). *La vie parisienne à travers le XIXe siècle: Paris de 1800 à 1900 d'après les estampes et les mémoires du temps...* Paris: Plon, Nourrit et cie., 1900–1901. 3 vols.

Techener, J. *Bulletin du bibliophile.* Paris: Techener, 1834–1840. 6 vols.

Trahard, Pierre, ed. *Le romantisme défini par 'Le Globe'.* Paris: Presses Françaises, 1924.

E. Printing and Bookselling

Bossange père, Martin. *A messieurs les membres de la Chambre des Députés (au sujet du prêt fait en 1830 par le Trésor au commerce de la librairie).* Paris: Imp. Bourgogne et Martinet, 1830.

―――. *Courtes observations de M. Bossange père à MM. les membres de la Chambre des Députés, relatives au prêt sur nantissement fait à la librairie par le gouvernement.* Paris: Imp. Dupont et Laguionie, [n.d.].

―――. *Nouvelles observations...relatives au prêt fait à la librairie...* Paris: F. Didot frères, 1833.

La commission d'enquête de la librairie de Paris. *Requête présentée à LL. EE. MM. les ministres du Roi.* Paris: F. Didot, [1829].

La commission de recherches des moyens de soutenir la librairie française contre la contrefaçon belge. *Compte rendu.* Paris: Panckoucke, 1837.

Crapelet, G.-A. *Etudes pratiques et littéraires sur la typographie.* Paris: Crapelet, 1837.

Daru, Pierre A. N. B. *Notions statistiques sur la librairie, pour servir à la discussion des lois sur la presse.* Paris: F. Didot, 1827.

Didot, Firmin. *L'exposition de 1844.* Paris: Didot, 1845. 3 vols.

Ducessois. *Notes sur la proposition de M. Benjamin Constant relative aux imprimeurs...* Paris: Ducessois, [1830].

Dupont, Paul. *Histoire de l'imprimerie.* Paris: Dupont, 1854. 2 vols.

Fouque, Victor. *De quelques abus en librairie et des moyens de les combattre.* Chalon-sur-Saône: Fouque, 1841.

Hébrard, J. *De la librairie, son ancienne prospérité, son état actuel...* Paris: Hébrard, 1847.

Levacher-Duplessis. *Requête au Roi et mémoire sur la nécessité de rétablir les corps de marchands et les communautés des arts et metiérs...* Paris: Imp. Smith, 1817.

Mosse, J.-M. *Du commerce de la librairie, des moyens de le rendre plus florissant et de déjouer les contrefacteurs étrangers.* Paris: Imp. Goetschy, 1824.

Panckoucke, C. L. F. *Budget statistique d'un éditeur.* Paris: Panckoucke, 1837.

Pic., F.-A. *Code des imprimeurs, libraires, écrivains et artistes...* Paris: Corby, 1827. 2 vols.

Plassan, J. R. *Mémoire à M. le comte de Montalivet, Ministre de l'Intérieur, sur l'imprimerie et sur la librairie.* Paris: Imp. Terzuolo, 1839.

Scott de Martinville, A. T. *Lettres à M. Plassan, ancien imprimeur, sur les intérêts matériels de la typographie.* Paris: Imp. Bachelier, [1838].

Werdet, Edmond. *Etudes bibliographiques sur la famille des Didots...1713–1864.* Paris: Dentu, 1864.

———. *De la librairie française, son passé, son présent, son avenir...* Paris: Dentu, 1860.

F.   Newspapers and Other Periodicals

L'artisan, 1830–1831.

Le constitutionnel, 1827–1835.

La gazette des tribunaux, 1827–1858.

Le globe, 1827–1835.

Le journal des débats, 1835.

Le journal des économistes, 1840–1845.

Le moniteur, 1854.

La muse française, 1823–1824.

La revue de Paris, 1829–1834.

La revue des deux mondes, 1828–1848 (3ᵉ série).

L'universel, 1829.

III. PRINTED SECONDARY SOURCES

A.   Methods and Theory

Bourdieu, Pierre. "Le marché des biens symboliques," *L'année sociologique* 21(1970): 49–126.

Cain, Julien et al. *Le livre français: hier, aujourd'hui, demain.* Paris: Imprimerie Nationale, 1972.

Cawelti, John. *Adventure, Mystery, and Romance: Formula Stories as Art and Popular Culture.* Chicago: University of Chicago Press, 1976.

Darnton, Robert. *The Business of Enlightenment: A Publishing History of the Encyclopédie, 1775–1800.* Cambridge: Harvard University Press, 1979.

———. "Reading, Writing, and Publishing in Eighteenth-Century France: A Case Study in the Sociology of Literature." In *Historical Studies Today,* ed. Felix Gilbert and Stephen Graubard, pp. 238–80. New York: Norton, 1972.

Davis, Natalie Zemon. *Society and Culture in Early Modern France.* Stanford: Stanford University Press, 1975.

Duncan, Hugh Dalziel. *Language and Literature in Society: A Sociological Essay on Theory and Method in the Interpretation of Linguistic Symbols.* Chicago: University of Chicago Press, 1953.

Eisenstadt, S. N. *From Generation to Generation: Age Groups and Social Structure.* Rev. ed. New York: Free Press, 1971.

Eisenstein, Elizabeth. "The Advent of Printing in Current Historical Literature: Notes and Comments on an Elusive Transformation," *American Historical Review* 75,2(1970): 727–43.

———. *The Printing Press as an Agent of Change: Communication and Cultural Transformation in Early Modern Europe.* Cambridge: Cambridge University Press, 1979. 2 vols.

Escarpit, Robert, ed. *Le littéraire et le social: éléments pour une sociologie de la littérature.* Paris: Flammarion, 1970.

———. *Sociologie de la littérature.* Paris: Presses Universitaires de France, 1958.

Furet, François et al. *Livre et société dans la France du XVIIIe siècle.* Paris: Mouton, 1965–1970. 2 vols.

Gans, Herbert J. *Popular Culture and High Culture: An Analysis and Evaluation of Taste.* New York: Basic Books, 1974.

Geertz, Clifford. *The Interpretation of Cultures.* New York: Basic Books, 1973.

Hauser, Arnold. *The Social History of Art.* Trans. Stanley Godman. New York: Vintage, [n.d.]. Vols. 3 and 4.

Henretta, James. "Social History as Lived and Written," *American Historical Review* 84,5(1979): 1293–1322.

Kress, G. R. "Structuralism and Popular Culture." In *Approaches to Popular Culture,* ed. C. W. E. Bigsby, pp. 85–105. Bowling Green, Ohio: Popular Press, 1977.

Lewis, George H. "The Sociology of Popular Culture," *Current Sociology* 26,3(1978): 1–157.

Lowenthal, Leo. *Literature, Popular Culture, and Society.* Englewood Cliffs, N.J.: Prentice-Hall, 1961.

McLuhan, Marshall. *Understanding Media: The Extensions of Man.* New York: McGraw-Hill, 1964.

Mannheim, Karl. *Essays on the Sociology of Knowledge.* Ed. Paul Kecskemeti. Oxford: Oxford University Press, 1952.

Marías, Julián. *Generations: A Historical Method.* Trans. Harold C. Riley. University, Ala.: University of Alabama Press, 1970.

Mornet, Daniel. "Les enseignements des bibliothèques privées, 1750–1780," *Revue d'histoire littéraire de la France* 17(1910): 449–92.

Ortega y Gasset, José. *Man and Crisis.* Trans. Mildred Adams. New York: Norton, 1958 [1933].

Panofsky, Erwin. *Studies in Iconology: Humanistic Themes in the Art of the Renaissance.* New York: Oxford University Press, 1939.

Pareto, Vilfredo. *The Rise and Fall of the Elites: An Application of Theoretical Sociology.* Totowa, N.J.: Bedminister Press, 1968.

Redfield, Robert. *The Little Community/Peasant Society and Culture* Chicago: University of Chicago Press, 1963.

Rosenberg, Bernard and White, David Manning, eds. *Mass Culture: The Popular Arts in America.* New York: Free Press, 1957.

Schücking, L. L. *The Sociology of Literary Taste.* Trans. Brian Battershaw. Chicago: University of Chicago Press, 1966 [1923].

Sorokin, Pitirim. *Society, Culture, and Personality: Their Structure and Dynamics. A System of General Sociology.* New York: Harper and Brothers, [1947].

Spitzer, Alan. "The Historical Problem of Generations," *American Historical Review* 78,5(1973): 1353–85.

Stone, Lawrence. "The Revival of Narrative: Reflections on a New Old History," *Past and Present* 85(1979): 3–24.

Trilling, Lionel. *Sincerity and Authenticity.* Cambridge: Harvard University Press, 1972.

Veysey, Laurence. "The Plural Organized Worlds of the Humanities." In *The Organization of Knowledge in Modern America, 1860–1920,* ed. Alexandra Oleson and John Voss, pp. 51–106. Baltimore: Johns Hopkins University Press, 1979.

Warren, Austin and Wellek, René. *Theory of Literature.* New York: Harcourt, Brace and World, 1956.

White, Hayden. "Structuralism and Popular Culture," *Journal of Popular Culture* 7(1973): 759–75.

Zoltowski, Victor. "Les cycles de la création intellectuelle et artistique," *L'année sociologique* 3(1952): 163–206.

Zuckerman, Michael. "Dreams That Men Dare to Dream: The Role of Ideas in Western Modernization," *Social Science History* 2(1978): 332–45.

B. History

Agulhon, Maurice. *Le cercle dans la France bourgeoise, 1810–1848: étude d'une mutation de sociabilité.* Paris: Colin, 1977.

———. "Le problème de la culture populaire en France autour de 1848," *Romantisme* 13(1975): 50–64.

———. *La république au village: les populations du Var de la Révolution à la II*e *République.* Paris: Plon, 1970.

———. *1848, ou l'apprentissage de la république.* Paris: Editions du Seuil, 1973.

Ariès, Philippe. *Centuries of Childhood: A Social History of Family Life.* Trans. Robert Baldick. New York: Vintage, 1962 [1960].

Bell, Daniel. *The Cultural Contradictions of Capitalism.* New York: Basic Books, 1976.

Bertier de Sauvigny, Guillaume de. *The Bourbon Restoration.* Trans. Lynn M. Case. Philadelphia: University of Pennsylvania Press, 1966 [1963].

———. *Nouvelle histoire de Paris: la restauration, 1815–1830.* Paris: Association pour la publication d'une histoire de Paris, 1977.

Bienaymé, Gustave. *Prix des principaux objets de consommation à Paris depuis deux siècles environ...* Paris: Imprimerie Municipale, 1898.

Bollème, Geneviève. *Les almanachs populaires aux XVIIe et XVIIIe siècles.* Paris: Mouton, 1969.

Bouchard, Gérard. *Le village immobile: Sonnely-en-Sologne au XVIIIe siècle.* Paris: Plon, 1972.

Bourgeois-Pichat, J. "The General Development of the Population of France Since the Eighteenth Century." In *Population in History: Essays in Historical Demography*, ed. D. V. Glass and D. E. C. Eversley, pp. 474–506. London: Arnold, 1965.

Buchez, P. J. B. and Roux, P. C. *Histoire parlementaire de la révolution française, ou journal des assemblées nationales, depuis 1789 jusqu'en 1815...* Paris: Paulin, 1834. Vol. 11.

Burke, Peter. *Popular Culture in Early Modern Europe.* New York: Harper and Row, 1978.

Camp, Wesley D. *Marriage and the Family in France Since the Revolution.* New York: Bookman Associates, 1961.

Carter II, Edward C. et al., eds. *Enterprise and Entrepreneurs in Nineteenth- and Twentieth-Century France.* Baltimore: Johns Hopkins University Press, 1976.

Chabert, Alexandre. *Essai sur les mouvements des prix et des revenus en France de 1789 à 1820.* Paris: Librairie de Medicis, 1945–1949. 2 vols.

Charléty, Sébastien. *La monarchie de juillet (1830–1848).* In *Histoire de France contemporaine depuis la révolution jusqu'à la paix de 1919*, ed. Ernest Lavisse, vol. 5. Paris: Hachette, 1922.

Chauvet, Paul. *Les ouvriers du livre en France, de 1789 à la constitution de la Fédération du livre.* Paris: Marcel Rivière, 1956.

Chevalier, Louis. *Dangerous Classes and Labouring Classes in Paris during the First Half of the Nineteenth Century.* Trans. Frank Jellinek. London: Routledge, Kegan Paul, 1973 [1958].

―――. *La formation de la population parisienne au XIXe siècle.* Paris: Presses Universitaires de France, 1950.

Clark, Priscilla P. "The Beginnings of Mass Culture in France: Action and Reaction," *Social Research* 45,2(1978): 277–91.

Cobb, Richard. *Reactions to the French Revolution.* London: Oxford University Press, 1972.

Collins, Irene. *The Government and the Newspaper Press, 1814–1881.* London: Oxford University Press, 1959.

Crouzet, François. "Essai de construction d'un indice annuel de la production industrielle française au XIXe siècle," *Annales: E.S.C.* 24(1970): 56–99.

Crubellier, Maurice. *Histoire culturelle de la France, XIXe–XXe siècles.* Paris: Colin, 1974.

Daumard, Adeline. *La bourgeoisie parisienne de 1815 à 1848.* Paris: S.E.V.P.E.N., 1963 [*Les bourgeois de Paris au XIXe siècle.* Paris: Flammarion, 1970].

————. "Le peuple dans la société française à l'époque romantique," *Romantisme* 13(1975): 21–28.

Dunham, Arthur Louis. *The Industrial Revolution in France, 1815–1848.* New York: Exposition Press, 1955.

Duveau, Georges. *1848: The Making of a Revolution.* Trans. Anne Carter. New York: Vintage, 1967 [1965].

Esler, Anthony. "Youth in Revolt: The French Generation of 1830." In *Modern European Social History,* ed. Robert J. Bezucha, pp. 301–334. Lexington, Mass.: D.C. Heath, 1972.

Fohlen, Claude. "The Industrial Revolution in France." In *Essays in French Economic History,* ed. Rondo E. Cameron, pp. 201–226. Homewood, Ill.: Richard D. Irwin, 1970.

Foucault, Michel. *The Order of Things: An Archeology of the Human Sciences.* New York: Vintage, 1973 [1966].

Frey, Michel. "Du mariage et du concubinage dans les classes populaires à Paris (1846–1848)," *Annales: E.S.C.* 33,3(1978): 801–826.

Frye, Northrop. *The Secular Scripture: A Study of the Structure of Romance.* Cambridge: Harvard University Press, 1976.

Gillis, John R. *Youth and History: Tradition and Change in European Age Relations, 1770–Present.* New York: Academic Press, 1974.

Goblot, Edmond. *La barrière et le niveau: étude sociologique sur la bourgeoisie française moderne.* 2ᵉ éd. Paris: Presses Universitaires de France, 1968 [1925].

Gonnet, Paul. "Esquisse de la crise économique en France de 1827 à 1832," *Revue d'histoire économique et sociale* 33(1955): 264–89.

Hazard, Paul. *The European Mind, 1685–1715.* Trans. J. Lewis Day. Cleveland: World, 1964 [1935].

Hobsbawm, Eric. *The Age of Revolution, 1789–1848.* New York: American Library, [1962].

Hughes, H. Stuart. *The Obstructed Path: French Thought in the Years of Desperation, 1930–1960.* New York: Harper and Row, 1968.

Kemp, Tom. *Economic Forces in French History.* London: Dobson, [1971].

Kent, Sherman. *Electoral Procedure under Louis-Philippe.* New Haven: Yale University Press, 1937.

Kuhn, Thomas. *The Structure of Scientific Revolutions.* Chicago: University of Chicago Press, 1970.

Landes, David. "French Entrepreneurship and Industrial Growth in the Nineteenth Century," *Journal of Economic History* 9(1949): 45–61.

————. *The Unbound Prometheus: Technological Change and Industrial Development in Western Europe from 1750 to the Present.* Cambridge: Cambridge University Press, 1969.

Lees, Lynn and Tilly, Charles. "Le peuple de juin 1848," *Annales: E.S.C.* 29(1974): 1061–1091.

Lefebvre, Georges. *The Coming of the Revolution: 1789.* Trans. R. R. Palmer. Princeton: Princeton University Press, 1947 [1939].

Leplay, Frédéric. *Les ouvriers européens...* Tours: Mame et fils, 1877–1879. 6 vols.

Levasseur, Pierre-Emile. *Histoire des classes ouvrières en France depuis 1789 jusqu'à nos jours.* Paris: Hachette, 1867. 2 vols.

Lévy-Leboyer, Maurice. "Croissance économique en France au XIXe siècle," *Annales: E.S.C.* 23(1968): 788–807.

McPhee, Peter. "Popular Culture, Symbolism and Rural Radicalism in Nineteenth-Century France," *Journal of Peasant Studies* 5(1978): 238–53.

Mandrou, Robert. *De la culture populaire aux 17e et 18e siècles.* Paris: Stock, 1975 [1964].

———. *Introduction to Modern France, 1500–1640: An Essay in Historical Psychology.* Trans. R. E. Hallmark. New York: Harper and Row, 1975 [1961].

Marczewski, Jean. "Some Aspects of the Economic Growth of France, 1660–1958," *Economic Development and Cultural Change* 9,3:(1961): 369–86.

Markovitch, Tihomir J. *Industrie française de 1789 à 1964.* Paris: Institut de science economique appliquée, 1966. 3 vols.

Mazoyer, Louis. "Catégories d'âge et groupes sociaux: les jeunes générations françaises de 1830," *Annales d'histoire économique et sociale* 10(1938): 385–423.

Moss, Bernard H. *The Origins of the French Labor Movement: The Socialism of Skilled Labor.* Berkeley: University of California Press, 1976.

Newman, Edgar Leon. "What the Crowd Wanted in the French Revolution of 1830." In *1830 in France,* ed. John Merriman, pp. 17–40. New York: New Viewpoints, 1975.

Pinkney, David H. *The French Revolution of 1830.* Princeton: Princeton University Press, 1972.

Pouthas, Charles. *La population française pendant la première moitié du XIXe siècle.* Paris: Presses Universitaires de France, 1956.

Price, Roger, ed. *Revolution and Reaction: 1848 and the Second French Republic.* London: Croom Helm, 1975.

Ragon, Michel. *Histoire de la littérature prolétarienne en France.* Paris: Albin Michel, 1974.

Regaudes-Weiss, Hilde. *Les enquêtes ouvrières en France entre 1830 et 1848.* Paris: Alcan, 1936.

Robertson, Priscilla. "Home as Nest: Middle-Class Childhood in Nineteenth-Century Europe." In *The History of Childhood,* ed. Lloyd deMause, pp. 407–431. New York: Harper and Row, 1975.

Rougerie, Jacques. "Remarques sur l'histoire des salaires à Paris au XIXe siècle," *Mouvement social* 63(1968): 71–108.

Rowntree, B. Seebohm. *Poverty and Progress: A Second Social Survey of York.* London: Longmans, 1941.

Rudé, George. *The Crowd in the French Revolution.* New York: Oxford University Press, 1959.

Shaffer, John. "Family, Class, and Young Women: Occupational Expectations in Nineteenth-Century Paris," *Journal of Family History* 3,1(1978):62–77.

Simiand, François. *Le salaire, l'évolution sociale et la monnaie; essai de théorie expérimentale du salaire, introduction et étude globale.* Paris: Alcan, 1932. 3 vols.

Singer-Kérel, Jeanne. *Le coût de vie à Paris de 1840 à 1954.* Paris: Colin, [1961].

Statistique générale. *Statistique de la France...2ᵉ série. Tome XII: Prix et salaires à diverses époques.* Strasbourg: Berger-Levrault, 1863.

Stearns, Peter N. "Patterns of Industrial Strike Activity in France during the July Monarchy," *American Historical Review* 70,2(1965): 371–94.

Thibaudet, Albert. *Histoire de la littérature française de la révolution à nos jours.* Paris: Stock, 1936.

Thompson, E. P. "The Moral Economy of the English Crowd in the Eighteenth Century." *Past and Present* 50(1971): 76–136.

Tilly, Louise and Scott, Joan. "Women's Work and the Family in Nineteenth-Century Europe," *Comparative Studies in Society and History* 17,1(1975): 36–64.

Tolédano, A. D. *La vie de famille sous la restauration et la monarchie de juillet.* Paris: Albin Michel, [1943].

Vidalenc, Jean. *La société française de 1815 à 1848.* Paris: Marcel Rivière, 1973. 2 vols.

Weber, Eugen. *Peasants into Frenchmen: The Modernization of Rural France, 1870–1914.* Stanford: Stanford University Press, 1976.

Whitehead, Alfred North. *Science and the Modern World.* New York: Free Press, 1953.

Wohl, Robert. *The Generation of 1914.* Cambridge: Harvard University Press, 1979.

Zeldin, Theodore. *France, 1848–1945*, vol. 1: *Ambition, Love, and Politics*; vol. 2: *Intellect, Taste, and Anxiety.* New York: Oxford University Press, 1975–1977.

C. Romanticism

Albert, Maurice. *Les théâtres des boulevards, 1789–1848.* Paris: Société française d'imprimerie et de librairie, 1902.

Avenel, Henri. *Chansons et chansonniers.* Paris: Marpon et Flammarion, [1889].

Aynard, Joseph. "Comment définir le romantisme?" *Revue de littérature comparée* 5(1925): 641–58.

Babbitt, Irving. *Rousseau and Romanticism.* Boston: Houghton, Mifflin, 1919.

Baldensperger, Ferdinand. *'Romantique': ses analogues et ses équivalents. Tableau synoptique de 1650 à 1840.* Cambridge: Harvard University Press, 1937.

Barbéris, Pierre. *Balzac et le mal du siècle, contribution à une physiologie du monde moderne.* Paris: Gallimard, 1970–1971. 2 vols.

———. "Le mal du siècle, ou d'un romantisme de droit à un romantisme de gauche." In *Romantisme et politique, 1815–1851.* Colloque d'histoire littéraire. Ecole Normale Supérieure de Saint-Cloud, 1966, pp. 164–87. Paris: Colin, 1969.

————. "Napoléon: structure et signification d'un mythe littéraire," *Revue d'histoire littéraire de la France* 70,5–6(1970): 1031–1058.

Barrère, Jean-Bertrand. "Sur quelques définitions du romantisme," *Revue des sciences humaines*, Fsc. 62–63(1951): 98–110.

Barzun, Jacques. *Berlioz and the Romantic Century*. New York: Columbia University Press, 1969. 2 vols.

————. *Classic, Romantic, and Modern*. Chicago: University of Chicago Press, 1975 [*Romanticism and the Modern Ego*, 1943].

Béguin, Albert. *L'âme romantique et le rêve: essai sur le romantisme allemand et la poésie française*. 2ᵉ éd. Paris: Corti, 1960.

Bellen, E. C. van. *Les origines du mélodrame*. Utrecht: Kimink and Zoon, 1927.

Bénichou, Paul. *Le sacre de l'écrivain, 1750–1830*. Paris: Corti, 1973.

————. *Le temps des prophètes: doctrines de l'âge romantique*. Paris: Gallimard, 1977.

Boas, George. "Il Faut être de son Temps," *Journal of Aesthetics and Art Criticism* 1,1(1941): 52–65.

Boulenger, Jacques. *Sous Louis-Philippe. Les dandys*. Paris: Ollendorff, 1907.

Bray, René. *Chronologie du romantisme, 1804–1830*. Paris: Boivin, 1932.

Brombert, Victor. "The Happy Prison: A Recurring Romantic Metaphor." In *Romanticism: Vistas, Instances, Continuities*, ed. David Thorburn and Geoffrey Hartman, pp. 62–82. Ithaca: Cornell University Press, 1973.

Brooks, Peter. *The Melodramatic Imagination: Balzac, Henry James, Melodrama, and the Mode of Excess*. New Haven: Yale University, 1976.

Carter, Marion Elizabeth. *The Role of Symbolism in French Romantic Poetry*. Washington, D.C.: Catholic University Press, 1946.

Chantavoine, Jean and Gaudefroy-Demombynes, Jean. *Le romantisme dans la musique européenne*. Paris: Albin Michel, 1955.

Clark, Kenneth. *The Romantic Rebellion: Romantic versus Classic Art*. New York: Harper and Row, 1973.

Clement, N. H. *Romanticism in France*. New York: P.M.L.A., 1939.

Donakowski, Conrad L. *A Muse for the Masses: Ritual and Music in an Age of Democratic Revolution, 1770–1870*. Chicago: University of Chicago Press, 1977.

Donnard, Jean-Hervé. *Balzac. Les réalités économiques et sociales dans La comédie humaine*. Paris: Colin, 1961.

Doolittle, James. "Four Elements in Romantic Writing: Mountain, Blue, Twilight, I," *Symposium* (Winter 1969): 216–24.

Einstein, Alfred. *Music in the Romantic Era*. New York: Norton, 1947.

Evans, David Owen. *Le drame moderne à l'époque romantique, 1827–1850*. Paris: Vie Universitaire, 1923.

————. *Social Romanticism in France, 1830–1848*. Oxford: Oxford University Press, 1951.

Frye, Northrop, ed. *Romanticism Reconsidered*. New York: Columbia University Press, 1963.

George, Albert Joseph. *The Development of French Romanticism: The Impact of the Industrial Revolution on Literature.* Syracuse: Syracuse University Press, 1955.

―――. "The Romantic Revolution and the Industrial Revolution in France," *Symposium* (Winter 1952): 281–89.

Gérard, Albert. "On the Logic of Romanticism," *Essays in Criticism* 7(1957): 262–73.

Guerard, Albert L. *Reflections on the Napoleonic Legend.* London: Unwin, 1924.

Honour, Hugh. *Romanticism.* New York: Harper and Row, 1979.

Houston, John Porter. *The Demonic Imagination: Style and Theme in French Romantic Poetry.* Baton Rouge: Louisiana State University Press, 1969.

Howarth, W. D. *Sublime and Grotesque: A Study of French Romantic Drama.* London: Harrap, 1975.

Hunt, Herbert J. *Le socialisme et le romantisme en France: étude de la presse socialiste de 1830 à 1848.* Oxford: Clarendon Press, 1935.

Iknayan, Marguerite. *The Idea of the Novel in France: The Critical Reaction, 1815–1848.* Geneva: Droz, 1961.

Johannet, René. *L'évolution du roman social du XIXe siècle.* Reims: Action Populaire, [1910].

Killen, Alice. *Le roman terrifiant, ou roman noir de Walpole à Ann Radcliffe et son influence sur la littérature française jusqu'en 1840.* Paris: Champion, 1923.

Laserre, Pierre. *Le romantisme français.* Paris: Garnier, 1919.

LeBreton, André. *Le roman français au XIXe siècle, avant Balzac.* Paris: Boivin, 192?.

Lotte, G. "Le vers romantique," *Revue des cours et conférences* 32,1(1930–1931): 44–58, 179–92, 214–26, 437–52, 538–51, 632–48, 689–704.

Lovejoy, Arthur O. "On the Discrimination of Romanticisms," *P.M.L.A.* 39,2(1924): 229–53.

Lucas-Dubreton, Jean. *Le culte de Napoléon, 1815–1848.* Paris: Albin Michel, 1959.

Lukács, Georg. *The Historical Novel.* Trans. Hannah and Stanley Mitchell. Boston: Beacon Press, 1963 [1937].

Maigron, Louis. *Le roman historique à l'époque romantique: essai sur l'influence de Walter Scott.* Paris: Hachette, 1898.

―――. *Le romantisme et la mode, d'après les documents inédits.* Paris: Champion, 1911.

Man, Paul de. "Structure intentionnelle de l'image romantique," *Revue internationale de philosophie* 14(1960): 60–84.

Marsan, Jules. *La bohème romantique, documents inédits.* Paris: Cahiers Libres, 1929.

Matoré, Georges. *Le vocabulaire et la société sous Louis-Philippe...* Genève: Droz, 1951.

Mazinghien, Georges. *Les ouvriers poètes.* Versailles: Imp. Vve. E. Aubert, 1893.

Milner, Max. *Le romantisme, I: 1820–1843.* Paris: Arthaud, 1973.

Mitzman, Arthur. "Roads, Vulgarity, Rebellion, and Pure Art: The Inner Space in Flaubert and French Culture," *Journal of Modern History* 51,3(1979): 504–524.

———. "The Unstrung Orpheus: Flaubert's Youth and the Psycho-Social Origin of Art for Art's Sake," *Psychohistory Review* 6,1(1977): 1–16.

Moreau, Pierre. *Le romantisme*. Paris: de Gigord, 1932.

———. "Le romantisme et la 'fraternité' des arts," *Symposium* (Winter 1969): 319–24.

Neff, Emery. *The Poetry of History: The Contribution of Literature and Literary Scholarship to the Writing of History Since Voltaire*. New York: Columbia University Press, 1947.

Newman, Edgar Leon. "L'Arme du Siècle, C'est la Plume: The French Worker Poets of the July Monarchy and the Spirit of Revolution and Reform," *Journal of Modern History* 51(1979): 4: offprint.

Peckham, Morse. "Toward a Theory of Romanticism," *P.M.L.A.* 61(1951): 5–23.

———. "Toward a Theory of Romanticism, II: Reconsiderations," *Studies in Romanticism* 19,1(1961): 1–8.

Peyre, Henri. *Qu'est-ce que le romantisme?* Paris: Presses Universitaires de France, 1974.

Poulet, Georges. *The Metamorphoses of the Circle*. Trans. Carley Dawson and Elliott Coleman. Baltimore: Johns Hopkins University Press, 1966 [1951].

———. "Timelessness and Romanticism," *Journal of the History of Ideas* 15(1954): 3–22.

Praz, Mario. *The Romantic Agony*, 2nd ed. Trans. Angus Davidson. London: Oxford University Press, 1951 [1930].

Remak, Henry H. H. "Trends in Recent Research on West European Romanticism." In *"Romantic" and its Cognates: The European History of a Word*, ed. Hans Eichner, p. 475–500. Toronto: University of Toronto Press, 1972.

———. "West European Romanticism: Definition and Scope." In *Comparative Literature: Method and Perspective*, ed. Newton P. Stallknecht and Horst Frenz, pp. 223–59. Carbondale, Ill.: Southern Illinois University Press, 1961.

Riasanovsky, Nicholas V. "On Lamennais, Chaadaev and the Romantic Revolt in France and Russia," *American Historical Review* 82,5:(1977): 1165–86.

Riffaterre, Hermine. *L'orphisme dans la poésie romantique: thèmes et style surnaturalistes*. Paris: Nizet, 1970.

Saunders, J. J. *The Age of Revolution*. New York: Hutchinson, 1949.

Schenk, H. G. *The Mind of the European Romantics: An Essay in Cultural History*. Garden City, N.J.: Anchor Books, 1969 [1966].

Shroder, Maurice Z. *Icarus: The Image of the Artist in French Romanticism*. Cambridge: Harvard University Press, 1961.

———. "France: Roman-Romanesque-Romantique-Romantisme." In *"Romantic" and its Cognates: The European History of a Word*, ed. Hans Eichner, pp. 263–92. Carbondale, Ill.: Southern Illinois University Press, 1961.

Sutherland, Donald. *On, Romanticism*. New York: New York University Press, 1971.

Talmon, J. L. *Romanticism and Revolt: Europe 1815–1848*. New York: Harcourt, Brace and World, 1967.

Tieghem, Paul van. *Le romantisme dans la littérature européenne*. Paris: Albin Michel, 1969 [1948].

Wellek, René. "The Concept of 'Romanticism' in Literary History," *Comparative Literature* 1,2(1949): 1–23, 147–72.

———. "Romanticism Re-Examined," In *Concepts of Criticism*, ed. Stephen G. Nichols, pp. 199–221. New Haven: Yale University Press, 1963.

Wood, John S. *Sondages, 1830–1848: romanciers français secondaires*. Toronto: University of Toronto Press, 1965.

D. Production, Distribution, and Consumption of Reading Matter

Alkan ainé. *Notice sur L.C. Silvestre, ancien libraire-éditeur...* Paris: Aubry, 1868.

Atkinson, Nora. *Eugène Sue et le roman-feuilleton*. Nemours: Imp. Lesot, 1929.

Audin, Maurice. *Histoire de l'imprimerie*. Paris: Ricard, 1972.

Avenel, Georges d'. *Les revenus d'un intellectuel de 1200 à 1913: les riches depuis sept cent ans*. Paris: Flammarion, 1922.

Beebe, Maurice. *Ivory Towers and Sacred Founts: The Artist as Hero in Fiction from Goethe to Joyce*. New York: New York University Press, 1964.

Bellanger, Claude et al. *Histoire générale de la presse française*. Paris: Presses Universitaires de France, 1971. 2 vols.

Bellos, D. "The *Bibliographie de la France* and its Sources," *The Library: Transactions of the Bibliographical Society* 28,1(1973): 64–67.

———. "Le marché du livre à l'époque romantique: recherches et problèmes," *Revue française d'histoire du livre* 47(1978): 647–60.

Biré, Edmond. *Dernières causeries historiques et littéraires*. Paris: Emmanuel Vitte, 1898.

Bollème, Geneviève. *La bibliothèque bleue: littérature populaire en France du XVIIe au XIXe siècle*. Paris: Julliard, 1971.

Borgal, Clément. *De quoi vivait Gérard de Nerval?* Paris: Deux Rives, 1950.

Boussel, Patrice and Dubois, Madeleine. *De quoi vivait Victor Hugo?* Paris: Deux Rives, 1952.

Brochon, Pierre. *Le livre de colportage en France depuis le XVIe siècle...* Paris: Julliard, 1954.

Brun, Robert. *Le livre français*. Paris: Larousse, 1945.

Cacérès, Benigno. *Histoire de l'éducation populaire*. Paris: Editions du Seuil, [1964].

Carteret, Léopold. *Le trésor du bibliophile romantique et moderne, 1801–1875*. Paris: Carteret, 1924–1928. 4 vols.

Chevallier, Pierre and Grosperin, Bernard. *L'enseignement français de la révolution à nos jours*. La Haye: Mouton, 1971. 2 vols.

Chollet, Roland. "Un épisode inconnu de l'histoire de la librairie: la société d'abonnement général," *Revue des sciences humaines* 36, 141(1971): 55–84.

Cipolla, Carlo M. *Literacy and Development in the West*. Baltimore: Penguin, 1969.

Clark, Priscilla P. "Stratégies d'auteur au 19e siècle," *Romantisme* 18(1977): 92–102.

Cloche, M. "Un grand éditeur du XIXe siècle, Léon Curmer," *Arts et métiers graphiques* 33(1933): 28–36.

Darmon, Jean-Jacques. *Le colportage de librairie en France sous le second empire...* Paris: Plon, 1972.

Darnton, Robert. "The High Enlightenment and the Low Life of Literature in Prerevolutionary France," *Past and Present* 51(1971): 81–115.

———. "Le livre français à la fin de l'ancien régime," *Annales: E.S.C.* 28,3(1973): 735–44.

Dérôme, Léopold. *Causeries d'un ami des livres, les éditions originales des romantiques.* Paris: Rouveyre, 1886–1887. 2 vols.

Dopp, Herman. *La contrefaçon des livres français en Belgique, 1812–1852.* Louvain: Librairie Universitaire, 1932.

Duboy, Hippolyte. *La presse, l'imprimerie, la librairie, le colportage: guide légal de l'écrivain, du journaliste, de l'imprimeur et du libraire.* Paris: Chevalier, 1869.

Duchartre, Pierre-Louis and Saulnier, René. *L'imagerie parisienne* (l'imagerie de la rue Saint-Jacques). Paris: Gründ, 1944.

Dumont, Francis and Gitan, Jean. *De quoi vivait Lamartine?* Paris: Deux Rives, 1952.

Easton, Malcolm. *Artists and Writers in Paris: The Bohemian Idea, 1803–1867.* New York: St. Martin's Press, 1965.

Escarpit, Robert et al. "La lecture." In *La vie populaire en France du moyen âge à nos jours,* 2:279–356. Paris: Editions Diderot, 1965.

Febvre, Lucien and Martin, Henri-Jean. *L'apparition du livre.* Paris: Albin Michel, 1971 [1958].

Felkay, Nicole. "Les libraires de l'époque romantique d'après les documents inédits," *Revue française d'histoire du livre* 5,3(1975): 31–86.

Fleury, Jules. *Les vignettes romantiques: histoire de la littérature et de l'art, 1825–1840.* Paris: Dentu, 1883.

Fleury, Michel and Valmary, Pierre. "Le progrès de l'instruction élémentaire de Louis XIV à Napoléon III," *Population* 12(1957): 71–92.

Fosseyeux, M. "Les écoles de charité à Paris sous l'ancien régime et dans la première moitié du XIXe siècle," *Mémoires de la Société de l'Histoire de Paris et de l'Ile de France* 39(1912): 225–367.

Franqueville, A. C. F. de. *Le premier siècle de l'Institut de France.* Paris: Rothschild, 1895–1896. 2 vols.

Furet, François and Ozouf, Jacques. *Lire et écrire: l'alphabétisation des français de Calvin à Jules Ferry.* Paris: Editions de Minuit, 1977. 2 vols.

Furet, François and Sachs, Wladimir. "La croissance de l'alphabétisation en France, XVIIIe–XIXe siècles," *Annales: E.S.C.* 29(1974): 714–37.

Gérin, Marius. *Eugène Renduel, 1798–1874, éditeur romantique.* Nevers: Imp. Lebel, 1929.

Girard, H. "Le livre, l'illustration et la reliure à l'époque romantique." In *Le romantisme et l'art*, ed. Louis Hautecoeur et al., pp. 288–317. Paris: Laurens, 1928.

Girou de Buzareingues, Claire. "Les cabinets de lecture et les débuts de l'époque romantique," *Bulletin de la librairie ancienne et moderne* 140(1971): 220–25.

Goebel, Théodore. *Frédéric Koenig et l'invention de la presse mécanique.* Trans. Paul Schmidt. Paris: Schmidt, 1885.

Gontard, Maurice. *L'enseignement primaire en France de la révolution à la loi Guizot (1789–1833): des petites écoles de la monarchie d'ancien régime aux écoles primaires de la monarchie bourgeoise.* Paris: Belles Lettres, 1959.

Goody, Jack, ed. *Literacy in Traditional Societies.* Cambridge: Cambridge University Press, 1968.

Graff, Harvey J. *The Literacy Myth: Literacy and Social Structure in the Nineteenth-Century City.* New York: Academic Press, 1979.

Graña, César. *Modernity and its Discontents: French Society and the French Man of Letters in the Nineteenth Century.* New York: Harper and Row, 1967 [*Bohemian versus Bourgeois.* New York: Basic Books, 1964].

Guise, René. "Le roman-feuilleton et la vulgarisation des idées politiques et sociales sous la monarchie de juillet." In *Romantisme et politique, 1815–1851.* Colloque d'histoire littéraire. Ecole Normale Supérieure de Saint-Cloud, 1966, pp. 316–24. Paris: Colin, 1969.

Hatin, Eugène-Louis. *Histoire politique et littéraire de la presse en France...* Paris: Poulet-Malassis et de Broise, 1859–1861. 8 vols.

Humblot, Alfred. *L'édition littéraire au XIXᵉ siècle.* Paris: Evreux, [1911].

Jourda, Pierre. "Un cabinet de prêt en province en 1832," *Revue d'histoire littéraire de la France* 44(1937): 540–50.

Jullien, Adolphe. *Le romantisme et l'éditeur Renduel, souvenirs et documents sur les écrivains de l'école romantique...* Paris: Fesquelles, 1897.

Kaës, René. *Les ouvriers français et la culture: enquête 1958–1961.* Paris: Institut de Travail, 1962.

Lauzac, Henry. *Galerie historique et critique du dix-neuvième siècle. Martin Bossange.* Paris: "Galerie Historique," 1865.

Ledré, Charles. *La presse à l'assaut de la monarchie, 1815–1848.* Paris: Colin, [1960].

Lehman, Harvey C. "The Creative Years in Science and Literature," *Scientific Monthly* 43(1936): 151–62.

Lelièvre, Pierre. "Livres et libraires en Avignon à l'époque romantique." In *Mélanges d'histoire littéraire et de bibliographie offerts à Jean Bonnerot*, pp. 269–75. Paris: Nizet, 1954.

Levasseur, Emile. *L'enseignement primaire dans les pays civilisés.* Paris: Berger-Levrault, 1897–1903. 2 vols.

Lough, John. *Writer and Public in France from the Middle Ages to the Present Day.* London: Clarendon Press, 1978.

Ministère de l'Instruction Publique. *Statistique de l'enseignement primaire*, Tome II: *Statistique comparée de l'enseignement primaire, 1829–1877.* Paris: Imprimerie Nationale, 1880.

Mistler, Jean. *La librairie Hachette de 1826 à nos jours.* Paris: Hachette, [1964].

Montagne, Edouard. *Histoire de la société des gens de lettres.* Paris: Librairie Mondaine, 1889.

Moran, James. *Printing Presses: History and Development...* Berkeley: University of California Press, 1973.

Neret, Jean-Alexis. *Histoire illustrée de la librairie et du livre français.* Paris: Lamarre, 1953.

Nisard, Charles. *Histoire des livres populaires, ou la littérature de colportage depuis l'origine de l'imprimerie...* Paris: Amyot, 1854. 2 vols.

O'Boyle, Lenore. "The Problem of an Excess of Over-Educated Men in Western Europe, 1800–1850," *Journal of Modern History* 42(1970): 471–95.

Odin, Alfred. *Genèse des grands hommes: gens de lettres français modernes.* Lausanne: Mignot, 1895. 2 vols.

Orecchioni, Pierre. "Presse, livre et littérature au XIXe siècle," *Revue française d'histoire du livre* 4,7(1974): 33–44.

Parent, Françoise. "Les cabinets de lecture dans Paris: pratiques culturelles et espace sociale sous la Restauration," *Annales: E.S.C.* 34,5(1979): 1016–1038.

Parménie, A. and Bonnier de la Chapelle, C. *Histoire d'un éditeur et de ses auteurs: P.-J. Hetzel (Stahl).* Paris: Albin Michel, [1953].

Pelles, Geraldine. *Art, Artists and Society: Origins of a Modern Dilemma. Painting in England and France, 1750–1850.* Englewood Cliffs, N.J.: Prentice-Hall, 1963.

Peyre, Henri. *Les générations littéraires.* Paris: Boivin, 1948.

Pichois, Claude. "Pour une sociologie des faits littéraires. Les cabinets de lecture à Paris durant la première moitié du XIXe siècle," *Annales: E.S.C.* 14,3(1959): 521–34.

Plon, Eugène. *Notre livre intime de famille.* Paris: Plon, Nourrit et cie., 1893.

Pottinger, David. *The French Book Trade in the Ancien Régime, 1500–1791.* Cambridge: Harvard University Press, 1958.

Quérard, J.-M. *Quelques mots sur M. Bossange père, doyen des imprimeurs et des libraires de Paris.* Paris: Imp. Lainé et Havard, 1863.

Radiguer, Louis. *Maîtres imprimeurs et ouvriers typographes, 1470–1903.* Paris: Société Nouvelle, 1903.

Resnick, Daniel and Resnick, Lauren. "The Nature of Literacy: An Historical Exploration," *Harvard Educational Review* 47(1977): 370–85.

Rosseeuw Saint-Hilaire, E. F. A. *Notice sur Charles Furne.* Paris: Imp. Claye, 1860.

Salvan, Paul. "Un moment de la diffusion du livre: livres et lectures en 1825." In *Humanisme actif: mélanges d'art et de littérature offerts à Julien Cain,* vol. 2. pp. 165–78. Paris: Hermann, 1968.

Seguin, Jean-Pierre. *Canards du siècle passé.* Paris: Pierre Horay, 1969.

———. *Nouvelles à sensation. Canards du XIXe siècle.* Paris: Colin, 1959.

Tirol, M. "Les cabinets de lecture en France, 1800–1850," *Revue des bibliothèques* 33(1926): 77–98, 198–224, 401–23; 34(1927): 13–25.

Whitmore, Harry Earl. "The *Cabinets de Lecture* in France, 1800–1850." Ph.D. Diss., University of Wisconsin-Madison, 1975.

———. "Readers, Writers, and Literary Taste in the Early 1830s: The *Cabinet de Lecture* as Focal Point," *Journal of Library History* 13,2(1978): 119–30.

INDEX

POPULAR FRENCH ROMANTICISM

was composed in 10-point Mergenthaler Linoterm Caledonia, leaded two points,
with display type in Deepdene,
printed on 55-pound P & S acid-free Offset Vellum
by Joe Mann Associates, Inc.;
Smythe-sewn and bound over boards in Columbia Atlantic Vellum
by Maple-Vail Book Manufacturing Group, Inc.;
and published by

SYRACUSE UNIVERSITY PRESS
SYRACUSE, NEW YORK 13210